METROLINA ATLAS

prepared with assistance from the

DEPARTMENT OF GEOGRAPHY AND EARTH SCIENCES

THE UNIVERSITY OF NORTH CAROLINA AT CHARLOTTE

METROLINA ATLAS

edited by
JAMES W. CLAY and DOUGLAS M. ORR, JR.

Institute for Urban Studies and Community Service
The University of North Carolina at Charlotte

chief cartographic assistant
JEFFERSON L. SIMPSON

The University of North Carolina Press
Chapel Hill

Manufactured in the United States of America.
Printed by Kingsport Press, Kingsport, Tennessee.
ISBN 0-8078-1186-6.
Library of Congress Catalog Card Number 75-179657.

CONTENTS

CONTRIBUTORS

JULIUS ALKER, *Assistant Professor of Geology,
The University of North Carolina at Charlotte*

R. ERIC ANDERSON, *Assistant Professor of Art,
The University of North Carolina at Charlotte*

THOMAS F. BAUCOM, *Research Analyst,
Charlotte Chamber of Commerce*

CARLOS G. BELL, JR., *Professor of Civil Engineering,
The University of North Carolina at Charlotte*

G. JACKSON BURNEY, *Vice-President and Director of
Marketing Research, North Carolina National Bank*

JAMES W. CLAY, *Associate Professor of Geography and
Earth Sciences, The University of North Carolina
at Charlotte*

TED R. FLETCHER, *Instructor, Mechanical Engineering,
Central Piedmont Community College*

BARBARA A. GOODNIGHT, *Associate Professor of
Sociology, The University of North Carolina
at Charlotte*

SAM HEARN, *Soil Scientist, Soil Conservation Service,
United States Department of Agriculture*

JERRY HENDRICK, *Research Manager,
Charlotte Chamber of Commerce*

J. NORFLEET JARRELL, *Instructor in Geography and
Earth Sciences, The University of North Carolina
at Charlotte*

DENNIS LORD, *Assistant Professor of Geography,
The University of North Carolina at Charlotte*

SCHLEY R. LYONS, *Associate Professor of Political
Science, The University of North Carolina
at Charlotte*

WILLIAM J. McCOY, *Assistant Professor of Political
Science, The University of North Carolina
at Charlotte*

DOUGLAS M. ORR, JR., *Assistant Professor of Geography,
The University of North Carolina at Charlotte*

EDWARD S. PERZEL, *Associate Professor of History,
The University of North Carolina at Charlotte*

ROBERT E. RANDOLPH, *Assistant Executive Director,
Health and Hospital Council*

BENJAMIN H. ROMINE, JR., *Assistant Professor of
Education, The University of North Carolina
at Charlotte*

GEORGE K. SELDEN, JR., *State Forecast and Rate
Supervisor, Southern Bell Telephone and Telegraph
Company*

MORTON SHAPIRO, *Assistant Professor of English,
The University of North Carolina at Charlotte*

JEFFERSON L. SIMPSON, *Instructor in Geography,
The University of North Carolina at Charlotte*

ALFRED W. STUART, *Associate Professor of Geography,
The University of North Carolina at Charlotte*

WAYNE A. WALCOTT, *Instructor in Geography,
The University of North Carolina at Charlotte*

SALLY A. ALLISON, KIRK S. ASHTON, CHARLIE W.
BARNES, DAVIANNE BILLMIRE, PHILIP M.
EDWARDS, JR., LINWOOD M. HARTON, JR.,
JANET F. HINCE, JOHN R. JAMES, ANDREI A.
KAMININ, ROBERT S. MACEY, WILSON A.
MATTHEWS, JR., and KURT TAUBE (*Student
Assistants*), *The University of North Carolina at
Charlotte*

Since its inception in 1970 the Institute for Urban Studies and Community Service has been devoted to the investigation of the Piedmont Carolinas as its primary laboratory. The institute provides a focal point at The University of North Carolina at Charlotte for new approaches to continuing urban problems. It also serves as a catalyst, convener, and coordinator of urban studies, community service, and urban-community research programs.

It is from this perspective that the *Metrolina Atlas* project was developed. The *Atlas* is the result of more than two years of planning and research coordinated by James W. Clay, associate professor of geography, and Douglas M. Orr, Jr., assistant professor of geography, both institute associates. The special effort of the Department of Geography and Earth Sciences was invaluable. The assistance of faculty, students, and community personnel was sought to provide needed expertise.

The study is an excellent example of a cooperative effort between the university and the area it serves. The *Atlas* would not have been possible without the aid and support of the organizations and individuals listed in the acknowledgments.

The *Metrolina Atlas* has been viewed as a challenge and an opportunity. The most comprehensive study of our region ever undertaken, this graphic-explanatory examination of Metrolina deals with such urgent societal concerns as population growth patterns, commercial and industrial development, air and water pollution, educational programs and developments, voting trends, and transportation needs. Although Metrolina is an area undergoing rapid urbanization, its stage of development still provides opportunity for decisions that may prevent haphazard growth. The *Atlas* is intended to provide information from a regional perspective in meeting this challenge.

Accordingly, the book is intended to be helpful to a variety of decision-makers from Metrolina as well as those residing elsewhere who desire to learn more about the region. The topics illustrated and discussed in the *Metrolina Atlas* should bring about a better understanding of Metrolina's complex regional characteristics.

Norman W. Schul, Director
Institute for Urban Studies
and Community Service

ACKNOWLEDGMENTS

The publication of the *Metrolina Atlas* is the result of a collective effort that has been more than simply the production of a book; it has been literally a university and community project. We therefore want to extend our deepest gratitude first to those individuals, as listed on the contributors page, who joined us in this effort. They generously gave their time and expertise to this project, and the blending of their talents makes possible the broad view of our regional community in all its dimensions.

The *Atlas* could not have been produced without support from several sources at The University of North Carolina at Charlotte. The project was sponsored by the university's Institute for Urban Studies and Community Service. Its support of this applied research represents one of many ways the institute is attempting to serve the needs of the surrounding urban region, and the cooperation and assistance received from the institute's staff have been instrumental in the realization of a *Metrolina Atlas*. A grant from the UNCC faculty research fund helped defray expenses during the early stages. Within the university's Department of Geography and Earth Sciences we have received substantial resource assistance, both human and material. A number of students in the department have been of great help in data collection and assimilation, and in the cartographic work. The departmental secretary, Elizabeth A. Chipley, not only typed the entire manuscript, but also assisted in project coordination, information collection, cartography, and the never-ending task of helping make all the pieces fit.

The Charlotte Chamber of Commerce has been instrumental in helping to develop the Metrolina regional idea from the concept's beginning. Members of the organization's Metrolina Committee have provided us with valuable suggestions and assistance throughout the project. In addition, representatives from each of the twelve Metrolina counties, who comprise the Metrolina Coordinating Committee, have acted as a sounding board and a source of information about their respective counties.

We are indebted to a number of individuals who reviewed several of the chapters and provided many useful comments. Charles Hickman and others on the staff of the Charlotte-Mecklenburg Board of Education reacted to the chapter on education. Stephen S. Birdsall of the Department of Geography of the University of North Carolina at Chapel Hill reviewed the transportation and utilities chapter, and Bobby G. Hightower of the Charlotte-Mecklenburg Planning Commission commented on the "Regional Overview." Alfred W. Stuart of the UNCC Department of Geography and Earth Sciences gave useful assistance on many sections of the book and in other ways as well. We also wish to thank Bob Byerly, assistant to the general manager of the *Charlotte Observer*, for permitting us to use photographs from the *Observer*'s outstanding collection. Dan O. Duncan of Duncan-Parnell, Inc. provided technical advice in countless ways relating to the cartographic function.

Special gratitude is extended to the staff of our publisher, The University of North Carolina Press. No one could have asked for more and too often such efforts go unreported.

Finally, we express our deep appreciation to our wives, whose understanding throughout the project was an immense help.

To each of these people and to many others who contributed to this volume directly or indirectly, we again extend our lasting gratitude.

James W. Clay
Douglas M. Orr, Jr.

METROLINA ATLAS

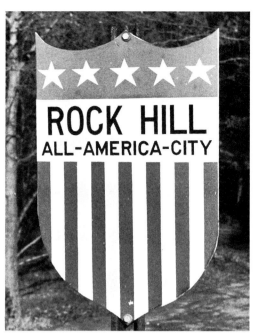
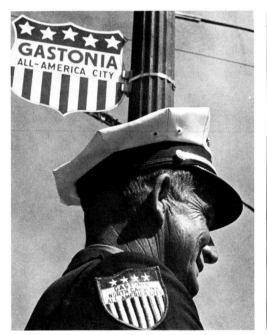

1. INTRODUCTION

JAMES W. CLAY
and
DOUGLAS M. ORR, JR.

"Some consider that a new environment for our civilization, which may be called the urban region, is in the making."— Peter Self, Frederick Gutheim, and H. V. Hodson, The Regional City.

A new spatial order is emerging across the landscape of American society. It encompasses more than the continued diminishment of the old high-density central city concept, whereby cities grew by monopolizing a strategic geographic position. And it is far more than the oversimplified pattern of a string of bedroom communities springing up in the suburbs and funneling their inhabitants into the central city each day for work. What is evolving today and for the future might be best called an "urban region." The phenomenon has been described also by such generic terms as regional city, spread city, strip city, and urban field. Recognizing this new urbanization pattern, the U. S. Bureau of the Budget has attempted to keep pace by expanding the meaning of its metropolitan area definition from "metropolitan district," to "standard metropolitan area," and finally to "standard metropolitan statistical area" (SMSA). The definition remains inadequate and the bureau continues to search for a workable meaning.

At the root of this enlarged scale of living is a much greater mobility of the populace; a mobility that creates a dispersed but footloose population in perpetual flow for many of its activities. An urban region therefore is not simply a spilling over of the city but rather a population tied together by a unity of behavior and a common accessibility to opportunities. In such a community there are shared interests oriented more toward specific functions than a fixed territorial base. As difficult as it may be, however, such a fluid population must be focused within a delimited area in order for effective planning to be possible.

The interdependency of the citizenry demands it.

Throughout much of the nation and in some other parts of the world there can be found this blurring of the frontier between city and countryside. (See Fig. 1.1.) It has been particularly prevalent along the eastern seaboard of the United States, where the massive Washington to Boston "Megalopolis" corridor includes a number of urban regions coalescing into the world's most intensive urban sprawl. Just to the southeast of Megalopolis there is evolving another large-scale urban strip covering approximately as much territory but not nearly so densely populated. Stretching from Lynchburg, Virginia, to Anderson, South Carolina, this region, called the Southern Piedmont, will become the fifth largest urban area in the country by the year 2000 according to population projections by the Urban Land Institute. Its population by that time is predicted to reach over five million people, boosted by a population growth rate more rapid than that of the nation as a whole.

Located in the heart of this larger Southern Piedmont region and straddling the North and South Carolina border is a grouping of twelve counties known as "Metrolina." It represents, we feel, a good example of the phenomenon of the emerging urban region. (See Fig. 1.2.)

The development of the Metrolina idea grew out of an interest expressed in 1968 by Cabarrus County officials in joining the Charlotte SMSA, which is comprised of Mecklenburg and Union counties. (The Bureau of the Budget assigns such an SMSA designation to facilitate collection and reporting of statistical data. Although never intended to be, the SMSA has become an important marketing tool for the attraction of new business.) As a result of the Cabarrus inquiry, the research staff of the Charlotte Chamber of Commerce went to work and discovered a "strong interrelationship economically and socially" beyond Meck-

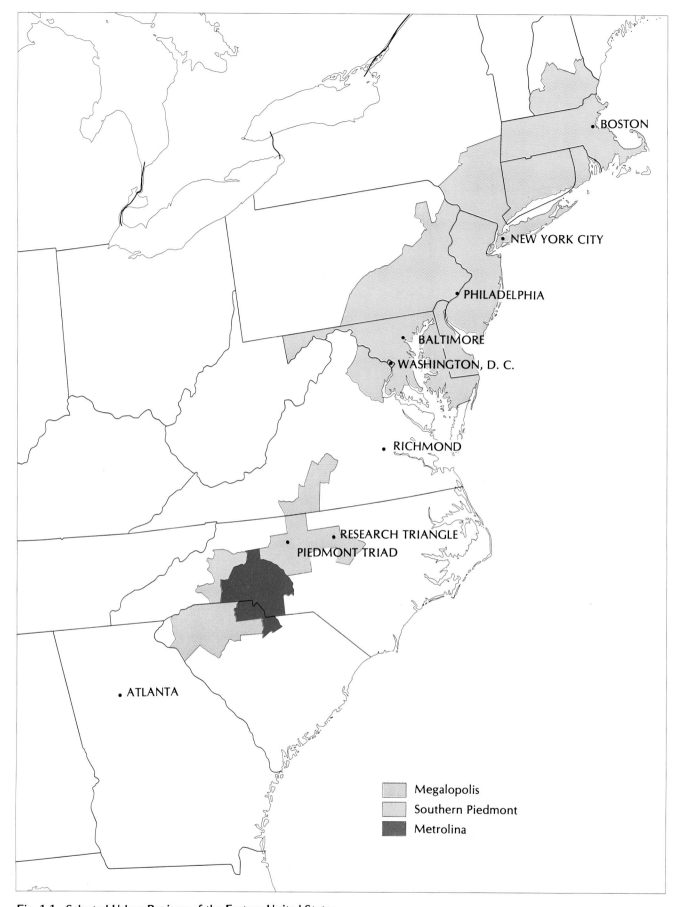

Fig. 1.1. Selected Urban Regions of the Eastern United States

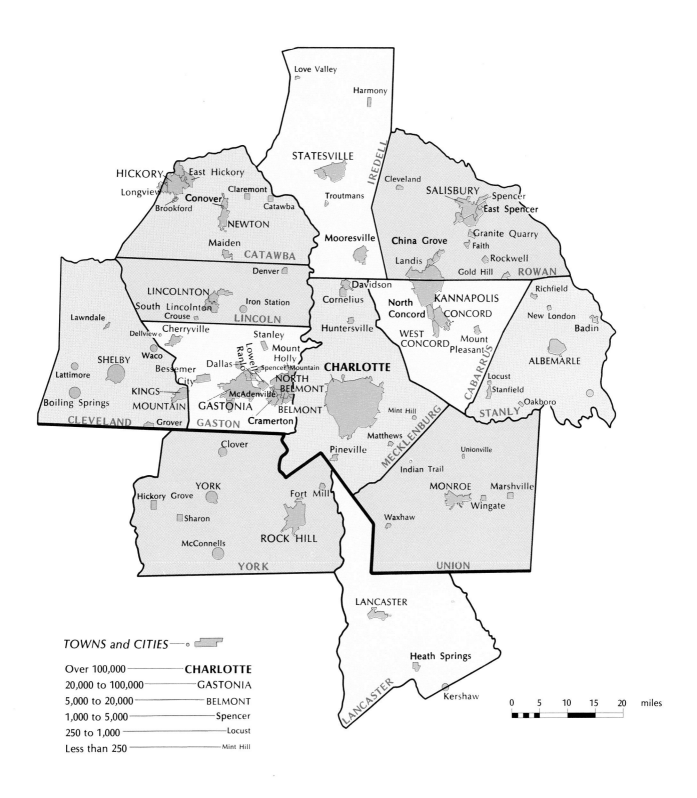

Love Valley

Harmony

STATESVILLE

IREDELL

HICKORY   East Hickory
Longview   Conover   Claremont
Brookford   Catawba
NEWTON
Maiden   CATAWBA
Denver

Troutmans

Mooresville

Cleveland   SALISBURY   Spencer
East Spencer
China Grove   Granite Quarry
Faith
Landis   Rockwell
Gold Hill   ROWAN

LINCOLNTON
South Lincolnton   Iron Station
Crouse   LINCOLN
Cherryville
Dellview   Stanley
Waco   Mount
Dallas   Holly
Lowell   Spencer Mountain
Bessemer   NORTH
City   BELMONT
KINGS   McAdenville
MOUNTAIN   GASTONIA   BELMONT
Grover   GASTON   Cramerton

Davidson
Cornelius   North
Concord   KANNAPOLIS
Huntersville   CONCORD
WEST   Mount
CONCORD   Pleasant
CABARRUS

Richfield
New London
Badin
ALBEMARLE

Locust
Stanfield
Oakboro
STANLY

Lawndale

SHELBY
Lattimore

Boiling Springs
CLEVELAND

CHARLOTTE
Mint Hill
Matthews
Pineville   MECKLENBURG

Clover

Unionville
Indian Trail
MONROE   Marshville
Wingate
Waxhaw

YORK
Hickory Grove
Sharon
McConnells   ROCK HILL
YORK

Fort Mill

UNION

LANCASTER

Heath Springs

LANCASTER   Kershaw

0   5   10   15   20   miles

TOWNS and CITIES

Over 100,000 — **CHARLOTTE**
20,000 to 100,000 — GASTONIA
5,000 to 20,000 — BELMONT
1,000 to 5,000 — Spencer
250 to 1,000 — Locust
Less than 250 — Mint Hill

Fig. 1.2. Metrolina Political Divisions

lenburg-Union-Cabarrus to include a twelve-county region of ten North Carolina and two South Carolina counties. This revelation was perhaps enhanced by an earlier announcement from a national publication that an area around Charlotte roughly corresponding to the Metrolina borders was one of the nation's top forty markets for quality merchandise. In any event the new trading area concept was an attempt to establish a well-defined entity for the twelve-county area that could be used as a more workable delimitation than the SMSA. A contest was conducted to choose a name for the newly conceived region, and out of 450 names received, five contestants submitted "Metrolina"—a name reflecting the area's metropolitan and two-state nature. It has since been used, with an accompanying logo design, to identify and promote the interlocking strengths of the twelve counties. It is heard daily in everything from "Metrolina weather" forecasts to automobile dealerships.

Yet despite the fact that the Metrolina idea began as a means of breaking out of the unnecessarily tight fit of the SMSA designation and as a way to promote regional trade, the delimited area has considerable validity as a cohesive urban region. For example, even though Charlotte would best be designated as the regional capital, it by no means dominates the area the way that a central city like Atlanta overshadows its surrounding territory. This is illustrated by the fact that in Metrolina one out of five commuters going to his job crosses a county line en route but a majority of this group is not Charlotte-bound. And as Fig. 1.3 shows, the region's 1.1 million inhabitants are distributed in a widely dispersed manner. Like other parts of the Southern Piedmont, individual cities are not particularly large but they are numerous and fairly close together. The physical framework also represents a binding force. The 5,700 square miles of land area is arranged in a very compact manner, almost completely within about a fifty-mile radius of the center. However, Metrolina's physical cohesiveness is reinforced most of all by the two historical corridors of the Catawba and Yadkin River Basins and the existing or planned expressways that radiate through the core of the region. There are, in addition, a significant array of other features that give Metrolina identity but that should become apparent throughout later sections of this book.

As is usually expected after the announcement of any Chamber-of-Commerce-inspired regional marketing concept, some negative reaction to the Metrolina idea has appeared from place to place. It is suspected as being an attempt by the big-city business interests to reach out and consume local trade in area communities. Such a reaction is understandable and can be anticipated in similar situations elsewhere. The problem is moreover intensified by extending the boundaries of such a newly devised region across the state line (as well as greatly complicating the collection of data).

Yet we are satisfied that Metrolina makes sense as a multidimensional urban region. That has been our attraction to the development of this project. It is not the exact boundaries that are of overriding importance in any case but rather the urgent and overdue need for a greater regional awareness and cooperation. The era of municipalities' being able to work in a vacuum of narrow local interests is ending. The trend toward a regional urbanization that transcends political units is irreversible. Such an expansion can provide a number of opportunities for an area: increased commercial activities, burgeoning markets, a broader manpower base, and a better offering of cultural amenities. On the other hand, the region's potential for problems will become much more acute, including everything from environmental quality to public education. How well all of these expansionary forces are controlled depends on a recognition of our regional interdependence and effective planning for coordinated action.

Metrolina, which was not meant to be an action body or to possess a government of its own, does provide an umbrella under which its political units can collect and exchange information, coordinate their efforts in planning, conserve and market their resources. As a first step toward better planning, we must more fully understand ourselves. Herein developed the idea for the *Metrolina Atlas.* With the 1970 census becoming available, this seemed the appropriate time to closely examine our urban region as it begins an important period of growth and change during the decade of the 1970s.

The *Metrolina Atlas* is not the typical sort of atlas, that is, one that sets out principal places and products. Rather, it is structured to deal with major themes in the region's total life style. This is attempted through a series of graphics: maps, graphs, charts, and photographs that visually portray intraregional relationships and trends. An explanatory text accompanies these illustrations. Such a format, built on several themes, allows us the unique opportunity to examine the various elements of the region within one cover—just as the closed and interacting system that our total environment certainly is. In order to carry out the multidisciplinary approach and bring as much specialized expertise as possible to this broad study, we have invited various individuals with talents in particular fields to contribute to the project. The *Atlas* is a collective effort by several faculty members at the University of North Carolina at Charlotte as well as by business and institutional leaders in the area. As such each of its themes is unique within its own special circumstances of time and space. Some sections lend themselves naturally to a regional-wide analysis, others must be examined within smaller political units, and some—like Politics, for example—cannot be divorced from the larger political context of the state. Yet we would encourage the reader to look for the various interrelationships and patterns that reoccur from section to section throughout the *Atlas.*

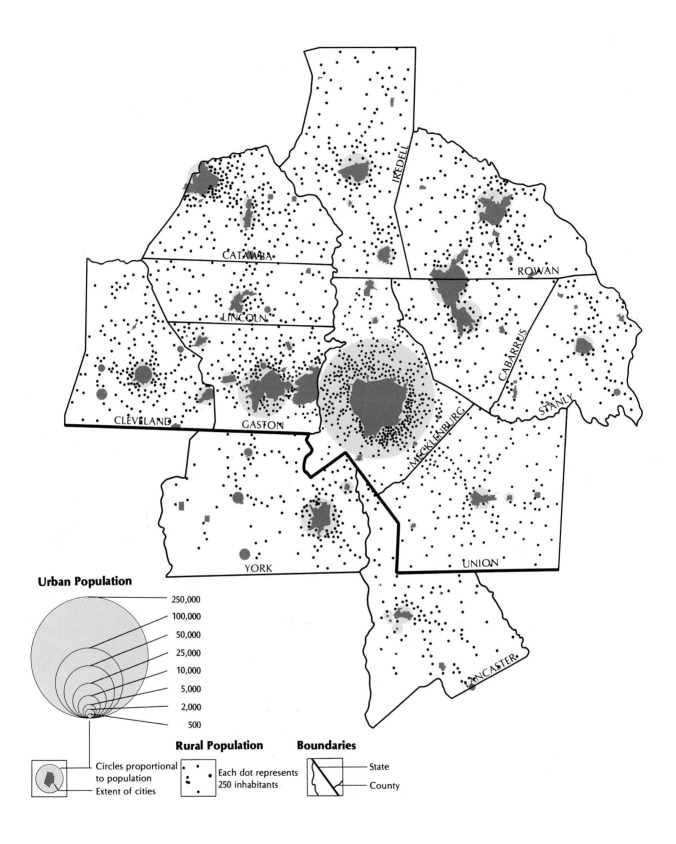

Urban Population

250,000
100,000
50,000
25,000
10,000
5,000
2,000
500

Rural Population   **Boundaries**

Circles proportional
to population   Each dot represents   State
Extent of cities   250 inhabitants   County

Fig. 1.3. Population Distribution in Metrolina, 1970

We have tried to look at Metrolina as objectively as possible, depicting the region not in the manner we would like ourselves and others to see it but simply as we found it. Also, it is not the purpose of the study to present a blueprint for future action. Regional planning schemes are developed after an understanding of the region's personality is achieved. And an in-depth probe of any of these complex topics of course requires more space than this volume permits. The list of major references at the end of each section is included to facilitate that kind of task. It is hoped, however, that each section will inform, allow for comparisons, point to trends, and raise questions that can be pursued further as well as acted upon in the future.

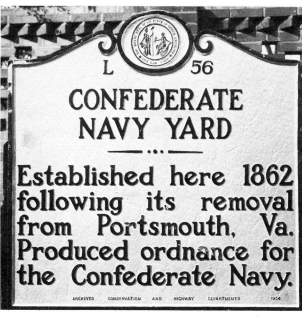

CONFEDERATE
NAVY YARD
···
Established here 1862
following its removal
from Portsmouth, Va.
Produced ordnance for
the Confederate Navy.

ARCHIVES   CONSERVATION   AND   HIGHWAY   DEPARTMENTS   1954

2. REGIONAL HISTORY

EDWARD S. PERZEL

"Our local environment and history are the mirror in which are reflected every aspect of our history as a nation. Here are to be observed, and what is more important—under-stood—the every process through which we built a nation out of a wilderness. . . . Just as the botanist examines the cell structure of a plant to study its growth, so should we approach the study of history as a means of understanding the nation's heritage."—Albert B. Corey, Clifford L. Lord, and S. K. Stevens, Making Our Heritage Live.

Early Settlement

At first glance Metrolina's north-south orientation, split-ting state lines and generally following the axis of the Catawba River Basin, might seem to run against the grain of the larger east-west configuration of North and South Carolina. The area's communication and trading routes, however, have traditionally been oriented in this north-south manner.

The first main access route, coming into the area from the north, was the Great Trading Path, the trail used by the Indians who came from the James River in Virginia across North Carolina to a point below the South Fork and Catawba Rivers. This path, along with the Great Philadelphia Wagon Road, channeled the Scotch-Irish and Pennsylvania Germans into what became the Metrolina area. Later in the nineteenth century the North Carolina Railroad would generally follow the old trading path. (See Fig. 2.1.)

The earliest inhabitants of this part of the Piedmont were the Indians. (See Fig. 2.2.) The Metrolina counties cover an area located between two major tribes, the Tusca-rora on the east and the Cherokee on the west. The area

itself was inhabited by a number of small tribes such as the Sapona, Sugaree, and the Waxhaws. The first recorded knowledge of these tribes was observations of two well-known explorers of early North Carolina, John Lawson and John Lederer. These small tribes were weakened by war and disease, and by the early 1700s had been absorbed by the most noted tribe in the area, the Catawba.

The Catawba, enemies of the Cherokee and Tuscarora tribes, were a sedentary agricultural people. They became ready friends of the whites who moved into the area, but were often exploited by their new allies. In 1743 Governor James Glenn of South Carolina incited the Catawbas to drive settlers out of the area disputed with North Carolina; but King Haigler, the great leader of the Catawbas, was able to maintain control of his people and restore peace to the area. His death in 1762 at the hands of a Shawnee war party from Ohio brought about the decline of the Catawba tribe. The Indians were eventually pushed onto a reservation on the Catawba River and in 1848 the United States Congress appropriated money for their removal west of the Mississippi River. Some remained on the reser-vation in South Carolina.

White settlers did not flood into the area until the mid-dle of the eighteenth century. By that time North and South Carolina, which had been granted as one single colony, had been divided and established as separate royal colonies directly under the crown of England. Beginning in the late 1740s German settlers began winding their way down the Great Trading Path and settled in what was to become Catawba County. These German immigrants repre-sented the Lutheran, German Reformed, and Moravian churches and by the time of the American Revolution numbered approximately fifteen thousand. The scarcity of land in the more settled northern colonies forced other

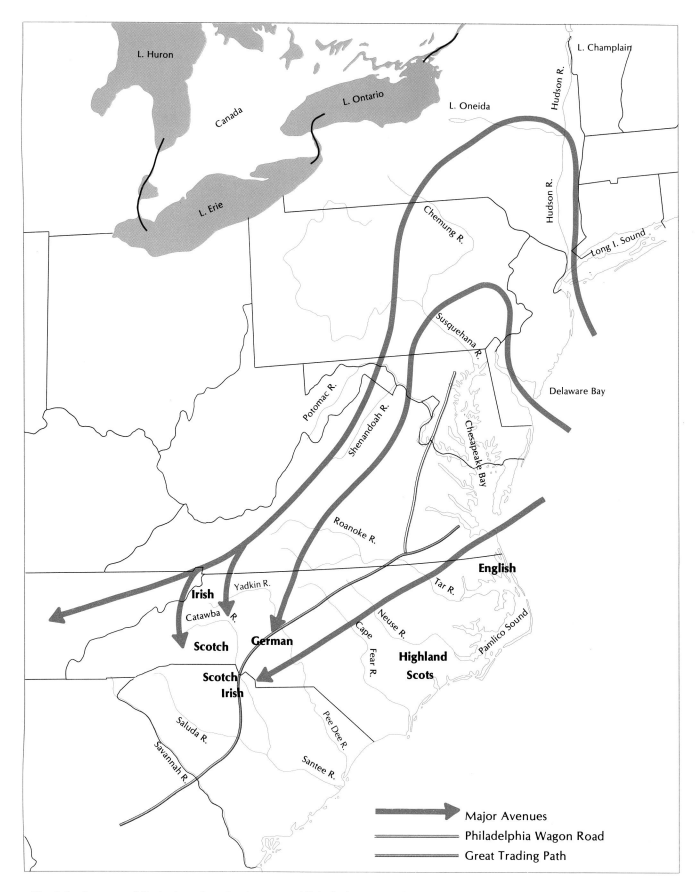

Fig. 2.1. Avenues of Early American Settlement and Ethnic Concentrations

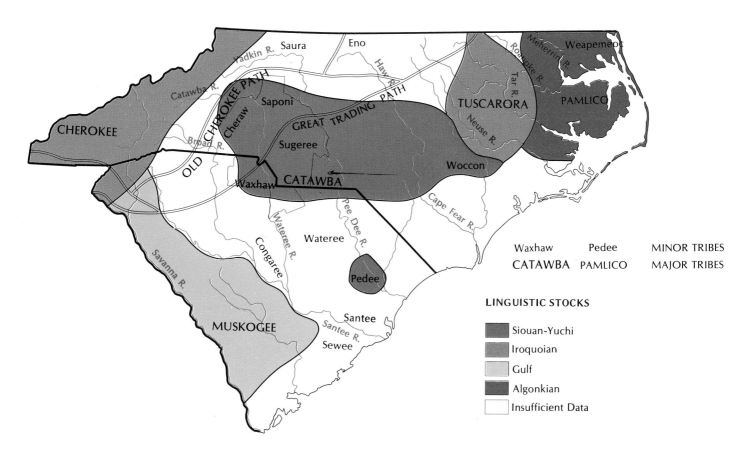

Fig. 2.2. Early Indian Tribes in the Carolinas

groups southward into the Piedmont. The largest of these groups was the Scotch-Irish, who came in the 1750s. By 1790 only New York and Pennsylvania had a larger percentage of non-English in their population than North and South Carolina. The German settlements were thickest in the area of southeast Rowan County while the Scotch-Irish were spread up and down the Catawba River.

The American Revolution

The Mecklenburg Declaration of Independence. The first major event in Metrolina related to the American Revolution was the reaction of the citizens, particularly in Mecklenburg, when news arrived from Massachusetts of the battles of Lexington and Concord. The historical record of what exactly happened in Mecklenburg during the spring of 1775 is very uncertain. Although most professional historians disagree, Mecklenburgers claim that their ancestors issued a document proclaiming them free and independent of Great Britain on May 20, 1775. (This date, along with the April 12, 1776, date of the state resolution, appear on the North Carolina state flag.) The controversy over this claim arises because there is no original copy of the so-called Mecklenburg Declaration of Independence.

Not only is there no original copy but Thomas Jefferson and John Adams, both prominent members of the Continental Congress, the body to which this proclamation was supposedly delivered, denied that they ever heard of it before 1819. There are other factors which cast doubt on the historical validity of the Mecklenburg Declaration. There were several important patriotic newspapers in the Carolinas in 1775 and none of them made the slightest mention of what should have been a momentous, headlining event. The names of the men who supposedly signed the Mecklenburg Declaration were determined in 1831 by act of the North Carolina General Assembly.

On the other hand, it is a proven historical fact that on May 31, 1775, the Committee of Public Safety of Mecklenburg passed a series of resolutions known in history as the Mecklenburg Resolves. This was a well-known event. The Resolves was a milder statement concerning a break in the relationship of the government of Mecklenburg with the crown. Many of the same men who were supposedly involved in the statement of May 20 were important in the drafting of the Resolves. The consensus of most historians is that several of the individuals involved with the Resolves recalled the incident years later in the slightly exaggerated form of the Mecklenburg Declaration. The major difference between the two documents is that the Declaration supposedly proclaimed the people of Mecklenburg to be free and independent, while the Resolves suspended royal authority and was a more moderate and cautious statement.

The War and Metrolina. The military activities of the American Revolution were brought to Metrolina by way of Charleston with the British invasion of the South in 1780. On May 12, after a long siege, the Americans were forced to surrender the city of Charleston to the British. The British learned that Colonel Abraham Buford and four hundred Virginia Continentals were nearing Charleston to aid the Americans. Buford learned of the surrender and turned around but the British sent Lieutenant Colonel Banastre Tarleton, a cavalry officer, in pursuit of Buford. Tarleton caught up with Buford in the Waxhaws on May 29 and slaughtered Buford's men, killing 113, wounding 150, and capturing 53—this, despite the fact that Buford tried to surrender. Tarleton gained the nickname of "Bloody," and the term "Tarleton's quarter," meaning the butchering of surrendered men, swept through the ranks of the American military. The fall of Charleston and Buford's massacre were followed by a major British victory at Camden, South Carolina, where the American general, Horatio Gates, lost his reputation after leading a hurried retreat of sixty-five miles to Charlotte and later to Hillsborough.

In light of these British victories the loyalists of the Carolinas began to organize to aid the British cause. On June 13, 1780, two hundred Tories gathered at Ramsour's Mill in Lincolnton under the leadership of John Moore. Within a week the number had increased to thirteen hundred. Word reached the patriots, and a force under Colonel Francis Locke of Rowan, consisting of four hundred men from Rowan, Mecklenburg, and Lincoln counties, marched on Ramsour's Mill. The suddenness of Locke's attack and the disorganization of the Tories carried the day for the patriots. Though losses were equal on both sides, the battle was an important victory for the patriots because it brought an end to Tory resistance in the Piedmont.

After the battle of Camden Lord Cornwallis decided to move toward Charlotte and advance through North Carolina. Cornwallis camped at the Waxhaws, on the Catawba River at Wahab's plantation. On the morning of September 21 the American Colonel William Davie launched a surprise attack on part of Cornwallis's force and collected 96 horses and 120 weapons at the cost of one man wounded. Davie, though greatly outnumbered, continued to harass Cornwallis's forces as the British moved into Charlotte. Cornwallis's army reached Charlotte on September 25 and Governor Josiah Martin, who accompanied Cornwallis, announced a week later that royal government had been restored in North Carolina. Evidently Cornwallis did not agree. He noted that, although Charlotte was an agreeable village, the people in the area were "more hostile to England than any in America." The news he was to receive in the next few days would support this statement.

Major Patrick Ferguson was foraging the countryside of the west, supporting the left flank of Cornwallis's army. Ferguson pushed into North Carolina at what is now Rutherfordton (then called Gilbert Town) on September 7, 1780. There he issued his famous threat that unless the American patriots of the mountain region "speedily dispersed and desisted from further resistance to the king's troops, he would cross the mountains, hang their leaders, and lay waste to their settlements with fire and sword." Such a threat would not and could not go unnoticed by the frontiersmen of the Appalachians. They gathered at Quaker Meadows, the plantation of Colonel Charles McDowell near Morganton, and then began to pursue Ferguson, who now, seeing the buildup of troops, called for reinforcements from Cornwallis. (The message was received after the battle.) At Cowpens on the South Carolina border Frederick Hambright and fifty men from Lincoln County joined the patriots in their pursuit. Ferguson decided to take his stand and await reinforcements atop Kings Mountain, a ridge about sixteen miles long running from Cleveland County, North Carolina, into York County, South Carolina. On October 7, despite the seemingly secure position of Ferguson on top of the ridge the patriots attacked his forces. The battle lasted about one hour and was a complete victory for the frontiersmen. Though Ferguson had the advantage of height, the frontiersmen took advantage of the high tree line, which gave these expert marksmen excellent cover as they moved toward the top. Of Ferguson's troops, 119 were killed including himself, 123 were wounded, and 664 were taken prisoner. The American losses were 28 killed and 62 wounded. The battle of Kings Mountain was sweet revenge for the earlier American losses. When Cornwallis learned of Ferguson's terrible defeat he was forced to withdraw southward to protect his flank now left open.

Meanwhile the American Congress, upset with the cowardliness of General Gates and the loss of the South, named General Nathanael Greene commander over the southern forces. Greene took command in Charlotte on December 2, 1780. He realized his force was too small to act directly against Cornwallis and decided to split his force and harass Cornwallis's flanks. He sent Daniel Morgan and one thousand men into western South Carolina and Greene himself took the rest of the army to operate in southeastern North Carolina and northeastern South Carolina. Cornwallis had eleven thousand men under his command but they were spread out so that he never had more than four thousand directly at his disposal. He could, however, have moved against either half of the American army and defeated it before the other half would have been able to join the battle. Instead of moving in force Cornwallis sent Colonel Banastre Tarleton after Daniel Morgan. They met at Cowpens just across the York county line on January 17, 1781. In a brilliant move Morgan defeated Tarleton's forces, killing or wounding 330 and capturing 600. Morgan then headed north with the British army in pursuit. On January 30 he crossed the Catawba at Sherrills' Ford where General Greene, having learned of the victory, met him. Cornwallis reached Ramsour's Mill on January 25, and, realizing that he was two days behind Morgan, burned most of his wagons and surplus baggage. As Cornwallis pursued Morgan through the Metrolina area the local militia units harassed his progress. General William Davidson organized some eight hundred militia men to guard the four fords crossing the Catawba River. These eight hundred men were stretched out along thirty miles of the river, the largest force guarding Beattie's Ford. General Davidson was in direct command of the troops at Cowan's Ford. As Cornwallis approached the river, on February 1, 1781, he made a feint at Beattie's Ford and then headed south to cross at Cowan's Ford before the American troops could organize. The British approached Cowan's Ford in the dark and had almost made it completely across before the Americans sounded the alarm. General Davidson courageously tried to rally his men but was shot and killed instantly. With the death of their commander the American troops scattered. (General William Davidson's heroics were rewarded in 1835 when the Presbyterians named a college after him.) Another encounter took place at Torrence's Tavern where "Bloody" Tarleton scattered a force of an undetermined number of militiamen.

Greene and Morgan decided the best strategy was to draw Cornwallis as far from his supply base as possible and then attack. The plan almost worked. The British and Americans met at Guilford Court House on March 15, 1781, with the British winning a victory that was so costly it was actually a defeat. Cornwallis left North Carolina shortly after the battle of Guilford Court House and moved to Yorktown where his defeat by Washington ended the war.

Thus three important events took place in the Metrolina counties that helped shape the outcome of the American Revolution: the early defeat of the Tories at Ramsour's Mill and the victories of Kings Mountain and Cowpens. (See Fig. 2.3.)

The Civil War

The Metrolina counties did not play a significant role as a battlefield during the Civil War. The only serious military action was Stoneman's raid. But the area was an important source of manpower for the Southern cause. And two cities, Charlotte and Salisbury, were important supply and railroad centers. Charlotte was also the site of the Confederate Naval Yard, and an important Confederate prison was located in Salisbury. (See Fig. 2.4.)

Metrolina was not a strong proslavery area; in fact, there was much antislavery sentiment, especially among the Germans of the area. For example, Rowan County's Hinton Rowan Helper, in his 1857 book, *The Impending Crisis of the South: How to Meet It,* argued that "slavery, and nothing but slavery, has retarded the progress and prosperity of our portion of the Union." Helper, who took an antislavery stand based on economic arguments, was not the least bit concerned with the welfare of the Negro. He simply felt that slavery endangered the economic position of the small white farmer. Helper considered the Negro a competitor and held the typical anti-Negro prejudices of the small farmer. Since it was a Southern repudiation of slavery, however, the book was used as political propaganda for the Republican party in the election of 1860.

Most citizens of the Metrolina area did not become overly excited as the events leading to the outbreak of the war unfolded. A secession meeting was held in Cleveland County in November, 1860, but proslavery feelings did not pervade much of the region, particularly the Metrolina counties of North Carolina. Stronger local support for the Southern cause became ardent, however, when North Carolina joined the Confederacy following President Lincoln's call for troops to put down rebellious South Carolina. The governor of North Carolina during these trying months was John Ellis of Rowan County. It was he who ordered the seizure of the federal mint at Charlotte following Lincoln's call for troops.

North Carolina led the Confederacy in providing troops for the army. With only one-ninth of the Confederacy's population, the state supplied one-sixth of the army. Although the exact number cannot be determined, the military personnel provided by the Metrolina counties of North Carolina was probably greater than that provided by any other section of the state. Counties such as Rowan and Mecklenburg sent one-fifth of their white population into the Confederate army.

The city of Charlotte received what had to be the most unusual task of any location during the Civil War. In the spring of 1862 the Confederate states faced the impending loss of their navy yard at Portsmouth, Virginia. Therefore, it was decided that this military installation would be moved to Charlotte, which, being far inland, was safe from Federal attack yet had good railroad connections with the seaboard. Thus in May, 1862, the Charlotte navy yard, as high and dry as it was, began operations. The city was also important for its production of gun powder. The Southern Chemical Works contracted with the Confederate government for the production of sulphuric acid.

The most important city in the Metrolina area during the Civil War era was Salisbury. Besides possessing a plant for the manufacture of arms, Salisbury had a major war prison. The prison was established in 1863 in an old cotton factory with a yard of approximately six acres enclosed by a twelve-foot stockade. Previous to the fall of 1864 the Federal troops imprisoned there were well treated. Major John H.

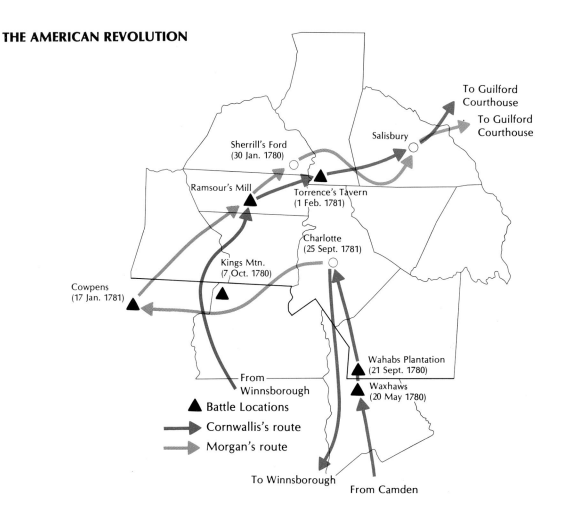

To Guilford
Courthouse

To Guilford
Courthouse

Salisbury

Sherrill's Ford
(30 Jan. 1780)

Ramsour's Mill

Torrence's Tavern
(1 Feb. 1781)

Charlotte
(25 Sept. 1781)

Kings Mtn.
(7 Oct. 1780)

Cowpens
(17 Jan. 1781)

Wahabs Plantation
(21 Sept. 1780)

From
Winnsborough

Waxhaws
(20 May 1780)

▲ Battle Locations

➤ Cornwallis's route

➤ Morgan's route

To Winnsborough

From Camden

Fig. 2.3. Prominent Metrolina Sites and Routes of the American Revolution

Gee of Selma, Alabama, was made commandant. Under his rule the Salisbury prison gained a reputation almost as dreadful as the infamous Andersonville. In 1864 there were 14,000 prisoners within the walls suffering a death rate as high as 75 per day and over a three-month period averaging not less than 40 deaths a day. At one point 526 men supposedly died in eight days. This establishment became a target of Federal raids into the Piedmont. In June, 1864, Colonel George W. Kirk, a federal officer who conducted guerrilla warfare in the mountains, raided Morganton with the idea of capturing a train on the Western North Carolina Railroad and moving to Salisbury to free the prisoners. He was turned back.

Although the Piedmont was not the site of any major battle the people faced frustrations similar to those of a battle zone. The major problem was a shortage of food. For example, at one point a group of angry women in Salisbury marched on the store of Michael Brown and began to ransack it. They were stopped only by the promise of being given several barrels of flour. More distressing than the irate women were the bands of deserters who roamed and plundered the Catawba and Iredell county areas. As the war dragged on this group became larger.

It was Major General George H. Stoneman of the Federal army who brought the largest military action into the Metrolina area. His purpose was to disrupt rail connections in the western Virginia and North Carolina area, such as the North Carolina Railroad. Stoneman reached Salisbury on April 12, 1865. The city, with its prison, hospitals, and warehouses receiving goods shipped north in front of Sherman and south from Richmond, was a virtual gold mine. The fact that the prisoners had been moved out almost a month earlier did not dampen the eagerness of the attacking Federal troops who had heard of the atrocities at the prison. The city fell to Stoneman with very little resistance. Before destroying supplies and buildings

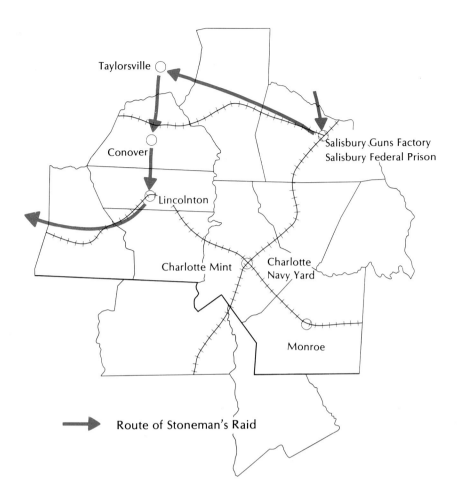

Fig. 2.4. Prominent Metrolina Sites and Routes of the Civil War

worth over $100,000, Stoneman allowed the poor whites and Negroes to take what they wanted. At the same time Stoneman showed amazing control over his men, preventing them from looting the town.

Stoneman's troops spent the next two weeks roaming from Salisbury to Statesville to Lincolnton. A detachment moved into South Carolina and burned a bridge of the Charlotte and South Carolina Railroad. Shortly after this raid Stoneman moved his troops to Asheville by way of Blowing Rock and Boone.

Stoneman's forays into the area south of Salisbury caused great concern in the Charlotte area, with its navy yard and mint. The concern was heightened by the fact that the Confederate treasure, or public funds of the government, had recently arrived at the mint. Captain H. A. Ramsay of the navy yard was ordered to raise two companies from the navy yard's employees. Despite the close scare, no action took place.

In a sense, it could be said that the Civil War ended in Charlotte. President Jefferson Davis arrived in the city on April 19, 1865, and departed on April 26, the last day of the Confederate government.

The Negro

The Negroes have traditionally comprised a substantial proportion of the Metrolina population. Their importance has not corresponded to their number. This doesn't mean they have not played an important part in the growth and formation of the region, but their contribution has not always been visible. The history of the Negroes in Metrolina can be divided into four phases: (1) Negroes under slavery, (2) free Negroes before the Civil War, (3) Negroes after emancipation, and (4) Negroes as citizens.

The first and most obvious role played by the Negro was

as a slave. The 1790 census, however, the first ever taken in the United States, indicates that slavery was not a vital part of the economy of the Metrolina counties at that time. This is best illustrated by Fig. 2.5. It is evident that the two South Carolina counties made a greater use of slaves but that slavery was not a major source of labor throughout the region. Metrolina counties tended to be well below the state averages in the percentage of families holding slaves and in the average number of slaves per slave-holding family. In 1790 the largest number of slaves held by one man in Lancaster County was 135, and in York only 84. These two counties were the most important as far as slavery was concerned because of the greater significance of the cotton culture within those areas. Yet, unlike some important cotton-producing parts of the South, Lancaster and York counties were largely devoid of the large plantation owner with control over hundreds of slaves. Only twenty-three men in the two counties owned more than

fifteen slaves; sixteen of these men owned more than twenty; and only ten of this group owned twenty-five or more slaves. In comparing these figures with Lincoln County, which had the fewest slaves per family, we find that the slaveholder owning the largest number of slaves in Lincoln County, Arthur Graham, owned only twenty-two slaves and that the two owners holding the next largest number in that county held eighteen and sixteen.

Since these statistics pertain to 1790 they can be somewhat misleading. After all, Lancaster County's population in 1790 was only 23 percent Negro as compared to 49 percent Negro in 1860. Lincoln County's population expanded from 10 percent Negro to 27 percent Negro. Does this mean that slaveholding became more widespread by 1860 in Metrolina? One study has shown that by 1840 the cotton production of the southwestern counties of North Carolina began to rival the eastern counties' output and that there was an accelerated rate of growth of the slave

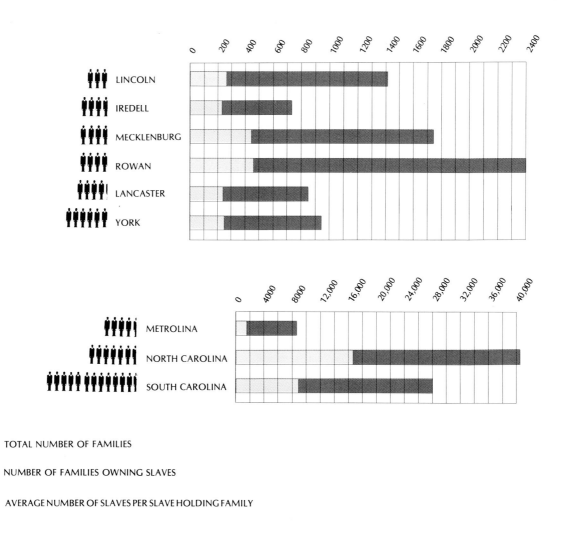

Fig. 2.5. Families and Slaveholding in Metrolina and North and South Carolina, 1790

Table 2.1. Percentage Growth of Slave and White Population in Eastern and Western North Carolina Counties, 1790-1860

	West	East
Slave	387	161
White	182	61

Table 2.2. Extent of Slaveholding in North and South Carolina, 1790-1860

	Percentage of Slaveholding Families		Average Number of Slaves per Family	
	1790	1860	1790	1860
North Carolina	31.0	26.8	6.8	10.2
South Carolina	34.2	48.4	12.1	15.0

population in the west. (See Table 2.1.) Other reports tend to soften the impact of the above study. For example, the percentage of families holding slaves and the average number of slaves held per family in North and South Carolina does not reflect this magnitude of increase. (See Table 2.2.) In Gaston County, where there were 2,199 slaves in 1860, the owner who held the largest number of slaves held 40 slaves and only 33 owners held 10 or more. There were only 360 slaveholders out of 1,273 families. The 1850 census contained but three families in Mecklenburg County that held more than 50 slaves: Davidson, with 109; Torrence, with 65; and Davis, with 54.

Thus slavery in Metrolina was characterized by many families owning a few slaves but very few families owning a large number. Despite trends in surrounding areas toward an increase in slaveholding, Metrolina's situation remained relatively stable.

What about the free Negro? How did he fare and what did he do? Free Negroes before the Civil War were never a large percentage of the total population or even of the Negro population. It seems that the small white farmer, especially in the Piedmont, was against slavery and used poor landless whites or free Negroes as laborers. Thus in counties where there was little slaveholding there were substantial numbers of free Negro farm laborers. The counties of Cabarrus, Cleveland, Gaston, and Rowan were examples of this. Farm laborers or common laborers accounted for the occupations of most of the free Negroes in Metrolina. Some of them served as apprentices and became skilled craftsmen, however, particularly in Mecklenburg, Lincoln, and Cleveland counties. They entered such trades as blacksmithing, masonry, carpentering, and wagonmaking. Little opportunity existed for free

Negroes to obtain a formal education; thus the illiteracy rate was very high among them. It was possible for a free Negro to hold slaves, but only one such occurrence was recorded in the Metrolina counties (in Lancaster County in 1790). There were few free Negroes who owned any kind of property. Figures for the ten North Carolina counties show that out of 1,001 free Negroes only 42 owned realty and only 97 claimed any personal property.

As the Civil War approached the lot of the free Negro steadily deteriorated. A statement presented by a grand jury of Cleveland County, a county with a very low percentage of Negro population, summed up the situation in 1858: "We, the Grand Jury of Cleveland County, North Carolina, do present, that free Negroes in general are a nuisance to society; and that it would be expedient to have a law requiring them to leave the State, and for a failure to do so, that they should be exposed to public sale, the proceeds arising therefrom be applied to the Literary Fund of our State. Adopted by unanimous consent."

The Civil War did not change the plight of the black man. He gained his freedom but could do very little with it. In the decade following the Civil War the Negro population remained stable in all the Metrolina counties. A steady out-migration typical of much of the South began soon, however, and the period 1880 to 1960 recorded a halving of the percentage of Negro population in eight of the twelve counties and a decrease in three others. Cleveland County has been the only county to show an increase in the percentage of Negroes in its population during the last century. This development is paralleled by statistics showing Cleveland as having one of the largest percentage increases in Negro farmers in the state. At the same time the number of Negro farmers was decreasing in most of the other Metrolina counties.

By the turn of the twentieth century the Negro was experiencing a reduction of his freedom on many fronts. In 1900 a statewide suffrage amendment disfranchised Negro voters in North Carolina. Every North Carolina Metrolina county except Lincoln voted in favor of the amendment. The trend continued as segregation was imposed on the Negro by the so-called "Jim Crow laws" allowed by the separate but equal ruling of the United States Supreme Court. The effectiveness of "separate but equal" school systems was reflected by the low literacy rates among the Negro population. For example, the 1930 statistics, which come under the separate but equal Supreme Court ruling, reveal the following expenditures per student.

	White	Black
Cabarrus	$25.03	$11.55
Catawba	28.17	15.42
Cleveland	23.83	9.11
Gaston	33.06	14.14
Iredell	27.06	13.74
Lincoln	20.46	10.31
Mecklenburg	40.53	14.90
Rowan	31.91	17.16
Stanly	24.16	13.46
Union	25.72	8.70
Lancaster	32.62	7.18
York	37.72	7.70

The New Deal legislation of Franklin D. Roosevelt brought some relief to this situation in the 1930s and 1940s but not enough to prevent many of the issues facing our system of public education today. It was not until the 1960s that the Negro's second class citizenship began to dissipate. As late as 1963 only three urban areas in Metrolina had desegregated their public facilities—Charlotte, Hickory, and Statesville. Many of the other urban areas had not integrated any of their facilities.

Thus the history of the plight of the Negro, while it has been no worse than in many sections of the country, has really not been better in Metrolina. The future has brightened but there is much to be done.

The Development in Counties

With the exception of minor boundary changes, the present boundaries of the Metrolina counties were completed in 1846 by the formation of Gaston County from land formerly in Lincoln County. (See Fig. 2.6.) At the beginning of the region's political development, all the land area which makes up Metrolina, excluding the two South Carolina counties York and Lancaster, was within the boundaries of Anson County when it was created in 1750.

As settlement spread into the Piedmont, particularly with the influx of Scotch-Irish and Germans, Anson became too large a territory to administer and thus Rowan County was established. Formed in 1753, the county was named in honor of Matthew Rowan, who was acting governor of North Carolina at the time. The county seat established in 1755 was known as Rowan Court House and became the city of Salisbury. As the county's population grew, its area was destined to shrink. Between 1770 and 1836 six different counties—Guilford, Surry, Burke, Iredell, Davidson, and Davie—were formed either entirely or partly from Rowan.

Rowan County was the center of activity of the Piedmont area for almost a century. Its population was a cross section of European immigrants with varying social and religious backgrounds. Because of its central location Rowan became a center of trade and transportation.

Continued migration down the Yadkin and Catawba River Basins caused a further division of Anson County with the creation of Mecklenburg. The county was named in honor of the wife of George III, king of England, Princess Charlotte Sophia of Mecklenburg-Strelitz. The county officially came into existence on February 1, 1763, and Charlotte became the county seat in 1776. Mecklenburg's

Fig. 2.6. Development of Metrolina County Boundaries and County Seats, 1775-1972

size diminished during the next three-quarters of a century with the creation of Tryon, Cabarrus, and Union counties.

Mecklenburg was a major agricultural area in its early years of existence. A major reason that Lord Cornwallis decided to use Charlotte as his headquarters during the American Revolution was the abundance of grain and gristmills in the area. Mecklenburg was to be surrounded by several counties of industrial importance and its relationship to these counties and its location as a transportation center would contribute later to Mecklenburg's importance as a commercial trade center.

The area west of Mecklenburg filled in rapidly and created the need for Tryon County in 1768. Named after the royal governor involved in the Regulator movement who was not a particular favorite of the back-country settlers, Tryon County was dissolved in 1779 and Lincoln County created. The county received its name from General Benjamin Lincoln, an American general in the Revolution. Lincolnton was selected as the county seat in 1785. Lincoln County was the largest and most heavily populated of the Metrolina counties, and also had the most potential for industrial development. Through the strange twists of geography and politics, however, Lincoln County became one of the smaller and more rural of the counties in the area. This transition took place with the carving up of Lincoln to create Cleveland, Catawba, and Gaston counties. Lincoln County was unique in the Piedmont in one respect as it was the only county in the area whose delegates voted in favor of ratification of the United States Constitution.

In 1785 two counties, Lancaster and York, were formed on the western edge of the so-called Camden district in South Carolina. Until after the Civil War South Carolina used the district rather than the county as its major political unit. A district consisted of several counties. This causes some difficulty in dealing with the pre-Civil War history of South Carolina on a county basis.

Lancaster County, with its original county seat of Hanging Rock, was established on March 12, 1785, and named after Lancaster, England. The county seat was moved to the town of Lancaster in 1793. Lancaster County was to remain a rural farm area until later in the nineteenth century when textile mills started to develop there. Despite this development the area stayed basically agricultural.

York County and its county seat of Yorkville (later renamed York) was formed on the same date as Lancaster. It was named for the Duke of York. The county would become an important cotton-producing area and would attract a considerable number of textile mills.

In 1788 James Iredell of Edenton was honored by having a county created in his name. Iredell was a leading advocate of the United States Constitution and became one of the earliest justices of the Supreme Court. Iredell County was formed from land belonging to Rowan. Statesville became the county seat in 1789. Iredell's area remained relatively stable despite four boundary changes with Burke and Wilkes counties. A very small part of Iredell was included in the creation of Alexander County in 1847. Iredell developed mainly as an agricultural area and always has ranked high in the number of farms and average size of farms among the Metrolina counties. This agricultural development was eventually paralleled by substantial industrial growth, giving the county a better economic balance.

Shortly after the formation of Iredell County, another Edenton man, Stephen Cabarrus, was honored with the formation in 1792 of Cabarrus County. The naming of these counties to honor the great leaders from the eastern part of the state was no accident. It pacified eastern legislators who were reluctant to create new counties which reduced that section's political control in a legislature apportioned by counties. The land used to create Cabarrus County was formerly part of Mecklenburg County. Concord was incorporated as the county seat in 1806.

Cabarrus County was a farming area producing large quantities of corn and wheat. The major industry until the end of the nineteenth century was flour-milling. The county became a major textile manufacturing area, especially with the development of Cannon Mills.

Cabarrus was the last county to be formed in the Metrolina area during the eighteenth century. It was not until over fifty years later that the county boundaries were completed. The five years from 1841 to 1846 witnessed the creation of the five counties that completed Metrolina. These were Cleveland, Stanly, Catawba, Union, and Gaston. This sudden rash of county building resulted from a movement to amend the North Carolina constitution and give better representation to the western half of the state.

The first of these counties to be created was Cleveland. It was formed in 1841 from parts of Rutherford and Lincoln and named for Colonel Benjamin Cleaveland, one of the American leaders at the battle of Kings Mountain. In 1887 the "a" was dropped, creating the present spelling of the county's name. Shelby became the county seat in 1843. Cleveland County was basically agriculturally oriented and in past decades its land yielded more cotton per acre than the Mississippi delta lands.

On the eastern extremity of Metrolina, Stanly County was formed in 1841 along with its county seat of Albemarle. The county was named in honor of John Stanly, a leading North Carolina legislator and Speaker of the House. Montgomery County was split in order to create Stanly. Stanly County, like Cleveland, has retained an agricultural economy from its conception.

Lincoln County suffered most from this rising tide of county proliferation. In 1842 Lincoln lost even more of its land area with the creation of Catawba County, named for the Indian tribe. Newton became the county seat in 1845. Catawba County was to become one of the major industrial areas in Metrolina.

Union County was formed in 1842, rounding out the eastern side of Metrolina, and Monroe was selected as the county seat. The county, created from parts of Anson and Mecklenburg, caused a minor dispute between the Whigs, who wanted to name the area Clay County, and the Democrats, who favored the idea of calling it Jackson County. The present name was adopted as a compromise on the rationale that the county was created from parts of two others. Union, like most of these newer counties, was mainly a farm area.

The most devastating blow to Lincoln County came in 1846 with the creation of Gaston County. This area was destined to become a manufacturing center of Metrolina, while Lincoln County, after losing the Catawba and Gaston area, was relegated to a rural existence. Gaston County was named for William Gaston, who served in Congress and was also a judge of the North Carolina Supreme Court. In the 1840s Gaston was the banner whiskey county of the state, but the distilling industry would eventually yield to social pressure and finally to the growth of the textile industry. Dallas, named for George Mifflin Dallas, vice-president of the United States, was the original county seat. It became a bustling town with schools, hotels, and taverns surrounding the still existing courthouse. When the railroad bypassed Dallas and, instead, came through Garibaldi Station, Dallas was doomed. On the site of Garibaldi Station grew the town of Gastonia, whose citizens began to pressure the voters to move the county seat to their town. After several unsuccessful attempts, the voters decided on August 5, 1909, that beginning in 1911 Gastonia would be the county seat.

REFERENCES

Alexander, J. B. *Mecklenburg County from 1740-1900.* Charlotte: Observer Printing House, 1902.

Brawley, James S. *The Rowan Story: 1753-1953.* Salisbury: Rowan Printing Co., 1953.

Catawba County Historical Association, Inc. *A History of Catawba County.* Salisbury: Rowan Printing Co., 1954.

Cope, Robert F., and Manly Wade Wellman. *The County of Gaston: Two Centuries of a North Carolina Region.* Charlotte: Gaston County Historical Society, 1961.

Corbit, David Leroy. *The Formation of the North Carolina Counties, 1663-1943.* Raleigh: State Department of Archives and History, 1950.

Franklin, John Hope. *The Free Negro in North Carolina, 1790-1860.* New York: Russell and Russell, 1969.

Gilbert, John, and Grady Jeffrerys. *Crossties Through Carolina.* Raleigh: Helios Press, 1969.

Hammer, Carl, Jr. *Rhinelanders on the Yadkin.* Salisbury: Rowan Printing Co., 1965.

Hobbs, S. Huntington, Jr. *North Carolina: An Economic and Social Profile.* Chapel Hill: University of North Carolina Press, 1958.

Johnson, Charles S. *Statistical Atlas of Southern Counties.* Chapel Hill: University of North Carolina Press, 1941.

Powell, William S. *North Carolina Gazeteer.* Chapel Hill: University of North Carolina Press, 1968.

Ramsey, Robert W. *Carolina Cradle: Settlement of the Northwest Carolina Frontier, 1747-1762.* Chapel Hill: University of North Carolina Press, 1964.

Rights, Douglas L. *The American Indian in North Carolina.* Winston-Salem: J. F. Blair, 1957.

Rumple, The Reverend Jethro. *A History of Rowan County, North Carolina.* Salisbury: Elizabeth Maxwell Steele Chapter, Daughters of the American Revolution, 1929.

Separk, Joseph H. *Gastonia and Gaston County, North Carolina, 1846-1949.* Gastonia: The author, 1949.

Sherrill, W. L. *Annals of Lincoln County, North Carolina, 1749-1937.* Charlotte: Observer Printing House, 1937.

Tompkins, D. A. *Mecklenburg County and Charlotte, 1740-1903.* Charlotte: Observer Printing House, 1903.

Wallace, David Duncan. *South Carolina: A Short History, 1520-1948.* Columbia: University of South Carolina Press, 1961.

3. PHYSICAL ENVIRONMENT AND PRIMARY INDUSTRIES

JAMES W. CLAY

"We travel together, passengers on a little space ship, dependent on its vulnerable supplies of air and soil . . . preserved from annihilation only by the care, the work, and I will say the love we give our fragile craft."

—Adlai Stevenson

Planning for the future of the region must be based on a better understanding of the interaction between human activities and the natural environment, and the ability of the environment to sustain and renew itself. Our society is increasingly aware of the esthetic value of the environment. Climate, air, geology, water, and soils have each had a central role in molding the character of the region. A primary aim throughout this section is to increase awareness and appreciation for this role and to increase sensitivity to the vulnerability of the environment.

This section also attempts to narrow the information gap about the general characteristics of the physical environment. Most Americans know of and appreciate such remarkable and spectacular phenomena as the Grand Canyon, Petrified Forest, Painted Desert, and the Florida Everglades. But too often these same people are unaware of some fascinating features of the landscape of their own region. Metrolina has a most interesting and varied landscape. It has a choice climate, extremely diversified geology, and a great asset in its many streams and lakes. In this section each of the major components of the environment is examined and some emphasis is also given to the human interactions with them.

CLIMATE

Metrolina lies in a humid subtropical climate region which extends north from the Gulf of Mexico to Maryland and west from the Atlantic coast to Arkansas. This climatic region, corresponding roughly with "the South," is characterized by short, mild winters, long, hot summers, and a relatively uniform distribution of rainfall throughout the year. Spring and fall seasons are very long and temperatures are typically quite pleasant. Metrolina's climate, in a general way, is representative of this southern climate, but climate regions are generalizations while places within them have unique conditions. To describe those unique conditions as they occur in Metrolina, its basic climatic components are examined.

Sunshine

The sun is the single noteworthy source of heat for the earth's atmosphere and is the ultimate cause of all atmospheric changes and motions. Thus the distribution of its radiation over the earth's surface and those factors accounting for variations in receipt of radiation are of paramount significance to an understanding of climate.

The most fundamental of these factors is the angle at which the sunrays strike the earth. Oblique rays are spread out over a larger surface than are vertical ones and thus deliver less energy per unit area. As is the case in all continental locations of the United States the rays from the noon sun throughout Metrolina are oblique and southerly. The altitude (angular distance from the horizon) of the noon sun at a location near the center of Metrolina ranges from a low of 31½ degrees on December 22 to a high of 78½ degrees on June 21.

The length of the day is a second factor accounting for variations in solar energy receipts: the lower the number of hours of sunshine during a twenty-four hour period, the

Fig. 3.1 (a). Hours of Sunshine by Months Throughout the Year in Metrolina

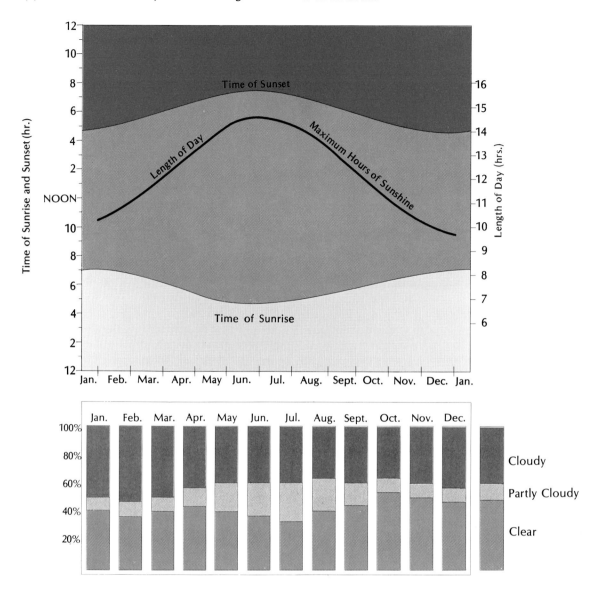

Fig. 3.1 (b). Characteristic Monthly Cloud Cover in Metrolina

lower the receipt of solar energy. The time of sunrise and sunset and thus the length of the day varies directly with the noon sun altitude. (Sunrise and sunset are considered to occur when the upper edge of the disk of the sun appears to be exactly on an unobstructed horizon.) As can be observed in Fig. 3.1 (a), on June 21, when the sun's altitude is highest, the sun rises at approximately 5:09 A.M. (Eastern Standard Time) and sets at approximately 7:41 P.M. for Metrolina observers. On December 22, when the sun's altitude is lowest, the sun rises at 7:29 A.M. and sets at approximately 5:16 P.M. Thus the length of day varies from nine hours and forty-seven minutes on December 22 to fourteen hours and thirty-two minutes on June 21, a difference of four hours and forty-five minutes.

As solar radiation passes through the atmosphere a varying amount of energy is lost through absorption by water vapor and carbon dioxide in the air and through scattering by particles such as dust. The amount of energy lost by these processes can be correlated with the intensity of cloud cover. Fig. 3.1 (b) illustrates the characteristic monthly cloud cover in Metrolina by giving the average percentage of each month that the sky was clear, partly cloudy, or mostly cloudy. The sun shines more than half of all daylight hours. On an annual basis clear skies occur approximately 42 percent of the year and partly clear skies occur 15 percent of the year. Although there is considerably more moisture and rain during the summer months, the number of cloudy days and the average amount of cloud cover is less in summer than in winter. This is explained by the fact that summers are characterized by

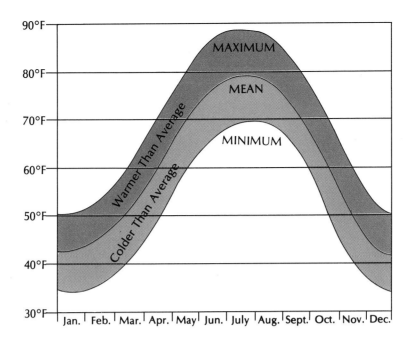

Fig. 3.2. Monthly Average, Minimum, Mean, and Maximum Air Temperatures at Charlotte

short intervals of cloudy periods followed by clear skies while winters characteristically have long unbroken periods of overcast.

Air Temperature

The seasonal cycle of the minimum, mean, and maximum monthly average temperatures of Charlotte, a typical Metrolina station, is shown in Fig. 3.2. At Charlotte mean air temperatures range from 42° F. in January to 78° F. in July. Variations from these mean temperatures at other Metrolina stations are slight. At Hickory they range from 41° F. to 77° F.; at Salisbury, from 42° F. to 79° F.

Ranges for the same periods at St. Louis, a midwestern city; New Orleans, a Gulf Coast city; and New York, a northeastern city, provide a basis for comparison. St. Louis, with an average January temperature of 32° F. and July temperature of 79° F. has colder winters and hotter summers. New York City, with an average January temperature of 32° F. and average July temperature of 76° F., has summers which are very similar but winters that are characteristically colder. New Orleans, with an average January temperature of 54° F., and a July temperature of 84° F. has milder winters but hotter summers.

Although the annual temperature range of approximately 35° F. is not large it does make for distinctive seasonal changes. During the summer months, when days are long, the sun high in the sky, and the cold polar air has retreated far to the north, the land becomes heated

and temperatures rise above levels of comfort. Occasionally extreme temperatures of 90° F. or higher occur and may persist for several days. These heat waves are characteristic over most of eastern North America and usually result from anticyclonic conditions (highs) that remain for several days over the area, bringing in warm, initially humid air from the south. Relatively clear skies and calm air associated with the high pressure cell allows the sun to warm the land and the air above to unusual high temperatures. These heat waves do not remain for more than a few days and are replaced by more moderate conditions. As a matter of fact, occasional mild invasions of air from the north continue to occur during the summer to bring short periods of greater relief.

July is Metrolina's warmest month and as illustrated by Fig. 3.3 (a) its average monthly temperature ranges from 77° F. in the northern and western portions to 80° F. in the south. As average temperatures drop about 1° for each three-hundred-foot increase, the lower temperatures in the northern and western portions are largely a result of the higher elevations characterizing those portions. The mean maximum temperature in the midafternoon at Charlotte is 88° F. with the thermometer frequently rising into the 90s on a given day. Night temperatures are about 20° cooler than at midday. Around dawn the thermometer drops to a mean minimum temperature of about 68° F. Again the lower temperatures are recorded in the western portions. Metrolina's July temperatures are slightly higher than those of New York City where the average maximum is 84° F. and average minimum is 67° F., very similar to St. Louis

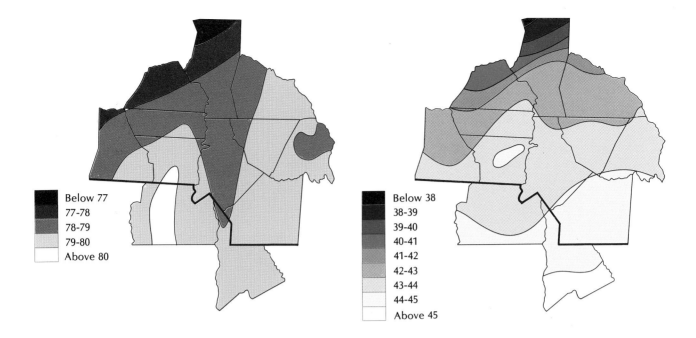

Fig. 3.3 (a). Average Metrolina July Temperature

Fig. 3.3 (b). Average Metrolina January Temperature

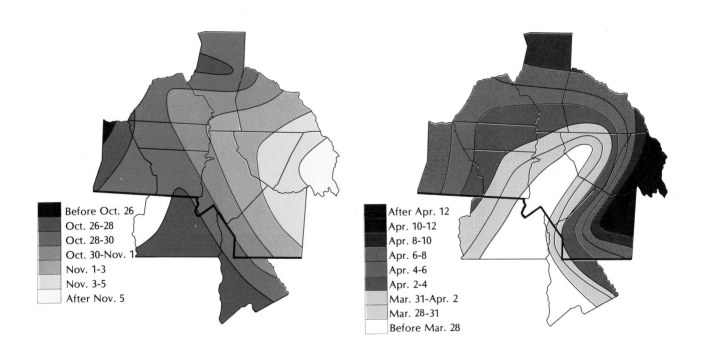

Fig. 3.3 (c). Average Date of First Fall Freeze in Metrolina

Fig. 3.3 (d). Average Date of Last Spring Freeze in Metrolina

where the average maximum is 88° F. and the average minimum is 70° F. and more comfortable than New Orleans where the average maximum is 90° F. and the minimum is 74° F.

Autumn is characteristically long, extending through most of November, and tends to bring clear weather with calm prevailing at this time more than at any other season. Temperatures are mild and pleasant. At Charlotte October has an average temperature of 62° F., an average maximum of 72° F., and an average minimum of about 51° F. As autumn progresses nighttime temperatures drop to increasingly lower values. Night temperature inversions occur with increasing frequency under calm, clear skies, bringing frost to the ground.

As the period of darkness lengthens and the surface receives less and less warmth from the lowering sun, the land becomes steadily cooler and the region experiences a distinct winter period starting in mid-December. Winters are mild for the latitude, however. The Blue Ridge Mountains and a number of smaller mountains between Metrolina and the Blue Ridge have a moderating effect on winter temperatures by providing partial protection from the frequent outbreak of polar air masses. When the cold air does penetrate these mountains, it is normally warmed by its descent on the eastern slopes. Thus extreme cold is rare throughout Metrolina. At Charlotte, for example, zero temperatures have occurred only four times since 1878. The lowest temperature ever, −5° F., was recorded in 1899. The lowest recorded temperatures at Hickory and Salisbury during the period 1937-66 were −2° F. and −11° F. respectively. There is comparatively little severe cold weather until mid-December with the coldest month of the year coming in January. As illustrated by Fig. 3.3 (b), January has average temperatures that range from 38° F. in the northern counties of Iredell and Catawba to 45° F. in several southern counties. The variation, although somewhat related to latitudinal differences, is largely a response to elevation. From the northwestern edge of Metrolina to the southeastern corner, the elevation drops more than twelve hundred feet.

In Metrolina the weather is very changeable since the area plays host to passing cyclonic storms and alternating polar and tropical air masses. In any given week the weather may fluctuate between mild, cool, or cold. Under such conditions averages often obscure real patterns by concealing extremes. Winter weather in Metrolina may be better understood by looking at such extremes. During each of the three winter months (December, January, and February) freezing temperatures on as many as eighteen days have been recorded, but there is a considerable variation from year to year. For example, at Charlotte subfreezing temperatures during January, the coldest month, have been recorded on as few as two days and as many as twenty-one. During December they have been recorded for as few days as one and for as many as nineteen, and for February for

as few as zero and as many as eighteen. In the last forty years average January temperatures have ranged from a low of 31° F. in 1940 to a high of 54° F. in 1950. In comparison, New York City experiences subzero temperatures during as many as three months and its January temperatures average between 16° F. and 37° F. St. Louis also has subzero temperatures during each of the three winter months and recorded January averages ranging from 14° F. to 43° F. Winters in New Orleans are milder. During the same period no subzero temperatures were recorded and January temperatures ranged from an average of 42° F. to 67° F.

Winters are relatively short and by mid-March temperatures are on the rise as the sun's rays exert an increasing heating effect upon the land. The storm systems that bring cold weather southward come less often and are replaced by the gradual northward penetration of warm, usually moisture-laden winds from the Atlantic or Gulf. Day-to-day variations in temperatures become less pronounced, and warm weather is more likely to occur with clear skies. The rise in temperature is usually greatest in April and residential heating is generally discontinued by late April or early May. Springs are relatively long, extending through two or three months, and tend to be quite pleasant. A typical April day would have a high of 60° F. and the night a low of 50° F.

Low Temperature Probabilities

Below freezing temperatures, particularly during nights and early mornings, occur frequently throughout the area from mid-November through mid-March. As indicated in Fig. 3.3 (c), the average dates of the first of these freezes range from October 25 in Stanly County to November 4 in the southern counties of Lancaster and York. As indicated in Fig. 3.3 (d), the average date of the last freeze in the spring varies from April 13 in Stanly County to March 28 in York County. Thus Metrolina's average annual freeze-free period or "growing season" ranges from about 200 days in the east to about 220 days in the south and west.

The longer growing season in the west seems, at first glance, contrary to what might be expected, for the higher elevation and latitude that characterizes the west should result in lower temperatures. This seemingly anomalous situation illustrates one of the unique climatic features of the area, the presence of "thermal belts" or "verdant zones." These belts are small areas that have higher temperatures than adjacent or nearby areas less favorably situated. The resultant "thermal belts" support frost-susceptible vegetation long after the greenery has disappeared in nearby areas. Often in early winter or even in midwinter a contrasting belt of green flanked above and below by brown may be seen. These green belts are thought to be locations along slopes that face the winter sun, are protected from cold northerly winds, and have cold air drainage to lower valleys.

Fig. 3.4. Annual Heating Degree Days at Charlotte

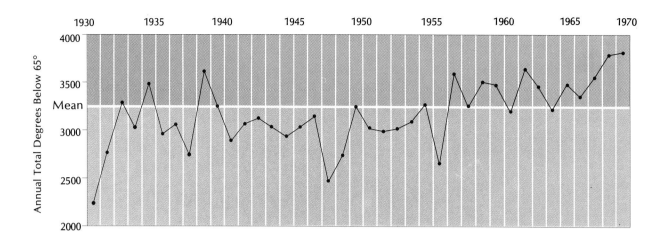

Fig. 3.5. Departures of Heating Degree Days at Charlotte from Annual Average

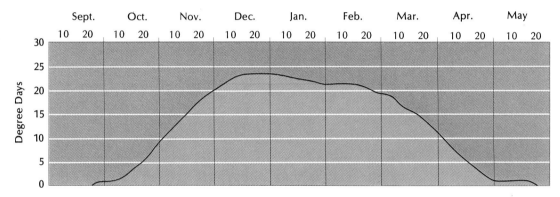

The Degree Day

The degree day concept is commonly used by the heating
industry to estimate heat deficiency and fuel needs. Fuel
companies and heating engineers utilize the records to determine fuel consumption loads and to schedule deliveries.
Records of heating degree days are also consulted by archi-
tects and engineers in designing or selecting heating systems. The degree day is based on the assumption that an
average daily temperature of 65° F. approximates the temperature above which artificial heating is not required. It
is calculated on a daily basis by measuring the negative departure of the mean air temperature from this specified
base and expressed in units called "heating degree day."
In other words, if the daily mean air temperature is 60° F.,
the heating degree days would be five; if the daily mean
air temperature is 50° F., the heating degree days would
be fifteen, and so on. The average annual heating-degree-
day total for a location would be the sum of negative departures of daily average temperature from 65° F. for all
days of the year, averaged over a period of years.

As shown in Fig. 3.4, mean annual heating degree days
total 3,186 at the Charlotte station. This compares to an
annual average of 1,327 at New Orleans; 4,758 at St.
Louis; and 4,930 at New York City. On a monthly basis
heating is required about seven months a year with very
little heating required before October and after late April.
November and March provide the transition from and to
the warmer season while December, January, and February
are the uniquely cold months. As illustrated in Fig. 3.4,
departures from the annual average are moderate with degree days ranging from about 2,200 in 1931 to about
3,800 in 1969.

Humidity and Sensible Temperature

Metrolina's average relative humidity is moderately high.
It does not vary greatly from season to season but is generally highest in summer and lowest in the spring. The annual
and daily humidity cycle at Charlotte is typical for the region. Here the average relative humidity at 7:00 P.M.

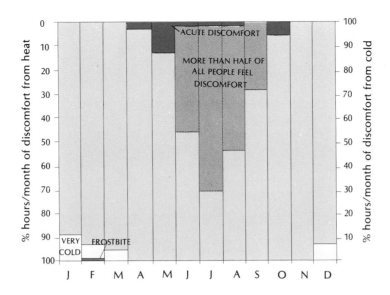

Fig. 3.6. Metrolina Discomfort Index

ranges from 51 percent in March and April to 67 percent in July and August. Summer humidity is higher because the repeated invasion of marine tropical air from the south brings very moist air into the area. Since the moisture saturation capacity of the air reduces as temperatures drop, the highest daily humidity levels usually occur during early morning and the lowest during early afternoon. During July the 7:00 A.M. humidity averages 89 percent, but as temperatures rise the humidity drops and by 1:00 P.M. the average drops to 58 percent. Although moderately high, Metrolina's summer humidity is, on the average, lower than any of the three comparison stations. During summer the daily average humidity ranges from 66 to 91 percent in New Orleans, from 58 to 78 percent in New York; and from 55 to 85 percent in St. Louis.

Humidity levels have a fundamental relationship to sensible temperatures (the body response to air temperature). On a damp day cold air is more penetrating while high temperatures are more oppressive. Thus when high summer air temperatures occur under conditions of high humidity acute discomfort may occur. Likewise a combination of high humidity and low temperature, though not common during winter days, may cause considerable discomfort. The extent of discomfort experienced as a result of the combined effect of temperature and humidity levels is illustrated in Fig. 3.6. In Metrolina June, July, and August are clearly months when discomfort from heat is experienced while December, January, and February are months when discomfort from cold may occur.

Precipitation

The region is well watered with average annual precipitation

varying from forty-three inches at Charlotte to forty-nine inches at Hickory. Precipitation is largely in the form of rain with only occasional snow or sleet. At Charlotte, for example, snow and sleet are usually recorded once or twice a year with an average snow accumulation of only five inches. Departures from normal precipitation are usually small, but as shown in Fig. 3.7, they can be substantial. Over the past forty years annual precipitation at Charlotte has ranged from a high of sixty-seven inches in 1936 to a low of thirty inches in 1933. Annual snowfall during this same period, averaging about five inches, has ranged from amounts too small to record during each of several winters to twenty-two inches in the winter of 1959-60. Snowfall variation from year to year is also illustrated in Fig. 3.7. Although precipitation is reasonably well distributed throughout the year, there are distinct seasonal variations in types and amounts.

Summers are Metrolina's rainiest period with monthly precipitation averaging between four and five inches. July is its wettest month, receiving an average of about five inches of rain. During July, 1944, Charlotte experienced its wettest month in forty years, recording 11.68 inches of rain. Convectional showers are the main source of summer rain as abundant moisture-laden air above and strong, daily heating of the land below result in frequent thermal updrafts which trigger precipitation-producing conditions. Summer rainfall is also the most variable. Although daily showers are common, so are periods of one to two weeks without rain. Occasionally during late summer or early fall tropical storms to the east bring moist air and heavy rains to the area. Another distinctive aspect of summer precipitation is the hail storm, which is a special feature of the well-developed convectional storm.

Autumn tends to bring clearer and drier weather as con-

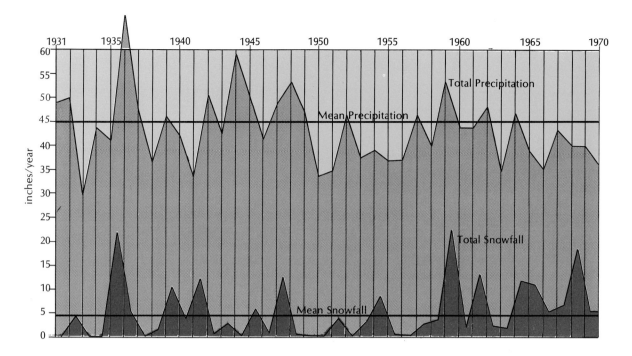

Fig. 3.7. Total Annual Precipitation in Metrolina

vectional activity decreases and winter cyclonic storms are not yet frequent. This period of less frequent rains with the gradual browning of summer foliage and periods of protracted calm allow dust particles to accumulate in the lower layers of air, creating a hazy condition known as Indian summer. October and November are the driest months with each receiving an average of less than three inches of precipitation. The transitional fall and winter months of September and December receive only slightly more precipitation. September, particularly during the early part, commonly experiences convective showers and by late December cyclonic storms are more frequent.

Frontal disturbances, chiefly cyclonic storms, are responsible for most of the winter precipitation. The alternate passing of cyclones (lows) and anticyclones (highs) continue to dominate the weather of the area into early spring when, in March or April, a climax of cyclonic development takes place. Since most winter precipitation occurs with southerly through easterly winds it is seldom associated with very cold weather and thus is usually in the form of rain. When precipitation occurs in association with northeasterly winds, however, snow and sleet often result. Such conditions generally occur when a high pressure cell is over the continental interior of the northeastern United States and a local low pressure cell is over the North Atlantic. This results in an offshore flow of cool air parallel to the Carolina coastline, which brings in cool, moist air from the North Atlantic.

Water Balance

More basic to an area's moisture availability than monthly precipitation totals is the effectiveness of its precipitation. This may be estimated by comparing required moisture for evaporation and transpiration processes (potential evapotranspiration) with incoming precipitation plus stored surplus water. The difference indicates the average surplus or deficit of water in any given month.

When examining monthly precipitation totals for Metrolina stations, the summer months consistently appear to be wet months. Using the water budget concept, however, Fig. 3.8 demonstrates that these months do not have a moisture surplus because of higher potential evapotranspiration rates. As a matter of fact, potential evapotranspiration exceeds precipitation on an average of five months per year. Yet the moisture deficiency is not correspondingly large. Soils can store moisture during periods of surplus for utilization by plants during periods of deficit. The storage potential varies with texture, structure, and depth of soil. On the average a soil can absorb the equivalent of four inches of rainfall before becoming waterlogged. Therefore approximately four inches of surplus fall moisture will be absorbed and stored by the soil. Likewise the first four inches of deficit in the summer can be compensated for by the stored moisture in the soil; the remaining deficit will, of course, affect the plants.

Thus, viewed in this way, Metrolina has a considerable

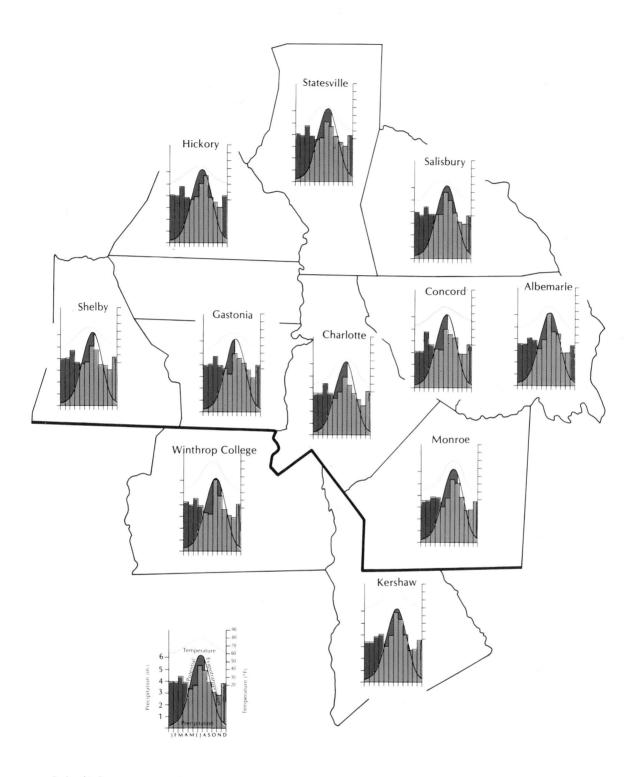

Dark red indicates moisture surplus, light red is a moisture deficiency
and green indicates adequate soil moisture.

Fig. 3.8. Metrolina Water Balance

moisture surplus from middle fall through early spring and a moisture deficiency from late spring through early fall. The deficit occurring in late spring and early summer, however, is compensated by drawing on surplus stored during the cooler season. The distinctive period of water deficiency varies somewhat throughout the region but is generally greatest during August and September. It is during this period that the greatest demands are made on municipal and county water systems since gardens and lawns usually need irrigating. Variations occur between and within individual counties. Minimum moisture deficiencies, if any, are experienced in Stanly, Rowan, Catawba, and Lancaster counties. Mecklenburg, Gaston, and Cleveland counties appear to have the largest average deficit. Year-to-year variations are also common. Often the fall season, characterized by a browning of summer foliage, will come early in response to a particularly high late summer and early fall moisture deficiency.

Winds

Metrolina is characterized by quite variable winds with percentage frequencies of prevailing wind direction on an annual basis as follows: N, 15.6; NE, 13.4; E, 6.8; SE, 9.5; S, 18.2; SW, 14.6; W, 7.7; NW, 11.3; and calm, 4.7. Winds are generally of a low speed averaging seven to ten miles per hour. Lowest wind speeds normally occur during the evening and early morning hours while higher wind speeds are usually observed during midafternoon.

As illustrated in Fig. 3.9, during the fall months of October and November prevailing winds are usually from the northeast and have an average speed of seven and a half miles per hour. By January the prevailing wind has shifted to the southeast and for most of the remainder of the year southerly winds persist. During winter months wind speeds are higher, averaging eight and a half to nine miles per hour reaching a maximum average of nine and a half miles per hour during March and April. In March, the windiest month, wind speeds of twenty-five miles per hour and over are frequently observed. The strong southwesterly flow of air in summer is a predominant feature of summer circulation as a result of onshore movement of oceanic air from the Bermuda High.

James W. Clay

AIR QUALITY

Like many urban regions of the United States, Metrolina faces a challenge in the maintenance of air quality at a level compatible with public health and welfare. The difficulty results from three principal factors: (1) regional meteorological conditions unfavorable for the rapid dispersion of air pollutants; (2) the extensive use of coal as an energy source; and (3) high densities of automotive traffic. A knowledge of existing air quality levels and an awareness of regional air pollution potential is necessary if clean air is to be maintained on a long-term basis.

Air Pollution Emissions

Almost all human activity results in some form of air pollution, either directly or indirectly. Every house, every automobile, truck, bus, factory, refuse disposal, and power plant is polluting the open air. As shown in Fig. 3.10, Metrolina's air pollution derived from five types of emission in 1970: transportation, thermoelectric power generation, industrial processing, space heating, and refuse disposal. Of these, transportation and thermoelectric power generation were by far the most important emission sources of air pollutants. They accounted for 87 percent of all sulfur dioxide, 90 percent of all particulates, 86 percent of the nitrogen oxides, 94 percent of all carbon monoxide, and 91 percent of all hydrocarbons. Secondary sources for sulfur oxides and particulates were the region's industrial plants. Significant emissions of particulate materials also derived from open dumps, stone and brick processing, lumber mills, feed plants, foundries, and other industrial activities. Secondary sources of hydrocarbons were space heating and refuse disposal.

Dispersion of Pollutants

Unfortunately Metrolina does not have meteorological conditions favorable for the rapid and continual dispersement of air pollutants. The earth's atmosphere is continuously in motion, dispersing air pollutants from areas of emission. There are upper limits on this self-cleansing capacity, however, which vary over space and through time with meteorological characteristics. The most important of these are horizontal wind speed, vertical turbulence, and precipitation. In Metrolina vertical movement is minimal, as a result of frequent anticyclones (highs), air temperature inversions, and low horizontal wind speeds.

In anticyclones, since air is subsiding and diverging from the center of high atmospheric pressure, there is little upward movement of air to carry pollutants. Further, anticyclones are characteristically accompanied by clear skies and low horizontal wind speeds. As illustrated in Figs. 3.11 (a) and 3.11 (b) Metrolina lies in an area that experiences the highest incidence of stagnating anticyclones in the eastern United States. This high frequency results from the common domination of the area by the western extension of the Bermuda High. During the thirty-year period 1936-65, air mass stagnations, extending over four or more days each, were noted eighty times and those ex-

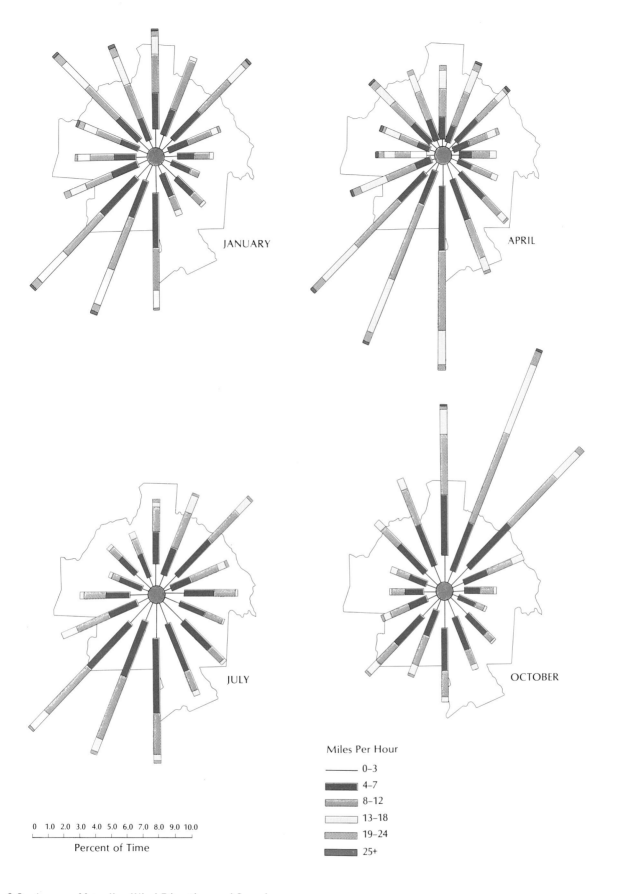

JANUARY

APRIL

JULY

OCTOBER

Miles Per Hour

———— 0–3
4–7
8–12
13–18
19–24
25+

0   1.0 2.0 3.0 4.0 5.0 6.0 7.0 8.0 9.0 10.0

Percent of Time

Fig. 3.9. Average Metrolina Wind Direction and Speed

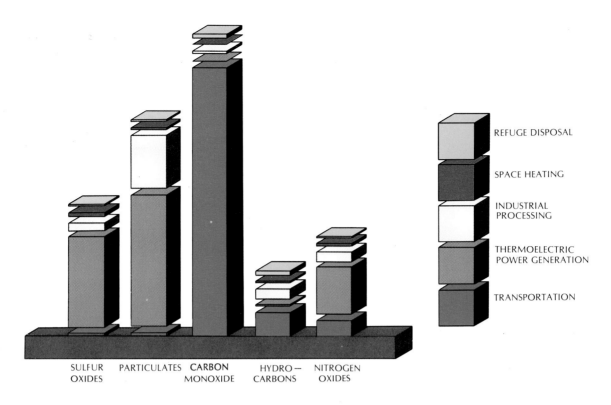

Fig. 3.10. Air Pollution Emissions in Metrolina

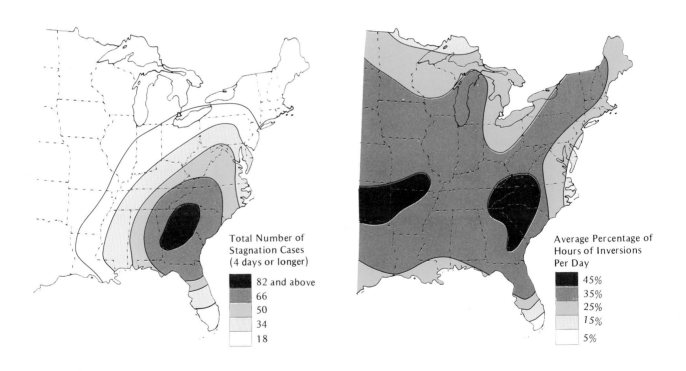

Source: Public Health Service; U.S. Department of Health, Education, and Welfare.

Fig. 3.11 (a). Frequency of Large-Scale Stagnating
Anticyclones in the Southeast, 1936-1965

Fig. 3.11 (b). Average Percentage of Hours of
Inversions per Day in the Southeast, 1936-1965

tending seven days or more were noted six times.

Dispersion problems resulting from such stagnating anticyclones are compounded by frequent temperature inversions. Under normal conditions temperature falls as altitude increases, and vertical dispersion occurs freely. Under certain meteorological conditions, however, the temperature increases with increasing altitude, a condition called an inversion. This limits vertical mixing by preventing air, and thus pollutants in the air, from rising. Metrolina experiences, on the average, inversion conditions fully 45 percent of the time. They occur most commonly during clear nights when ground temperatures and air near the ground are cooled.

Although not comparable in magnitude to the above factors, an inadequately considered phenomenon is the intraregional variation in air pollutant dispersion capability. Although insufficient data are available to describe the local pattern, differences in topography, and to a lesser degree, vegetation, soils, and various architectural features, can affect wind patterns and vertical air movement. In local and regional planning identification and consideration of such variations should be made in order to effect an improvement in the dispersion of air pollutants. For instance, the zoning of industrial activities in areas where the natural air flow would spread the pollutants with greater facility could be undertaken. When appropriate, stacks might be designed to vent emissions at a higher level in the atmosphere.

Dispersion capability also varies through time, both seasonally and daily. Thus, although day-to-day variations in the production of air pollutants are not very great, day-to-day variation in their concentration can be considerable.

In Table 3.1 seven meteorological factors basic to the dispersion of air pollutants are integrated on a seasonal basis for the Metrolina area. This table illustrates the relative seasonal potential for the dispersion for air pollutants. The figures in parentheses are seasonal rankings for the variables considered, with (1) representing the lowest relative air pollution potential and (4) the highest. Assigned rankings were averaged, assuming equal contribution to attempt seasonal ranking. Winter, fall, and summer appear to have low dispersion capability in Metrolina, and thus are periods during which air pollution potential is highest. During spring the dispersion potential increases considerably. Day-night variations in dispersion are also substantial. Typical nighttime temperature inversions combined with low wind speed result in a much lower potential for dispersion of air pollutants than do day periods. When designing operational plans, consideration of such variations by industry and regulatory agencies is necessary if dispersion is to be maximized.

Concentration and Control of Air Pollutants

Of primary concern to the people of an area are the types and concentrations of pollutants in the ambient (surrounding) air, for they affect man's health, property, and the overall quality of his environment. In accordance with provisions of the Clean Air Act, as amended December 31, 1970, the administrator of the Environmental Protection Agency has published proposed national primary and secondary ambient air quality standards for six pollutants as shown in Table 3.2. The purpose of the standards is

Table 3.1. Summary of Factors Affecting Dispersion of Air Pollutants in Metrolina

Season	Frequency of Inversions (% total hrs.)	Ventilation (Mixing Depth X Wind Speed)	Stability (Difference Between Max. & Min. Temp.)	Number of Stagnation Cases 4 Days	Monthly Average Precip.	Wind Speed
				(1936-65)	(inches)	(mph)
Winter	43	4,513	18.3	7	11.27	8.4
(2.9)	(4.0)	(4.0)	(4.0)	(1.0)	(2.6)	(1.8)
Spring	32	10,852	21.3	17	10.70	8.8
(1.4)	(1.0)	(1.0)	(1.0)	(2.0)	(2.3)	(1.0)
Summer	33	10,863	19.6	19	13.94	7.2
(2.5)	(1.3)	(1.0)	(2.7)	(2.2)	(4.0)	(4.0)
Fall	40	8,171	20.0	37	8.31	7.6
(2.7)	(3.2)	(2.3)	(2.3)	(4.0)	(1.0)	(3.3)
Annual average per season	37	8,600	19.8	20	44.22	7.9

Table 3.2. Proposed Minimum Ambient Air Quality Standards and Levels of Adverse Effect on Health and Welfare

Pollutant	Proposed Federal Standards		According to Federal Criteria, Levels of Adverse Effects	
	Primary	Secondary	Health	Welfare
Particulates (Mg/M₃)				
Annual geometric mean	75	60	80 (Increased death rate, persons over 50)	60 (Corrosion of steel panels)
Maximum 24-hour concentration	260	150	200 (Increased illness in industrial workers)	150 (Reduces visibility to as low as five miles)
Sulfur oxides (Mg/M₃)				
Annual arithmetic mean	80	60	115 (Increased death from bronchitis)	85 (Plant injury, excessive leaf drop)
Maximum 24-hour concentration	365	260	300 (Increased hospital admissions for respiratory disease, persons over 50)	285 (Reduces visibility to as low as five miles)
Carbon monoxide (Milligrams/M₃)				
Maximum 8-hour concentration	10	10	11.5 (Driving reaction impaired. Heart patients die after long exposure.)	—
Maximum 1-hour concentration	40	40	58	—
Photochemical oxidants (Mg/Mg)				
Maximum 1-hour concentration	160	160	130 (Impairs performance of student athletes)	100 (After 4 hours, leaf injury to sensitive plants, like petunias)
Hydrocarbons (Mg/Mg)				
Maximum 3-hour concentration, 6-0 A.M.	160	160	—	—
Nitrogen dioxide (Mg/Mg)				
Annual arithmetic mean	100	100	113 (Increased bronchitis in infants and school children)	—
Maximum 24-hour concentration	250	250	—	225 (Level of human odor perception)

clearly to protect the health and welfare of people who have suffered, are suffering, or might suffer from pollutants in the air. Primary ambient standards are designed to protect human health while secondary standards are designed to protect against effects on water, soil, plants, material, weather, visibility, and personal comfort and well-being.

In Metrolina only two pollutants are monitored on a regional basis, sulfur dioxide and particulate matter. Measured sulfur dioxide concentrations do not appear to be a problem anywhere in the region. The highest concentrations are reported in Cabarrus, Rowan, and Stanly counties, but with measured levels averaging only 20 micro-

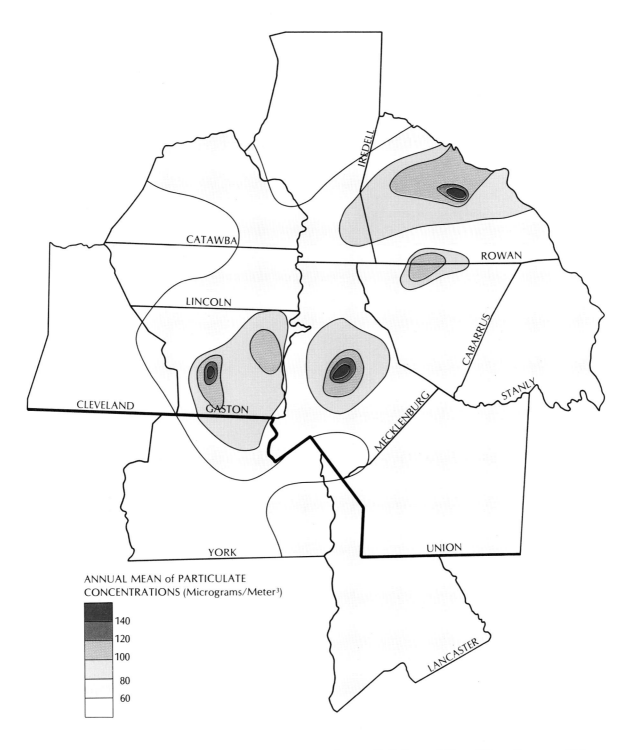

ANNUAL MEAN of PARTICULATE
CONCENTRATIONS (Micrograms/Meter^3)

140
120
100
80
60

Source: N. C. Dept. of Air and Water Resources 1970.

Fig. 3.12. Concentration Levels of Particulate Matter in Metrolina

grams per cubic meter, the environment should not be adversely affected. The lower concentrations reportedly result for two reasons: first, the conventional usage of gas and number 2 oil, both of which are low in sulfur, as a basic fuel of domestic heating; second, Duke Power, the single largest coal consumer in the region, which utilizes a low sulfur coal.

Particulate concentrations, on the other hand, are very high and of serious concern. As a matter of fact, most stations in Metrolina report concentrations in excess of amounts compatible with public health and welfare. Air quality criteria for suspended particulates published by the Environmental Protection Agency are shown in Table 3.2. Adverse health effects are noted when the annual mean level of particulate matter exceeded 80 micrograms per cubic meter. Visibility reduction can be observed at concentrations of 150 micrograms per cubic meter, and adverse effects on material occurs at annual means exceeding 60 micrograms per cubic meter.

As shown in Fig. 3.12, particulate concentrations are particularly high in Gaston, Mecklenburg, and Rowan counties. These higher levels are largely the result of emissions from Duke Power's steam generating plants along the Catawba and Yadkin rivers. Aware of the problem, Duke Power is updating existing electrostatic precipitators, which should considerably reduce emissions from these plants. Officials from the North Carolina Department of Air and Water Resources are of the opinion that this action will reduce concentrations to a level compatible with proposed primary and secondary ambient air quality standards.

In Mecklenburg County such transportation-related pollutants as carbon monoxide, nitrogen dioxide, and photochemical oxidants are monitored. Carbon monoxide concentrations have been surprisingly low, but concentrations of both nitrogen dioxide and photochemical oxidants exceed national primary and secondary ambient air quality standards. Of eight stations in the Charlotte metropolitan area, five reported an annual arithmetic mean concentration of nitrogen dioxide in excess of 100 micrograms per cubic meter (national air quality standard) and three of these reported concentrations of 200 micrograms per cubic meter or higher.

James W. Clay

GEOLOGY

Metrolina lies almost entirely in the Piedmont Province of the Appalachian Highlands. In the southeast it extends slightly onto the Coastal Plains and in the northwest isolated spurs of the Blue Ridge Mountains are prominent. Rocks of Metrolina are among the oldest in the United States with some having formed in Precambrian times. Subsequently the area experienced volcanic and other igneous activity,

faulting and metamorphism, and several erosional cycles. The resulting geological landscape is not only interesting but is directly related to local mining activities, ground water resources, surface drainage patterns, soils properties, and other environmental features.

Landforms

The typical landscape throughout most of the area is a series of rounded hills and rolling ridges with a general northeast-southwest trend. The landscape results largely from dissection of an old, slightly southeasterly tilted, erosional surface called a peneplane (near flat). This southeasterly slope accounts for the general drainage pattern of the Broad, the Catawba, and the Yadkin rivers. In turn the rolling topography of the area has been shaped largely by these rivers and their tributaries through their erosion of rocks having unequal resistance. When streams cut through ridges of resistant rocks, narrow steep valleys were formed providing excellent sites for the numerous dams now found along the Yadkin and Catawba rivers. The southeasterly slope remains today with the elevation rising gently from about 250 feet in the southeast corner of Stanly County at the confluence of the Rocky and Yadkin—Pee Dee rivers, to almost 3,000 feet in the western portion of Metrolina.

The generally moderate relief of the region is broken by a number of small mountains called monadnocks, which mark the level of the old erosional resistance of the rocks that form them. The Kings Mountain Range, extending from South Carolina in the south across Cleveland, Gaston, and Lincoln counties and into Catawba County in North Carolina provides a series of prominent peaks. The best known are the Pinnacle, at 1,705 feet, Crowders Mountain, at 1,624 feet, and Anderson Mountain, at 1,547 feet.

In Stanly County Morrow Mountain stands as a remnant of one of the oldest mountain ranges in North America, the Ocoee Mountains. Having an elevation of only 936 feet at its highest point, the mountain nevertheless provides a spectacular panoramic view of the surrounding landscape. The Yadkin River, by separating this mountain from the larger Uwharrie range to the east, illustrates the role of river dissection in the evolution of the region's topography. The range has a typical northeast-southwest orientation and is cut by a southeast flowing stream, which, upon passing through a more resistant rock, forms a narrow valley. The valley provides the site for Badin Dam, one of the region's largest.

Along the northern and western border of Cleveland County, Metrolina's elevation rises dramatically. Here the South Mountains, cut off from the Blue Ridge by the Catawba River, are Metrolina's highest. In this range, along the northern border of Cleveland County, rises Benn Knob, which at its highest point stands at 2,894 feet. In Catawba County several small mountains rise rapidly to provide

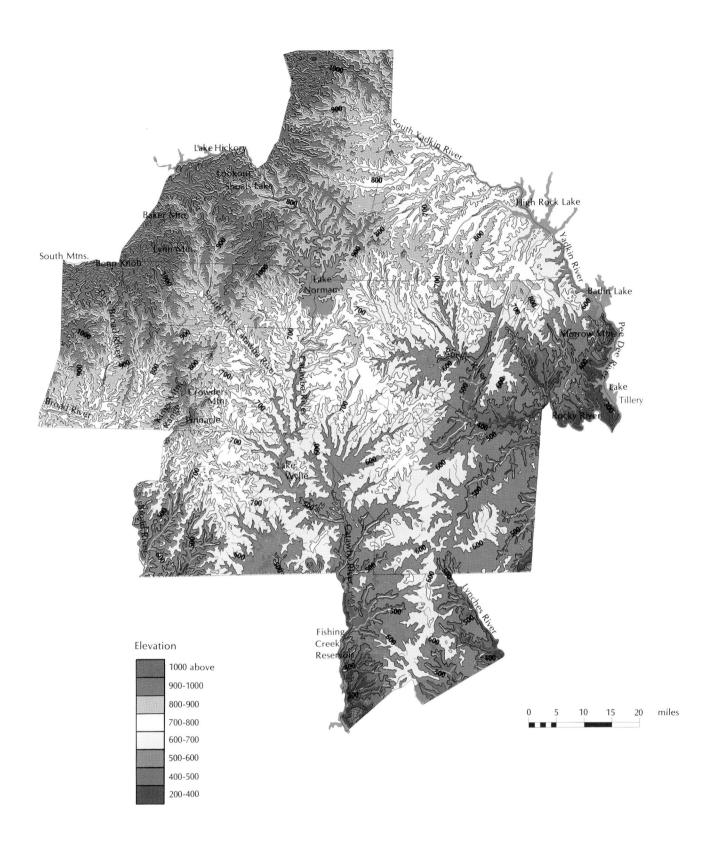

Fig. 3.13. Topography of Metrolina

higher relief. The most notable of these are Lynn Mountain, which has an elevation of 1,480 feet, and Baker Mountain, 1,820 feet.

These small mountains throughout Metrolina are becoming increasingly significant to the citizenry by providing an interesting ecological habitat and a retreat from the increasing urban character of life in the region. Kings Mountain in York County and Morrow Mountain in Stanly County now provide sites for state parks. Following strong local opposition to the possible mining of Crowders Mountain and support for a state park, the North Carolina State Parks Committee has recently recommended to the Board of Conservation and Development the acquisition of the Kings and Crowders mountain area for the establishment of a state park. (See Fig. 3.13.)

Lithology and Mineral Resources

Rocks and minerals common to Metrolina number in the hundreds, and the many varieties of minerals and gems of museum quality are a great attraction to rock and mineral collectors. Precious metals and gems, though not mined commercially today, have enriched the history of the area. The region that is now Metrolina was the country's major gold-producing area during the early part of the nineteenth century. Small quantities of such gem stones as diamonds, rubies, emeralds, and many less well-known gem stones have been found or mined in Metrolina counties.

Today, however, granite is the leading mineral product, followed by sand and gravel, mica, clay, lithium minerals, kyanite, and traprock. Other mineral products include limestone, barite, graphite, beryllium, thorium, and rare-earth metals. Although the region produces only a small amount of minerals used in metal processing at the present time, it has produced or is a potential producer of iron, cobalt, manganese, nickel, copper, lead, zinc, silver, tin, cromium, titanium, tungsten, niobium-tantalum, and zirconium.

The map in Fig. 3.14, compiled from existing North and South Carolina state geological maps, illustrates the general lithological pattern. The many rock types recognized and mapped are grouped into four major belts: (1) Sedimentary and Coastal Belt, (2) Carolina Slate Belt, (3) Charlotte Belt, and (4) Inner Piedmont Belt. In the discussion that follows the lithology and related mineral resources of each of these belts are examined.

Sedimentary and Coastal Belt. Small areas of sedimentary rocks are found in two Metrolina counties. In southeastern Lancaster County unconsolidated sands, clays, and gravel of unknown age mark the boundary of the Coastal Plain Province. Underlying these sediments is the Cretaceous Tuscaloosa formation characterized by arkosic sands interbedded with conglomerates, sands, and clays. Large quantities of sand and gravel are extracted from the unconsolidated

sediments of this formation in counties adjacent to Metrolina. They are thus a potentially valuable resource to Lancaster County.

In southeastern Union County a small area of Triassic sediments of the Newark group have formed red, brown, purple, or gray claystones, shales, sandstones, or conglomerates. Weathered argillite bolders and pebbles common to the area indicate that the Carolina Slate Belt to the west was the source for the sediments. Although not extracted from Union County, the Triassic brownstones from the Newark group have been extensively used in public buildings in Statesville and Charlotte.

Carolina Slate Belt. Immediately to the west of the sedimentary belt, the "Carolina Slate Belt" (Carolina Sedimentary-Volcanic Belt) underlies nearly all of Stanly County, most of Union County, and smaller portions of Cabarrus, Rowan, and Lancaster counties. Rocks of this Slate Belt are thought to have formed during a period of intermittent volcanic activity probably during the Ordovician period. Periods of quiet upwelling of lava and explosive activities resulted in deposition of tuff, breccia, ash, and other volcanics. Following were quieter periods when weathering and erosion of volcanics and deposition of silt and clay occurred. Such an environment resulted in a volcanic-sedimentary series that was later to be slightly metamorphosed (changed in form as a result of heat and pressure). The wide variety of resulting rock types can be grouped into bedded argillites (volcanic slates) and volcanics.

Of the two the bedded argillites are the more abundant, underlying most of Union and Stanly counties. They are usually dark or bluish in color, are in the form of slate or shale, and are massive and thick-bedded. The slate often resembles chert in places where contact metamorphism has occurred.

The many types of volcanic rocks resulting from lava flow and fragmental deposits may be categorized into two principal types: acidic volcanics and basic volcanics. The acidic volcanics formed from rhyolitic flows and fragmentals that were rhyolitic to dacitic in composition. The rhyolite is dark gray to bluish in color and in some specimens the minerals plagioclase, orthoclase, and quartz can be identified. The basic volcanics were formed largely from volcanic flows of andesite and basalt or from andesitic fragmentals. They range in color from green, when the flow was andesitic, to black, when the flow was basaltic. Such minerals as epidote, plagioclase, and quartz commonly occur in the rocks.

It was here in the Carolina Slate Belt, following the discovery of a large gold nugget on the Reed farm in Cabarrus County in 1799, that America was to experience its first gold rush. The lump of gold, weighing about seventeen pounds, was accidentally discovered by a twelve-year-old boy, Conrad Reed. Later searches here and in nearby areas uncovered many other nuggets, including the largest nugget ever found, a twenty-eight-pound lump dug up by a Negro

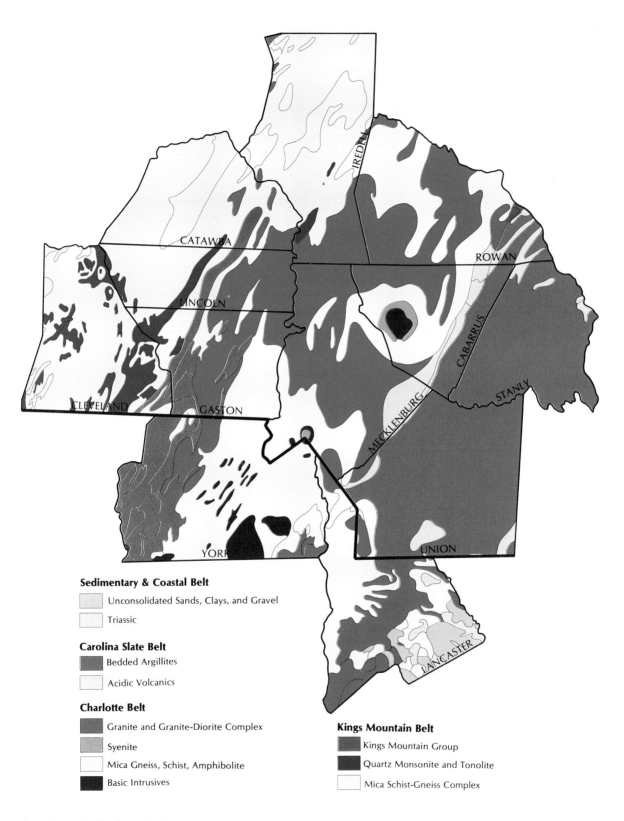

CATAWBA

IREDELL

ROWAN

LINCOLN

CABARRUS

MECKLENBURG

STANLY

CLEVELAND

GASTON

YORK

UNION

LANCASTER

Sedimentary & Coastal Belt

☐ Unconsolidated Sands, Clays, and Gravel

☐ Triassic

Carolina Slate Belt

■ Bedded Argillites

☐ Acidic Volcanics

Charlotte Belt

■ Granite and Granite-Diorite Complex

▨ Syenite

☐ Mica Gneiss, Schist, Amphibolite

■ Basic Intrusives

Kings Mountain Belt

■ Kings Mountain Group

■ Quartz Monsonite and Tonolite

☐ Mica Schist-Gneiss Complex

Fig. 3.14. Metrolina Surface Geology

boy on an adjacent plantation. More than one million dollars worth of gold was ultimately to be mined from the subsequent Reed gold mine. Following these discoveries, scores of mines began to open, the best known of which was the Barringer mine in Stanly County. The Barringer mine is of particular interest because it was the first lode mine in the Southern Piedmont. Although the vein was thin, it is said to have been very rich. One of the largest gold mines in the eastern United States was the Haile mine in Lancaster County. At the time of its closing in 1942 it had produced $6,500,000 in gold. Unlike that of the Barringer mine, the ore was of a low grade occurring in irregular bodies. Much of the ore averaged less than ten dollars per ton of gold.

During the early part of the nineteenth century considerable gold was mined in the belt and for a twenty-year period nearly all the country's gold production came from this and adjacent areas. Although production of gold, along with silver, lead, zinc, copper, and other associated metals, has long been discontinued, the metals can still be found throughout the belt. The potential for gold production in the region has not been adequately tested in terms of modern exploration and production techniques.

Of greater commercial importance today is the production of nonmetallic minerals. The Carolina Slate rocks provide a number of commercial products. They have been used since early colonial times for building stone and flagstone. When unweathered the stone makes an excellent crushed aggregate and when weathered to clay it is suitable for the manufacture of clay products such as brick and tile.

Charlotte Belt. West of the Carolina Slate Belt is a group of igneous and associated metamorphic rocks referred to as the Charlotte Belt. The belt underlies most of Mecklenburg, Iredell, Rowan, and Cabarrus counties and the eastern portion of Catawba, Lincoln, Gaston, and Lancaster counties. It is widely fractured and has numerous intruded dikes and sills. These plutonic rocks are too small to be included in Fig. 3.14. In Fig. 3.14 and in the text that follows rocks of this belt are grouped into four categories: (1) granite and granite-diorite complex; (2) syenite; (3) mica gneiss, schist, and amphibolite; and (4) basic intrusives.

Large bodies composed essentially of granite occur in Rowan, southern Iredell, and southeastern Catawba counties. Large areas of granite-diorite in which granite predominates occur in Rowan, Cabarrus, Mecklenburg, and eastern Gaston, Lincoln, and York counties. Both units vary from fine-grained through medium-grained to porphyritic in texture. Colors vary from white through various shades of gray and pink to almost red. The rocks consist of orthoclase, plagioclase, quartz, biotite, muscovite, and various accessory minerals.

In addition to a number of syenite bodies too small to be included at the scale of the map in Fig. 3.14, two large,

coarse-grained augite syenites are found in Metrolina. The smaller intrusive, a porphyritic plug, is found in a mafic dike on the North and South Carolina boundary. The larger body is a ring dike approximately twenty-two miles in circumference, located in the west-central part of Cabarrus County. This structure forms one of the most interesting geological and topographic features in Metrolina. The syenite is more resistant to erosion than the surrounding mica gneiss and the gabbro-diorite core and thus stands out strongly in relief. The area of outcrop is generally marked by large boulders and pedestal rocks. The rock is composed largely of bluish-gray feldspar and augite. It is uniformly of coarse texture and massive in structure showing no effects of metamorphism. The absence of a fine-grained matrix permits the syenite to disintegrate into a residual granular matter that makes excellent road material.

The basic intrusives include a wide number of dark-colored rocks the most important of which are pyroxenite, norite, andesites, and gabbro. They are best represented in York County but occur commonly in units too small to map in several other counties. The largest basic intrusive body in the Carolinas is the gabbro-diorite core of the syenite ring dike of Cabarrus County. Since basic rocks are less resistant to erosion than are acidic rocks, topographic depressions often result from their weathering and erosion.

A mica gneiss, mica schist, and amphibolite unit extends from York and Lancaster counties in South Carolina north through Mecklenburg, Gaston, Cabarrus, and Rowan counties in North Carolina. In South Carolina the unit has been described as light to dark gray in color, fine to medium grained in texture. In South Carolina hornblende is commonly found in the schist and gneiss and in North Carolina granite and diorite-granite layers are commonly interspersed.

The Charlotte Belt has several interesting and important mineral deposits. In terms of value granite and related crystalline rocks rank first. An excellent granite varying from light gray to pink in color occurs in the vicinity of Granite Quarry and Faith, south and southeast of Salisbury. It has been extensively developed as a monumental and building stone for more than fifty years. Trade names under which this pink granite is sold include Balfour Pink, Salisbury Pink Granite, Coral Pink, and Arabian Pink. The large body of granitic rock outcropping in Mecklenburg County is quarried in Mecklenburg County at Charlotte, Pineville, and Davidson.

As late as 1938 gold was mined from one of the important gold mines of the belt. The Rudisil mine opened in 1830 near the present intersection of Trade and Tryon streets in Charlotte. It was one of the largest of the old gold mines of the Carolinas and it has been reported to have produced approximately one million dollars in gold. For the thirty-year period between 1837 and 1867 the mine supplied the Charlotte mint with its gold supply.

Although no longer commercially significant, iron ores

occur in many locations throughout the belt. Crystalline siderite known as spathic ore occurs in many of the old gold mines. A tungsten ore, scheelite, occurs near the boundary of the Carolina Slate Belt along with pyrite, chalcopyrite, barite siderite, calcite, and gold in Cabarrus County. Thus far no commercial deposits of these tungsten minerals have been found, however.

Inner Piedmont Belt. For purposes of convenience rocks lying between the Charlotte Belt and the Blue Ridge Mountains are grouped into a belt called the Inner Piedmont. They underlie all of Cleveland County, most of Iredell and Catawba counties, and the western portion of York, Gaston, and Lincoln counties. The rocks are organized into (1) the schists and phyllites of the Kings Mountain group; (2) the Yorkville, Toluca, and Cherryville quartz monzonite and tonolite; and (3) the mica schist-gneiss complex.

The Kings Mountain group extends northeasterly from York County through Cleveland, Gaston, and Lincoln counties into Catawba County. It is composed largely of gneiss, schists, and phyllites that contain distinctive beds of quartzite, kyanite quartzite, conglomerate, limestone, and pyroclastic volcanics. Considerable mineral resources are associated with this group. Crystalline limestone has been quarried intermittently for years and beds of barite, iron and manganese ores, and gold are all known to the Kings Mountain area. The most important mineral resource at present, however, is the lithium mineral spodumene associated with pegmatite dikes. The mineral is currently mined by several mining companies in Gaston and Cleveland counties and accounts for North Carolina's prominent position in lithium production. One of the largest beryl deposits of the United States is located in the tin-spodumene range extending from Grover to Lincolnton. The mineral is used as the raw material for the strategically important beryllium metal. It is mined from pegmatite dikes in Cleveland, Gaston, and Lincoln counties. About fifteen thousand dollars worth of emeralds, dark green gem-quality beryl, was recovered from pegmatites about four miles west of Patterson Springs in Cleveland County before the abandonment of the operation in 1913. Aquamarine, the blue- and light-green-colored gem-quality beryl, is found south of Shelby in Cleveland County. Tin was mined from the range until 1902 and the columbite-tantalite deposits are still a potential source for tin. Pyrite, the raw material for sulfuric acid production, was a byproduct of tin recovery. Today it is produced as a byproduct of kyanite milling in York County.

Iron was the first commercially extracted metal in Metrolina. The iron ore came from magnetite deposits found in a belt extending from Iron Station in Lincoln County to Anderson Mountain in Catawba County. The Buffalo furnace in Cleveland County was built before the American Revolution and in 1795 the Vesuvius furnace was built in Lincoln County. By the early nineteenth century seven iron-processing plants (furnace and foundry) were smelting the ore in Metrolina. Mining of the iron minerals was discontinued in 1936 and attempts to reactivate the industry during World War II failed. Unfortunately the good quality iron ores were not large enough to support an extensive mineral mining and smelting operation.

The Kings Mountain group also yielded gold intermittently from the date of its discovery in 1834 until 1931. The chief mine was the Long Creek gold mine located about six miles northeast of Dallas in Gaston County. For a short period absolite, a black cobalt oxide containing nickel and manganese, was mined during the early 1900s. Lead-zinc-silver was mined from the Kings Mountain group in Gaston County intermittently, but production of these metals was never important.

Of recent importance are the kyanite deposits common to the area. Large quantities of the mineral have been strip-mined from Henry Knob in York County. A large deposit has been identified in Crowders Mountain and mining interests are now considering active mining. Protest against strip-mining of this local landmark may discourage mining activities. Gem-quality kyanite has been recovered as a byproduct of the kyanite mining.

Three different quartz monzonites underlie Metrolina. The Yorkville quartz monzonite in western York County is medium to dark gray in color and fine- to coarse-grained in texture. The Cherryville quartz monzonite is a broad, irregular belt in eastern Cleveland, western Gaston, and central Lincoln counties. It is a medium-grained rock and may contain microcline, quartz, muscovite, and biotite. Usually deeply weathered, the rocks support a light tan to gray sandy soil. The Toluca quartz monzonite is a scattered unit consisting of many bodies in a general belt along the central and western portions of Cleveland County. The rock is typically a gray, medium-grained gneissic biotite-quartz monzonite. The chief minerals are feldspar, quartz, biotite, and garnet.

The tonalite (quartz diorite) intrusive of York and Gaston counties is a coarse-grained, massive, gneissic rock, rich in oligoclase and often containing biotite schist, staurolite, garnet, and kyanite.

The monzonites are mined in several locations. In Cleveland County they are mined for thorium oxides, rare-earth metals, and zirconium. To a lesser degree, and declining in importance, monzonite deposits of adjacent counties are providing mineral products. In future years these rocks may provide dimension stones and crushed rocks. Associated rocks are potential sources of chromium, nickel, titanium, tungsten, and niobium-tantalum.

The mica schist-gneiss complex is the most abundant of any unit in the belt. The rocks are generally metasediments and, dating from Precambrian times, are probably the oldest of any in Metrolina. Included in this unit are the hornblende schists of Catawba and Iredell counties. The schists are green to black in color, fine- to coarse-grained in texture, and contain layers of hornblende gneiss and actinolite schist,

Table 3.3. Geologic History of Metrolina

Million Years Before Present	Time	Events in Metrolina
0-0.01	Recent Pleistocene	Development of the Fall Line, present drainage, soils, and the deposition of alluvium in stream channels. Terracing along the streams due to fluctuation of sea level associated with glacial advance and retreat.
1-70	Tertiary	Rejuvenation and tilting of the Fall Line Peneplane; deposition of sediment on the Coastal Plain as the seas retreated.
70-135	Cretaceous	Rejuvenation of the Fall Line Peneplane; last great inundation of the Coastal Plain and the deposition of the Tuscaloosa formation.
135-180	Jurassic	Weathering and erosion reduced the Piedmont and the Appalachian Mountains to a peneplane; intrusion of diabase dikes.
180-225	Triassic	Palisade disturbance causing faults forming the Triassic basins (Deep River Basin); coal swamps and peneplanation of the area.
225-270	Permian	Appalachian orogeny uplifts the entire area; intrusion of many igneous bodies, including the syenites and the Yorkville quartz monzonite.
270-350	Carboniferous	Erosion of the Acadian surface; some intrusion.
350-400	Devonian	Acadian orogeny reelevates the Piedmont; associated intrusions, including the Cherryville quartz monzonite, and metamorphism of Carolina Slates.
400-440	Silurian	Erosion of the Taconic uplands (Piedmont to New England), possibly some granitic intrusions.
440-500	Ordovician	Volcanic and sedimentary rocks of the Carolina Slate Belt deposited; Taconic orogeny elevates the Piedmont, Goldhill Fault and intrusions, including the Toluca quartz monzonite, and metamorphism of older rocks.
500-600	Cambrian	Deposition of sand, clay, and carbonates.
600-	Precambrian	Deposition of the oldest rocks of the Charlotte and Inner Piedmont belts, which were later metamorphosed to gneiss and schists.

interbedded with quartzites, metashales, marbles, dolomites, and limestones. The gneissic rocks are usually light to dark gray in color and weather to a dull gray, yellow, or various shades of red.

The mica gneiss-schist group is the main producer of ground and scrap mica and good quality sheet mica comes from pegmatitic quarries operating in Cleveland County and in the Shelby-Hickory district of Gaston, Lincoln, Catawba, and Iredell counties. Stone, clays, and sand and gravel are mined in several localities of this group. Limestone is mined for cement manufacturing in Cleveland County; clay is produced from shales, metashales, slates, and weather rocks; and sand and gravel come from alluvial deposits.

The geological history of the region is a small part of a large-scale series of events over a period of a billion or more years. A detailed discussion of these events in Metrolina does not seem appropriate. To provide the reader with some reference, however, Table 3.3 dates those geological events most relevant to Metrolina.

Julius Alker and James W. Clay

SURFACE WATER RESOURCES

A growing concern of many well-informed people is the limited availability and declining quality of water for domestic, agricultural, industrial, and recreational use. The Metrolina region has a large and well-developed water supply and its availability, in an absolute use of the term, is not a problem. The incidences of pollution, however, are such that there must be a major emphasis upon the safe-guarding of these waters against deterioration.

Water Supply

Metrolina's plentiful supply of surface waters may be delineated into three large river basins: the Yadkin, the Catawba, and the Broad. The flow rate of the three major rivers is large, totaling almost 13,000 cubic feet per second (cfs). Of the three, the Yadkin River is the largest with a flow rate of 7,749 cfs. The Catawba River has an average flow rate of approximately 3,000 cfs and the Broad has a flow rate of 1,384 cfs.

These high flow rates, combined with relatively steep slopes and good dam sites, has encouraged the extensive development of the main basin streams. A series of hydro-electric power dams has been built along the Catawba and Yadkin rivers. Indeed there are only a few short sections along these rivers that remain undeveloped. Lakes associated with these dams are being used to great advantage and are included among the region's most important resources. They are used for recreational purposes such as fishing, boating, and swimming and supply large quantities of water for domestic and industrial water supplies. Collectively reservoirs along the Catawba and Yadkin rivers have usable storage capacities of more than 60 billion cubic feet. The largest of these reservoirs is Lake Norman with a usable storage capacity of almost 27 billion cubic feet. The capacities of the other reservoirs are shown in Table 3.4.

Stream Classification

The natural ability of streams and rivers to absorb wastes through dilution and bacterial decomposition is being severely challenged in a great many of the country's river basins. The accelerated growth of population centers, attended by an increasing industrialization and urbanization, has increased and concentrated organic and chemical waste loads. These increased concentrations require large amounts of oxygen for decomposing and can, in the process, exhaust the river's dissolved oxygen content. When the oxygen levels become low, life in the river literally suffocates and the ability of the stream to decompose organic material becomes severely restricted. Such streams are little more than open sewers. Toxic wastes and excessive plant nutrients from industrial sewage and from urban and agricultural runoff often lead to the same harmful results.

Metrolina's major streams—the Catawba, the Yadkin, and Broad rivers, and associated reservoirs—are not seriously polluted. Many of the smaller tributaries, however, are overtaxed and of a very low quality and are adversely affecting the main streams.

High quality water resources are basic to the general well-being of citizens of the region and must be protected from pollution. Since these resources are of the public sector, they belong to all the people and their usage should correspond to that which is in the best interest of the citizenry. The states, as representatives of the people, have the ultimate responsibility for the preservation and development of these resources and for the prevention of use contrary to the people's best interest.

Recognizing this responsibility, the states of North and South Carolina have classified streams within their boundaries in accordance with their interpretation of best use. Once classified, the maintenance of water quality compatible with that use becomes the responsibility of governmental agencies.

Great difficulty is often experienced in determining the best use for a particular stream. Public hearings are held before classification for the purpose of balancing conflicting considerations. This classification process, and related water-quality standards, is most important to the preservation and development of a region's water resources. Interested citizens and organizations should appear at these hearings to express their concerns and viewpoints. Of interest perhaps is the flexibility of this system. Stream classifications are not permanent; streams may be reclassified upward or downward in accordance with the public need.

Metrolina's rivers and streams have been classified into the four classes shown in Fig. 3.15: A-II, B, C, and D. A generalized description of best usage and related water-quality standards for each of these classes follows.

Sources of water supply for drinking, cooking, or food-processing are classified as A-II. Of a uniformly excellent quality, water from these streams is considered safe for drinking after approved treatment. The streams may be used for any other usage requiring waters of lower quality provided such usage does not conflict with a higher specified usage.

The bacteriological quality of the water must be high. Accordingly, the most probable number (MPN) of coliform bacteria must not exceed 5,000 per 100 milliliters of water as a monthly average. The coliform bacteria concentration is used as a general indicator of the density of parasitic organisms infectious to man. Further, the MPN of fecal coliform is not to exceed a log mean of 1,000 per 100 milliliters based on at least five consecutive samples during any thirty-day period. As normal inhabitants of the intestines, coliform bacteria are discharged in large number in the human feces.

The dissolved oxygen (DO) should be near saturation values (the daily average should not be less than five milligrams per liter). Dissolved oxygen is essential to natural purification of the stream as well as maintenance of fish or other aquatic life. A deficiency of DO in a stream indicates the presence of polluting substances which causes a reduction of oxygen in the stream and, thus, is an index of the degree of pollution. To flourish at normal water tempera-

Table 3.4. Metrolina Reservoirs and Their Capacities

Lake	Total Capacity Cubic Feet	Usuable Capacity Cubic Feet	Elevation Range In Feet
Catawba Basin			
Lake Hickory	5,552,985,000	2,277,800,000	85-100
Lookout Shoals	1,355,190,000	208,200,000	95-100
Lake Norman	47,586,200,000	26,910,400,000	75-100
Mtn. Island Lake	2,495,988,000	845,000,000	93-100
Lake Wylie	4,022,000,000	2,520,500,000	95-100
Fishing Creek Reservoir	963,100,000	667,000,000	95-100
Yadkin Basin			
High Rock Lake	11,090,000,000	10,230,000,000	625-655
Tuckertown Reservoir	1,852,400,000	293,800,000	593-596
Badin Lake (Narrows Reservoir)	10,497,960,000	6,202,584,000	505-541
Lake Tillery	7,274,520,000	5,927,040,000	200.5-239.5

tures, most fish require DO values of 4 and trout require values of 5.

Class A-II streams should also be essentially free of the following substances: oil or grease; odor; floating solids; scum; and untreated sewage or industrial wastes, or toxic wastes. The pH should be near neutral (6.0-8.5), for changes may throw out of balance the tolerance of fish to high temperature and low DO concentrations. Acid wastes are especially detrimental. Additionally the temperature should be within 5° F. of natural temperatures.

In A-II streams hardness is not to exceed 100 parts per million as calcium carbonate. Water is considered soft if it contains less than 60 parts per million of carbonate. A hardness of 60 to 120 does not seriously interfere with the use of water for most purposes, although the consumption of soap is increased somewhat. Water having a hardness of more than 120 parts is rated as hard and is commonly softened mechanically when used for domestic and some industrial purposes. Finally, specified minimum levels of radioactive substances are to be observed. When alpha emitters and strontium-90 are essentially absent, the gross beta concentrations must not exceed 1,000 piocuries per liter.

Sections of each of the three major streams, their accompanying reservoirs, and several of the smaller tributaries are classified as A-II.

Best usage of Class B streams is bathing (swimming, skiing, etc.) and any other use except as a source of water supply for drinking, cooking, or food-processing. Standards are specified so as to maintain water quality at a safe and satisfactory level for bathing purposes. Again the most important considerations relate to bacteriological quality. The maximum permissible fecal coliform count during summer months (log mean of 200/100 ml from five consecutive samples) is five times the allowable number for drinking water. The reason for this is that the risk of contracting an enteric infection at these levels is about the same as through drinking water conforming to public health standards. Specified levels of DO, pH, phenols, and temperatures are identical to those of A-II streams. Floating and setteable solids; sewage and industrial wastes, toxic wastes, oils and greases; and, other general wastes must be compatible with best use. Specific maximum limits are covered in other regulations. For safe conditions the water should be clear and without visible sewage matter. Total coliform should not exceed 1,000/100 ml as a monthly average.

Except for a small section in Rowan County all sections of the Yadkin, Catawba, and Broad not classified as A-II are classified as B streams. Elsewhere in Metrolina few streams have a B classification.

Best usage for Class C streams include fishing, boating,

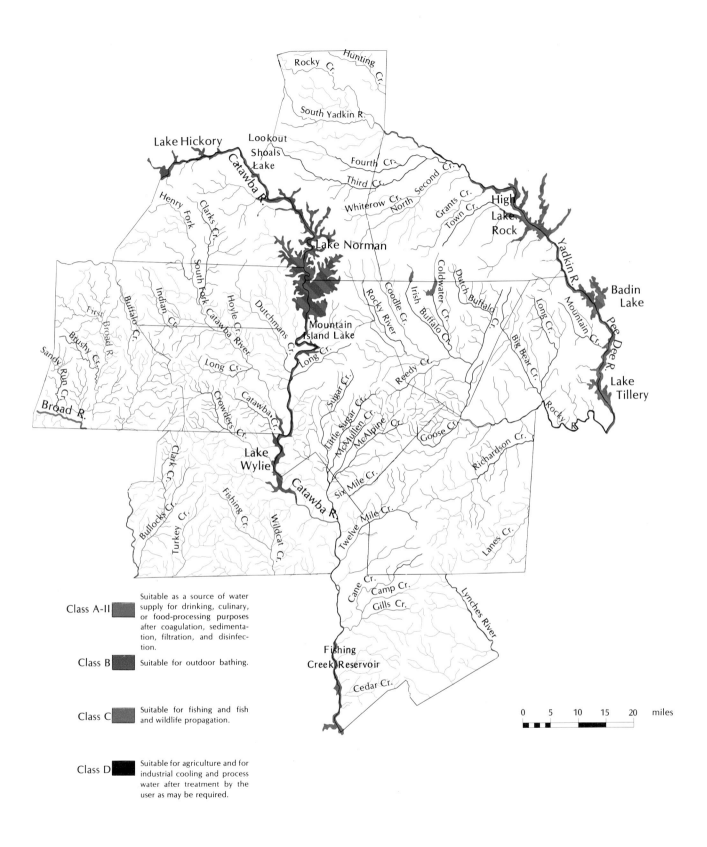

Class A-II — Suitable as a source of water supply for drinking, culinary, or food-processing purposes after coagulation, sedimentation, filtration, and disinfection.

Class B — Suitable for outdoor bathing.

Class C — Suitable for fishing and fish and wildlife propagation.

Class D — Suitable for agriculture and for industrial cooling and process water after treatment by the user as may be required.

0   5   10   15   20   miles

Fig. 3.15. Classification of Metrolina Rivers and Streams

wading, and any other usage except for bathing or as a source of water for drinking, cooking, or food-processing. For streams to be suitable for fishing, the DO should not fall below four milligrams per liter, the pH should remain between 6.0 and 8.5, and toxic substances including insecticides and organic phosphorus compounds as well as a broad range of trace metals should be carefully monitored. Accordingly, specifications require that DO, pH, and temperature levels remain at those required of A-II and B streams. Required level of sewage and industrial waste treatment and maximum total coliform and phenol levels are not specified. Further, the maximum fecal coliform count is raised to 1,000 per 100 milliliters. The fact that some wastes, including sewage, contribute to the fertility of aquatic meadows in which fish browse for food does not necessarily justify excessive organic material. If streams are overloaded with organic matter DO levels may be seriously reduced. Further, Class C streams often discharge into streams of higher classification, making it more difficult for the receiving streams to maintain the desired quality.

There are not a large number of Class C streams in Metrolina. The largest of these include the South Yadkin River in Iredell and Rowan counties, and the First Broad River and Buffalo Creek in Cleveland County.

Best usage of Class D streams includes agriculture, industrial processing, fish survival, and any other usage except fishing, bathing, or as a source of water for drinking, cooking, or food-processing. Specifications regarding quality are essentially the same as for C streams with the following exceptions: minimum dissolved oxygen levels are reduced to 3.0 milligrams per liter, and specified maximum coliform counts only apply to those streams used for irrigation of fruits and vegetables.

It is unfortunate that so many of the small streams in Metrolina have a D classification. In densely populated areas Class D streams are particularly common. In Mecklenburg County, for example, nearly all streams other than the Catawba are classified as D and great difficulty is still experienced in maintaining many of these streams at a quality compatible with this low classification.

Chemical Characteristics and Bacteriological Quality

Metrolina is underlain by hard, relatively insoluble crystalline rocks and thus natural waters have little dissolved mineral matter. As shown in Fig. 3.16, silica, iron, manganese, sodium, potassium, sulfates, chlorides, flourides, and nitrates are almost always below levels of significant adverse effects. The pH, averaging about 6.5, is almost everywhere within a satisfactory range. Only on Irish Buffalo Creek, where pH readings of 11 and above have recently been reported, is this a problem. It is hoped that this is a temporary problem resulting from local industrial effluent that will soon be corrected.

Waters are generally soft, averaging less than 30 parts per million of carbonates. Areas where population is dense and industrial and municipal effluent contributes large amounts of carbonates have moderately hard water. For example, at sampling stations along Steele, Irwin, Little Sugar, Briar, and McMullen creeks in the Sugar Creek Basin hardness of 100 parts per million and above are reported. Each of these streams is of the D Class where such levels are compatible.

The reported occurrence of gold, copper, mercury, zinc, lead, and arsenic in a wide number of streams is of concern. Reported concentrations are below hazardous levels, but testing has not been inclusive and an expanded monitoring program seems appropriate.

A large number of stations have observed low DO levels and high coliform counts indicating a low bacteriological quality. It is quite apparent that this is a regional problem. The low quality largely results from inadequate treatment of domestic sewage.

Greater emphasis is needed on stream-monitoring. Agencies charged with stream-monitoring are limited by a shortage of funds, equipment, and manpower. Most stations average only three readings per year. In sampling, there is limited consistency concerning the hour of the day, day of the week, or month of the year. Further differences in flow rates, water temperatures, and other variables often mask the results.

James W. Clay

GROUND WATER

Ground water is an important resource of the region. Thousands of wells have been drilled and large quantities of water are used daily. In general yields of wells throughout Metrolina are low, averaging about 15 to 20 gallons per minute (gpm). These low yields result from the underlying igneous and metamorphic rocks, which, when solid, have porosities between 1 and 3 percent. The few pores that are present are small and generally not interconnected. Thus ground water can only move through interconnected joints and fractures in the rocks and between the individual mineral grains in the soil and weathered rock.

Differences in well yield, except for a small southeastern zone where sedimentary rocks are tapped, are usually a function of variations in weathering or fracturing rather than in rock type. Each rock unit, however, normally has distinctive fracturing and weathering characteristics and thus the rock type has an indirect influence. Well yields are also related to topography. Wells on flat uplands, valleys, and ravines tend to yield larger amounts of water than wells on slopes and hilltops. The lack of water on or near the steeper slopes can be explained by the fact that erosion has removed much of the weathered and more per-

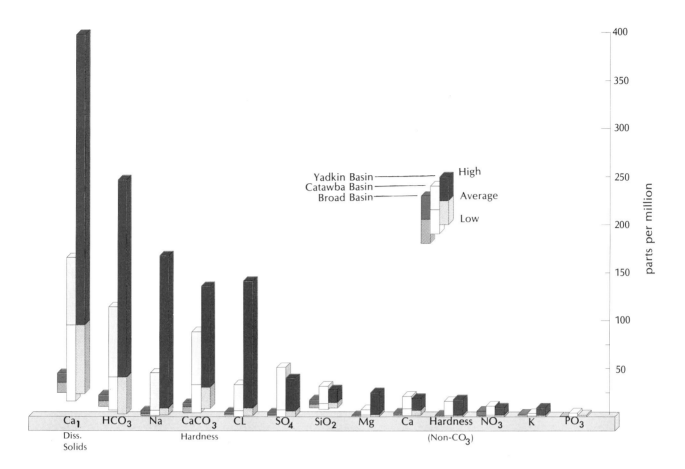

Fig. 3.16. Chemical Characteristics of Surface Waters in Metrolina

meable rock. Water levels are also further below the surface on slopes because ground water drains to points of discharge in adjacent lowlands. Ravines have an added advantage since they often develop along permeable fault zones where permeability and flow rates are typically higher.

Depth of wells varies from a few feet to over a thousand feet, but most of the available ground water in Metrolina is less than three hundred feet deep and greater drilling depths are seldom justifiable. The weathered material extends to an average depth of about thirty-five to forty feet, but ranges from a few feet to more than a hundred. In general the size and number of fractures decrease with depth. Thus below a depth of three hundred feet porosities and permeabilities are normally extremely low.

The chemical quality of water throughout Metrolina is almost always excellent. Water from granite, gneiss, mica schist, and rhyolite tends to be slightly acid and has median total dissolved solids of only 71 ppm (parts per million) and a median hardness of only 23 ppm. In contrast, water from gabbro, diorite, hornblende gneiss, and andesite is slightly alkaline with median total dissolved solids of 233

ppm and a median hardness of 145 ppm.

Biological contamination of ground water is a problem where soil is thin or absent over the water-bearing rocks. Even though fractures may be less than one millimeter wide, pathogenic organisms will move much more efficiently than in normal alluvial aquifers. The problem is aggravated by dug wells that penetrate only a short distance into the rock, particularly in wells not properly protected against direct storm runoff.

There are significant intraregional variations in ground water properties. Following is a discussion of flow rates and chemical quality of each of the four lithological belts shown on the surface geology map.

The Sedimentary and Coastal Belt

In the southeast, where the igneous and metamorphic rocks give way to the unconsolidated sands of the coastal belt, well yields are the highest in Metrolina. Here in Lancaster County yields of 200 to 400 gallons of soft water per minute are common and by using gravel-packed or screened wells, yields can often be doubled.

In the Triassic sediments of Union County yields are typically low. Sandstones and conglomerates have undergone postdepositional composition and cementation and thus have very low permeability. Wells yield about 15 gallons per minute (gpm) and the water is frequently hard and locally may contain objectionable amounts of iron and chloride.

The Carolina Slate Belt

Wells in the Carolina slate belt have the lowest average yields in Metrolina. Wells yield about 13 gallons per minute with the per foot ratio decreasing below a depth of about 150 feet. Rocks having pronounced cleavage may yield up to 60 gpm. Others, however, yield less than 10 gallons per minute. The water is generally moderately hard, containing low to moderate amounts of iron.

The general tendency for the weathered material of rocks in this belt to provide poor filtering action has been reported to commonly result in septic tank failure. Throughout Metrolina this problem reappears. The generally low permeability of the weathered material requires a much larger area for proper filtering than would more pervious material such as sand. A second problem common to the belt is well pollution. A preliminary report recently compiled by interns from the Institute for Urban Studies and Community Service of The University of North Carolina at Charlotte and the Stanly County Medical Society revealed a high incidence of polluted wells throughout Stanly County. The North Carolina Department of Air and Water Resources attributes this problem to poorly constructed wells rather than to a widespread pollution of the ground water supply. In areas where bedrock fracturing is common and the weathered layer is thin, pathogens may be transported moderate distances to pollute nearby wells. Thus care should be exercised to provide wide spacing between septic tanks as well as other sources of biological contamination, and wells. Further, wells should be properly constructed and finished to protect against surface and near-surface seepage and contamination.

The Charlotte Belt

Ground water in the Charlotte belt is almost everywhere of good chemical quality. The acidic rocks are relatively insoluble in water and thus water from them is low in mineral content. As illustrated in Table 3.5, water from granite, granite-diorite, and mica gneiss normally has less than 100 parts per million of dissolved solids and is low in iron and calcium. The basic rocks such as diorites and gabbros are readily soluble and thus host water lower in chemical quality. Well water from these rocks commonly contains 200 to 300 ppm of dissolved solids and even higher amounts of iron, calcium, and other chemicals.

Wells in the Charlotte belt yield between zero and several hundred gallons per minute, averaging about 24 gallons per minute. The highest yields are associated with the more basic gabbros and diorites with flow rates averaging about twice that of granitic rocks.

The Inner Piedmont Belt

Ground water in the Kings Mountain group is often moderately hard because of the presence of weathered beds of marble and calcareous shales that are relatively soluble in water. Wells in the area yield on the average about 26 gallons per minute, but as elsewhere in Metrolina the range is considerable depending on lithology, intensity of fracturing, thickness of weathered material, and topography. The quartz monzonites yield on the average about 20 gpm but flow rates of more than 200 gpm have been reported. The water is of a high quality having very low amounts of iron and calcium.

Ground water in the mica schist-gneiss complex is transmitted largely through intersecting sets of fractures. The water is low in mineral content and has a median hardness of about 50 parts per million. In the schist the average flow rate is about 25 gpm though rates may be much larger. The gneissic rocks have slightly higher average yields, about 35 gpm.

In this belt and throughout Metrolina there appear to be considerable underdeveloped ground water supplies in floodplains. Fiber Industries has installed a well in a floodplain along Buffalo Creek in Cleveland County. It has been reported that the well yields more than 600 gallons per minute. The water is low in dissolved solids and of a high quality.

James W. Clay

SOILS

Fig. 3.17 is an extremely broad, general, pictorial presentation of Metrolina's soil resources. It can be used to assist in planning orderly growth and development on a regional basis. Detailed soil surveys are generally made on a county basis at a much larger scale by the Soil Conservation Service. These detailed surveys, properly interpreted, provide one of the best tools for planning and applying the proper land use. Individual properties or characteristics of a soil series determine how it will respond to specific usage, such as sediment control, water management, parks, school grounds, septic-tank filter fields, sanitary land fills, woodland, general agriculture, and others.

The map, prepared by a soil scientist, groups the many

Table 3.5. Summary of Chemical Analyses of Well Water in the Statesville Area, North Carolina (parts per million)

| | Granite[a] | | | | Diorite[b] | | | | Granite & Diorite[c] | | | |
| | | Range | | | | Range | | | | Range | | |
	Median	Mean	Low	High	Median	Mean	Low	High	Median	Mean	Low	High
Silica (SiO_2)	27	27.5	10	39	32	33.8	21	50	30	29.9	24	36
Total iron (Fe)	.11	.26	.02	1.70	.21	.60	.06	5.70	.09	.21	.02	.76
Calcium (Ca)	8	9.3	2	37	21	35	4	174	7	12	6	22
Magnesium (Mg)	2	2.9	1	8	5	6.3	1	22	3	3	2	5
Sodium & potassium $(Na+K)$	7	7.7	4	13	10	11.7	3	35	8	7.8	6	11
Carbonate (CO_3)	0	0	0	0	0	0	0	0	0	0	0	0
Bicarbonate (HCO_3)	43	45.6	12	132	86	87.6	33	229	50	61.3	40	99
Sulfate (SO_4)	2	5.7	1	34	10	38.6	1	391	4	6.5	2	13
Chloride (Cl)	2	4.5	1	18	3	16	1	204	1	1.4	1	2
Fluoride (F)	.1	.29	0	1.5	.1	.3	0	2.2	.1	.14	.1	.2
Dissolved solids	80	84.4	25	187	175	196.6	70	696	80	93.4	77	120
Total hardness as $CaCO_3$	27	34.5	8	124	94	113.1	17	449	28	42.4	22	71
pH	6.5	6.55	5.8	7.0	7.0	7.12	6.3	8.2	6.7	6.88	6.6	7.6

a. Water from wells in granite and granite gneiss. Represents fourteen samples.
b. Water from wells in diorite, gabbro, and hornblende gneiss. Represents twenty-five samples.
c. Water from wells that penetrated both granite and diorite, and both granite and hornblende gneiss. Represents eight samples.
Source: Harry E. Legrande, *Geology and Ground Water in the Statesville Area, North Carolina*, 1954.

recognizable soils into four major resource areas and eleven soil associations. A soil association is named for the soil series that make up the major portion of an area. The name results from combining series names in a declining order by acreage. Series names are subject to change and several of those discussed herein have not been correlated under the most recent classification system. The extremely brief, general interpretations that follow give some of the significant characteristics of the associations and the soil series. Limitations or hazards for nonagricultural usage are expressed as "slight," "moderate," or "severe." To compensate for these limitations, the treatment is "simple,"

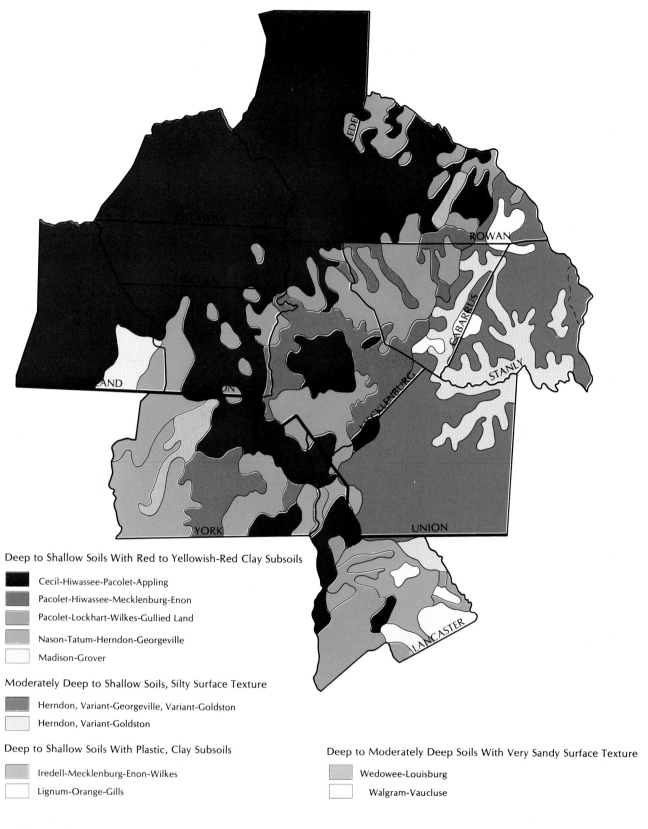

Deep to Shallow Soils With Red to Yellowish-Red Clay Subsoils

■ Cecil-Hiwassee-Pacolet-Appling

▨ Pacolet-Hiwassee-Mecklenburg-Enon

▨ Pacolet-Lockhart-Wilkes-Gullied Land

▨ Nason-Tatum-Herndon-Georgeville

☐ Madison-Grover

Moderately Deep to Shallow Soils, Silty Surface Texture

▨ Herndon, Variant-Georgeville, Variant-Goldston

☐ Herndon, Variant-Goldston

Deep to Shallow Soils With Plastic, Clay Subsoils

▨ Iredell-Mecklenburg-Enon-Wilkes

☐ Lignum-Orange-Gills

Deep to Moderately Deep Soils With Very Sandy Surface Texture

▨ Wedowee-Louisburg

☐ Walgram-Vaucluse

1. This map is based on current limited information and is subject to revision.
2. Information on Lancaster and York Counties, S. C. was furnished by SCS, Columbia, S. C.
3. Soil names are tentative and subject to change. Several of them have not been correlated under the most recent classification system.

Prepared by USDA-Soil Conservation Service

Fig. 3.17. Metrolina's Soil Resources

"moderate," and "intensive" respectively.

Cecil-Hiwassee-Pacolet-Appling

These well-drained soils make up the northwest quadrant of the area and the largest of the associations. The Cecil, Hiwassee, and Appling occupy the broad, gently sloping ridge crest with the Pacolet and inclusions on the steeper terrain. Limitations or hazards for nonagricultural uses are predominantly moderate with minor acreages having severe limitations. There are numerous large, caving gullies in Lincoln County and occasional gullies in the other counties that contribute enormous loads of sediment to the drainage system annually. Erosion is the major hazard for all of these soils. That portion of the area, designated by a dotted line in Fig. 3.17, in the northwest part of Cleveland County, is the foothills of the mountains. It is steep, rocky, mixed woodland. That portion in central Mecklenburg County is the Charlotte metropolitan area.

Pacolet-Hiwassee-Mecklenburg-Enon

These are well-drained soils with the majority of the acreage in Mecklenburg, York, Cabarrus, and Rowan counties. The Hiwassee and Mecklenburg occupy the broader, gentler slopes with Pacolet, Enon, and most of the inclusions on the steeper terrain. Limitations for Pacolet and Hiwassee are predominantly moderate for nonagricultural uses. Primarily because of their plastic, slowly permeable clay subsoils that have a high "shrink-swell" ratio, Mecklenburg and Enon have severe limitations for nonagricultural uses.

Pacolet-Lockhart-Wilkes-Gullied Land

These are well-drained soils with the association restricted to Lancaster County. This area is predominantly strongly sloping to steep, and a large portion of it is severely eroded. Because of slope and erosion, Pacolet and Lockhart have moderate to severe limitations for most nonagricultural uses. The shallow (less than twenty-four inches to rock) Wilkes and the Miscellaneous Land Class Gullied Land have severe limitations or hazards for nonagricultural use.

Nason-Tatum-Georgeville

Most of this acreage is in Gaston, Cleveland, York, and Lancaster counties. These are well drained soils with a fine-textured surface layer. The area in Lancaster County occupies a gently to strongly sloping broad ridge crest while the remainder is predominantly steep, wooded land

around the Pinnacle and adjacent ridges of Kings Mountain. Excluding the steep slopes and rocky areas, the soils have moderate limitations for most nonagricultural uses. Rock ledges, loose boulders, and rocky spires are quite common. This latter portion is well suited to certain recreational uses.

Madison-Grover

These are well-drained soils that occupy broad, gently sloping ridges in Cleveland County. Limitations for nonagricultural uses are predominantly moderate. There are small areas where loose boulders, stones, and rock outcrop are common. The subsoils have a high mica content, are very susceptible to erosion, and soil compaction is extremely difficult.

Herndon, Variant-Georgeville, Variant-Goldston

These well-drained soils make up the major portion of Union and Stanly counties with smaller areas in Cabarrus, Rowan, and Mecklenburg. Topography is predominantly undulating with the great majority of the slopes ranging from 3 to 8 percent. Goldston is a "slaty," shallow (less than twenty inches to bedrock) soil and the Herndon and Georgeville variants are about twenty to thirty-six inches thick. They contain 5 to 50 percent slate fragments by volume and are underlain by "Carolina Slate" rock. The bedding plane, fracture, and mineralogy of this rock, and comparatively poor filtering actions of the silty soils have significant effects on:

1. Sanitation. Septic field failure is quite common. Many individual water wells are polluted.

2. Water. There are very few "all weather" springs and most streams go dry or to "pool stage" during the dry months. Many drilled wells do not yield an adequate supply of water for an individual family and some of the water is unpalatable.

3. Bearing Strength. The interbedding of silt/clay layers with the slate rock often presents problems.

Limitations for most nonagricultural uses range from moderate to severe.

Herndon, Variant-Goldston

This association, located in Stanly, Union, Cabarrus, and Lancaster counties is comparable to the Herndon, Variant-Georgeville, Variant-Goldston association with three exceptions: (1) the percentage of Goldston is much higher; (2) the Herndon contains more slate fragments and is shallower; and (3) slopes are much steeper, loose stones and rock outcrop are common, topography is very broken. Because of these exceptions, the limitations for most nonagricultural uses are severe.

Iredell-Mecklenburg-Enon-Wilkes

The Iredell is moderately well drained while the other series are well drained. This association occurs in all counties except Catawba, Cleveland, Stanly, and Union. The Iredell and Mecklenburg occupy broad areas with slopes of 1 to 7 percent while Enon and Wilkes occur on the steeper terrain. Primarily because of their plastic, slowly permeable, clay subsoils that have a high "shrink-swell" ratio, all of these soils have severe limitations for most nonagricultural uses. If the slopes are less than 3 percent, excess surface water presents a serious secondary problem.

Lignum-Orange-Gills

This association, composed of somewhat poorly drained soils, occurs in Cabarrus, Lancaster, Rowan, and Stanly counties. These soils occupy nearly level to gently sloping areas with slopes of 0 to 5 percent. Water-tolerant shallow-rooted hardwoods are the dominant natural vegetation. The plastic, slowly permeable clay subsoils that have a high "shrink-swell" ratio and the problem of excess water, both surface and subsurface, present extremely difficult problems for use and management. The soils have severe limitations for nonagricultural uses.

Wedowee-Louisburg

These are well to excessively drained soils. This association is located in York and Rowan counties. These soils occupy broad, gently sloping ridges with occasional, distinct knobs. Rock outcrop, very large boulders, and stones are quite common. There is some commercial quarrying in Rowan. Hard rock is usually encountered at a depth of less than six feet. Excluding the rocky areas and steeper slopes, limitations for most nonagricultural uses range from slight to moderate.

Wagram-Vaucluse

This association, composed of well-drained soils, is located in Lancaster County. This area is the beginning of the "Sand Hills" section and the soils are derived from ocean sediment. They occupy broad, nearly level to gently sloping ridges. Vaucluse soils are often underlain by platy iron-stone sheets; permeability is moderately slow. Wagram has slight to moderate limitations for most nonagricultural uses; limitations for nonagricultural uses of Vaucluse range from slight to severe.

Sam Hearn

AGRICULTURE

During the past several decades the agricultural structure of the United States has demonstrated several distinctive trends. These national trends have been apparent in the states of North Carolina and South Carolina, particularly in urban-oriented regions such as Metrolina.

First, there has been an increase in the average size of farm units as a result of the absorption of smaller farms by larger operators. In 1964 the average size farm in Metrolina consisted of 112 acres as compared to 71 acres in 1950. Further, Metrolina farms are considerably larger than farms in North Carolina as a whole. In North Carolina, for example, the average farm size was slightly less than 100 acres in 1964, while the average farm size exceeded 100 acres in all except two Metrolina counties.

Second, there has been a reduction in the acreage of cropland harvested. Many previous farms have ceased crop production entirely as idle land has come to dominate land use in many rural areas. Even during the short period from 1959 to 1964 the amount of cropland harvested in Metrolina decreased from 640,139 acres to 473,433 acres, a decline of 26 percent.

Third, and related to the above trends, there has been a dramatic decrease in the number of farm units. The general decline in the number of farm units began around 1930. In Metrolina the number of farm units decreased by 60 percent between 1950 and 1964. In a few counties the rate of decline even exceeded 70 percent. These rates of decline can be compared to a decrease of 52 percent in North Carolina and South Carolina during the same period. The decrease in the number of Metrolina farms by county is revealed in Fig. 3.18.

In the context of these trends several characteristics of Metrolina's agricultural structure as related to tenure and production can be noted. It is apparent that the typical farm operator in the Metrolina region can only be considered as a part-time farmer since for many farmers frequently the nonfarm source of income exceeds the farm income. Over one-third of the farm operators in North Carolina and South Carolina have off-farm incomes that exceed farm income and this proportion is increasing. In two regions of North Carolina, however, the proportion of farm operators with off-farm incomes greater than farm incomes is exceptionally large. One of these regions consists of counties in the mountainous western portion of the state. The other region is Metrolina, where as early as 1959 well over one-half (58 percent) of the farm operators had off-farm incomes greater than farm incomes. This can be compared to values of 33 percent and 42 percent for the entire areas of North Carolina and South Carolina respectively and a value of less than 20 percent for the tobacco-production area of eastern North Carolina.

The Metrolina region historically has not accounted for a large share of North and South Carolina's volume and

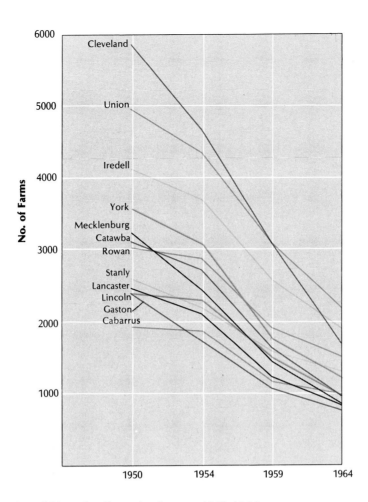

Fig. 3.18. Decline in the Number of Metrolina Farms by County, 1950-1964

value of agricultural production. Nevertheless several important characteristics of Metrolina's agricultural structure can be noted. This region differs markedly from the entire areas of North Carolina and South Carolina in terms of the proportion of income derived from crops as compared to the proportion derived from livestock and livestock products. For North Carolina and South Carolina as a whole in 1964 crops accounted for approximately 72 percent of the value of farm products sold whereas livestock and livestock products accounted for only 28 percent. These percentages were exactly reversed within Metrolina as crops accounted for only 28 percent of the value of farm products and livestock and livestock products accounted for approximately 72 percent. In all Metrolina counties the value of livestock and livestock products exceeded the value of crops. Stanly and Union are the two counties most dominated by the sale of livestock and livestock products where, in 1964, this category accounted for 85 percent and 79 percent respectively of farm incomes. The dominance of livestock as a source of farm income compared to crops is characteristic of the entire Piedmont area of the two Carolinas. The principal location of many of the major cash crops of the state historically has been the coastal plain region. In both North Carolina and South Carolina, however, the proportion of total farm income that is accounted for by income from crops is declining.

Fig. 3.19 reveals the total value of farm products sold by county and the relative significance of each major source. Union, Stanly, and Cleveland counties far exceed any other Metrolina counties in terms of the value of livestock and livestock products. The major portion of the income in these three counties from livestock products comes from the sale of poultry and poultry products, principally the sale of broiler chickens and eggs, which are two of North Carolina's fastest growing agricultural-business products. The Metrolina region is located on the western fringe of one of North Carolina's major poultry production areas.

In addition, Metrolina contains a large dairy industry with the greatest concentration in the northern counties of Iredell and Rowan. In fact these two counties respectively led the state in 1968 in the number of dairy cows. The dairy industry in these two counties is well located to serve the large urban markets centered on Charlotte and the High Point—Greensboro—Winston-Salem urban conur-

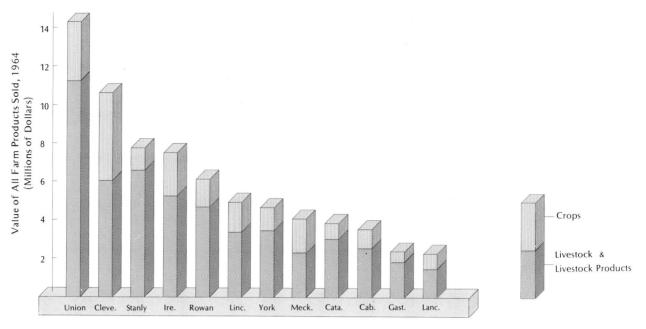

Source: 1964 Census of Agriculture.

Fig. 3.19. Value of Farm Products Sold by County in Metrolina

bation.

North and South Carolina's major field crops in terms of value of products sold are tobacco, corn, soybeans, cotton, and peanuts. These crops historically have been grown in the sandy soils of the coastal plain area of the two Carolinas and thus have been virtually absent from the Metrolina region. Only two of these crops, cotton and soybeans, are presently grown to any extent in the Metrolina counties. Cleveland and Union counties ranked third and seventh respectively in North Carolina in volume of cotton production for 1967. But cotton production has been declining very rapidly in these two counties as well as throughout the two Carolinas. In the short period from 1964 to 1967 production in Cleveland County dropped from 20,400 bales to 2,559 bales, a decline of 88 percent. Union County also ranked third in North Carolina in the volume of soybean production for 1967. Soybean is a comparatively new crop to the southeastern United States, and production of this crop in North and South Carolina has more than doubled between 1960 and 1970. Much of the expansion in production in Union County has occurred since 1965.

Only the production of two small grain crops, wheat and oats, is concentrated to any extent in the Metrolina area. The counties of Rowan, Stanly, and Union respectively were the three leading North Carolina counties in wheat production for 1967 whereas Rowan, Iredell, and Union ranked as the top three North Carolina counties in oats production.

Dennis Lord

REFERENCES

Carney, Charles B.; Albert V. Hardy; and Henry V. Marshall, Jr. *Climate of North Carolina Research Stations*, Agricultural Experiment Station bul. 433 (July 1967).

Environmental Protection Agency. "Requirements for Preparation, Adoption, and Submittal of Implementation Plans," *Federal Register* 36, no. 158, part 2 (August 14, 1971).

Fair, G. M.; J. C. Geyer; and D. A. Okum. *Water Purification and Wastewater Treatment and Disposal*. New York: John Wiley & Sons, 1968.

Harris, K. F. *Chemical Character of Surface Waters of South Carolina, 1945-60*, South Carolina State Development Board, bul. no. 16C. Columbia: The Board, 1962.

Holzworth, George C. "Mixing Depths, Wind Speeds and Air Pollution Potential for Selected Locations in the United States." Cincinnati: Air Resources Field Research Office, August 1967.

Korshover, Julius. "Climatology of Stagnating Anticyclones, East of the Rocky Mountains, 1936-1965." Cincinnati: National Center for Air Pollution Control, 1967.

North Carolina Board of Water and Air Resources. *Rules, Regulations, Classifications and Water Quality Standards Applicable to the Surface Water of North Carolina*. Raleigh: The Board, 1970.

North Carolina Department of Agriculture. *North Carolina Agricultural Statistics*. Raleigh: The Department, 1968.

North Carolina Department of Conservation and Development and the Geological Survey, U.S. Department of the Interior. *Geology and Ground Water in the Statesville Area, North Carolina*, bul. no. 68. Raleigh: The Department, 1954.

North Carolina Department of Water and Air Resources. *Ground Water Resources of Cleveland County*, North Carolina Division of Ground Water. Raleigh: The Department, December 1966.

North Carolina Department of Water and Air Resources. *Ground Water Resources of Cleveland County*, North Carolina Division of Ground Water. Raleigh: The Department, December, 1966.

North Carolina Department of Water and Air Resources. *Ground*

Water Quality in Stanly County, North Carolina Division of Ground Water, Ground Water cir. no. 15. Raleigh: The Department, 1970.

Phibbs, E. J., Jr. *Chemical and Physical Character of Surface Waters of North Carolina 1966-67*, North Carolina Department of Water and Air Resources, Water Pollution Control Division, bul. 1, vol. 9. Raleigh: The Department, 1969.

Stromquist, Arvid A., and Harold W. Sundelius. *Stratigraphy of the Albemarle Group of the Carolina Slate Belt in Central North Carolina*, U.S.G.S. bul. 1274-B, 1969.

Stucky, Jasper L., and Stephen G. Conrad. *Explanatory Text for Geologic Map of North Carolina.* Raleigh: North Carolina Department of Conservation and Development, 1958.

U.S. Department of Commerce. *Local Climatological Data*, Annual Summary with Comparative Data. Washington, D.C.: The Department, 1966.

U.S. Department of Commerce, Bureau of the Census. *United States Censuses of Agriculture.* Washington, D.C.: The Department, 1950-64.

U.S. Department of Commerce, Weather Bureau. *Summary of Hourly Observations, Charlotte, N.C.*, Climatography of the U.S. no. 82-31. Washington, D.C.: U.S. Government Printing Office, 1963.

U.S. Department of Health, Education, and Welfare. *Report for Consultation on the Metropolitan Charlotte Interstate Air Quality Control Region (N.C. and S.C.).* Washington, D.C.: National Air Pollution Control Administration, May 1970.

U.S. Department of the Interior, Geological Survey. *Water Resources Data for North Carolina, Part 1. Surface Water Records.* Washington, D.C.: The Department, 1969.

U.S. Department of the Interior, Geological Survey. *Water Resources Data for South Carolina, Part 1. Surface Water Records.* Washington, D.C.: The Department, 1966.

4. POPULATION PROFILE

BARBARA A. GOODNIGHT

"The most important thing in the world is people. As people, you and we and billions of our kind spread over the face of the earth are at once the means and the end of all society's endeavors."—T. Lynn Smith and Paul E. Zopf, Jr., Demography: Principles and Methods, 1970.

The principal component of Metrolina, or any region, is its people. People create and consume, modify and interpret the physical, technological, and cultural environments of the region and in turn are molded and influenced by them. Thus, to understand the characteristics and challenges of Metrolina as an urbanizing region, one must know something about the distribution and composition of its population.

In the pages that follow some of the more salient characteristics of the inhabitants of Metrolina are analyzed. This profile features seven basic themes: number and geographic distribution of inhabitants, rural-urban distribution, racial distribution, age and sex composition, marital status and family composition, quality of housing, and population growth and change. These themes are developed for the region, the 12 counties that comprise it, and, when practicable, the 125 townships within their boundaries. Unless otherwise specified, the themes are developed from data contained in the First Count Summary Tapes from the 1970 Census of Population and Housing.

Barbara A. Goodnight

Number and Geographic Distribution of Inhabitants

Perhaps the most important facts to be learned about Metrolina and the twelve counties that comprise this urbanizing region are the number of its inhabitants and their geographical distribution. Not only are these facts among the principal defining characteristics of an urbanizing region, but they also function as indicators of the general level of living or quality of life of the population. They are basic to the computation of more specific indexes of the quality of life—indexes of criminality, dependency, marriage, and so on—and thus are essential for various research and administrative purposes.

Two types of data pertaining to the number and geographical distribution of the inhabitants of Metrolina are available: (1) the total number of inhabitants, an enumerative or descriptive measure; and (2) the density of population, a simple analytical measure calculated by dividing the total number of inhabitants by the number of square miles in an area. These measures are especially instructive when analyzed in terms of the subareas of the region or compared to other urbanizing regions.

Data from the Bureau of the Census indicate that Metrolina had a population numbering 1,162,123 persons on April 1, 1970—an 18 percent increase over the 984,372 persons residing there in 1960. It ranks fourth in population and thirteenth in land area (5,790 square miles) among the market areas and urbanizing regions of the southeastern United States. Included within the region is the Standard Metropolitan Statistical Area (SMSA) of Charlotte, comprised of Mecklenburg and Union counties.

The population of the region is unevenly distributed throughout its twelve counties, which range in size from the 308 square miles of Lincoln County to the 685 square miles of York County. (See Fig. 4.1.) Approximately one-half of the population (557,785 or 48 percent) is concentrated in Mecklenburg, Union, and Gaston Counties. Slightly more than one-third (409,370 or 35.23 percent) resides in the Charlotte SMSA; slightly less than one-third (354,656 or 30.52 percent) is concentrated in Mecklenburg

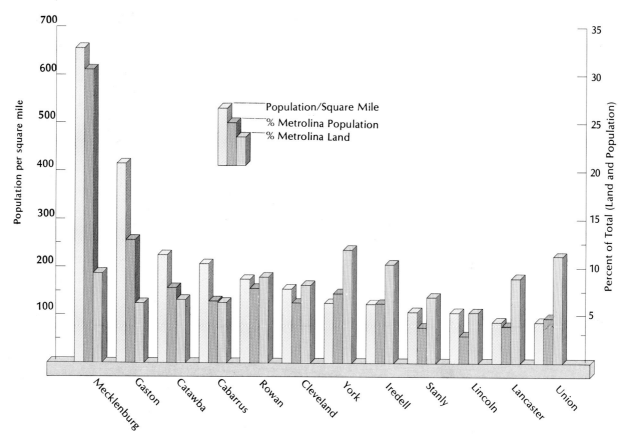

Source: 1970 Census of Population.

Fig. 4.1. Area and Population of Metrolina Counties, 1970

County. Approximately one-fifth of the region's population (241,178 or 20.75 percent) lives in Charlotte, the largest city within Metrolina and the Carolinas.

In terms of the man-land ratio, that is, the density of population, Metrolina ranks fourth among the urbanizing regions of the Southeast, with 201.09 persons per square mile. (It is outranked only by Miami, Florida, 314.00 per square mile; Atlanta, Georgia, 287.27 per square mile; and Tampa—St. Petersburg, Florida, 231.21 per square mile.) Metrolina's density is considerably greater than the approximately 57 persons per square mile of the United States or the 86 per square mile of South Carolina and the 104.5 per square mile of North Carolina, the states in which the region is located.

Mecklenburg County has the greatest concentration of population with 654.35 persons per square mile, followed by Gaston County with 414.57. The least densely populated counties within the region are Union, 85.09 per square mile, and Lancaster, 85.97 per square mile.

The concentration of population around urban centers is demonstrated in Figs. 4.2 and 4.3, which show the population density of Metrolina by township for 1970 and 1960.

The general pattern is one of decreasing density with increasing distance from urban centers. The townships vary in density of population from the 3,993.91 per square mile of tiny Lancaster Township with its 2.3 square miles of land area in Lancaster County to the 16.7 per square mile of McConnells Township (74.6 square miles) in York County. The Charlotte Township currently has 2,781.75 persons per square mile in contrast to its 3,199.47 per square mile in 1960. This generally unexpected decrease is at least partially the result of the annexation of 23.7 square miles of less densely settled land area to the 63 square miles that comprised the township in 1960.

Further examination of Figs. 4.2 and 4.3 reveals a pattern of increasing concentration of population. This is certainly to be expected in light of the increasing number of inhabitants in the area.

Barbara A. Goodnight

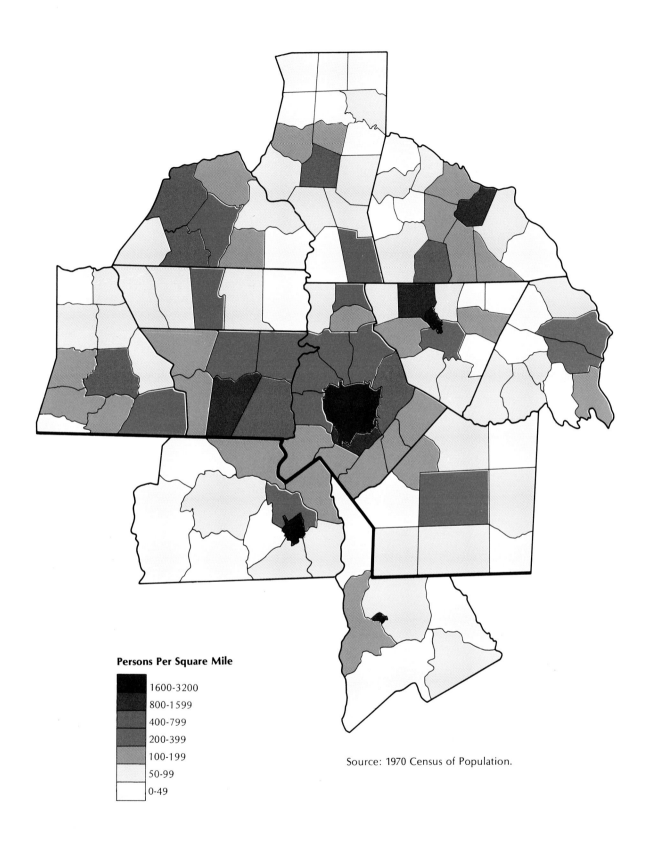

Persons Per Square Mile

1600-3200
800-1599
400-799
200-399
100-199
50-99
0-49

Source: 1970 Census of Population.

Fig. 4.2. Population Density of Metrolina, by Township, 1970

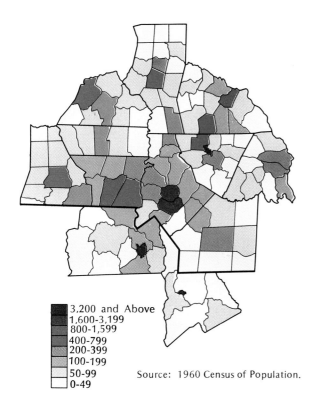

3,200 and Above
1,600-3,199
800-1,599
400-799
200-399
100-199
50-99
0-49

Source: 1960 Census of Population.

Fig. 4.3. Population Density of Metrolina, by Township, 1960

Rural-Urban Distribution

One of the most striking features of a region is the distribution of its population according to place of residence. The significance of this demographic fact may be changing somewhat as a result of improvements in transportation and communication that have made possible the development of a large rural-nonfarm, suburban population and a general homogenization of cultural patterns and life-styles. Nevertheless sufficient dissimilarities remain in the physical, cultural, and social environments of rural and urban dwellers to produce distinctive personalities and life-styles for each.

As an urbanizing region Metrolina is characterized by a preponderance of urban dwellers (persons living in incorporated and unincorporated places of 2,500 inhabitants or more or in the densely settled area around central cities, or twin cities, of 50,000 or more) and a significant proportion of nonurban dwellers who are associated with and dependent upon urban centers economically and/or culturally. Although the only Metrolina counties having a majority of urban inhabitants are Mecklenburg (79.1 percent), Cabarrus (64.0 percent), Gaston (60.3 percent), and York (55.1 percent), 55.4 percent of the total population of Metrolina is classified as urban. (See Fig. 4.4 (a).) This represents a very slight increase over the 55.3 percent of the population categorized as urban by the 1960 census (see Fig. 4.4 (b)) and does not adequately portray the increasingly urban

quality of life in the region. It does not, for instance, include the growth of the urban-oriented suburban population, which will be classified as rural nonfarm. Some indication of this growth may be seen in Figs. 4.4 and 4.5, which show the urban and rural distribution for 1960 and 1970. These maps reflect the general trend toward increasing concentration of population in urban fringe areas. The trend is especially evident in the areas just outside Charlotte, Hickory, and Gastonia, and is largely responsible for the increase in the rural population of the region (79,012 or 18 percent) during the decade preceding 1970.

Although tabulations of the 1970 rural farm and nonfarm populations are not yet available, there is every indication that they will reveal patterns similar to the 58 percent decrease in the rural farm and the 48 percent increase in the rural nonfarm populations of Metrolina during the 1950s. The fact that each county within the region gained rural inhabitants during the period from 1960 to 1970 and that eight of them experienced a higher rate of increase in their rural populations than in their urban populations is a further indication that Metrolina is experiencing the often-cited "flight to suburbia." This includes the nationwide trends to relocate industry in outlying areas and to build recreationally oriented "planned communities" featuring both single-family and multifamily dwelling units.

Charlotte, with its population of 241,178, is the dominant urban center and focal point of the region. Although it is sometimes described as a "small town grown large" in comparison to the more cosmopolitan centers of the Northeast and the West Coast, it offers a sharp contrast in tempo and pattern of living to the other cities of the region, the largest of which are Gastonia (47,142), Kannapolis (36,293), Rock Hill (33,846), Salisbury (22,515), and Hickory (20,569).

Barbara A. Goodnight

Racial Distribution

The human characteristics conceived as race must be taken into account by the student of population, not because of their inherent biological significance but because of the significance attributed to them by society. Race functions as a determining factor in the establishment and patterning of social relationships. As a demographic fact, it serves as an important indicator of cultural background, socioeconomic status, and other aspects of the quality of life.

Of the 1,162,123 inhabitants of Metrolina included in the 1970 census, 944,242 (81.2 percent) were classified as white; 215,280 (18.5 percent) as Negro; and only 2,709 (.2 percent) as belonging to other races. By focusing on the size and proportion of the Metrolina population that is Negro, some understanding may be gained of the nature and significance of the racial composition of the region.

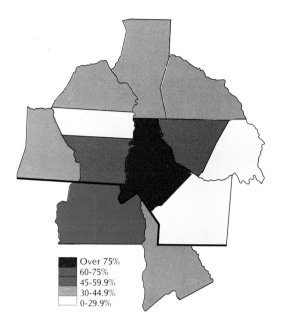

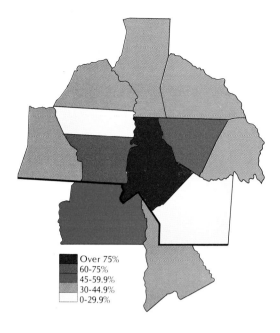

Source: 1970 Census of Population.

Fig. 4.4 (a). Percentage of Metrolina's Population That Was Urban, 1970

Fig. 4.4 (b). Percentage of Metrolina's Population That Was Urban, 1960

The number of Negroes in Metrolina has been increasing steadily throughout the years, but the proportion of Negroes in the population has declined just as steadily. This is evidenced by an increase in the size of the Negro population from 191,024 in 1960 to 215,280 in 1970 and an accompanying decline in the proportion of the population that is Negro from 19.4 percent to 18.5 percent. Correspondingly, there was a gain of 21,643 Negroes in North Carolina at the same time that the Negro proportion of the population declined from 25 percent in 1960 to 22 percent in 1970. Within the region only Lincoln and York counties experienced a decline in the size of their Negro populations during the decade ending in 1970, whereas the only counties that did not experience a decline in the Negro proportions of their populations were Cabarrus, Catawba, and Stanly.

This was not the pattern for the United States as a whole, for it had not only an increase in the size of the Negro population (from 18.5 million in 1960 to 22.6 million in 1970) but also an increase in the Negro proportion of the population (from 10.5 percent to 11.2 percent). This suggests that the heavy out-migration of Negroes from Metrolina and the South in general is continuing. Analysis of the components of population change—births, deaths, and migration—indicates that this is indeed the case.

Figs. 4.6 and 4.7 reveal that Negroes are overrepresented both in the more rural townships of the region and in Charlotte, its metropolitan center. This corresponds to the general pattern of migration from the rural South to metropolitan centers usually in the North or on the West Coast. That the distribution of Negroes in Metrolina is gradually moving toward that of the nation as a whole can be seen in Fig. 4.8.

Mecklenburg is the only county in the region that experienced a net in-migration of Negroes in the 1960s. The Metrolina counties having the largest proportion of Negroes in their populations are Lancaster (24.7 percent), York (24.3 percent), and Mecklenburg (23.8 percent), and those having the smallest proportions are Catawba (10.3 percent), Lincoln (10.6 percent), and Stanly (11.0 percent).

The implications of these facts and the use of race as an indicator of other sociocultural variables can be more readily seen when other variables and population characteristics are cross-tabulated with the racial distribution.

Barbara A. Goodnight

Age and Sex Composition

Age and sex are two of the most fundamental characteristics of an individual and serve as fairly reliable indicators of his status and life-style. Also, the distribution of the population among age and sex groups is a basic demographic fact which has important sociocultural and economic rami-

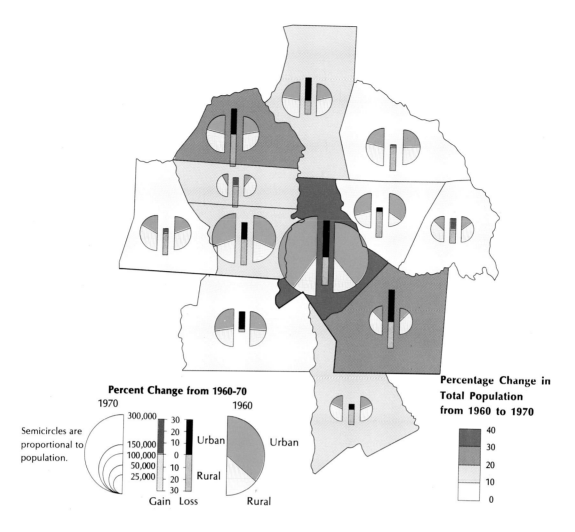

Percent Change from 1960-70

1970   300,000 ┐ ┌ 30   1960
                      │ │ 20
Semicircles are   │ │ 10
proportional to 150,000│ │ 0   Urban   Urban
population.   100,000│ │
                50,000 │ │ 10
                25,000 │ │ 20   Rural
                       └ └ 30   Rural
              Gain   Loss

Percentage Change in Total Population from 1960 to 1970

- 40
- 30
- 20
- 10
- 0

Source: 1970 Census of Population.

Fig. 4.5. Urban and Rural Population Change in Metrolina, by County, 1960 and 1970

fications and must be taken into account in any population analysis.

Several measures are available to aid in the presentation and interpretation of data pertaining to the age-sex composition of Metrolina. They range from such basically descriptive measures as (1) the size and proportion of the population in selected age groups and (2) the size and proportion of the population in various age-sex groups, which can be portrayed by age-sex pyramids, to such analytical measures as (3) the dependency ratio—the number of dependents (persons under fifteen years of age and sixty-five years of age and over) per one hundred contributors (persons between fifteen and sixty-five years of age) in the population— and (4) the sex ratio, the number of males per one hundred females in the population. Each of these measures is presented for the total and Negro populations of the region and its twelve counties. Other significant measures, including the median age and the age-sex composition of the rural and urban populations, have not yet been calculated from the 1970 census.

There are considerably fewer males (558,501) than females (603,622) in the population of Metrolina; the same is true for each of the counties within the region. As indicated by the sex ratios, this imbalance between the sexes is greatest in York County, which has only 87.6 males per 100 females and least in Union County where there are 97.7 males per 100 females. Metrolina's sex ratio of 92.5 falls midway between these extremes.

The imbalance between the sexes in the Negro population is even greater than it is in the total population. Although there are 97.4 males per 100 females in the Negro population of Union County, there are only 85.7 in Catawba County and 89.1 in Metrolina. Only in York County is the Negro sex ratio, 88.8, higher than that of the total population of the county, 87.6.

These variations in the sex ratio and the balance between the sexes they represent are indicative of differences in the style and tempo of life from one population to another. They result from variations in mortality rates and occupational structures as well as patterns of migration. The lower

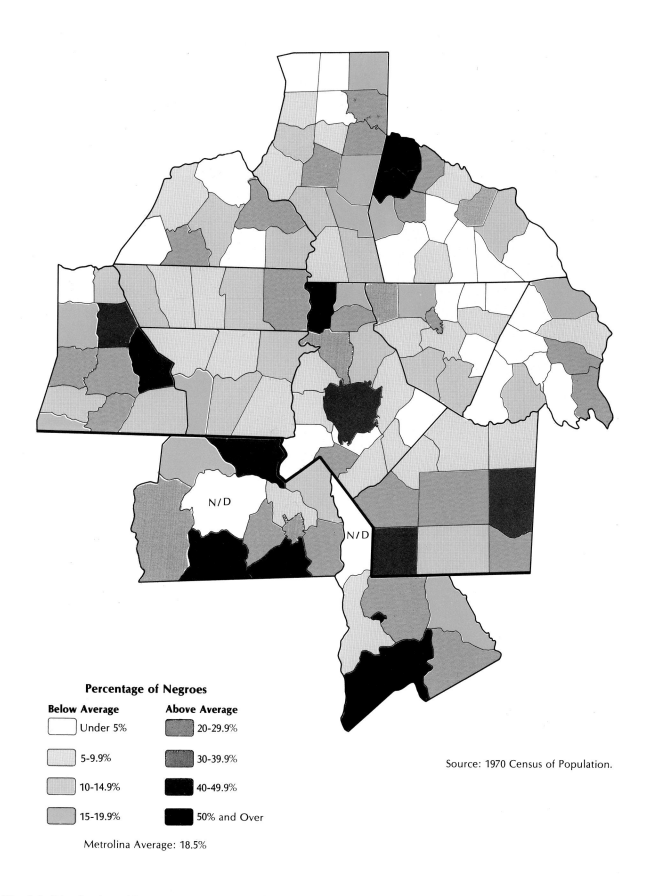

Percentage of Negroes

Below Average

☐ Under 5%

☐ 5-9.9%

☐ 10-14.9%

☐ 15-19.9%

Above Average

▨ 20-29.9%

▧ 30-39.9%

■ 40-49.9%

■ 50% and Over

Metrolina Average: 18.5%

Source: 1970 Census of Population.

Fig. 4.6. Distribution of Negroes in Metrolina, by Township, 1970

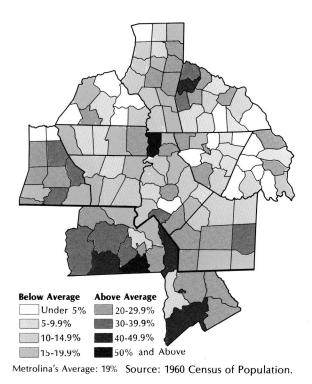

Fig. 4.7. Distribution of Negroes in Metrolina, by Township, 1960

sex ratio of the Negro population may also partially be the result of an underenumeration of Negro males, especially in urban areas.

The age distribution of Metrolina's population varies significantly according to sex and race as shown in Fig. 4.9. In the age-sex pyramids[1] presented there, it can be seen that the female population tends to be somewhat older than the male population and the Negro population tends to be somewhat younger than the total population. The latter is confirmed by the fact that Negroes are overrepresented in the zero to fourteen years age group, which includes 36.0 percent of their population as compared to 29.0 percent of the total population, and underrepresented in the group aged sixty-five years and over, which contains 6.3 percent of their population and 7.7 percent of the total population. These variations, as do most in the age-sex distribution, result from differential birth and mortality rates. Negro birth and death rates, for instance, tend to be higher than those for the total population. Fluctuations in the birth or death rates over a period of time are also indicated by the age-sex pyramids. The disproportionately

1. Deviation from the customary format of using five-year intervals in the construction of age-sex pyramids was necessitated by the form of data pertaining to Negroes that was available on the First Count Summary Tapes of the 1970 Census.

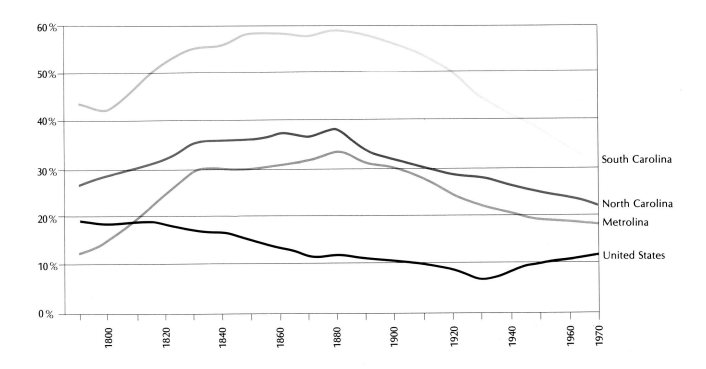

Source: 1970 Census of Population.

Fig. 4.8. Percentage of Negroes in the Population of Metrolina, 1790-1970

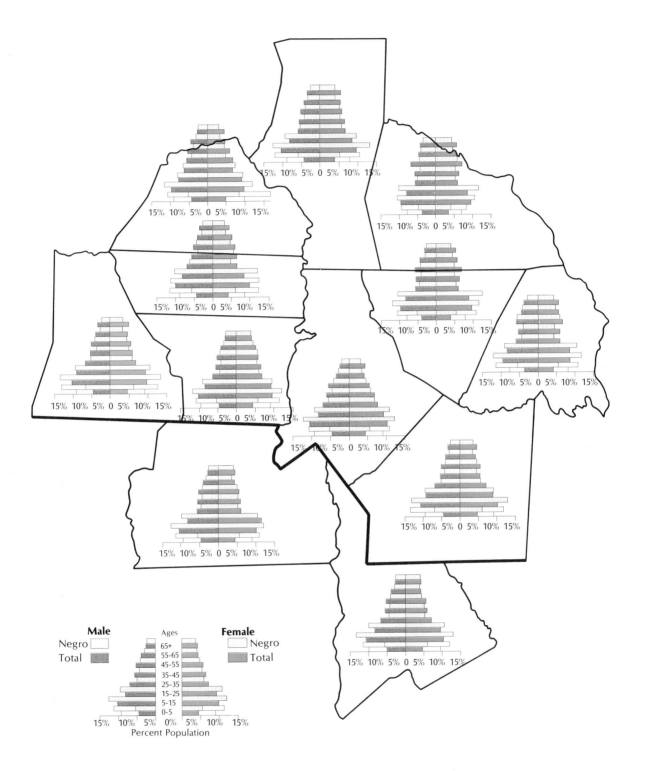

15% 10% 5% 0 5% 10% 15%

15% 10% 5% 0 5% 10% 15%

15% 10% 5% 0 5% 10% 15%

15% 10% 5% 0 5% 10% 15%

15% 10% 5% 0 5% 10% 15%

15% 10% 5% 0 5% 10% 15%

15% 10% 5% 0 5% 10% 15%

15% 10% 5% 0 5% 10% 15%

15% 10% 5% 0 5% 10% 15%

15% 10% 5% 0 5% 10% 15%

15% 10% 5% 0 5% 10% 15%

15% 10% 5% 0 5% 10% 15%

15% 10% 5% 0 5% 10% 15%

Male

Negro ☐

Total ▨

Ages

65+
55-65
45-55
35-45
25-35
15-25
5-15
0-5

Female

☐ Negro

▨ Total

15% 10% 5% 0% 5% 10% 15%
Percent Population

(Note: Age group 0-5 has been extended but un-colored to reflect the smaller interval used.)

Source: 1970 Census of Population.

Fig. 4.9. Age and Sex Composition of the Total and Negro Populations of Metrolina, 1970

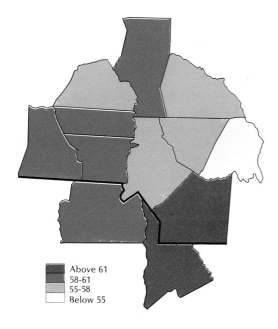

Above 61
58-61
55-58
Below 55

Fig. 4.10 (a). Dependency Ratio,
Total Metrolina Population

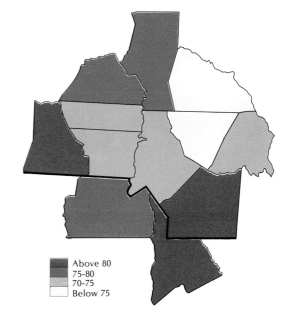

Above 80
75-80
70-75
Below 75

Source: 1970 Census of Population.

Fig. 4.10 (b). Dependency Ratio,
Negro Population of Metrolina

large difference in the sizes of the groups aged twenty-five to thirty-four and fifteen to twenty-four, for example, is the result of fluctuations in the birth rate due to the Great Depression and the Second World War. The influence of selective migration patterns on the age-sex distribution can also be seen in the more rural areas, particularly in the underrepresentation of the twenty-five to thirty-four and thirty-five to forty-four age groups. The out-migration of Negroes in the thirty-five to forty-four age group of Cleveland and Stanly Counties is a case in point.

Perhaps an even clearer indication of the influence of the age distribution of a population on its style and level of living is furnished by the analytical measure known as the dependency ratio. As explained earlier, the dependency ratio gives a crude estimation of the number of dependents per one hundred contributors or providers in the population and is thus inversely related to the level of living. The dependency ratio for the total population of Metrolina is 58.0; the comparable measure for its Negro population is considerably higher, 73.3 (see Fig. 4.10). Since Negro dependents are disproportionately young, they constitute an even greater dependency load than the ratios indicate. Dependency ratios within the region vary from a low of 54.8 for the total population of Stanly County to a high of 85.2 for the Negro population of Union County. It is interesting that the lowest dependency ratio for Negroes in the region, 63.1 in Rowan County, is higher than the high-

est for the total population, 62.0 in Lancaster County. These differences in the dependency loads of the Negro and total populations indicate that if all other factors were equal—education, occupation, income, and so forth—the level of living of the Negro population would still be somewhat lower than that of the total population.

Barbara A. Goodnight

Marital Status and Family Composition

The marital status of an individual, whether or not he lives in a family, and the composition of his family are important indicators of his life-style. Likewise, the mode of living of a region such as Metrolina is greatly influenced by the proportions of its population that are married and living with their mates, separated, widowed, divorced, or never married and the proportions of its population living in families centered around a husband and wife, another male head, or another female head. These measures may be used to assess the prevalence and strength of the family institution, to trace its changing structure, and to ascertain variations in it among population groups.

Of the 848,734 persons in Metrolina fourteen years old and over in 1970 a substantial majority (64 percent) are currently married and less than one-fourth (23 percent)

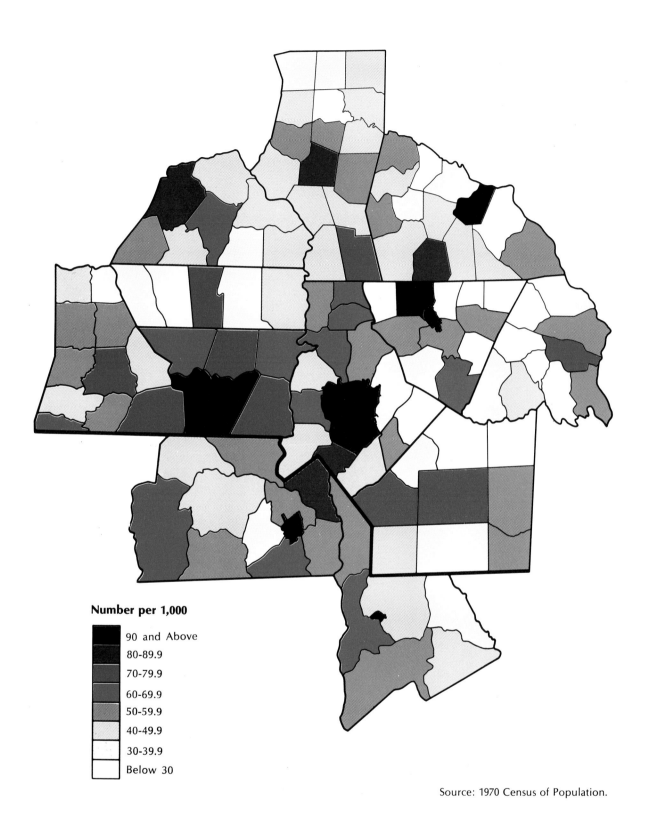

Number per 1,000

- 90 and Above
- 80-89.9
- 70-79.9
- 60-69.9
- 50-59.9
- 40-49.9
- 30-39.9
- Below 30

Source: 1970 Census of Population.

Fig. 4.11. Marital Unrest: Number of Divorced or Separated Persons per 1,000 Married Persons in Metrolina, by Township

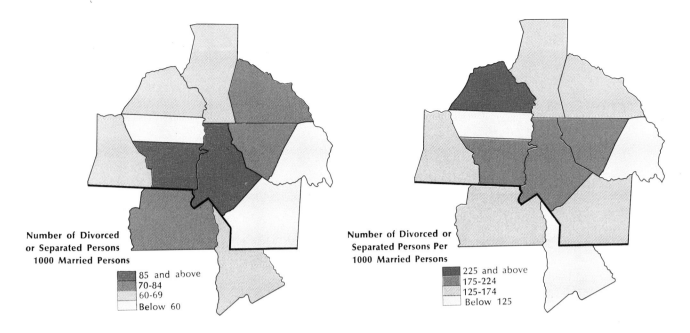

Source: 1970 Census of Population.

Fig. 4.12 (a). Index of Marital Unrest,
Total Metrolina Population

Fig. 4.12 (b). Index of Marital Unrest,
Negro Population of Metrolina

have never married. The remainder of these persons have been married but are now widowed (7 percent), divorced (2 percent), or separated (3 percent). The general marital condition of the population in each of the counties comprising the region is virtually the same as that of the region itself.

When this population is analyzed in terms of race and sex, however, significant variations in its marital condition are revealed. For instance, less than one-half (48 percent) of the region's 143,252 Negroes fourteen years old and over is now married, and slightly more than one-third (34 percent) is reported as never having married. Approximately 10 percent are widowed, 2 percent are divorced, and 7 percent are separated. Although a larger proportion of males (68 percent) than females (61 percent) is reported as now married, a larger proportion of males (25 percent) than females (21 percent) is also reported as never having married. When we look at disrupted marriages, however, we find larger proportions of the female than the male population in each category. This is especially true of the widowed, who comprise 12 percent of the female population and only slightly more than 2 percent of the male population. Approximately 3 percent of the females and 2 percent of the males are divorced and roughly the same proportions of each group are separated.

A somewhat more sophisticated analytical measure of the marital status of the region is the index of marital un-

rest, the ratio of divorced and separated persons per 1,000 married persons in the population. This index for the total population of Metrolina is 79; that is, there are 79 divorced and separated persons per 1,000 married persons in the region. This measure varies within the region from a low of 49 in Stanly County to a high of 97 in Mecklenburg County. Examination of the indexes of marital unrest for each township shown in Fig. 4.11 confirms the predominantly urban nature of this phenomenon.

Applying this same measure to the Negro population of Metrolina, we find that there are 184 divorced and separated persons per 1,000 married persons in the region, more than twice the number in the total population. This measure varies from a low of 107 in Lincoln County to a high of 315 in Catawba County. It should be noted that the lowest county index of marital unrest for Negroes exceeds the highest county index for the total population (see Figs. 4.12 (a) and 4.12 (b)). It should also be noted that the higher index of marital unrest for Negroes is due to the much larger proportion of their population that is separated rather than divorced. Although separation is often referred to as the "poor man's divorce," it does not have the same effect of returning the individual to single status and making him eligible for remarriage. It may be hypothesized that a significant number of the Negroes listed as never married are living as husband or wife with a person they cannot legally marry because a previous marriage has been

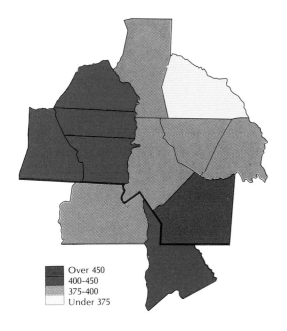

Over 450
400-450
375-400
Under 375

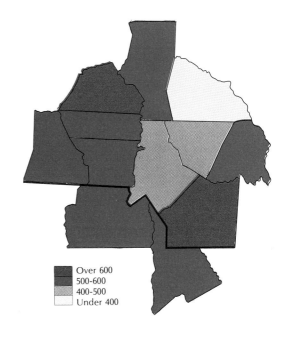

Over 600
500-600
400-500
Under 400

Source: 1970 Census of Population.

Fig. 4.13 (a). Metrolina Fertility Ratio, Total Population

Fig. 4.13 (b). Metrolina Fertility Ratio, Negro Population

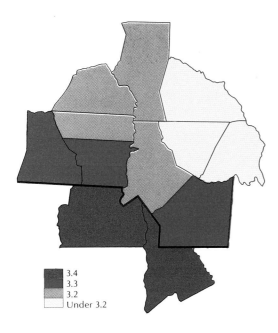

3.4
3.3
3.2
Under 3.2

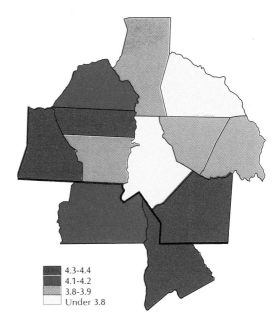

4.3-4.4
4.1-4.2
3.8-3.9
Under 3.8

Fig. 4.13 (c). Average Number of Persons per Household, Total Metrolina Population

Fig. 4.13 (d). Average Number of Persons per Household, Negro Population of Metrolina

terminated by separation.

In terms of family composition, by far the most prevalent family type in Metrolina is that centered around a husband and wife (86.3 percent). A substantial proportion has a female head of the household (11.2 percent), and a much lesser proportion (2.5 percent) has a male head. These figures include the entire population of the region except the 35,422 female and 16,293 male primary individuals (persons living alone or in nonfamily households) and the 34,549 persons who are roomers or boarders, inmates of institutions, or residents of other group quarters.

Although it is used primarily as a measure of reproduction, another indicator of family composition is the fertility ratio, the number of children under five years per 1,000 females aged fifteen to forty-four years. The fertility ratio of 398 for the total population of Metrolina is substantially lower than that of the 502 of its Negro population (see Figs. 4.13 (a) and 4.13 (b)), and both of these ratios are dramatically lower than the corresponding ratios of 521 and 709 in 1960. The declining fertility ratio reflects the general urban pattern of smaller families and is an excellent indicator of the increasing urbanization of the region.

Also indicative of Metrolina's increasing urbanization is the decline in average household size. (See Figs. 4.13 (c) and 4.13 (d).) Average (mean) household size for the total population of the region decreased from 3.6 in 1960 to 3.2 in 1970, a decline of 11.1 percent. This compares to a 5.5 percent decline in household size for the nation from 3.29

in 1960 to 3.11 in 1970. Average household size for Negroes within the region declined even more rapidly than that of the total population. It decreased from 4.3 in 1960 to 3.8 in 1970, a decline of 11.6 percent.

Barbara A. Goodnight

Quality of Housing

Although housing is not technically a population variable, quality of housing is an invaluable indicator of interaction patterns and life-styles. Housing not only constitutes a physical setting in which much human interaction occurs but it also serves as an important status symbol.

Five measures may be used to assess the physical quality and indicate the status symbolized by the housing of Metrolina's population: the owner-occupancy rate, the average value of owner-occupied housing, the average monthly contract rent of renter-occupied housing, the rate of overcrowding, and the proportion of housing units lacking complete plumbing facilities. (See Figs. 4.14, 4.15, 4.16, and 4.17.)

Of the 354,535 housing units in Metrolina enumerated in terms of occupancy in the 1970 census, about two-thirds (236,687 or 66.8 percent) were owner occupied. The rate of owner occupancy within the region ranged from a low of 60 percent in metropolitan Mecklenburg County to a high of 76 percent in rural Lincoln County. Although Ne-

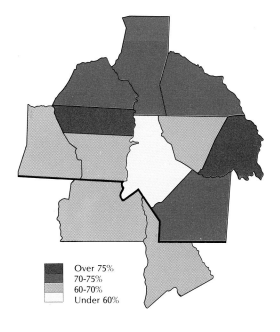

Fig. 4.14 (a). Owner Occupancy,
Total Metrolina Population

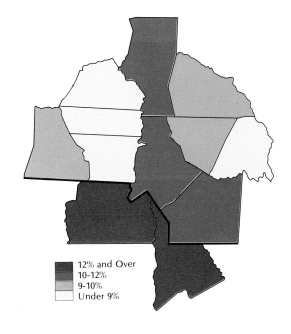

Source: 1970 Census of Population.

Fig. 4.14 (b). Owner Occupancy,
Negro Population of Metrolina

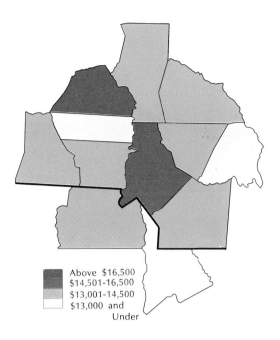

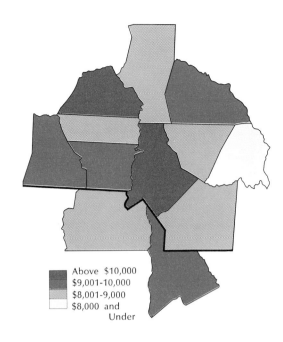

Fig. 4.15 (a). Average Value of Owner-Occupied Housing, Total Metrolina Population

Fig. 4.15 (b). Average Value of Owner-Occupied Housing, Negro Population of Metrolina

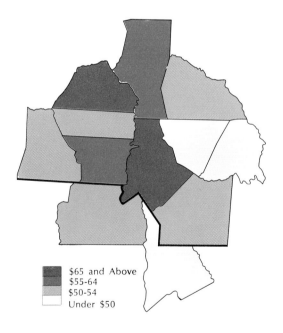

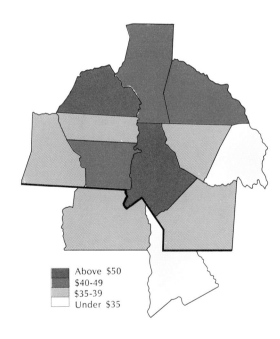

Source: 1970 Census of Population.

Fig. 4.15 (c). Average Monthly Rent of Occupied Housing, Total Metrolina Population

Fig. 4.15 (d). Average Monthly Rent of Occupied Housing, Negro Population of Metrolina

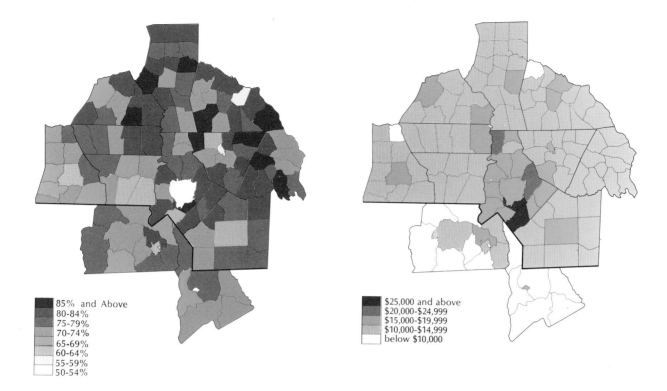

85% and Above
80-84%
75-79%
70-74%
65-69%
60-64%
55-59%
50-54%

$25,000 and above
$20,000-$24,999
$15,000-$19,999
$10,000-$14,999
below $10,000

Fig. 4.16 (a). Owner-Occupancy Rate, by Township, in Metrolina, 1970

Fig. 4.16 (b). Average Value of Owner-Occupied Housing, by Township, in Metrolina, 1970

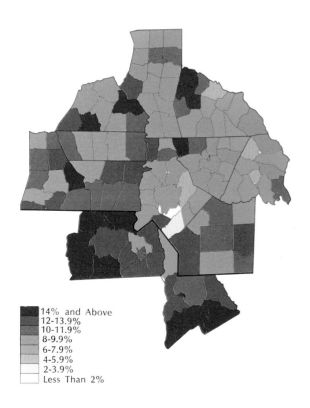

14% and Above
12-13.9%
10-11.9%
8-9.9%
6-7.9%
4-5.9%
2-3.9%
Less Than 2%

Fig. 4.16 (c). Percentage of Occupied Housing Over-crowded, by Township, in Metrolina, 1970

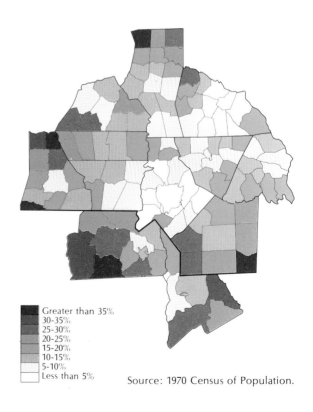

Greater than 35%
30-35%
25-30%
20-25%
15-20%
10-15%
5-10%
Less than 5%

Source: 1970 Census of Population.

Fig. 4.16 (d). Percentage of Occupied Housing with Incomplete Plumbing, by Township, in Metrolina, 1970

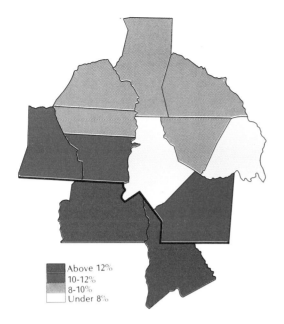

Fig. 4.17 (a). Percentage of Housing Units Overcrowded, Total Metrolina Population

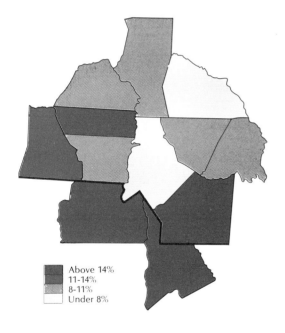

Fig. 4.17 (b). Percentage of Housing Units Overcrowded, Negro Population of Metrolina

Source: 1970 Census of Population.

Fig. 4.17 (c). Percentage of Housing Units with Incomplete Plumbing, Total Metrolina Population

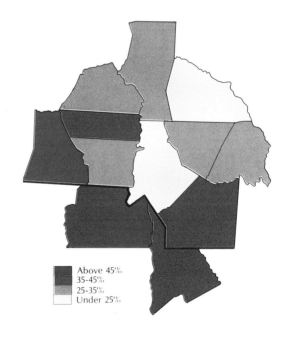

Fig. 4.17 (d). Percentage of Housing Units with Incomplete Plumbing, Negro Population of Metrolina

groes occupy 54,634 or 15.4 percent of the region's housing units, only 9.8 percent (23,296) of the owner-occupied units are Negro. Stated differently, only 42.6 percent of Negro housing is owner occupied. Fig. 4.16 (a) reveals the tendency of urbanization to lower this measure.

The average value of the 194,003 owner-occupied units for which values were given in the 1970 census was approximately $15,900. The average values of owner-occupied units within the region range from a low of $11,900 in Stanly County to a high of $20,500 in Mecklenburg County. These are very crude measures obtained by dividing the aggregate value of the units (the respondents' estimations of their current market value) by the number of units, and are useful largely for purposes of comparison. Fig. 4.16 (b), showing the average value of owner-occupied units by township, reveals the influence of urbanization on the value of housing as well as the tendency of the affluent to build in the suburbs. The value of Negro owner-occupied units ranges from $6,800 in Stanly County to $12,100 in Mecklenburg County, with a regional average of $10,200. The average value of housing units within the region that are vacant and for sale is $18,300, well above the average value of all owner-occupied units. This is an interesting pattern which may result from any one of several factors, including the tendency to overprice real estate for purposes of bargaining, the slowness of a few especially expensive houses to sell, or the present mortgage market.

The average contract rent of the 103,035 renter-occupied units in Metrolina for which rental information was available in 1970 was $70. This compares to $51 for the 27,744 Negro renter-occupied units. The most expensive average monthly rent within the region is the $91 ($62 for Negroes) in Mecklenburg County. The least expensive rent is the $46 per month in Cabarrus County or the $33 per month for Negroes in Stanly County. These rents reflect the generally higher cost of living in urban centers, a pattern that includes more luxurious accommodations and a wider range of services.

An especially important indicator of interaction patterns and style of living is the rate of overcrowding, which may be expressed in terms of (1) the number of housing units with 1.01 or more persons per room or (2) the number of persons living in housing with 1.01 or more persons per room. Of the 354,535 housing units in Metrolina enumerated in terms of occupancy, 33,601 (9.5 percent) are overcrowded. In addition, 217,349 or 20.9 percent of the 1,039,883 persons in the region enumerated in occupied units live in overcrowded housing. This is in dramatic contrast to the situation of the Negro component of Metrolina's population. A little over one-fourth (25.5 percent) of the Negro-occupied housing units and approximately one-half (46.4 percent) of the Negro population is overcrowded. Analyzed on the township level, the data reveal a fairly uniform rate of overcrowding with the urban centers tending toward the average for the region. As would

be expected, lower rates of overcrowding are found in the more affluent areas just outside Charlotte.

Another useful indicator of quality of life is based on the completeness of plumbing facilities for each housing unit. (Plumbing is assessed as incomplete if one or more of the following facilities is lacking: hot piped water, flush toilet, or bathtub or shower.) Only 8.2 percent of the housing and 9.7 percent of the population of Metrolina have incomplete plumbing. This compares to 24.4 percent of the housing of the Negro population. Fig. 4.16 (d), showing the proportion of housing units with incomplete plumbing in each township, reveals the influence of urbanization in this instance to be one of raising the level of living.

Combining the indexes of overcrowding and incomplete plumbing, we find that approximately 5 percent (49,140 or 4.7 percent) of the population of Metrolina lives in housing that is both overcrowded and lacks complete plumbing facilities. Whereas only 1.1 percent of Mecklenburg County's population lives in such surroundings, 11 percent of Lancaster County's population has such an environment.

Although housing itself may neither cause nor prevent enumerable physical, social, and behavioral problems, it must be taken into account as a contributing factor. Overcrowding, for instance, may contribute to the spread of disease or increase the level of interaction and, hence, the possibility for conflict. Also, the quality and location of housing often serve as symbols of status which, in turn, influence patterns of interaction and the establishment of social relationships.

Barbara A. Goodnight

Population Growth and Change

The population of a region is never static, for it changes constantly in composition, size, and geographical distribution. The major tasks of the student of population, therefore, are to describe and measure change, to assess the relative significance of births, deaths, and migration as components of change, and to make projections of future growth (or decline) and redistribution of population. To do this for Metrolina, we must view its population growth and change from both a historical as well as a current perspective.

Barbara A. Goodnight

Historical Perspective. The population statistics concerning the growth of the Metrolina counties since 1790 reinforce the growing significance of the area in the politics and economics of North and South Carolina. There are no particular trends except an upward curve perhaps slightly ahead of most of the other counties in the Carolinas. At the turn

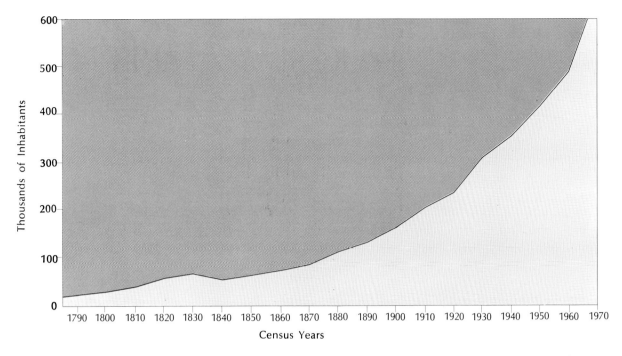

Source: 1970 Census of Population.

Fig. 4.18. Population of Metrolina, 1790-1970

of the century there was a definite increase in the number and size of the urban areas within Metrolina. (See Fig. 4.18.)

The population lead has been held by four different counties during the period 1790 to 1970. For the first three decades Rowan County had the largest number of people. In 1830 and 1840 Lincoln County's population surpassed all others until yielding to York County. Mecklenburg squeezed into the lead by thirteen people in 1870 and has maintained this population lead ever since. Some counties experienced dramatic losses in the early 1800s. These losses resulted from the creation of new counties by dividing existing counties. For example, Lincoln County dropped from 25,160 to 7,746 in the decade of the 1840s as a result of the creation of Gaston, Cleveland, and Catawba counties. It took Lincoln County a full century to match its population figure of 1840.

Three counties have shown exceptional growth in the past. Gaston County has twice increased its population by more than 50 percent. During the decade from 1890 to 1900 Gaston's population increased by approximately 57 percent. Then again between 1920 and 1930 there was a 52 percent increase. Both increases can be accounted for by the surge of textile production in that county. Cleveland County's population increased 51 percent during the decade of the twenties. But the largest gain of any Metrolina County was made by Mecklenburg during the period 1920 to 1930 when its population increased by 58.6 per-

cent.

Since 1850 only one county has suffered a loss in population. During the same period of the tremendous growth in Gaston, Cleveland, and Mecklenburg counties (1920 to 1930) the population of Lancaster dropped by 648 people. This was the only exception to more than one hundred years of solid population growth.

The 1960 census figures revealed that Mecklenburg was the fastest growing county, with a 38 percent increase over 1950. Its closest competitor was Catawba County, with an 18.4 percent increase. Cleveland County, with the smallest gain, had only a 2.6 percent increase over the previous decade. Catawba County led the decade of the 1950s in urban growth with a 55.1 percent increase of urban population and Stanly County had the largest rural increase, with 12.9 percent. Five of the Metrolina counties had a decrease in rural population during the 1950s as follows: Catawba (0.2 percent), Cleveland (3.1 percent), Gaston (2.2 percent), Rowan (1.5 percent), Lancaster (2.0 percent). Thus the trend in the 1960s was definitely toward the development of an urban population.

This trend toward an urban population is reflected in Metrolina's population density, which has been significantly higher than the density of both North and South Carolina during this century. With the exception of one or two counties, every Metrolina county has kept well ahead of the density rates for the two states. Gaston and Mecklenburg counties have been the most thickly settled areas.

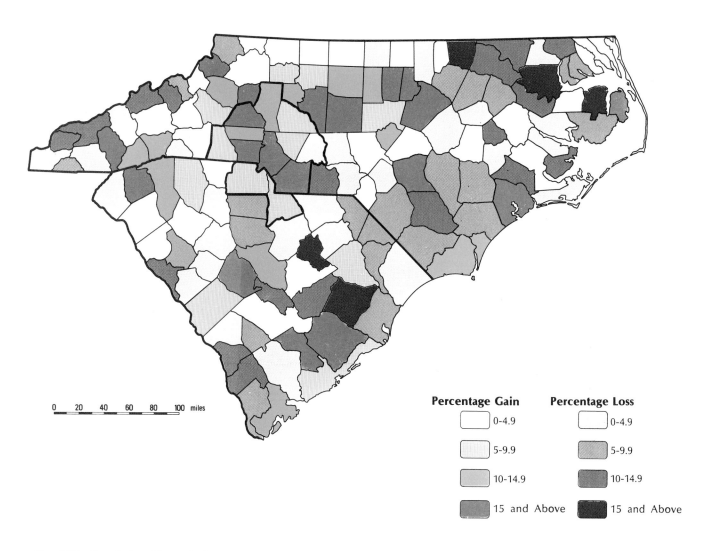

Percentage Gain
0-4.9
5-9.9
10-14.9
15 and Above

Percentage Loss
0-4.9
5-9.9
10-14.9
15 and Above

Fig. 4.19. Population Change in North and South Carolina, 1960-1970

The major urban area in Metrolina is the greater Charlotte area, but an overview of the region will reveal the important influence of several fringe urban areas of Metrolina. These areas stretch well beyond the Metrolina boundaries. The most important of them is Hickory. Others are Statesville, Salisbury, and Albemarle. It should be noted also that the Winston-Salem—Greensboro—High Point area, though outside Metrolina, has a definite influence on trade and transportation within Metrolina.

The sudden growth of the urban areas within Metrolina has been remarkable. The ten urbanized communities in Metrolina have shown population increases of over 100 percent eleven times during the century from 1860 to 1960 and have grown by 50 percent or more thirty-one times. The most notable were the increases in population of Albemarle between 1940 and 1950 by 190 percent, of Gastonia between 1910 and 1920 by 123 percent, and of Charlotte between 1950 and 1960 by 50 percent or 67,522 people.

In conclusion, the population growth patterns of Metrolina during the past century reveal a growing urban area

with a steady record of population expansion. The area is by no means overpopulated and has room for future expansion.

Edward S. Perzel

Current Population Changes. In Fig. 4.19, showing the population change in North Carolina and South Carolina from 1960 to 1970, it can be seen that Metrolina's rate of increase was significantly higher than either the 11.5 percent of North Carolina or the 8.7 percent of South Carolina. The region experienced a net in-migration of 3.6 percent in comparison to the net out-migration rates of 2.1 percent for North Carolina and 6.3 percent for South Carolina.

The rate and direction of Metrolina's population change has been essentially the same since 1940, showing increases of 17.9 percent in 1950, 16.5 percent in 1960, and 18.1 percent in 1970. There have been significant variations

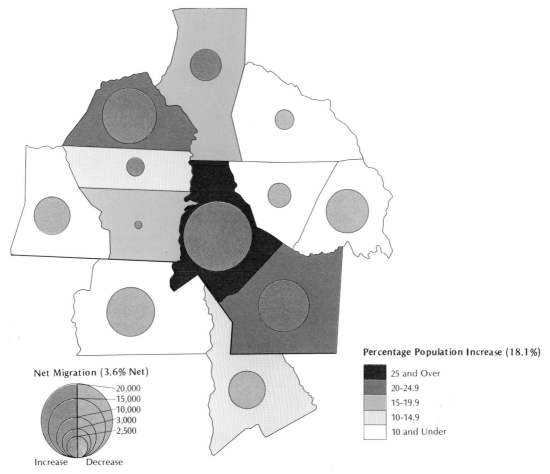

Net Migration (3.6% Net)

20,000
15,000
10,000
3,000
2,500

Increase   Decrease

Percentage Population Increase (18.1%)

25 and Over
20-24.9
15-19.9
10-14.9
10 and Under

Source: 1970 Census of Population.

Fig. 4.20. Percentage of Population Change in Metrolina and Net Migration by County, 1960-1970

within the region, however. As shown in Figs. 4.20 and 4.21, all twelve counties within the region experienced an increase in population during the decades ending in 1960 and 1970 in spite of the fact that eleven counties in 1960 and six counties in 1970 had a net out-migration of population, that is, more persons moved out of the area than moved into the area. This produced a net out-migration for the region of 4.0 percent in 1960 and a net in-migration of 3.6 percent in 1970. Thus the growth of the region in recent years has been primarily the result of natural increase (an excess of births over deaths) rather than migration.

Three counties increased in population more rapidly during the 1960s than did the region as a whole: Mecklenburg, 30.3 percent; Catawba, 24.2 percent; and Union, 22.5 percent. Six counties had rates of increase at least 5 percent lower than the region's 18.1 percent: Stanly, 4.8 percent; York, 8.2 percent; Rowan, 8.7 percent; Cabarrus, 9.5 percent; Cleveland, 9.9 percent; and Lancaster,

10.1 percent. It should be noted that these are the same six counties that had a net out-migration during the period under consideration.

During the 1950s the only counties that increased in population more rapidly than the region as a whole (16.5 percent) were Mecklenburg (38.1 percent) and Catawba (18.4 percent), and the increase in Gaston County (14.7 percent) was only slightly lower. The rate of increase in the remaining counties ranged from 2.6 percent in Cleveland County to 11.1 percent in Iredell County. Only Mecklenburg experienced a net in-migration during this period, an impressive 14.6 percent. Rates of net out-migration ranged from the 2.7 percent of Catawba to the 17.1 percent of Cleveland. The region's 16.5 percent rate of increase was somewhat higher than either the 12.2 percent of North Carolina or the 12.5 percent of South Carolina. Its rate of net out-migration (4.0 percent) was significantly lower than the 8.1 percent of North Carolina and the 10.5 percent of South Carolina.

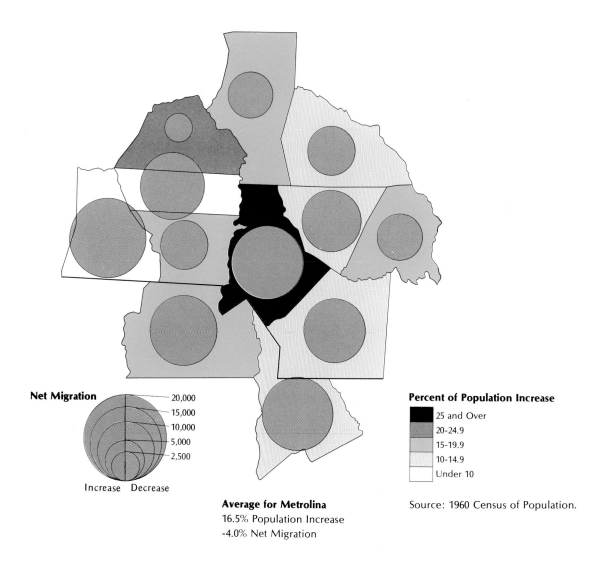

Net Migration

20,000
15,000
10,000
5,000
2,500

Increase   Decrease

Average for Metrolina
16.5% Population Increase
-4.0% Net Migration

Percent of Population Increase

■ 25 and Over
▨ 20-24.9
▨ 15-19.9
▨ 10-14.9
□ Under 10

Source: 1960 Census of Population.

Fig. 4.21. Percentage of Population Change in Metrolina and Net Migration by County, 1950-1960

Considerably more change occurred in the composition and distribution of Metrolina's population during the 1950s and 1960s than is readily observable from the data presented above, for the patterns of growth and change are comprised of a number of trends and countertrends that are obscured by summary data. The lower rate of natural increase in 1970, for instance, is more than cancelled out by the net increase in the population as a result of migration. The continuing but declining migration of Negroes from the rural farm areas of the region is obscured by the increasing movement of whites from urban centers to rural-nonfarm suburbia. This latter trend is documented by the fact that only Mecklenburg had a net in-migration of Negroes in the 1960s and the region as a whole had a net out-migration of Negroes of 6.8 percent. Fig. 4.22 very clearly

reveals the lower growth rates of urban centers in comparison to the fringe-area townships surrounding them. It also shows the lower growth rates and the population declines in the more rural townships of the region.

Barbara A. Goodnight

Conclusions

This section has portrayed Metrolina as an urbanizing region comprised of twelve counties dominated by Charlotte and its SMSA, a region in the process of developing and diffusing a distinctively urban style and mode of living. The most obvious and frequently employed indicators of its

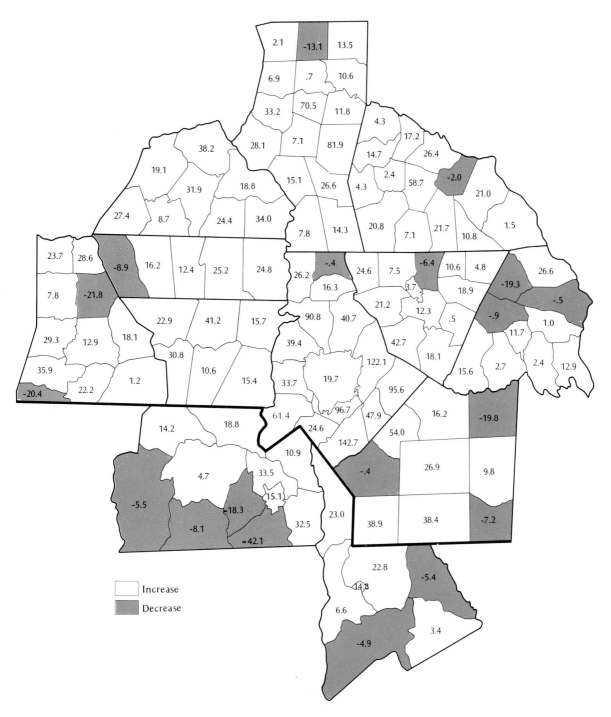

Source: 1970 Census of Population.

Increase

Decrease

Fig. 4.22. Percentage of Population Change in Metrolina, by Township, 1960-1970

Table 4.1. Selected Population Data for Metrolina, by County

	Cabarrus	Catawba	Cleve-land	Gaston	Iredell	Lincoln	Meck-lenburg	Rowan	Stanly	Union	Lancas-ter	York	Total for Metrolina
Total population													
1970	74,629	90,873	72,556	148,415	72,197	32,682	354,656	90,035	42,822	54,714	43,328	85,216	1,162,123
1960	68,137	73,191	66,048	127,074	62,526	28,814	272,111	82,817	40,873	44,670	39,352	78,760	984,372
Percent change	9.5	24.2	9.9	16.8	15.5	13.4	30.3	8.7	4.8	22.5	10.1	8.2	18.1
Population per square mile, 1970	207.3	223.8	155.7	414.6	122.2	106.1	654.4	174.2	107.3	85.1	86.0	124.4	201.1
Percent population urban, 1970	64.0	42.9	34.0	60.3	44.2	16.2	79.1	42.1	26.0	25.3	34.5	55.1	55.4
Percent population Negro, 1970	16.0	10.3	20.8	12.1	17.1	10.6	23.8	15.9	11.0	19.0	24.7	24.3	18.5
Dependency ratio, 1970													
Total	55.6	56.2	60.9	58.0	59.8	58.2	57.6	55.8	54.8	61.9	62.0	59.2	58.0
Negro	69.1	77.6	82.5	74.5	76.7	71.6	70.0	63.1	72.0	85.2	80.6	76.9	73.3
Sex ratio, 1970													
Total	92.4	92.9	94.4	93.3	93.0	95.8	91.2	93.7	94.2	97.7	93.3	87.6	92.5
Negro	87.3	85.7	90.7	86.4	91.6	92.5	87.9	91.9	93.0	97.4	89.8	88.8	89.1
Index of marital unrest, 1970													
Total	82	69	66	87	64	56	97	74	49	53	61	83	79
Negro	224	315	151	197	144	107	217	171	110	133	116	171	184
Fertility ratio, 1970													
Total	388	407	430	430	398	408	383	360	380	571	443	382	398
Negro	449	655	580	533	532	549	460	393	565	663	537	512	502
Percent owner-occupied housing, 1970													
Total	67.5	72.2	66.9	66.0	73.5	76.3	60.1	70.9	75.4	71.5	67.5	67.5	66.8
Negro	12.7	8.1	16.0	10.5	13.8	7.8	20.8	13.0	8.7	14.6	19.7	20.3	15.4
Percent overcrowded housing, 1970													
Total	9.5	9.1	11.1	11.6	9.2	9.7	7.7	8.1	7.4	10.7	13.8	12.9	9.5
Negro	27.7	27.9	32.1	26.4	27.8	31.1	21.3	22.0	26.8	33.2	34.9	29.2	25.5
Percent incomplete plumbing, 1970													
Total	8.4	8.4	13.7	8.9	10.2	14.6	2.3	6.9	9.5	16.6	16.6	14.6	8.2
Negro	34.7	26.6	40.1	29.7	31.0	50.3	5.9	23.9	34.5	54.0	52.8	47.7	24.4

urban character are the increasing size of its cities and the proportion of its population residing in them. Metrolina qualifies as an urbanizing region in terms of these measures of population growth and concentration, which have traditionally been highly correlated with urbanization. The extent of urbanization throughout the region may actually be underrepresented, however, for current patterns of migration and communication have taken the urban life-style well beyond the limits of its urban centers and into the suburbs and fringe areas.

The racial composition of the region characterized by an increasing concentration of Negroes in cities and a corresponding dispersal of whites to suburban areas displays basically the same patterns and trends as other metropolitan areas within the United States. Metrolina also approximates the typical urbanizing region in terms of its age and sex composition with its lower sex ratio and somewhat younger population.

In terms of marital status and family composition the impact of urbanization upon Metrolina is observed in the higher proportion of families with a female head than is found in more rural regions. It is also seen in the greater number of divorced and separated persons in its population. The generally higher quality and value of housing within the region are also indicative of the pervasiveness of urbanization.

Finally, the urbanizing character of the region is observed in its patterns of population growth and change. Metrolina continues to experience a rate of growth higher than that of the nation as a whole and evidences all the trends and countertrends currently found in other urban regions.

For selected population data for Metrolina, by county, see Table 4.1.

Barbara A. Goodnight

REFERENCES

Boskoff, Alvin. *The Sociology of Urban Regions.* New York: Appleton-Century-Crofts, 1970.
Chapin, F. Stuart, Jr., and Shirley F. Weiss, eds. *Urban Growth Dynamics in a Regional Cluster of Cities.* New York: John Wiley & Sons, 1962.
Gendell, Murray, and Hans L. Zetterberg, eds. *A Sociological Almanac for the United States.* New York: Charles Scribner's Sons, 1964.
Hamilton, C. Horace. *The USA South: Its Changing Population Characteristics.* Chapel Hill: Carolina Population Center, 1970.
Maddox, James G., ed. *Growth Prospects of the Piedmont Crescent.* Raleigh: The Agricultural Policy Institute, 1968.
Proceedings of the Southern Regional Conference on Urbanization, Athens, Georgia, May 28-31, 1967. Athens: Editorial Services, Department of Conferences, University of Georgia Center for Continuing Education, May 1967.
Smith, T. Lynn, and Paul E. Zopf, Jr. *Demography: Principles and Methods.* Philadelphia: F. A. Davis Company, 1970.
U.S. Bureau of the Census. *County Business Patterns.* Washington, D.C.: Government Printing Office (published annually for each state).
U.S. Bureau of the Census. "Components of Population Change, 1950-1960, for Counties, Standard Metropolitan Statistical Areas. . . ." *Current Population Reports,* Series P. 23, no. 7 (November 1962).
U.S. Bureau of the Census. "Components of Population Change by County: 1960 to 1970." *Current Population Reports,* Series P. 25, no. 461 (June 1971).
U.S. Bureau of the Census. "North Carolina" and "South Carolina," parts 35 and 42 in *Characteristics of the Population,* vol. 1 of *U.S. Census of Population,* 1960. Washington, D.C.: U.S. Government Printing Office, 1963.
U.S. Bureau of the Census. *U.S. Census of Population,* 1970. Forthcoming.
Zopf, Paul E., Jr. *North Carolina: A Demographic Profile.* Chapel Hill: Carolina Population Center, 1967.

5. MANUFACTURING

ALFRED W. STUART

". . . the student in the fortunate nation will study the manufacturing industries because more than any other single factor they have changed conditions of life in the last century and a half. Manufacturing is chiefly responsible for the urbanization which has become a hallmark of the industrialized nation."—Gunnar Alexandersson, Geography of Manufacturing.

Metrolina is one of the nation's major manufacturing regions, employing nearly 232,000 persons with an annual payroll of over 1.2 billion dollars in 1970. The value added (a technical term that expresses the difference between the value of the raw materials used and the value of the product) by manufacturing in the region was approximately two billion dollars in 1967, an amount equivalent to more than 30 percent of value added by manufacturing in all of North Carolina. Not only is manufacturing the dominant source of employment in the region but the pattern of its historical development was largely responsible for the unusual degree of population dispersion that is one of Metrolina's most striking characteristics. Historically and currently the story of manufacturing in Metrolina is largely that of textiles.

The Role of Manufacturing in the Regional Economy

Two out of every five persons employed in Metrolina work in a factory. As Table 5.1 shows, this ratio is substantially higher than that for the United States as a whole. In fact, the only major differences between the economic balance of Metrolina and the United States are the former's higher proportion in manufacturing and the latter's larger share in government. The emphasis on manufacturing is not uniform throughout all of the Metrolina counties but, as Fig.

5.1 indicates, all except Mecklenburg have very high proportions of employment in manufacturing. In six of the counties manufacturing is the source of employment for over half of all workers. In five others the manufacturing proportion ranges between 42 and 50 percent. Mecklenburg is obviously a special case with only about 20 percent of its employment in manufacturing. Areas that are as heavily specialized in manufacturing as are most of the Metrolina counties must look elsewhere for necessary supportive activities such as professional and business services, finance, and wholesale trade. The employment data suggest that this service and trade function is provided for Metrolina by Charlotte and Mecklenburg County.

Table 5.2 and Fig. 5.2 present data on actual amounts of manufacturing employment, rather than as proportions of all employment. Quite a different pattern emerges. One of the counties that has a high proportion of employment in manufacturing, Gaston, also has the most manufacturing employment, but Mecklenburg is not far behind despite its high employment in other sectors. Catawba is the only other county having over 30,000 manufacturing employees and Cabarrus is the only other one to have at least 20,000. But even the least industrialized of the Metrolina counties, Lincoln, has over 6,000 employees in manufacturing. The role of manufacturing in the economy of Metrolina may be summarized as follows: Manufacturing is the single largest employer in eleven of the counties and all of the counties are important concentrations of manufacturing.

As the data in Table 5.3 show, manufacturing in Metrolina is characterized by a heavy specialization in textiles and closely related industries. This fact is one that has given the region a rather unique character, the development of which is best seen in historical perspective.

Table 5.1. Employment by Industrial Group in Metrolina Counties, by Percent of Total Employment, 1969

Industry	Cabarrus	Catawba	Cleveland	Gaston	Iredell	Lincoln	Mecklenburg
Agriculture	2.2%	1.5%	6.0%	1.0%	5.2%	7.2%	0.4%
Manufacturing	63.5	55.3	47.0	58.7	49.5	52.7	19.9
Construction	2.2	4.1	2.9	2.3	4.0	2.5	6.3
Transport-utilities	1.4	4.8	1.6	5.1	2.0	1.9	9.9
Trade	9.9	13.1	11.6	10.4	11.9	9.6	24.0
Finance, insurance, real estate	1.5	1.5	1.9	1.5	1.3	1.2	6.2
Service & miscellaneous	12.8	15.0	19.3	14.5	18.1	17.8	24.0
Government	6.5	4.7	9.7	6.5	8.0	7.1	9.3
Total	100	100	100	100	100	100	100

Industry	Rowan	Stanly	Union	Lancaster	York	Total	U.S.
Agriculture	3.2%	4.7%	8.8%	4.2%	4.3%	2.5%	4.9%
Manufacturing	42.5	54.7	43.2	59.4	45.1	41.8	27.6
Construction	4.3	3.6	6.5	2.8	4.3	4.4	4.5
Transport-utilities	4.1	1.8	1.6	2.8	1.6	5.4	6.0
Trade	12.3	10.9	11.0	8.3	13.0	15.6	19.7
Finance, insurance, real estate	2.1	1.3	2.4	1.7	2.7	3.2	4.6
Service & miscellaneous	20.6	15.2	16.4	14.1	17.5	18.8	15.6
Government	10.9	7.8	10.1	6.7	11.5	8.3	17.1
Total	100	100	100	100	100	100	100

Source: South Carolina Employment Security Commission, *South Carolina's Manpower in Industry;* Employment Security Commission of North Carolina, *N.C. Work Force Estimates, 1969.*

Historical Evolution of Manufacturing in Metrolina

The people of English, German, and Scotch-Irish origin who settled the Piedmont were industrious people well skilled in the mechanical arts. They developed various products for self-consumption or for, at most, local markets. Before the Civil War there was very little manufacturing as a factory system in the area. An early start in that direction was overwhelmed by a preoccupation with cotton-growing that spread inland from the Coastal Plain and brought with it an agrarian-based set of attitudes that assigned a low social status to mechanical crafts. By 1860 there were only fifty-six textile mills in the two Carolinas and almost all of these were small, local-market-oriented facilities. After the catastrophe of the Civil War economic recovery was slow. An attempt was made to return to cotton cultivation but prices on the staple fell steadily throughout the 1870s. The thin soils of the Piedmont were becom-

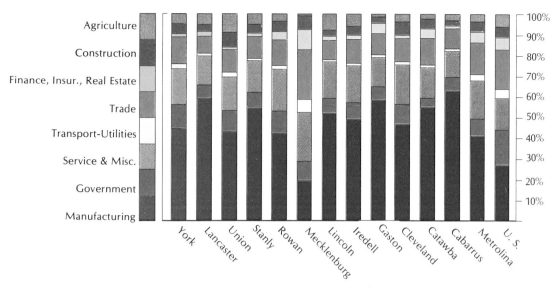

Agriculture
Construction
Finance, Insur., Real Estate
Trade
Transport-Utilities
Service & Misc.
Government
Manufacturing

York Lancaster Union Stanly Rowan Mecklenburg Lincoln Iredell Gaston Cleveland Catawba Cabarrus Metrolina U. S.

Sources: Employment Security Commission of N. C., *N. C. Work Force Estimates, 1969;* S. C. Employment Security Commission, *South Carolina's Manpower in Industry, Work Force Estimates, 1969.*

Fig. 5.1. Percent of Employment in Each Major Economic Sector of Metrolina, 1969

ing exhausted through desperate overcultivation with little resultant gain. Students of the economic history of the period credit the national election of 1880 with triggering one of the most remarkable episodes in American industrial history. The South generally was counting heavily on a Democratic victory to hasten the restoration of the region, and the election of a Republican president, James A. Garfield, was a bitter blow to those hopes. The Democratic defeat forced the South to recognize that revival must be found within the region, and what has been described as a true social movement began. Editorial writers and ministers alike began to preach the doctrine of self-help under the slogan, "Bring the mills to the cotton." Apparently they only reflected a widely held belief that economic salvation lay in turning fiber into cloth. This idea swept the South and was given impetus at the famous Atlanta Exposition of 1881.

The "Cotton Mill Campaign" that began in 1880 was a cooperative effort on the part of most of the people. In a typical sequence of events, community leaders in a small town would decide that a mill was needed to save the town. A financial drive would be initiated, with individual pledges of as little as fifty cents a week elicited. A local leader, rarely one with industrial experience, would be selected to head the proposed mill. One who lived through those days described what happened next: "A promoter had to have his home money first. He would get, say, $50,000; he would go to the machinery men and explain that he had so much subscribed, and would they sell him the equipment and how much would they take in stock.

Commission and machinery firms would give him 40 to 50 per cent of his total capital. If a man had no previous mill connections, his local subscriptions would be his sole backing."[1]

That so many mills succeeded under these circumstances is remarkable and is probably testimony to both the dedication of the operators and the rapidly rising market for textiles. It is extremely significant that these mills were developed as conscious agents of community economic recovery. The purpose was to create jobs rather than to satisfy the profit motives of a small entrepreneurial group. Virtually the entire capital stock of the community was committed to a venture that was seen as an alternative to the poverty of the present and recent past.

Although the "Cotton Mill Campaign" was manifested throughout the South, it was in the Piedmont regions of Virginia, the Carolinas, Georgia, and Alabama that it achieved its greatest appeal and success. This fact alone stands in refutation to the widely held belief that the main factor in the location of textile mills in the South was proximity to the source of raw materials. More cotton was actually grown on the Coastal Plain and even before the Civil War cultivation of the crop was rapidly shifting southwestward as growers raced to find areas of undepleted soils. The Piedmont was a cotton-growing area, but it was hardly the center of the crop's cultivation. Discriminatory freight rates often cancelled the apparent advantage of sheer prox-

1. Broadus Mitchell, *The Rise of Cotton Mills in the South* (Glouster, Mass.: Peter Smith, 1966), pp. 241-42.

Table 5.2. Employment by Industrial Group in Metrolina Counties, by Number of Employees, 1969.

Industry	Cabarrus	Catawba	Cleveland	Gaston	Iredell	Lincoln	Mecklenburg
Agriculture	920	870	1,860	690	1,710	860	770
Manufacturing	26,480	31,410	14,490	39,070	16,180	6,300	36,730
Construction	930	2,340	890	1,540	1,310	300	11,570
Transport-utilities	600	2,720	480	3,370	640	230	18,290
Trade	4,120	7,470	3,560	6,900	3,890	1,150	44,130
Finance, insurance, real estate	610	840	600	990	420	140	11,420
Service & miscellaneous	5,360	8,560	6,040	9,650	5,920	2,140	44,190
Government	2,710	2,680	2,990	4,340	2,630	850	17,100
Total	41,730	56,890	30,810	66,550	32,700	11,970	184,200

Industry	Rowan	Stanly	Union	Lancaster	York	Total	U.S. (000)
Agriculture	1,070	910	1,650	750	1,450	13,510	3,537
Manufacturing	14,420	10,650	8,050	10,700	15,350	229,830	19,740
Construction	1,470	690	1,220	500	1,450	24,210	3,259
Transport-utilities	1,380	340	290	500	550	29,390	4,348
Trade	4,180	2,110	2,060	1,500	4,400	85,470	14,111
Finance, insurance, real estate	700	250	450	300	900	17,620	3,357
Service & miscellaneous	7,000	2,960	3,070	2,550	5,950	103,290	11,129
Government	3,690	1,510	1,890	1,200	3,900	45,490	12,202
Total	33,910	19,420	18,680	18,000	33,950	548,810	71,683

Source: Table 5.1.

imity. One study pointed out that until several decades ago it was possible to ship Texas cotton to a Fall River, Massachusetts, mill more cheaply than it could be delivered to Atlanta.

Serious students of the Cotton Mill Campaign attribute its localization in the Piedmont, including Metrolina, to a combination of social and economic factors:

1. Despite the recent preoccupation with cotton, anti-manufacturing attitudes were not deeply rooted in the people of the Piedmont and were easily overcome. The popu-

lation had descended from a group of mechanically gifted settlers.

2. There was a stronger middle class to provide leadership from the supervisory through the managerial levels and to support fund-raising efforts.

3. There were more towns than in the Coastal Plain and in them there was not the rigid social stratification into planters, Negroes, and impoverished whites that characterized the Coastal Plain. A more homogeneous, town-based society served to make the Cotton Mill Campaign the

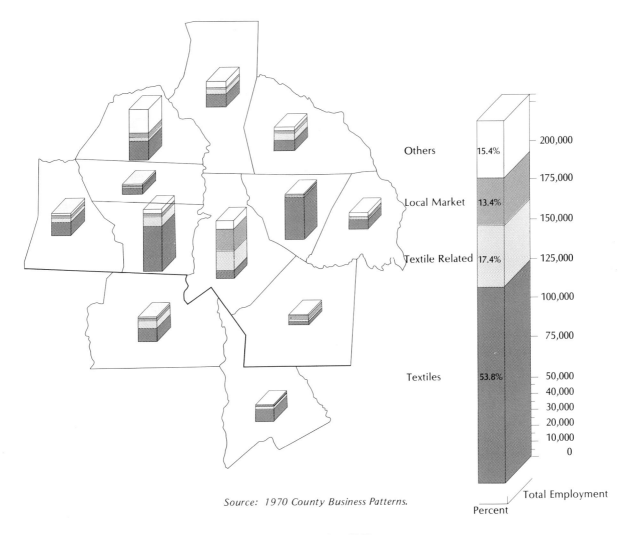

Others | 15.4%
Local Market | 13.4%
Textile Related | 17.4%
Textiles | 53.8%

200,000
175,000
150,000
125,000
100,000
75,000
50,000
40,000
30,000
20,000
10,000
0

Total Employment
Percent

Source: 1970 County Business Patterns.

Fig. 5.2. Total Manufacturing Employment in Metrolina Counties, 1970

broadly based social movement that it was.

4. Water power available on rapidly flowing Piedmont streams was an early localization inducement but its influence may have been exaggerated. Townspeople who decided they must have a mill would base their plans on coal-fired steam power if a stream were not available. Later the major streams were harnessed for the generation of electricity. This was the basis for the formation of Duke Power Company, which for many decades has realized nearly 85 percent of the hydroelectric potential of the Catawba River. For a long time the Piedmont, and especially Metrolina, has been an area of power surplus with consequently lower rates for electricity.

5. The Southern Railroad system was completed between Charlotte and Atlanta soon after 1870. Feeder lines up the valleys and the trunk line itself gave numerous small towns direct access to northeastern markets and provided an intraregional transport system as well. Obviously the development of a national market-oriented manufacturing complex would not have been possible without low cost access to that market. Less obvious is the fact that the early establishment of an intraregional network made it possible for many towns to succeed in their textile mill schemes and thus perpetuated the pattern of population dispersion that is characteristic of Metrolina.

6. The towns and countryside of the Piedmont had an underemployed population that was desperate for an alternative to ruinous cotton farming. Indeed, as was noted earlier, the prime motivation behind the Cotton Mill Campaign was the creation of jobs. Initially the workers came from the immediate vicinity of the mills, but word of job opportunities soon reached the more rural parts of the region and even into the mountains, and whole families arrived at the mill sites looking for work. By the end of the century mills were sending agents into the mountains to seek out still further labor.

Mills were developed rapidly throughout Metrolina although not without a number of false starts. In 1874, for

Table 5.3. Manufacturing Employment in Metrolina, 1970

	Cabarrus	Catawba	Cleveland	Gaston	Iredell	Lincoln	Mecklenburg	Rowan	Stanly	Union	Lancaster	York	Total
Food	744	523	623	604	347	204	4,982	814	265	817	---	174	10,097
Textiles	26,895	11,842	8,304	28,720	7,316	4,573	5,209	6,138	6,936	1,991	8,028	8,760	124,712
Apparel	380[a]	1,526	1,004	1,516	2,438	106	1,878	1,376	868	932	375[a]	432	12,831
Wood	---	725	73	52	233	119	373	84	154	691	131	258	2,893
Furniture	---	11,796	243	---	1,669	804	930	536	752	---	---	---	16,730
Paper	---	779	167	320[a]	275	---	956	244	---	---	---	900[a]	3,641
Print., publishing	185	311	154	470	120	---	4,393	190	---	---	124	139	6,086
Chemicals	---	105	1,250[a]	416	---	---	2,573	2,665[a]	---	---	---	2,160[a]	9,169
Rubber, plastics	---	1,054	---	510	---	---	1,270	205[a]	---	250[a]	---	50[a]	3,339
Stone, clay, glass	---	259	1,401[a]	121	420	---	1,130	433	159	322[a]	---	---	4,245
Primary metals	---	740[a]	---	---	---	---	1,122	200[a]	825[a]	468	---	---	3,355
Fabr. metals	---	840	---	379	---	---	2,192	195	---	634	---	---	4,240
Nonelec. machinery	---	194	---	3,725	667	175[a]	4,562	244	---	90	268	127	10,052
Elec. equip.	---	900[a]	---	---	502[a]	---	619	---	750[a]	---	---	---	2,771
Transport equip.	---	---	---	1,300[a]	---	---	372[a]	427	---	---	---	---	2,099
Instruments	---	---	---	---	475[a]	---	687[a]	---	---	---	---	---	1,162
Other	317	281	1,210	625	1,164	202	226	484	260	70	509	882	6,230
Admin.-aux.	423	416	178	401	---	---	3,735	115	175	---	744	2,129	8,316
Total	28,944	32,291	14,607	39,159	15,626	6,183	37,209	14,350	11,144	6,265	10,179	16,011	231,968

a. Estimated.

Source: *County Business Patterns, 1970.*

example, several meetings were held in Mecklenburg County in an effort to establish a mill at Spring's Shoals, on the Catawba River. An attempt was made to convert a Mecklenburg woolen mill into a cotton factory. Both efforts failed. Charlotte did not get its first spinning mill until 1881. Weaving operations were added to the mill soon after 1890 and by 1896 Charlotte had five cotton mills. By 1903 Mecklenburg County had twenty-one mills, seventeen in Charlotte and one each in Davidson, Pineville, Huntersville, and Cornelius.

At the turn of the century it was beginning to occur to the people of Metrolina that the region was emerging as a major textile manufacturing concentration and that Charlotte was the apparent focus of a great deal of this activity. The situation was described in 1903 in the following manner: "Within a radius of one hundred miles around Charlotte are nearly 300 cotton mills, operating more than 3,000,000 spindles and 85,000 looms, and having a capital of $100,000,000, which not only shows that Charlotte is a manufacturing centre [sic], but the remarkable fact that *one-half of the looms and spindles of the South are within one hundred miles of this city. In Charlotte are companies which build and equip cotton factories and [cotton seed] oil mills, and a number of other agencies for miscellaneous supplies and machinery."[2]*

For the first several decades a real wage differential for textile workers existed between New England and the Piedmont generally. This differential not only strengthened the competitive position of Piedmont textiles but also created profits that were plowed back into new or enlarged mills, thus creating more jobs. Apparently the Piedmont textile worker did not feel exploited, partly because his wages were far better than any he had known before and partly because he shared a sense of community with the whole operation. In any case, a strong wage differential assisted mightily in the rapid growth of textile mills in the southern Piedmont, while the New England industry grew slowly, hampered by a generally static management group that contributed to deteriorating labor relations, poor community relations, and high building and power costs.

The momentum of growth continued through the rest of the nineteenth century and up to the beginning of the First World War, which gave it fresh, if temporary, impetus. The industry was faced with overcapacity early in the 1920s and only at that point did a direct, major intrusion of northern capital become a part of the shift of textiles from New England to the southern Piedmont. That is, until about 1923 the interregional shift had been a matter of the relatively rapid growth of an indigenously organized Piedmont industry. Assistance had been provided by the machinery manufacturers and commission houses, while northern capital built the railroads, but the mills themselves had been built with southern capital and operated by southern management. This stands in contrast to a popular misconception that the textile industry was moved bodily from New England to the Piedmont. During the decade of the 1920s the southern Piedmont surpassed New England as a textile-producing region.

The continual growth that had occurred since 1880 peaked nationally about 1920 and since that time the industry has been faced with more lean years than good. Generally the industry has continued to grow in the Piedmont at the expense of other areas, mainly New England and the Middle Atlantic states. It seems that the Piedmont's timing was superb. The region chose to enter competition in an industry just as that industry was accelerating into an extended period of rapid growth. By the time the period of rapid growth ended, concentration in the Piedmont was so entrenched that the more experienced and highly developed competitor, New England, found itself unable to compete on equal terms. Had the period of growth been shorter or the Piedmont's entry later, the New England industry might have been obliged to solve its problems and terminate the upstart textile industry to the south.

2. D. A. Tompkins, *History of Mecklenburg County.* Charlotte: Observer Printing House, 1903. Italics in original.

As it was, the advantages of the region were so well established that the hard-pressed New England companies looked southward for operating efficiencies that would help them survive in the tightening market for textile products. A few companies literally moved their establishments southward but more either bought existing facilities or expanded operations by building new plants. This movement, begun in 1923, has been called "The Second Cotton Mill Campaign." It was different in character from the first in that northern interests were the prime agents in establishing or assuming control of mills. Piedmont communities competed vigorously for these new entrants with promotional campaigns, tax concessions, capital assistance in the form of subsidized land and buildings, and various other inducements.

Most of the textile industry of the South developed in the Carolinas with the single largest concentration in the large Piedmont area of North Carolina. To the north of Metrolina in North Carolina manufacturing diversified through the development of the furniture and tobacco-processing industries. Catawba County, alone among Metrolina counties, is in the northern Piedmont furniture belt, and tobacco manufacturing is virtually nonexistant in Metrolina. Metrolina was unique among Piedmont areas in its degree of specialization in textile manufacturing.

Attempts were made to develop other industries, but they were largely unsuccessful. For example, between 1909 and 1929 the Anderson Motor Company in Rock Hill, South Carolina, produced over six thousand automobiles. The company was only one of many small automobile companies to fail at this time as the large companies cut prices to low levels.

Thus by 1920 not only the basic economic structure of Metrolina had been established by a major specialization in textile manufacturing but also the tendency to build mills in most of the small towns and cities of the region made it possible for those towns to hold and increase their populations. Metrolina has experienced much less of the rural-urban population migration than most other developing regions in this country and in others (see Fig. 5.3). Migrations occurred but mostly from the edges of or beyond the region.

During the national depression of the 1930s a number of independent mills were bought by stronger rivals. A trend toward merger and the formation of large companies had begun to develop under the tight market conditions of the 1920s and it increased dramatically in the next decade. Burlington Industries, the largest textile company in the United States, had its official beginning in the city of Burlington in 1923 but a predecessor plant was bought in Gastonia in 1919 by the company's founder, J. Spencer Love. The Gastonia mill was sold a few years later and the operation moved to Burlington but the separation from Metrolina was only temporary. Today a number of Burlington Industries' 130 American plants are in Metrolina.

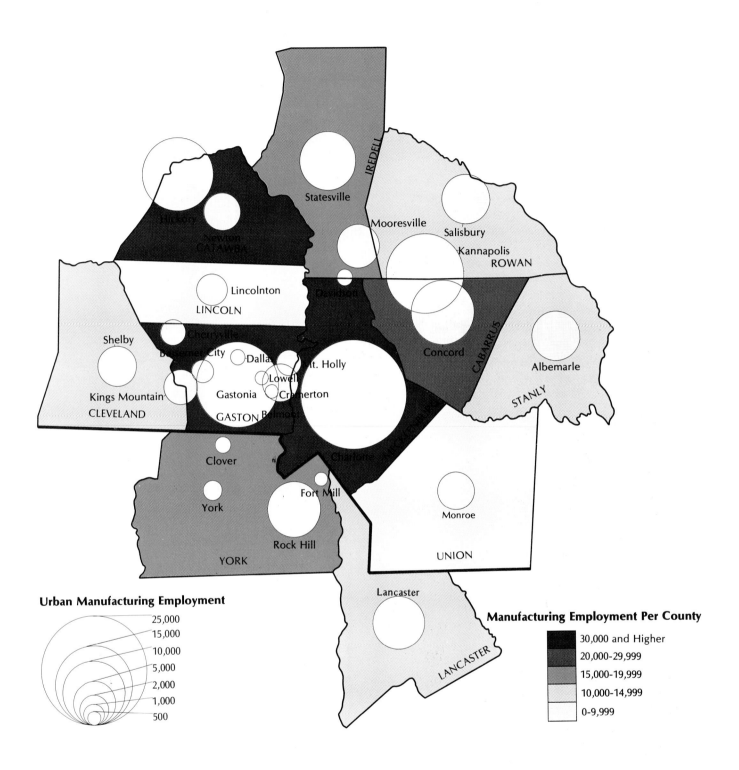

Urban Manufacturing Employment

25,000
15,000
10,000
5,000
2,000
1,000
500

Manufacturing Employment Per County

■	30,000 and Higher
▓	20,000-29,999
▒	15,000-19,999
░	10,000-14,999
□	0-9,999

Sources: 1967 Census of Manufactures, 1970 County Business Patterns.

Fig. 5.3. Manufacturing Employment in Metrolina's Urban Areas, 1967

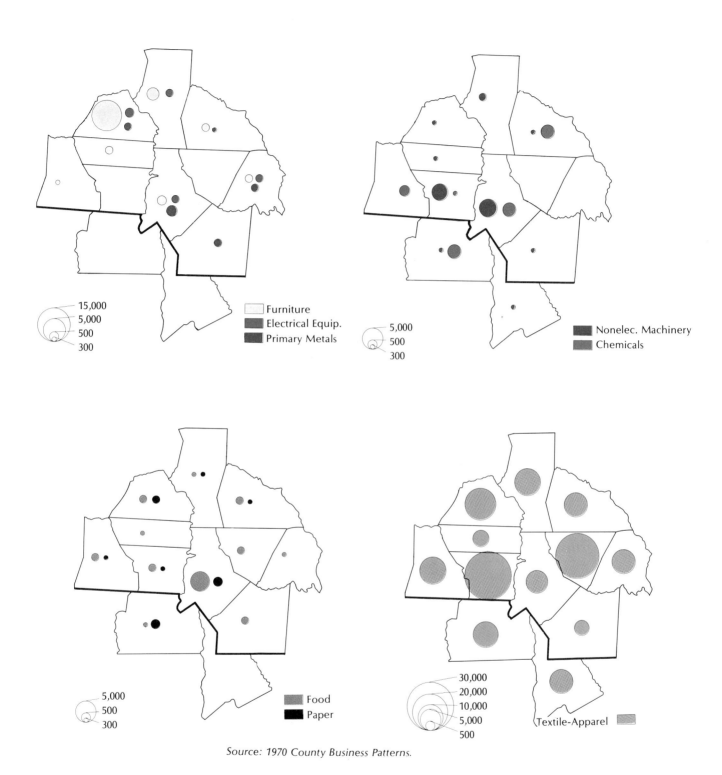

Source: 1970 County Business Patterns.

Fig. 5.4. Employment by County in Major Metrolina Industrial Groups, 1970

The trend toward the creation of larger companies was exemplified in Metrolina by the formation of Textiles Incorporated in Gastonia. The company was formed in 1931 from the consolidation of twenty-two other plants that were faced with failure. The stockholders of the company asked Albert G. Myers, a local banker, to effect a merger. By pooling resources, using more aggressive marketing, closing some obsolete mills, and modernizing the rest, Myers had the remaining twelve plants of the company out of receivership in only eight years. In 1941 the original indebtedness of the twenty-two companies had been canceled.

The Celanese Corporation is another large, multiplant company that has emerged since the 1920s. A chemical concern, it has had an important involvement in a more recent phase of the textile industry, synthetic fibers. The company has a number of manufacturing facilities in Metrolina and also employs about 1,400 persons in Charlotte in administrative, marketing, and research and development offices.

Cannon Mills Company began on a farm site near Concord in 1906. Today the company has mills throughout the South but most of the more than 20,000 employees live and work in Kannapolis. The company town was a common feature throughout the Piedmont and Kannapolis was probably the largest. Still unincorporated, it is one of the last towns in which the company still provides housing for workers and maintains various community services.

Springs Mills, Inc., is another local giant. Started in Lancaster County in 1888, this company now has its main office in York County and employs nearly 20,000 people, mostly in Lancaster and York counties.

Today textiles continue to dominate manufacturing in Metrolina and manufacturing continues to dominate the regional economy (see Fig. 5.4). Charlotte and Mecklenburg County have moved away from a major involvement with actual production in textiles, but have taken the role, as indicated by the Celanese offices, of a sales, marketing, and research center for the industry. Mecklenburg County also appears to be leading the way in the diversification of the Metrolina industrial base.

It appears that diversification both within textiles and in manufacturing generally will be necessary if the region is to continue enjoying sustained economic growth. More insight into such questions can be gained by examining employment in several textile-related industries and other groups that are not directly related to textiles. Also, analysis of the wage levels of the various Metrolina industries offers a fuller understanding of the impact of these economic activities on the region.

The Distribution of Textile Manufacturing

Gaston and Cabarrus counties lead Metrolina in textile employment, with over 25,000 employees each (see Table 5.3).

Catawba is the only other county having over 10,000 employees in the industry. In all the others, except Lincoln and Union, the totals range between 5,000 and 10,000.

Relative degrees of specialization exist among the counties (see Fig. 5.5). Cabarrus and Lancaster counties specialize in cotton broadwoven fabric facilities; Gaston and Stanly, in yarn and thread mills; Catawba and Union, in knitting mills; and Iredell, in synthetic broadwoven fabric plants. The others are more balanced: Cleveland, synthetic broadwoven, knitting, yarn-thread; Lincoln, knitting, yarn-thread; Mecklenburg, broadwoven cotton, knitting, yarn-thread; Rowan, broadwoven cotton, yarn-thread; York, broadwoven cotton and synthetics, textile furnishings.

Specialization is not total, of course, but rather a matter of emphasis. Each textile group has its own, somewhat different technology and this apparently causes like-minded producers to cluster. No doubt in some cases it is a matter of ambitious individuals who have come to know one operation well setting up their own plants in the same general area where they first gained their experience.

Textile-Related Industries

In addition to the actual making of textiles, there is a group of other industries that are closely related to it, either through using textile products as a raw material or through making products that in turn are raw materials for textiles. There is also important involvement in nonproduction operations, such as separate administrative and research facilities. A total of 40,368 persons (17.4 percent of all manufacturing in Metrolina) are in four industrial groups that have strong ties with textiles.

Apparel. In the fabrication of clothing and related products textiles are used as the primary raw material. In fact, it is often unclear where textiles end and apparel begins. In any case, the relationship between textiles and apparel is so obvious and close that it is surprising that apparel accounts for only about 5.5 percent of manufacturing employment in the region. Iredell County is the leading employer in this industry, followed closely by Mecklenburg, Catawba, and Gaston counties, in that order. As shown in Fig. 5.6, the larger apparel factories are located in a ring along the outer edge of Metrolina.

Chemicals. Four Metrolina counties have over 1,000 employees in chemicals with Rowan the leader, followed by Mecklenburg, York, and Cleveland in that order. In Rowan and Cleveland counties most of this employment is in the production of noncellulosic organic fibers while the major category in York is cellulosic man-made fibers. Mecklenburg County produces a variety of chemical products, many of them for the textile industry. The forty-five plants in Mecklenburg County average only 57 employees

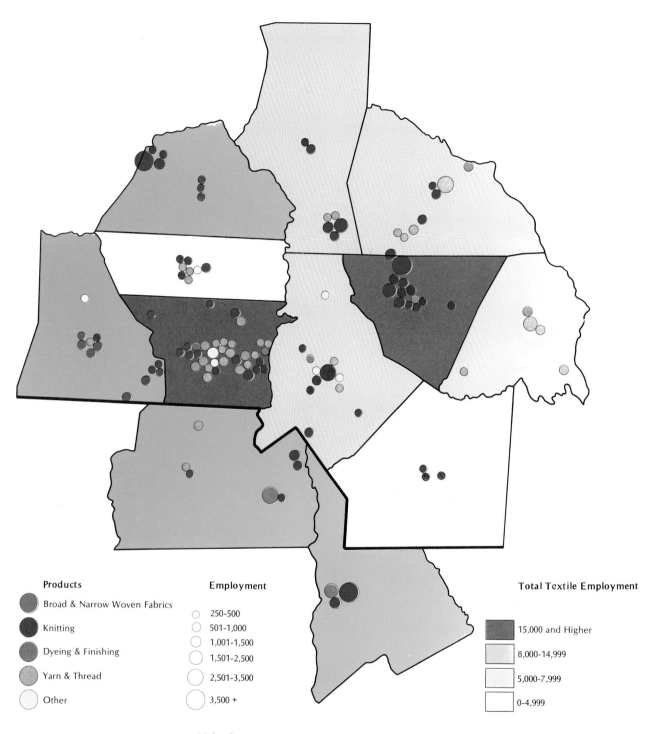

Major Sources: 1970 County Business Patterns, 1968 N. C. Directory of Mfg. Firms.

Fig. 5.5. Distribution of Large Textile Mills in Metrolina, 1970

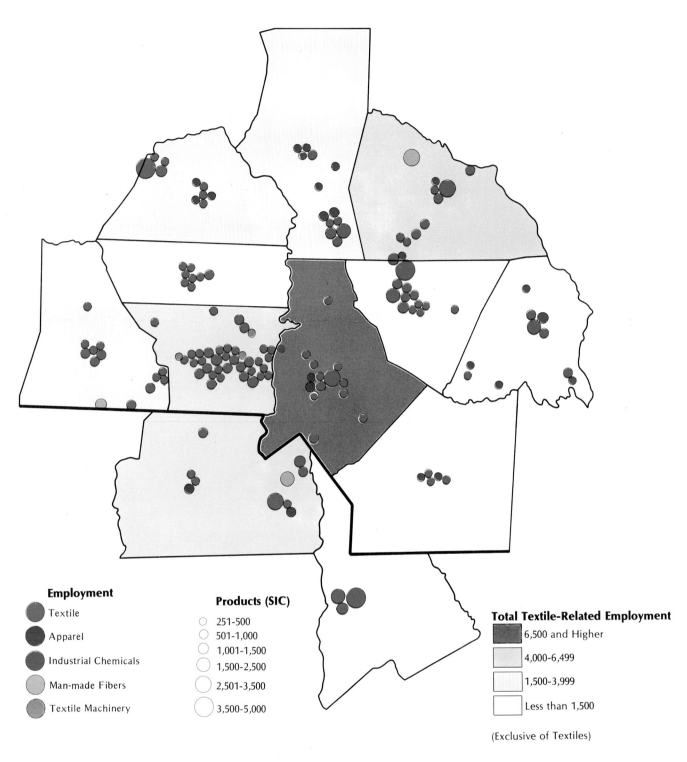

Employment

- Textile
- Apparel
- Industrial Chemicals
- Man-made Fibers
- Textile Machinery

Products (SIC)

- 251-500
- 501-1,000
- 1,001-1,500
- 1,500-2,500
- 2,501-3,500
- 3,500-5,000

Total Textile-Related Employment

- 6,500 and Higher
- 4,000-6,499
- 1,500-3,999
- Less than 1,500

(Exclusive of Textiles)

*Major Sources: 1970 County Business Patterns,
1968 N. C. Directory of Mfg. Firms.*

Fig. 5.6. Distribution of Large Textile Mills and Plants of Textile-Related Industries in Metrolina, 1970

while those in the other three average from 333 to 1,250 employees per plant. In fact, all of the Rowan County employment is in one plant and that in York is in two.

Nonelectrical Machinery. An important linkage with the textile industry is the making of special machinery for the industry. Though not all of the 10,052 employees in the nonelectrical-machinery industry make textile machinery, a substantial number do, especially in Gaston and Mecklenburg counties. The single largest plant that is not textile related is the recent nuclear turbine facility of Westinghouse in Charlotte. The design and manufacture of special machinery symbolizes the extent to which Metrolina is in the heart of the American textile industry.

Administrative and Auxiliary. This unique employment category includes separate establishments that are engaged not in actual manufacturing but rather in administration or research. Only when such administrative and research functions are large enough to require facilities on a different site than the factory is employment reported in this category. A substantial number of employees in this category signifies a headquarters role. In Metrolina over 8,000 employees are reported for this important function. Most are in Mecklenburg County, notably in the Celanese-Fiber Industries facilities in Charlotte, and in York County, largely in the Springs Mills offices.

Local Market Industries

Some industries exist primarily to serve the local population or other manufacturers. "Local" is defined roughly as the area of Metrolina itself. The four broad industrial groups that include most of this relatively ubiquitous type of manufacturing employed 31,202 persons in 1970, about 13.4 percent of total manufacturing. Though certainly a significant component of the local industrial system, these industries are not the ones that distinguish the industrial base of Metrolina from that of other areas.

Food Products. Almost half of the 10,097 employees in food-processing work in Mecklenburg County. No other county has as many as 1,000 employees in this industry. Dominant components are meat-packing plants, dairy product processors, and bakeries. Some of the establishments are large and ship products throughout a region larger than Metrolina, such as the Lance, Inc., plant in Charlotte, but most are preparing various edible products to be distributed to the population of Metrolina.

Lumber and Wood Products. This industry involves the processing of wood as a structural material but not the fabrication of furniture. Characteristic are saw mills, planing mills, hardwood and dimension flooring, millwork, and

plywood facilities. Much of this processing takes place near the source of the raw material and the product goes to the nearby construction industry. Employment in this group is reported in eleven of the twelve counties with the largest amounts in Catawba, Union, and Mecklenburg counties, in that order.

Paper and Allied Products. Paper is classified with the local market group because a large part of its product—principally paperboard boxes, containers, and the like—go to various other manufacturers in the area. Because many textile mills and apparel factories acquire packaging materials locally the paper industry might also be considered textile related. Many other local industries also use substantial quantities of paper packaging products, however. The major exception to the local market orientation of the paper industry is the big Bowater pulp mill in York County. This mill is of such a size that its market area probably extends farther into the southeastern United States than Metrolina.

Printing and Publishing. Printing shops and newspaper printing and publishing facilities are a common feature of any populated area and Metrolina is no exception. The large Charlotte *Observer* and *News* plant in Charlotte distributes newspapers to points beyond Metrolina but for the most part this industrial group, like food products, services the local population and business community.

Stone, Clay and Glass. In this industry a number of raw materials of the earth are processed to make either structural or packaging materials. Many of the 4,245 employees are engaged in making brick, prestressed concrete, cinder block, or ready-mixed concrete for use by the local construction industry. The one major exception to this is the large plant of the fiberglass division of Pittsburgh Plate Glass Industries, Inc., in Shelby.

Fabricated Metals. This group is less clearly devoted to the local market but it has such a strong involvement in it that this seems to be the best category in which to place it. Common products are metal doors, sash, and trim; sheet metal work; and fabricated structural steel. These are obviously products for the construction industry. Others, such as boiler shops, metal stampings, and metal services, are oriented to other manufacturing groups. The major exceptions to the apparent local market orientation of this group include wire products in Catawba County, nuts and bolts in Iredell, and hand and edge tools in Catawba, Mecklenburg, and Union counties.

Other Nontextile Industries

The final broad group of industries makes products that are

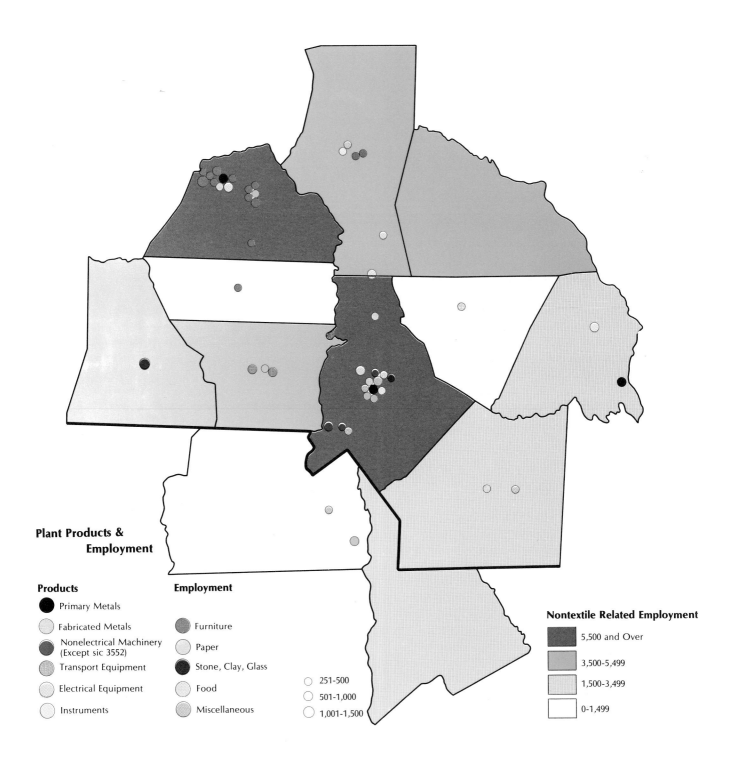

Plant Products & Employment

Products

⬤ Primary Metals

◯ Fabricated Metals

⬤ Nonelectrical Machinery (Except sic 3552)

◉ Transport Equipment

◯ Electrical Equipment

◯ Instruments

Employment

◉ Furniture

◯ Paper

⬤ Stone, Clay, Glass

◯ Food

◉ Miscellaneous

◯ 251-500

◯ 501-1,000

◯ 1,001-1,500

Nontextile Related Employment

▨ 5,500 and Over

▨ 3,500-5,499

▨ 1,500-3,499

☐ 0-1,499

Major Sources: *1970 County Business Patterns, 1968 N. C. Directory of Mfg. Firms.*

Fig. 5.7. Distribution of Nontextile-Related Plants in Metrolina, 1970

largely unrelated to textiles and are probably distributed mainly to regional and national markets, rather than to the local market. This group is of particular significance because it is involved in "exporting" products beyond the local area, thus adding substantially to the economic growth of the area, and because it is largely unrelated to textiles, thereby constituting the major segment of diversification in the area's industrial sector. In 1970 the seven broad industries that comprise this group employed 35,686 persons, 15.3 percent of total manufacturing. Their growth will largely determine the extent to which Metrolina will be able to develop a less specialized industrial base. An important characteristic of this group is that with the exception of furniture, employment is in a very few rather large plants. The size of these plants reflects the fact that they are mostly facilities of nonlocal firms that are producing for the regional or national market. (See Fig. 5.7.)

Furniture. Metrolina lies south of the main Piedmont furniture belt except for Catawba County where furniture rivals textiles as the principal employer. In fact, Catawba County contains just over 70 percent of Metrolina's total employment in furniture. Somewhat like textiles, the furniture industry began to develop in the Piedmont in the late nineteenth century through local initiative and by utilizing an available raw material supply. Since then the Piedmont district, including the concentration around Hickory, has achieved national prominence in the design, manufacturing, and marketing of furniture. Although seven of the Metrolina counties report some employment in furniture-making, only Iredell, in addition to Catawba, has more than 1,000 employees in the industry. Iredell and Catawba account for over 80 percent of the industry in Metrolina.

Rubber and Plastics. A wide variety of products is included in this group. In Catawba County there is an emphasis on foam plastic and rubber products for the furniture industry. In Gaston County products include rigid plastic parts, plastic moldings, and the like. The largest employment in this group is in Mecklenburg County, with the General Tire Company accounting for a big part of the total. Other products include plastic pipe and film.

Primary Metals. Primary metals production is handled by relatively few sizable plants. The Superior Wire Company plant in Hickory makes communications wire and cable. In Mecklenburg County the Charlotte Pipe and Foundry Company makes cast iron pipe and the Florida Steel Corporation plant turns out reinforcing steel. The largest primary metals facility in Metrolina is the Alcoa aluminum refinery at Baden, in Stanly County.

Electrical Equipment. A very few plants account for most of the nearly 2,800 employees in this industry. In Catawba County it is the General Electric transformer plant; in Iredell it is the transistor factory of the Continental Device Company; and in Stanly it is the electrical switch-gear facility of the Federal Pacific Electric Company. Mecklenburg County has somewhat greater variety but the bulk of employment is engaged in fabricating communications equipment in plants of the Union Carbide Corporation and Western Electric Corporation.

Transportation Equipment. The Wix Corporation in Gastonia, a maker of oil, air, and gas filters, largely accounts for Gaston County's lead in the transportation equipment industry. In Rowan the automatic air brake plant of Bendix-Westinghouse is the major component of the industry in that county. In Mecklenburg there are a number of representatives of this industry. Most of them specialize in truck bodies, equipment, and trailers, including a plant of the Freuhauf Corporation. Several types of electrical and special purpose vehicles are also manufactured there.

Instruments and Related Products. Only three plants make up most of Metrolina's employment in this varied group. The wood laboratory equipment facility of the Kewaunee Technical Furniture Company makes up most of Iredell County's part. In Mecklenburg the General Time Corporation plant in Davidson makes automobile clocks and in Charlotte the Pelton and Crane Company fabricates dental equipment.

Others. This category is a mixture of industries that were not included in the previous categories. Some categories had so few representatives that to give information about them would violate disclosure rules. The rest are classified as miscellaneous. In Metrolina that category usually means novelties and advertising display fabricators.

The Wage Level of Manufacturing Industries

Manufacturing concerns contribute to an area in many ways but the most direct expression of their role in the local economy is that of wages and salaries paid to employees. Particularly important are those industries that ship products to markets beyond the local area, thus providing a flow of incomes back into the area. The level of wages and salaries paid to workers is thus a vital characteristic of an area's industrial base. As a report prepared in 1968 for the governor on the condition of the North Carolina economy pointed out, the state has a relatively heavy dependence on wages for total income.

Generally speaking, industrial wage levels reflect the nature of the product and the process used in making it. Some processes are relatively capital intensive—that is, they are highly mechanized operations. Output per worker is

Table 5.4. Average Annual Earnings for Manufacturing Employees, 1970

	Cabarrus	Catawba	Cleveland	Gaston	Iredell	Lincoln	Mecklenburg	Rowan	Stanly	Union	Lancaster	York	Metrolina
Food	$4,608	$5,927	$5,149	$6,086	$6,190	$4,196	$5,470	$6,044	$4,906	$3,657	—	$4,966	$5,322
Textiles	4,407	4,435	5,058	4,861	4,991	4,886	5,216	4,830	4,557	4,356	5,411	5,350	4,802
Apparel	NA	3,688	5,331	4,003	4,466	3,208	3,781	3,762	3,613	4,425	NA	3,370	4,080
Wood	—	5,175	4,055	3,231	3,519	3,798	6,102	3,952	4,935	4,237	4,794	6,155	4,839
Furniture	—	5,413	4,543	—	4,570	4,821	6,447	5,515	5,351	—	—	—	5,346
Paper	—	5,705	6,395	NA	—	—	6,427	6,656	—	—	—	NA	6,188
Print., publishing	5,232	5,955	6,182	6,094	5,267	—	6,610	5,221	—	—	5,323	5,957	6,438
Chemicals	—	5,752	NA	8,087	—	—	8,322	NA	—	—	—	NA	8,203
Rubber, plastics	—	4,163	—	6,753	—	—	5,650	NA	—	NA	—	NA	5,296
Stone, clay, glass	—	6,008	NA	1,719	5,410	—	6,694	5,570	4,428	NA	—	—	6,036
Primary metals	—	NA	—	—	—	—	7,241	NA	NA	6,778	—	—	7,104
Fabr. metals	—	5,443	—	7,029	—	—	7,367	5,621	—	5,804	—	—	6,642
Nonelec. machinery	—	6,103	—	6,139	6,489	NA	7,482	7,525	—	6,178	6,612	6,394	6,833
Elec. equip.	—	NA	—	—	NA	—	6,837	—	NA	—	—	—	6,837
Transport equip.	—	—	—	NA	—	—	6,828	4,927	—	—	—	—	6,173
Instruments	—	—	—	—	NA	—	9,652	—	—	—	—	—	9,652
Other	—	—	—	—	—	—	—	—	—	—	—	—	4,648
Admin.-aux.	4,785	9,529	6,427	9,865	—	—	9,659	8,000	—	—	5,462	6,769	8,198
Average	4,428	5,067	5,549	5,214	5,147	4,846	6,710	5,523	4,964	4,751	5,445	5,851	5,391
											N.C.		5,477
											U.S.		7,688

Source: Derived from *County Business Patterns, 1970.*

high and so are wages. On the other hand, there are labor-intensive industries in which wages comprise a relatively large part of total costs. Labor productivity is lower and so are wages. Labor unions and other factors sometimes modify this relationship but the nature of the industry remains as the primary determinant of wage levels. As a result, the industrial wage levels that are prevalent in a region are a direct reflection of the mix of industries in that region. North Carolina has the lowest average manufacturing wage levels in the United States because the state's industrial base is dominated by furniture, textiles, and apparel—all labor-intensive and low-wage industries.

Table 5.4 summarizes the annual payrolls per worker in Metrolina for each county and each industry for which data were available. Average earnings in Metrolina were equivalent to 70.1 percent of the national average. Largely responsible for this low standing were three industries—textiles, apparel, and furniture—all of which had earnings below the Metrolina average and which together account for two-thirds of the industrial employment in Metrolina.

Table 5.5 summarizes weighted earnings for the three major groupings of industry. It is noteworthy that three of the textile-related groups (chemicals, machinery, and administrative-auxiliary) have relatively high earning levels and keep the whole textile and related group from being lower than it is. Unfortunately, there are nearly six low-

Table 5.5. Major Categories of Manufacturing Industries in Metrolina, 1970

Industry	Employment	
	Number	Percent of Total
Textile and related (average earnings $5,229 per employee, 1970)		
Textiles	124,712	53.9
Apparel	12,831	5.5
Chemicals	9,169	4.0
Nonelectrical machinery	10,052	4.3
Administrative-auxiliary	8,316	3.6
	165,080	71.3
Local market (average earnings $5,872 per employee, 1970)		
Food	10,097	4.4
Wood	2,893	1.2
Paper	3,641	1.6
Printing, publishing	6,086	2.6
Stone, clay, glass	4,245	1.8
Fabricated metals	4,240	1.8
	31,202	13.4
Others, nontextile related (average earnings $5,689 per employee, 1970)		
Furniture	16,730	7.2
Rubber, plastics	3,339	1.4
Primary metals	3,355	1.4
Electrical equipment	2,771	1.2
Transportation equipment	2,099	0.9
Instruments	1,166	0.5
Others	6,230	2.7
	35,686	15.3

wage jobs in textiles and apparel for every one in chemicals, machinery, or administrative-auxiliary. Even with the inclusion of the high-wage components of the textile and related group, the earnings for those industries still averaged nearly $250 below the average for North Carolina.

Since 1962 earnings in Metrolina have increased dramatically from the average of $3,648 of that year. The absolute gain of $1,743 to an average of $5,391 in only eight years is truly impressive but in comparison with North Carolina the gains are less notable. In 1962 the average for Metrolina stood at 99.9 percent of the state average ($3,652). By 1970, however, Metrolina's average had dropped to 98.4 percent of the state average of $5,477 (the lowest in the United States).

The spread in average earnings among the counties is very large, from $4,428 for Cabarrus to $6,710 for Mecklenburg. It is no accident that four of the five counties that have earnings below the Metrolina average are the four with the highest percent of employment in textiles. Even the spread within industries is substantial, ranging in textiles from a high of $5,411 in Lancaster to a low of $4,407 in Cabarrus County. A significant pattern that emerges is for earning levels within an industry group to be lower in the counties with low overall averages. Conversely, Mecklenburg County is consistently at or near the top in every industrial group. This suggests that as higher-wage industries enter a county they are able to draw labor away from the former lower-wage industries, causing the latter to have to either raise wage rates or to find labor elsewhere. That this mobility is less than perfect is shown by the considerable variations within counties, especially Mecklenburg (an incredible range of nearly $6,000). This is to be expected, however, unless one assumes that a sewing-machine operator in an apparel mill can quickly learn to operate precision machine tools, for example.

The existence of even a modest degree of labor mobility between industries is a highly significant finding for an area that is so heavily oriented to labor-intensive and, therefore, low-wage industries. It is, of course, advantageous for the long-term economic growth of an area to have a labor supply that can adapt to higher skill and higher-wage industries. But it also poses a major problem for the existing industries. How are they to respond to the challenge of higher wage-paying competitors for industrial labor?

Three kinds of positive responses seem to be open and all three are beginning to appear in Metrolina. First, some companies are leaving the relatively high-wage Piedmont and are moving to either the Coastal Plain or the mountains. Some of the rural counties in those areas are now experiencing their first real industrialization and this may help to stem the outmigration of population that has characterized rural North and South Carolina for so long. Second, some companies are seeking to bring more Negroes into the production force even though this sometimes requires more extensive training programs. The textile industry was once characterized as "lily white" but now it probably has a higher proportion of blacks in its employ than any other major American industry.

Third, some companies are seeking to mechanize their processes even further so that they will need fewer but more skilled laborers whom they can pay more. One textile executive put it this way: "The coming of new industry may hurt us for a little while. But our feeling is that higher paying industry probably will help—maybe even force—us to automate. And that'll mean greater efficiency, higher profits, and greater wages for our workers."[3]

Whatever the approach, it seems clear that the pressure is on textile and other labor-intensive employers to be more competitive for labor or leave the area. The result may mean higher income jobs for Metrolina's population and possibly for that of the Coastal Plain and mountains as well.

Industrial Diversification

Evidence of competition for labor by different industrial groups implies that the industrial base of Metrolina is becoming more diversified. Metrolina seems to be sharing a trend that is evident in the Carolinas. Between 1950 and 1969, for example, textiles' share of manufacturing employment dropped from 57.1 to 40.5 percent. Between 1962 and 1970 that same proportion dropped from 43.7 to 39.1 percent for the state and Metrolina's specialization in textiles dropped from 60.0 to 53.9 percent. Thus although Metrolina's share dropped faster than the state's it still has a much higher degree of specialization in textiles than does the entire state. The same is true for South Carolina where 41.6 percent of all manufacturing employees were in textiles by 1970.

While industry in Metrolina is becoming somewhat more diversified, a shifting has been taking place within the area. Between 1962 and 1970 eight of the counties had smaller proportions in textiles, including Mecklenburg and York counties in which there were actually fewer employees. Three of the four that had an increase in the proportion in textiles (Lancaster, Lincoln, and Union) were the three smallest industrial counties in Metrolina. The fourth, Iredell, ranked only sixth in total manufacturing employment. The four together have fewer industrial employees than Gaston County alone. This and the low average earnings in these four counties support the possibility that the diversification that is occurring in the other counties is beginning to push labor-intensive employers into these less industrialized counties.

Diversification really has three components. One is the group of textile-related industries other than apparel. These three high-wage industries (chemicals, nonelectrical

machinery, and administrative-auxiliary) are centered in Mecklenburg, Gaston, and York counties, with Mecklenburg alone having nearly 40 percent of all employees in this category—the only county to have more in these three than in textiles and apparel. Thus while Mecklenburg is unique in not having textiles as the leading employer, its involvement in the industry is very deep. Of course these data indicate only a direct manufacturing involvement and do not include Charlotte's very important textile-related sales, distribution, and financial functions.

Another element of diversification is the local-market sector. The making of consumer products, construction materials, and goods for other nearby industries is dominated by the two counties of the Charlotte Metropolitan Statistical Area, Mecklenburg and Union. Together they account for just over half of all Metrolina employment in this group. Again it is questionable just how much diversification this group really involves since much of its market derives directly or indirectly from the textile and related industries.

Finally there is the group of nontextile-related industries that market mainly to a broad region, including the rest of the United States. This group accounts for about 15 percent of all manufacturing employees in Metrolina. The furniture industry of Catawba County is the single largest element of this group. Excluding furniture because it is a relatively low-wage industry, one is left with about 20,000 employees (less than 9 percent of the Metrolina total) in industries that are not heavily dependent on textiles and can pay wages substantially higher than those now prevalent in the area.

There are many who are not concerned with Metrolina's heavy specialization in textiles. For example, one local authority on the industry recently wrote: "If Metrolina's fate seems to be inescapably bound to that of the textile industry, should it be a cause of concern to that area's citizenry? This writer thinks not. Even the most casual observer can hardly escape the point that there exists with[in] the Southern textile industry today an incredible range of product diversification. And while some economists may lament this heavy involvement in a 'one-industry economy,' it seems equally clear that any area of our nation which possesses so dominant a share of so basic an industry should consider itself fortunate indeed! Textile marketing experts estimate that by 1975 that industry will have to be one and one-half times as large as it is today to supply the needs of our growing, goods-hungry population. And as the industry grows, Charlotte and Metrolina will grow with it!"[4]

Maybe so, but objective analysis does not support the unquestioning optimism of the statement. One problem is that although the textile industry was undoubtedly responsible for the economic growth of this area over the years it is not capable of providing adequately for the various needs

3. Charlotte *Observer*, March 1, 1970, p. 8A.

4. Ed Smith, "Textiles," *Charlotte* (July-August 1969), p. 38.

of contemporary society. Another writer spoke to this point for the whole state but he could just as easily have applied his analysis to Metrolina: "How can a state be so intensely industrialized, in so far as employment is concerned, and yet lack so many of the features of an industrial region? The key to this seeming paradox lies in the fact that North Carolina has a preponderance of labor-intensive, low-profit margin, slow-growth economic sectors (e.g., textiles, furniture, apparel, food processing) where wage rates and the rates of capital investment to employment are well below the national norm. This helps to explain the below-average levels of income and retail sales, the more limited tax base, and the more modest expenditures for public instruction. Lower educational levels in turn make it more difficult for the state to attract high-wage firms which require more highly skilled personnel."[5]

Also, the first statement quoted implies that growth of the market for textiles will have a proportionate benefit for Metrolina. Ignored is the fact that modern mills produce more with fewer employees, thus benefiting those still working at the mill but not necessarily raising the income for the total economy. Furthermore, there is the question of imports. Although the American domestic market may be increasing, so are imports. The United States Tariff Commission a few years ago predicted that imports would capture 41 percent of the domestic market by 1975. A string of mill closings in recent years has been publicly blamed on imports, even though obsolescence also probably had a role. Recent agreements limiting certain textile imports, especially from Japan, will probably provide only temporary relief from the pressure of cheaper imports.

Finally there is the simple, unadorned fact that the textiles industry is declining as an employer. From 1939 to 1967, for example, while total manufacturing employment in the United States more than doubled, textiles was the only major industry in which fewer people worked in 1967 than in 1939. The growth of textile employment in Metrolina during this period means that the region has gained a larger share of a dwindling total, a dubious distinction.

There are historical precedents pointing to the dangers of commitment to a declining employer. Lancashire, England, was the world's first great industrial district, because of its cotton textiles. Today textile employment in that area is less than it was in 1840 and only about 25 percent of the immediate pre–World War II peak due mainly to the loss first of export markets and later of much of the domestic market. A distressed area today, Lancashire has closed hundreds of mills and the national government is bearing most of the cost of a desperate attempt to diversify the Lancashire economy.

5. Richard E. Lonsdale, "Is North Carolina an Industrial State?," *Quarterly Review*, First Union National Bank of North Carolina (Fall 1967).

New England had a somewhat less difficult adjustment to make when textiles began to leave the area and, largely because of a highly developed educational system, it was able to convert to higher skill and wage types of manufacturing and to expand nonmanufacturing sectors of the economy. It remains to be seen whether or not the Piedmont, including Metrolina, has the leadership, capital, and educational system that a similar conversion will require.

The prospects are not entirely pessimistic. The events of 1880 and later years have demonstrated that the region has the capacity for economic rejuvenation. Since that time it has developed an education, business-service, transportation, and amenities base that is attracting nonindustrial as well as manufacturing growth.

A good location in relation to national markets and an industrially experienced labor force are further advantages that will stand the region in good stead. In fact, chances are good that the region will be able to make the adjustment to a more diversified economy without major dislocation. Even though much of the actual making of textiles may be phased out, the region can probably hope to maintain strong leadership in research and administration and an important share of the various textile-related industries, especially machinery and chemicals.

"Natural" economic change may not be sufficient, however, and governmental policies aimed at encouraging diversification may be necessary, particularly in the face of the not uncommon attitude that the continued dominance of the regional economy by the textile industry is a totally unmixed blessing. A key aspect of these policies may be a major effort to retrain textile workers for higher-skill and higher-wage jobs.

As in so many aspects of contemporary life, change seems to be the only constant in the economic future of Metrolina. Change without planning could be tragic but with it the region should be able to continue the steady move forward that began in 1880 with the first Cotton Mill Campaign.

REFERENCES

Gilman, Glenn. *Human Relations in the Industrial Southeast.* Chapel Hill: University of North Carolina Press, 1956.
Mitchell, Broadus. *The Rise of Cotton Mills in the South.* Gloucester, Mass.: Peter Smith, 1966 (originally published by Johns Hopkins Press in 1921).
North Carolina Department of Labor. *North Carolina Directory of Manufacturing Firms*, 1968 (with 1970 supplement). Raleigh: The Department, 1970.
U.S. Department of Commerce, Bureau of the Census. *Census of Manufactures.* Washington, D.C.: U.S. Government Printing Office, published annually.
U.S. Department of Commerce, Bureau of the Census. *County Business Patterns.* Washington, D.C.: U.S. Government Printing Office, published annually.

6. TRANSPORTATION AND UTILITIES

WAYNE A. WALCOTT

"... It is not at all impossible that the rapid strides made in the realm of transportation (including energy transmission) and communication during the past two or three decades go further to explain America's prosperity than almost any other single factor."—Erich W. Zimmerman, Introduction to World Resources.

A vital element in the viable functioning of any urban region is the efficient movement of people, goods, and information. This is especially true in a societal setting where the complexity and volume of such movements are of a large scale.

Basic economic concepts have little practical application when taken out of the context of an efficient transportation system, which is in fact a part of the total communication system. For example, it would be impossible to have any degree of regional specialization or realize economies of scale without a highly efficient transportation and communication system. This is an extremely important fact of life for any geographic region whether it is Metrolina, the Piedmont, or the state of North Carolina. Efficient transportation and communication, however, should imply more than just efficient companies operating on modern, high-speed networks. It should entail also a co-ordinated effort to insure that all parts of the transportation and communication system are used when and where they are best suited to provide for the needs of the people.

It is easy to define the "parts" of this system: highway transport, railroads, airlines, pipelines, telephones, and so on. It is also easy to see that each of the parts has special functions in relation to the whole. That is, pipelines move different kinds of substances over different distances than do airplanes. What is most difficult to accomplish, however, is to explain in detail the extent to which each of the parts contributes to the overall functioning of the whole system. The reason for this is the lack of precise data on the amount of different commodities moving into and out of an area such as Metrolina and on the travel characteristics of the region's residents, as well as on many other items related to the movement of goods, people, and information. Although the scarcity of such data prohibits a thorough system-wide analysis of transportation and communication in Metrolina, it is still possible to examine some characteristics of individual modes. For example, in some of the sections to follow, statements are made about the relative "usability" of Metrolina's surface transport system; in other words, how well the parts of the surface transportation system serve the people of different sections of Metrolina. It will also be pointed out how parts of this transportation system are a reflection of previous economic and transport linkages. These would be important steps in a complete systems analysis of Metrolina's transportation and communication system. The emphasis here will not be on detail but in stressing those characteristics, both good and bad, that illustrate the usefulness of the system. It is hoped that this emphasis will be of interest to those planning future transportation facilities and those wanting to make better use of existing facilities.

A primary focus is on highway and rail transportation, since these modes seem to have the greatest impact on a region the size of Metrolina. Air travel has its principal effect on linkages with areas outside Metrolina. Subsequent pages deal with such utilities as pipelines (which of course are also a form of transportation), electric power, and telephone service. Although it may seem difficult to justify electric-power utilities as part of the transportation and communication system, their inclusion here is based on parallel problems concerning the provision of all of these facilities as well as the important element of governmental regulation.

Wayne A. Walcott

Historical Background

Quite often the structure of a modern transportation network is merely a refinement of one that has existed for many generations. An assessment of the current transportation and communication system is therefore not complete without a review of the historical development of transportation routes in the area.

The earliest transportation route in the Metrolina area was the Great Trading Path (see Part 2), established by the original inhabitants of the area, the Indians. Extending from eastern Virginia into the Piedmont of the Carolinas, it was used by the whites to trade with the tribes along the Catawba and Yadkin rivers and later to move their families into the area. One of the most important fords across the Catawba, the Tuckasseegee, was along this path. North of Tuckasseegee Ford was Beatty's, Cowan's, Toole's, and Trading fords, names still familiar to many in the area. To the south were Martin's, Armstrong's, and Armer's fords.

The major colonial routes in Metrolina were north-south oriented through the Piedmont, much to the dismay of the North Carolina Colonial Assembly. In 1762 the assembly therefore established the Cape Fear area as a trading center, hoping to divert the trade of Anson and Rowan counties, through which producers found it easier to reach markets in South Carolina. The attempt was futile. For example, records reveal that the iron products of Lincoln County (created from the Rowan area) were sent down the Catawba, eventually reaching Charleston, and the 1810 census for Mecklenburg County showed that the 103 cotton gins in the county produced 3,512 bags "all sent to market principally in Charleston, South Carolina."

The growth of railroad transportation routes in the nineteenth century had a tremendous economic impact on several towns and counties in Metrolina. In the 1830s the Cape Fear and Yadkin Railroad Company began discussing the possibilities of running a line through Lincoln and Mecklenburg counties, but nothing developed from this early effort. By 1845 business interests in Charlotte, discouraged with the lack of action by the North Carolina Railroad Company, turned to South Carolina in an attempt to tie into that state's system. In 1846 South Carolina authorized two lines: the Charlotte and South Carolina Railroad Company between Charlotte and Columbia, and the Kings Mountain Railroad Company from Yorkville to Chester, which joined the Charlotte and South Carolina line.

In the late 1840s an attempt was made to charter, without state financial aid, the Charlotte and Danville Railroad Company, but the Coastal Plain—dominated legislature feared it would compete with the struggling Raleigh and Gaston line. Instead of accepting the original proposal, the legislature decided to build a line from Charlotte to Raleigh that would link into the Raleigh and Gaston line. This became the North Carolina Railroad in which the state owned two-thirds of the stock. The railway ran through Metrolina parallel to the Great Trading Path.

Two more lines were added to the Metrolina system in the 1850s. The Wilmington, Charlotte, and Rutherfordton Railroad Company was one of the first attempts to link the Cape Fear area with the Piedmont. This line went from Wilmington to Rockingham to Charlotte through Gaston and Lincoln counties to Lincolnton and finally to Rutherfordton. After several years of financial difficulties it became part of the Seaboard Airline system. The other line added in the 1850s was the Western North Carolina Railroad Company line extending from Salisbury to Morganton. The 1860 census recorded the following companies and track mileage within the Metrolina area: Western North Carolina (41.5), Wilmington, Charlotte, and Rutherfordton (110), North Carolina Railroad (45), Charlotte and South Carolina (34). This total of 230.5 miles of track represented 25 percent of the track mileage in the entire state of North Carolina at the time. (See Fig. 6.1.)

In 1872 a decision concerning rail linkages made by the citizens of Dallas, in Gaston County, had important repercussions for that town. The newly established Atlanta and Charlotte Airline Railroad requested Dallas to make available several thousand dollars for building bridges across some of the creeks in the Dallas area. The Dallas citizenry refused. As a result, the engineers of the line detoured around Dallas and established the Gastonia station four miles to the south. That was the beginning of the end for Dallas as an important rail center and established Gastonia on what was to become one of the main cargo routes in North Carolina. Shortly thereafter the Chester and Lenoir Narrow Gauge Railroad was constructed between Yorkville, South Carolina, and Lenoir. It crossed the Atlanta and Charlotte Railroad at Gastonia, giving further impetus to growth in Gastonia. (See Fig. 6.2.)

Salisbury suffered also as a result of indecision regarding railroad development. After twenty-two years of disagreement the Yadkin Valley Railroad was established between Salisbury and Cheraw. But this did not occur until 1891 and by that time other railroads established through Charlotte asserted that city's dominance over Salisbury as a rail center. Another significant development in Rowan County's history of transportation was the location of a major repair shop in the small town of Spencer by the Southern Railroad in 1895. This was an important economic stimulus to the area and only recently have railway operations declined in Spencer.

From 1860 to the early 1900s the railways were an important factor in the economic development of the region,

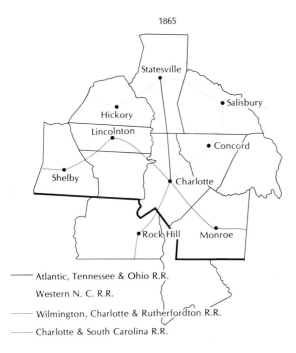

Atlantic, Tennessee & Ohio R.R.

Western N. C. R.R.

Wilmington, Charlotte & Rutherfordton R.R.

Charlotte & South Carolina R.R.

Fig. 6.1. Metrolina Railroad Network, 1860

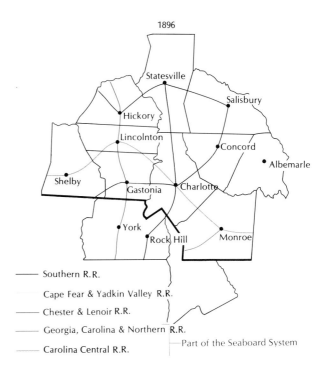

Southern R.R.

Cape Fear & Yadkin Valley R.R.

Chester & Lenoir R.R.

Georgia, Carolina & Northern R.R.

Carolina Central R.R.

Part of the Seaboard System

Fig. 6.2. Metrolina Railroad Network, 1890

helping to establish the basic transport corridors of Metrolina. By 1923 the age of intensive railway construction had essentially ended, as the total amount of track in Metrolina had increased 60 percent since 1860 to a total of 573 miles. (In 1970, there were 642 miles of track in the Metrolina counties.)

Today Metrolina has a good highway network. The development of an extensive road system in Metrolina and in the state of North Carolina has been credited to a bill passed by the North Carolina Assembly in 1879. The Mecklenburg Road Law, intended as a general state law but applied at the time only to Mecklenburg County, allowed property taxes to be used for the construction and maintenance of roads in the county.

Good transportation has been an important element in the rapid growth of Metrolina ever since the opening of the Great Trading Path. The people of the area, even when dominated by a rural economy, were vitally concerned with moving their products to market. The fact that state boundaries were unimportant was evidenced by Charlotte's desire in the 1840s to tie into the South Carolina railroad system. In general the primary factors in determining where transport facilities were placed were first, the geographic arrangement of the physical features and later, emerging economic needs. Early routes were established along lines of least physical resistance. These routes gave rise to the growth of towns and cities at certain strategic points, which in turn stimulated the further growth of transportation networks connecting these places. The result has been to give the region the rail and highway net-

works that exist today.

Edward S. Perzel

Highways

As in any metropolitan region, highway facilities are of utmost importance in the day-to-day functioning of the region's economy and play a vital role in determining the type and scope of future economic development. At the present time Metrolina offers a substantial amount of highway transport facilities for the movement of goods and people. There are over 11,000 miles of paved primary and secondary roads in Metrolina. Further, there are over 600,000 cars and trucks registered in the region with over one-third of them in Mecklenburg County. Seventy-five thousand of the 600,000 are truck-for-hire registrations. Fig. 6.8 shows the distribution of truck-terminal facilities in the twelve counties. The highest per capita concentration of truck-terminal facilities in the South is in the Metrolina region. Note the alignment of these facilities along the two interstates, I-40 and I-85, an obvious orientation of truck traffic along the Piedmont axis. In Charlotte alone there are 147 truck companies offering 3,000 scheduled runs a day, one of the highest figures of any city in the nation. Only Chicago has a higher per capita number of scheduled truck runs than Charlotte.

Bus connections are also well developed throughout the area, as Greyhound and Continental Trailways make regu-

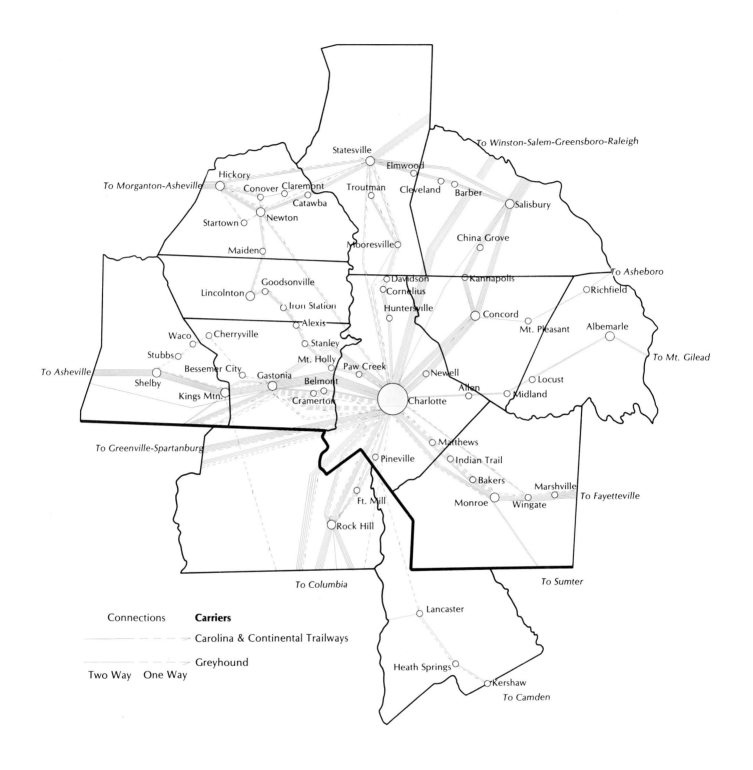

Fig. 6.3. Scheduled Metrolina Bus Service

a.

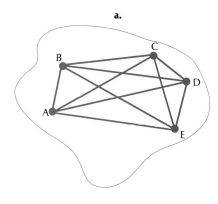

b.

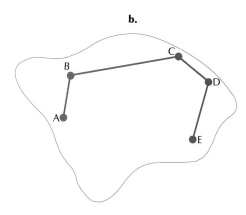

Fig. 6.4. Two Types of Optimum Network Linkages

larly scheduled stops in over fifty towns and cities in Metrolina. This is approximately one-half of all incorporated places. No point in Metrolina is further than twenty miles from a bus terminal. (See Fig. 6.3.)

An assessment of highway transportation facilities in Metrolina, as anywhere else, is a difficult task. The difficulty stems from the fact that the highway system is used for so many of the region's activities that it is almost impossible to devise a system that will satisfy all users. For example, Fig. 6.4 (a) shows what might be an optimum system for linking points A through E to serve the needs of commuting workers in a hypothetical area. This is not an optimum system for those who must fund the facilities, however, because of the expense involved in building and maintaining such a network. An optimum system for them would be the one shown in Fig. 6.4 (b), which links all points with a minimum number of miles of roadway.

Lack of data on who is using the system and how much is being moved also contributes to the general frustration of assessing a highway system. It is possible, however, to examine the network structure and come to some conclusions about the effectiveness of different parts of the system, as well as the system as a whole, in serving the needs of the people.

One can begin by examining the general structure of Metrolina's highway network. The network as shown in Fig. 6.5 appears roughly as part of a series of concentric circles centered on Charlotte. The circles are connected to each other by a number of routes that appear to radiate from that city. Most of the circle routes are the secondary highways and the radial routes are the primary roads. The interstates seem to be superimposed on this system, in some places acting as circle routes, in other places as radial routes. Fig. 6.6 is a simplification of the highway system of Metrolina with some roads eliminated to make the concentric circle pattern show more clearly.

The largest towns and cities of Metrolina lie at the junctions of one or more circle routes and one or more radial routes, while most of the smaller towns are located only on the radial routes. There are very few small towns on the circle routes. This suggests something about the orientation of the Metrolina highway network and also something of its major function. The majority of the radial routes (as well as the interstates) are oriented north-south, or more specifically to the other major urban centers of the Piedmont. The circle routes of course bend around Charlotte. It follows from this simple observation that the great majority of the traffic moving out of Metrolina would move over the radial routes and the circle routes would carry mostly intraregional traffic. Figs. 6.7 and 6.8, showing the volume of all traffic and the volume of truck traffic, which is predominantly to places outside the region, emphasize the importance of the radial routes in carrying goods into and out of Metrolina.

The pattern of circle and radial routes just described gives Metrolina one of the best-connected road systems of any similar-sized metropolitan area in the Carolinas. It is an efficient type of network for the movement of goods and people within the region since all the larger towns in Metrolina are not only connected directly to Charlotte (by radial routes) but each of these towns is also connected to the other by a well-developed, high-quality system of circle routes. A comparison of an idealized radial network pattern similar to that found in Metrolina having two concentric circles with a grid pattern having nearly the same number of intersections illustrates the above statement (see Fig. 6.9). First, in the idealized radial network it is quite apparent that one city is the primary focus of the entire network, but this is not the case in the idealized grid-type network. Second, it is possible to pass from "corner to corner," going through fewer junctions, in the Metrolina type, radial network (three junctions) than in the grid network (seven junctions), and since it is at road junctions where congestion is usually the heaviest, movement is facilitated when relatively few of these must be traversed.

For moves outside the region, beyond the perimeter of the circles, the Metrolina radial network is perhaps not as efficient as a grid type network because the former gives the region fewer connections to other areas than does the

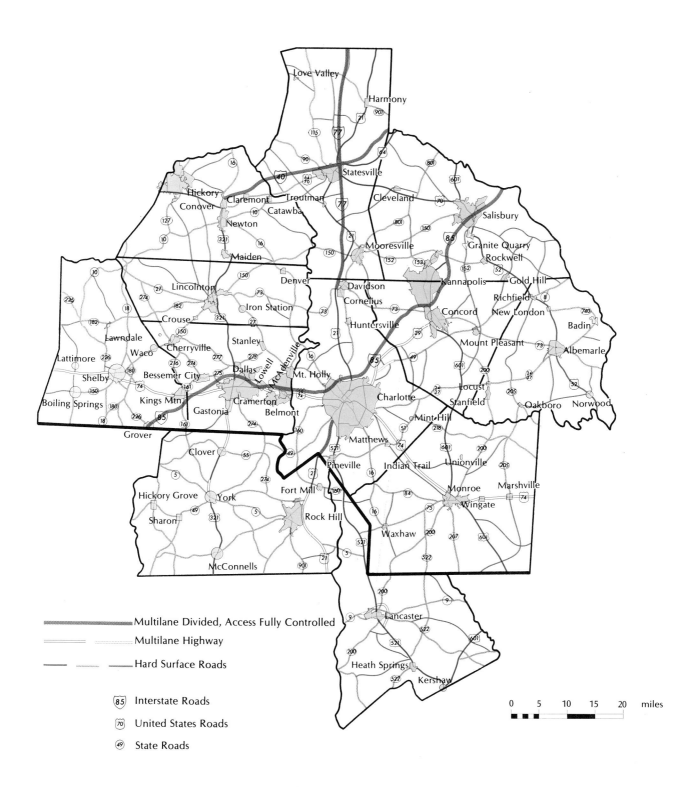

Legend:

Multilane Divided, Access Fully Controlled

Multilane Highway

Hard Surface Roads

(85) Interstate Roads

(70) United States Roads

(49) State Roads

0 5 10 15 20 miles

Fig. 6.5. Primary and Secondary Road Network in Metrolina

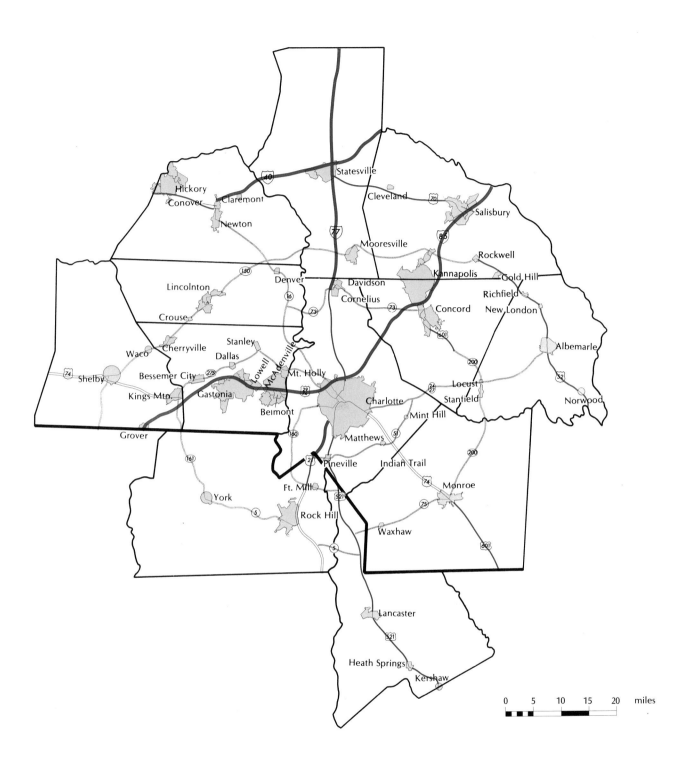

Fig. 6.6. Simplified Metrolina Highway Network Illustrating Concentric Circle Pattern

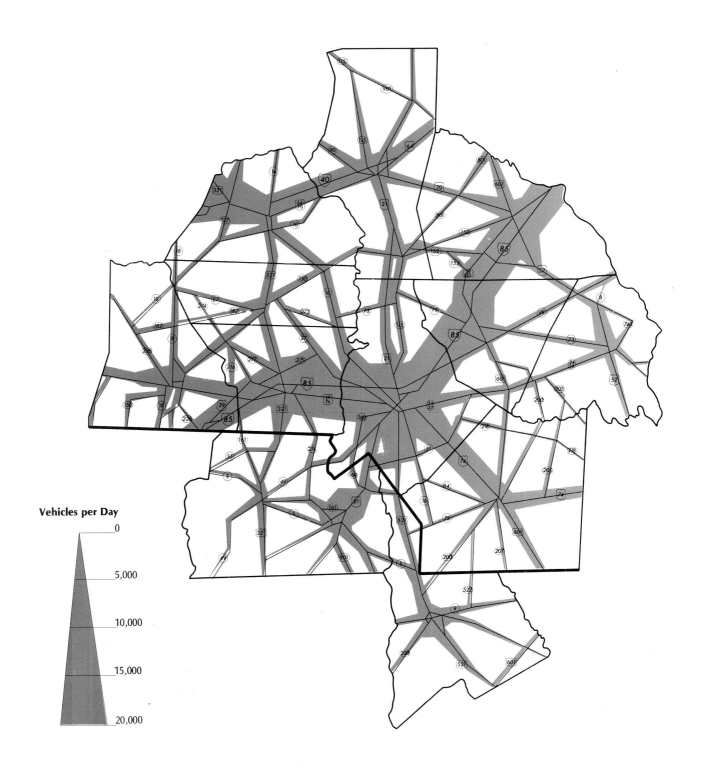

Vehicles per Day

Fig. 6.7. Vehicle Traffic Volume in Metrolina

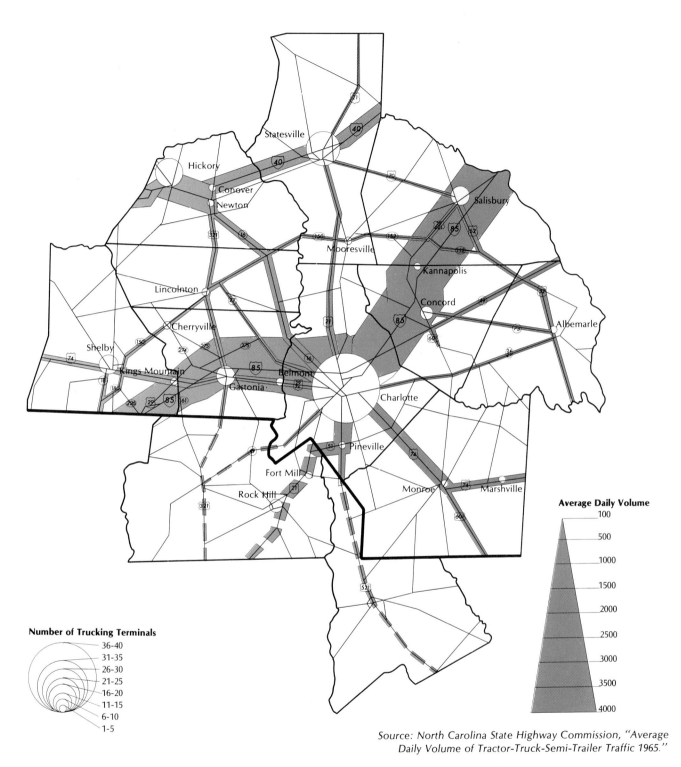

Number of Trucking Terminals
- 36-40
- 31-35
- 26-30
- 21-25
- 16-20
- 11-15
- 6-10
- 1-5

Average Daily Volume
- 100
- 500
- 1000
- 1500
- 2000
- 2500
- 3000
- 3500
- 4000

Source: North Carolina State Highway Commission, "Average Daily Volume of Tractor-Truck-Semi-Trailer Traffic 1965."

Dashed roads indicate insufficient data to calculate flow line width.

Fig. 6.8. Truck Traffic Volume in Metrolina

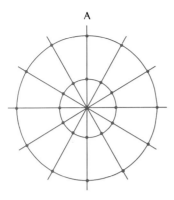

A

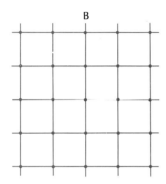

B

Fig. 6.9. Idealized Concentric Circle and Grid Networks

latter. In the idealized example above having an equal number of junctions there are only twelve exits for the radial network resembling the one in Metrolina but there are twenty for the grid pattern. Connections from Charlotte to places outside the Metrolina area are excellent, however, because of Charlotte's position in the center of the "wheel." But the very thing that makes Charlotte well connected to other places, its central location, indicates that other places will be relatively less well connected since the radial network tends to focus on one place rather than all places equally as in the grid network.

It is possible to measure the relative accessibility of points in the network, i.e., the relative ease of traveling between specific points in the network, by counting the number of cities and/or road junctions between two places. The assumption is that the more towns and junctions that must be passed through on any given trip, the more difficult will be the completion of that trip. It is possible then to assign numbers to given locations (cities) that will reflect the difficulty of moving from that point to some other common focal point. In the Metrolina region the obvious focal point of the highway network is Charlotte. Since Charlotte acts as the distribution center for many products and has the best facilities for "exporting" items outside the region, highway linkages to that city are vital

for cities located in Metrolina. Fig. 6.10 indicates the relative amount of difficulty encountered in moving from any place in the region to the city of Charlotte. The higher the number of highway junctions, the greater the relative inaccessibility of that area to Charlotte. Accessibility to Charlotte is best along Routes I-85, both toward Gastonia and Concord-Kannapolis; along U.S. Route 74 toward Monroe; and along N.C. Route 16 toward Hickory. It is expected that accessibility along I-77 toward Statesville will improve as the expressway becomes completed. Accessibility to Charlotte is relatively difficult from points in South Carolina. Fig. 6.10 shows that accessibility decreases rather markedly after the North Carolina–South Carolina boundary is crossed.

The same general notions of accessibility can be used to judge the accessibility of points in the system to all places, including those outside the region. By simply counting the number of routes emanating from a town one can get a crude indication of its connectivity with all places at once, on the assumption that the relative importance of a place as a link to other places can be measured by totaling the number of roads leading away from that place. Fig. 6.11 shows the accessibility patterns that result from making these calculations.

Charlotte of course is the dominant center with twelve links leading away. Four other cities also are relatively accessible: Lancaster, Gastonia, Statesville, and Monroe. Monroe is an unusual case. It is a city that is highly accessible, especially to places within the region. (Note that in Fig. 6.5 it appears as a sort of secondary hub with its own well-developed system of radial routes.) It ranks as a highway transportation center second only to Charlotte in Metrolina. This suggests that Monroe is in a very good position, from the standpoint of its connections with the rest of Metrolina, to utilize its highway facilities to enhance future growth. Monroe does, however, suffer from not being on the "mainline" of routes moving goods in and out of the region, and is handicapped by relatively poor rail connections.

In Fig. 6.11 the region has been categorized into areas having differing levels of accessibility. As would be expected, the Charlotte-Monroe area has the highest accessibility. Other large cities and their surrounding areas fall into a second category indicating somewhat lower accessibility. The least accessible areas in all of Metrolina are those areas between the cities. This pattern of course illustrates the concentration of traffic in and between the major cities. Congestion will increase, though, as the population of Metrolina increases and more people and activities occupy those relatively little-used areas between cities. Rarely does network development in these areas keep pace with the needs of the people. It is in these "developing" areas where there is little or no possibility of control that traffic congestion will become most menacing.

Wayne A. Walcott

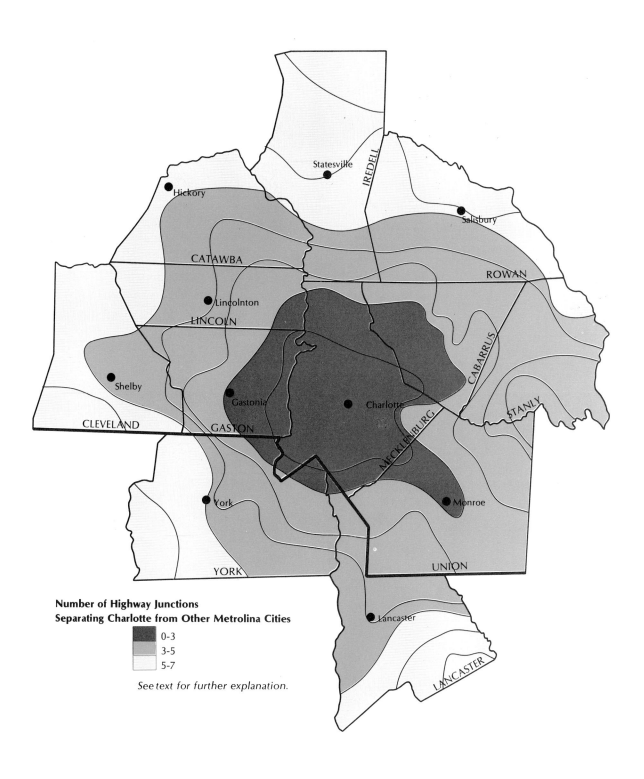

Number of Highway Junctions
Separating Charlotte from Other Metrolina Cities

0-3
3-5
5-7

See text for further explanation.

Fig. 6.10. Comparative Highway Accessibility to Charlotte

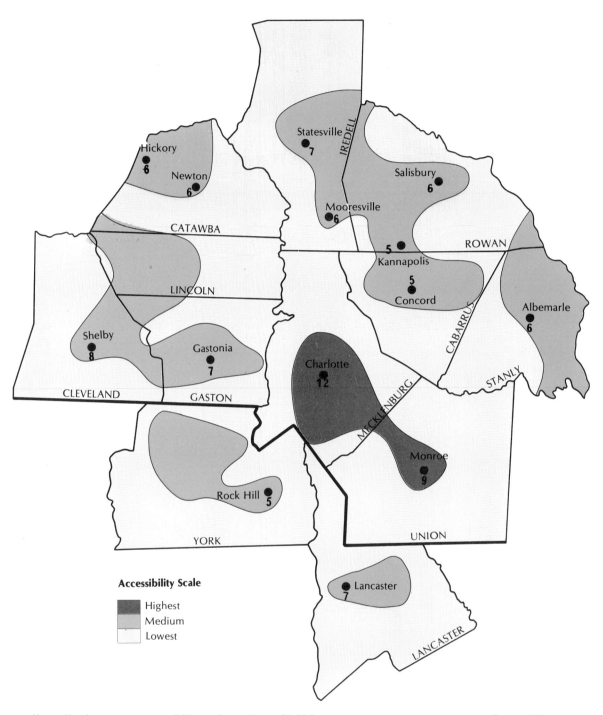

Note: Numbers measure accessibility at given points, with higher numbers indicating greater degrees of accessibility. The color scheme groups places with similar ratings to illustrate patterns.

Fig. 6.11. Comparative Highway Accessibility to Points in Metrolina and Beyond

Ideally one should attempt to assess rail facilities using techniques similar to those used with highways, which should make the results more directly comparable. Unfortunately in a region as small as Metrolina it is not possible to make the results exactly comparable because of the differences in the densities of the two networks. Nevertheless one can measure accessibility of the rail network in serving places in Metrolina even though the techniques must be varied somewhat. Here accessibility is more restricted in definition than it was in the discussion of highways. In an area the size of Metrolina there is little point in discussing the usefulness of the railroad in handling intraregional moves since the rail facilities are used very little for this purpose. Therefore accessibility is considered in terms of the connection that rail facilities provide with places or regions outside Metrolina. Accessibility here, then, means the ease with which rail transportation can be obtained for moving to areas outside Metrolina. The measurements are made at the rail terminals in Metrolina and are a combination of the number of scheduled trains serving a terminal place and the number of rail lines emanating from the terminal.

Fig. 6.12 shows three levels of rail accessibility, with blank areas indicating places without rail terminal facilities nearby. It is not surprising that Charlotte-Gastonia is the area with the best rail services. Surrounding this high-access area are areas of the lowest accessibility rating and on the periphery of Metrolina are the middle accessibility areas. This is explained by the fact that the larger cities of Metrolina are found generally in a ring around Charlotte-Gastonia near the periphery of the region, and we naturally expect greater accessibility in these larger urban places.

It is interesting to note the similarities between Figs. 6.11 and 6.12, indicating highway connectivity to areas beyond Metrolina and rail connectivity to other areas. Both center on the Charlotte area where rail and highway connectivity is best. Also on both maps there are gaps around all the larger urban areas where connectivity is poorer. Only in areas around Monroe in Union County does the consistency of this pattern on both maps break down. Monroe has very good highway connectivity, but, at least in relation to its highway facilities, poor rail connections. This is of course explained by its nearness to Charlotte, which provides many of Monroe's rail services. It also underlies the tendency for the strong economic ties Monroe has and will continue to have with Charlotte. The fact that both Monroe and Charlotte have good highway connections creates a type of axis between them where future growth potential is especially high. But the fact that rail connections out of Monroe are relatively poor means that this growth will have to be strongly oriented to highway traffic. Charlotte, with its better rail connections, will have an advantage in attracting industries, for example, that use large amounts of bulky raw materials or ship large amounts of low-valued finished products, since these activities depend heavily on rail transportation.

Having indicated which localities in Metrolina have good rail connections, it might be useful to point out the extensions of those connections. Metrolina is perhaps in the best of all possible locations for serving, with its railroads, both the older established markets of the North Atlantic coast as well as the newer and rapidly growing markets of the South. Charlotte is a focus for rail traffic moving north from both southern Piedmont cities and the Southern Atlantic coastal cities (Savannah, Jacksonville, Miami, etc.), and therefore stands to benefit greatly as a transport center as the South continues its vigorous growth. Virtually every major city east of the Mississippi is within three days' travel from Metrolina, and over 100 million people live within one and a half days' travel time to Metrolina.

One special service initiated by the railroads but which actually represents the cooperative effort of several transport modes is the rapidly growing practice of piggybacking. This procedure involves the movement of truck-trailers (with or without wheels) on railway flatcars. Because of substantial savings in terminal costs, piggybacking is becoming an important method of moving freight. And since piggyback terminals are frequently constructed outside congested urban areas, users of piggyback have noticed time savings as well as cost savings, adding to the attractiveness of the system.

The Piedmont and Northern Railway, the Seaboard Coast Line, and the Southern Railway Company all offer piggyback services in Metrolina. Two types of loading and unloading facilities are utilized. One, called a "Circus Ramp," is simply a ramp in which the trailers are hauled up and onto the flatcars. The other system utilizes a crane that straddles the flatcar and picks up trailers, setting them on the flatcar as it moves down the line of the train. The second method is by far the most efficient since it allows a trailer to be loaded or unloaded usually in less than sixty seconds. The Southern Railway Company has the most extensive piggyback service, with crane facilities operating at Charlotte, Gastonia, and Hickory.

Although accurate statistics are difficult to obtain, piggybacking probably accounts for about 5 to 10 percent of the total rail traffic moving in and out of Metrolina. This is not too significant in itself, but developments in piggybacking point to a very bright future for this transport mode. The service has been operational over the nation for a long enough time now so that terminals are becoming fairly widespread. This means that more and more shippers are going to be able to use the service. Also, railroads are beginning to encourage the use of wheelless trailers or containers rather than regular trailers. In this way the containers can be conveniently loaded onto other types of transport modes such as barges, ocean-going vessels, and even airplanes, thereby increasing the flexibility of the service.

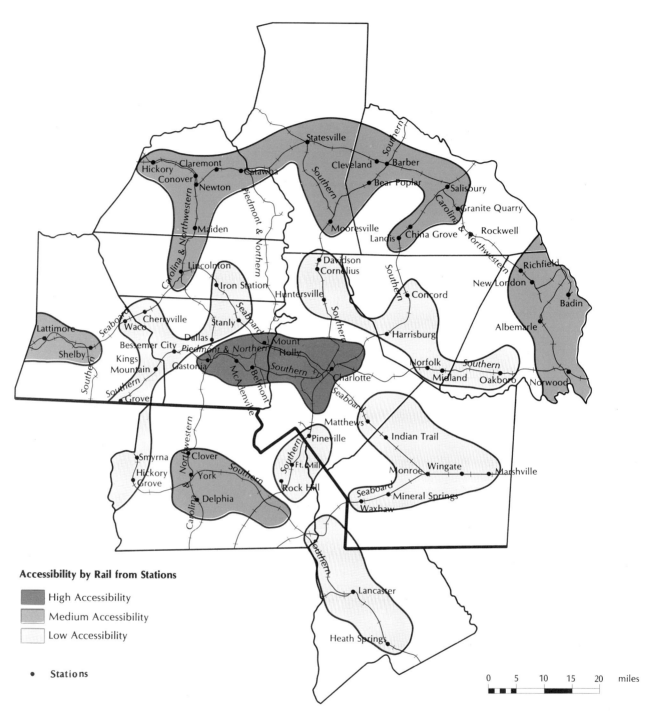

Accessibility by Rail from Stations

	High Accessibility
	Medium Accessibility
	Low Accessibility

●   **Stations**

0   5   10   15   20   miles

Note: Accessibility ratings apply to stations only; the color scheme was used solely to facilitate groupings of stations with a similar rating.

Fig. 6.12. Rail Facilities and Accessibility to Points in Metrolina and Beyond

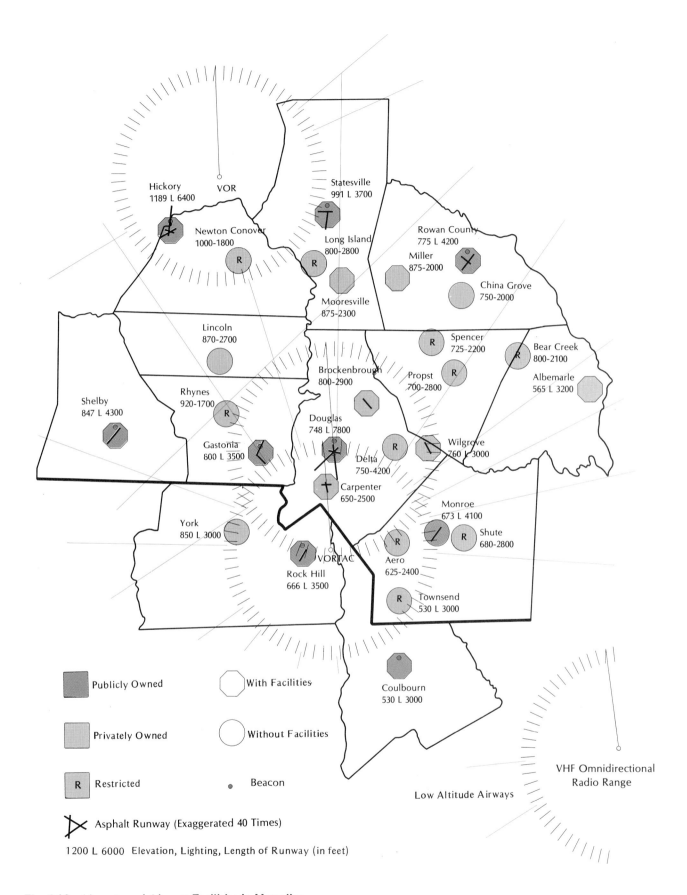

Hickory
1189 L 6400

VOR

Statesville
991 L 3700

Rowan County
775 L 4200

Newton Conover
1000-1800

Long Island
800-2800

Miller
875-2000

China Grove
750-2000

Lincoln
870-2700

Mooresville
875-2300

Spencer
725-2200

Bear Creek
800-2100

Brockenbrough
800-2900

Propst
700-2800

Albemarle
565 L 3200

Shelby
847 L 4300

Rhynes
920-1700

Douglas
748 L 7800

Delta
750-4200

Wilgrove
760 L 3000

Gastonia
800 L 3500

Carpenter
650-2500

Monroe
673 L 4100

Shute
680-2800

York
850 L 3000

Aero
625-2400

Townsend
530 L 3000

VORTAC

Rock Hill
666 L 3500

Coulbourn
530 L 3000

Publicly Owned

With Facilities

Privately Owned

Without Facilities

R Restricted

• Beacon

VHF Omnidirectional
Radio Range

Low Altitude Airways

Asphalt Runway (Exaggerated 40 Times)

1200 L 6000 Elevation, Lighting, Length of Runway (in feet)

Fig. 6.13. Airports and Airport Facilities in Metrolina

Such flexibility plus the cost savings involved in containerized shipping make piggybacking an important improvement in shipping technology. Metrolina, as one of the nation's leading trucking centers, can make better use of containerized shipping than most other places in the Southeast, and the future will undoubtedly see a rapid increase in the use of this service throughout the region.

Wayne A. Walcott

Air Travel

Airport facilities in Metrolina (see Fig. 6.13) include two airports that handle commercial flights: Charlotte's Douglas Airport and Hickory's Municipal Airport.

Douglas has airport facilities befitting a growing metropolitan region the size of Metrolina. It has a maximum runway length of 7,840 feet and a bearing capacity of 60,000 pounds for single-gear planes, 150,000 pounds for twin-gear, and 240,000 pounds for twin-tandem-gear. Sixty-nine direct flights daily to twenty-six cities in the eastern United States are provided by United Airlines, Delta, Eastern, Piedmont, and Southern Airlines. These cities include Chicago, Pittsburgh, Washington, Philadelphia, New York, Boston, Miami, Atlanta, and Memphis. (See Fig. 6.14.) (At peak periods it is not unusual to have fifteen take-offs and landings in an hour.) Equipment used by these airlines includes DC-6s, DC-8s, DC-9s, Electra LE-82s, Boeing 727s, Convair 44s, Martin 404s, and Viscounts. There are over 800,000 passengers enplaned annually at Douglas, ranking Charlotte as one of the top six cities in the nation in enplaned passengers per capita.

Detailed statistics on the amount of air freight moving through the Metrolina airports are not available. Douglas Airport handles by far the most air freight and in 1970 about 17,000 tons of air freight passed through the airport. Although air freight cannot be considered a major function of an airport's daily business, it is becoming an increasingly significant operation as the containerization of freight becomes more prevalent. For Charlotte this will necessitate the development of runway facilities to accommodate the large jets that will move most of the air freight as well as the development of facilities for the efficient handling of freight. Since Charlotte already is a trucking and warehouse center serving the entire Piedmont, it should logically develop as an air-freight center as that type of freight shipment becomes more widespread. Officials at Douglas Airport expect about a 20 percent increase per year in air freight business in the forseeable future.

The Municipal Airport at Hickory served by Piedmont Airlines has flights primarily to other cities and towns in North Carolina although there are also flights to large regional cities such as Washington and Atlanta. Maximum runway length is 6,400 feet, adequate for the largely local service provided by the airport. The airport terminal building is just over ten years old and provides complete service facilities and radio aids for its users. Charter service is also available at the airport.

Wayne A. Walcott

Perspective on Transportation

The preceding paragraphs dealing with highway, rail, and air transportation indicate that on balance the Metrolina region possesses a sound array of transportation facilities. On the other hand, it should not be assumed that the area is without transportation problems. The problems are numerous, and all too familiar to anyone acquainted with the traffic congestion that can occur in any urban region. In one way, however, the people of Metrolina are fortunate in that their problems are not yet unmanageable, and they can look to the experience of other larger urban areas for guidance in future transportation planning.

Problems that have developed already for the Charlotte area and soon may confront much of Metrolina include rush-hour congestion, inadequate parking facilities, the need for more airport facilities that are connected to the central city in an efficient manner, and the provision of more widespread bus transportation in the city. All of these are compounded by a burgeoning population with a greater demand for even more mobility. In the past most urban areas have sought to ease these pressures by continually increasing the amount of facilities, while the search goes on for some new "technology" to allow for more permanent solutions. Most new technologies, however, have involved developments such as jumbo jets, containerized freight service, and high-speed intercity rail service. Not many innovations have been developed to aid intracity transportation. But the creation of new technologies may not be the only answer to the problem. A far less costly approach might be to try to make better use of the transportation system on hand. For example, one of the better-developed sectors of the Metrolina transportation system is the highway network. Rather than building more and more multilane highways to carry increasing amounts of traffic in and out of downtown areas, perhaps it would be better to try to relieve traffic densities by cutting down on the number of vehicles using existing roads through providing a better bus service or making better use of the capacity of the vehicles (cars) using the system. And not to be overlooked is the construction of bicycle paths alongside highways, as practiced in some European countries, which have the dual advantage of reducing vehicular traffic as well as carbon monoxide pollution.

The city center is not the only area where serious problems result from the nature of the transport system. Of even more concern to Metrolina as a whole is the provision

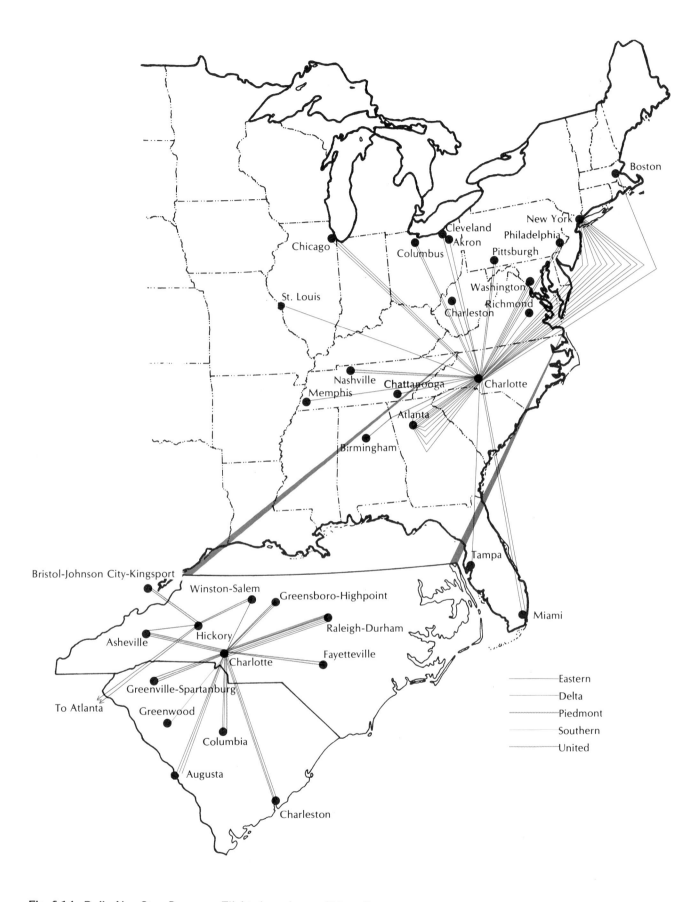

Fig. 6.14. Daily Non-Stop Passenger Flights in and out of Metrolina

Legend:
- Eastern
- Delta
- Piedmont
- Southern
- United

City labels (upper map): Boston, New York, Cleveland, Akron, Philadelphia, Chicago, Columbus, Pittsburgh, Washington, Richmond, Charleston, St. Louis, Nashville, Chattanooga, Memphis, Charlotte, Atlanta, Birmingham, Tampa, Miami

City labels (lower map): Bristol-Johnson City-Kingsport, Winston-Salem, Greensboro-Highpoint, Raleigh-Durham, Asheville, Hickory, Fayetteville, Charlotte, Greenville-Spartanburg, Greenwood, To Atlanta, Columbia, Augusta, Charleston

of adequate transportation facilities to allow commuting employees to reach places of work that are located throughout the urban region. The emphasis in most intraurban transportation planning seems to be on the movement from suburbs to city centers. As the "suburbs" in Metrolina continue to push out from many cities, more and more people are going to find themselves in what has been termed a "transport vacuum," an area between the well-connected city center and the suburbs, where transport connections are poor. In most cities these areas have been "forgotten" in transportation planning and they present some of the greatest problems in traffic congestion in urban areas.

Metrolina planners can learn from these experiences that attention must be directed to both suburb—city center and suburb—city fringe connectivity if the transport system is to keep pace with the region's growth.

Many of the transportation problems in Metrolina cannot, unfortunately, be solved internally. This reflects the difficulties that arise from the rules established by the Civil Aeronautics Board and the Interstate Commerce Commission for the operation of airplanes and trucks. These rules include the setting of fees for the use of government-owned facilities such as air terminals and highways and requests for rate adjustments to meet given circumstances. Too often they are made for one mode of transportation without regard to their effect on other modes or the competition between modes. Regulatory problems represent one of the greatest challenges to a more efficient transportation system for Metrolina as well as for the rest of the nation. Help may come from the Federal Department of Transportation, one of the charges of which is to coordinate the policies and activities of the various transport media. Until goals for the provision of a sound national transport system are set forth and methods for achieving them are devised, the chaotic system of unrelated individual decisions will continue, much to the detriment of coordinated transport systems for the nation's urban regions.

Wayne A. Walcott

Petroleum and Natural Gas Pipelines

Two major interstate petroleum-product lines cross Metrolina on their way from Texas and Louisiana refineries to the huge New Jersey terminals (see Fig. 6.15). The Paw Creek and other tank farms are served by Plantation Pipeline Company and by Colonial Pipeline Company. With their daily total capacity of 1,300,000,000 barrels of refined petroleum products, Metrolina has a steady, spill-proof source of petroleum products available under all weather conditions. Further, since transportation by pipeline is in many cases less expensive than by rail, highways, or barges and ships, relatively stable prices for these prod-

ucts are the rule. These two pipeline facilities handle many products refined by all the major oil companies serving Metrolina. Their customer's products are kept separate because all petroleum distillates have different specific gravities. These gravities can be determined quickly and accurately, so that control of the necessary valves can be made from the pipeline to the storage tanks.

Three natural gas facilities—Carolina Pipeline Company, Piedmont Natural Gas Corporation, and Public Service Company of North Carolina, Inc.—serve Metrolina and are under the regulation of the North Carolina Utilities Commission (see Fig. 6.15). These are transmission and distribution companies and they purchase their gas for resale from the Transcontinental Gas Pipe Line Corporation, the only interstate gas pipeline operating within the state. All portions of the Metrolina area are advantageously situated because of their proximity to this line. Transcontinental, in turn, purchases natural gas from producers in Texas and Louisiana and transports it to Metrolina and much of the North Atlantic area, where it is resold to the distributing companies at rates prescribed by the Federal Power Commission on the basis of three zones of distance from the point of origin. Metrolina lies within Zone 2, with an average cost to its utility customers of approximately 36.5 cents per thousand cubic feet. Because gas must be available at all times for all localities, even during the most severe and protracted periods of cold weather, for space-heating private dwellings, many industrial customers are supplied gas on an interruptable basis. These large-volume users purchase natural gas from the distribution companies with the understanding that they may have their supply interrupted or curtailed at times when the need is greater for space-heating of dwellings. For this reason interruptable gas is sold at a much lower price than that sold for private use.

Several cities, including Albemarle and Monroe, are serviced by municipally owned and operated facilities.

Considering that the natural gas industry is relatively new, having come into existence in the period immediately after World War II, its growth and the demand for its product has been an impressive one. It is not possible, however, to extrapolate its rate of growth into future decades, for the simple reason that *known* reserves of natural gas are limited. Federal and private sources estimate conservatively that at our present rate of consumption, current known natural gas reserves would last seventeen more years.

The safety record of the industry is an impressive one. Taking into consideration the gas-gathering operation in the producing field, high-pressure pumping (2,000 pounds per square inch and more) for great distances, and the subsequent distribution to domestic and industrial users both urban and rural, injury or loss of life or property damage by asphyxiation, fire, or explosion has been minimal. For the most part this has been made possible not by federal

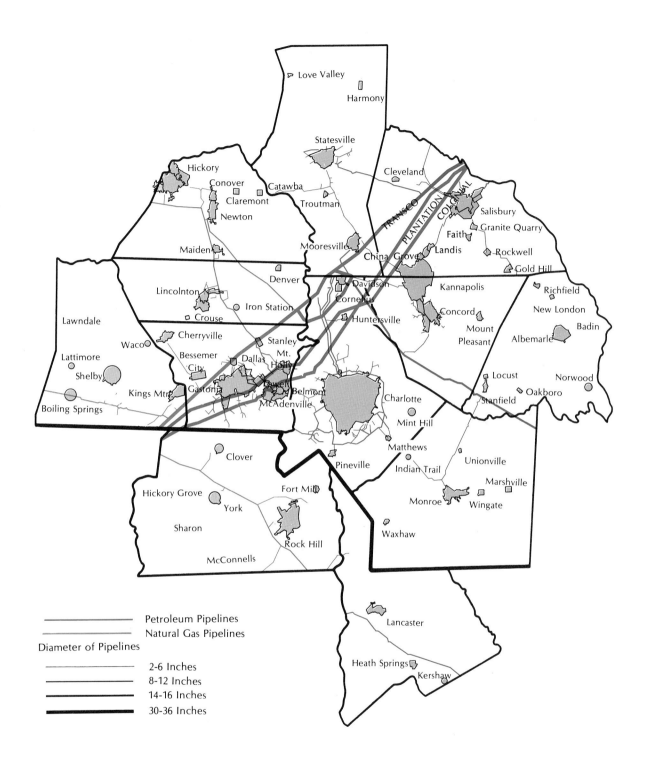

Fig. 6.15. Natural Gas and Petroleum Pipelines in Metrolina

or state controls but by industry-wide self-imposed regulations through self-policing methods.

Ted R. Fletcher

Electric Power

Hydroelectric Power Plants. Planning for publicly available electric power in Metrolina was initiated at the turn of the century, and by 1904 hydroelectric power was being generated at Catawba Station from a dam at the present site of Lake Wiley. Between 1907 and 1963 fourteen stations having a total capacity of 880.8 megawatts (1 megawatt equals 1,000 kilowatts) were installed to complete development of the Catawba River for generating electric power (see Fig. 6.16). Although hydroelectric development satisfies only a small percentage of the total current electric-power demand of Metrolina, these generating stations still are of particular importance. Since hydroelectric generating plants can both be brought to and taken off full power quickly and conveniently, they are used for peaking. Power demands vary through the day, and hydroelectric stations are generally turned on only during periods of peak demand. Thus the less quickly activated steam-generating stations can be kept on "base" load (minimum demand).

Fossil-Fuel Power Plants. More than 90 percent of the electricity generated for Metrolina is from combustion of coal. The first steam plant was built in 1910 and the oldest large plant still in operation was built in 1926. Other steam plants will be added, at least through 1974. (See Fig. 6.16.) Many of these plants burn pulverized coal, and fly-ash emission problems have necessitated the installation of new control devices. It is a reasonable expectation that more environmental limitations will be placed on coal-fired plant emissions. Four new sites for electric generating stations have been chosen within the Metrolina area: one is on the east side of Lake Norman in Iredell County off County Road 1100, another is on the east side of Lake Norman in Mecklenburg County off Road 2151, the third is on the west side of Lake Wylie in York County, South Carolina, and the fourth one is on Lake Wateree in South Carolina. No choice has been announced concerning whether coal or nuclear fuels will be used at these sites.

A small amount of the total electric power for Metrolina is generated by using combustion turbines. These are similar to aircraft jet engines and are connected through gear systems to generators. They serve the important function of augmenting the peaking capacity provided by the hydroelectric stations, as they can also be quickly brought to full power.

Nuclear Power Plants. Future base-load generating capacity may come predominantly from nuclear power, and since nuclear power plants can most economically be operated at their design power level for long periods, a pump-storage plant is being built south of Metrolina in which special pumps run by the nuclear power plants will lift water into the reservoir during low power demand for use in generating more hydroelectrical energy during peak demand (see Fig. 6.16). Although a significant portion (one-third) of the power is lost in the transfer, the additional peaking capacity makes the project economically advantageous. The installation of this facility further illustrates the value of the already installed hydroelectric plants. Two nuclear plants are scheduled to begin operation on Lake Norman at the McGuire station in 1975 and 1977. They will have a total rated generating capacity of 2,300 megawatts of electrical power. The nuclear power systems will be of the pressurized water-reactor type and will be supplied by the Westinghouse Electric Corporation. This single station will have a power level somewhat more than a third of the entire Duke Power Company's generating capacity in 1969. Since the ratio of the installation of new and expanded industry in the Piedmont to present capacity is approximately four times that of the remainder of North and South Carolina, such large power increases do not seem excessive.[1]

Interconnections and Reliability. Three large electrical power companies (Duke Power Company, Carolina Power and Light Company, and the South Carolina Electric and Gas Company), all of which are local or adjacent to Metrolina, are members of the Southeastern Electric Reliability Council (SERC), an organization of power utilities devoted to insuring an adequate and reliable power supply. A number of very high-voltage, high-capacity interconnection lines, some at 500,000 volts, are to be installed. These lines should give increased reliability and allow sharing of very large generating units, such as the McGuire station, thus leading to a more efficient operation. Some 450 miles of 500-kilovolt (one kilovolt equals 1,000 volts) transmission lines will be in service among the three companies in 1975, with a major portion completed by 1972. One 500-kilovolt line will run from McGuire northwards and somewhat east of Statesville into Virginia, another will connect Metrolina with the Oconee Nuclear Plant in South Carolina, and still another will run from Oconee into Union County.

1. Concern has been expressed by individuals in Metrolina as well as elsewhere on questions of the safety of nuclear power plants. Interested readers may wish to obtain copies of Public Law 85-256 (September 2, 1957) 42 U.S.C. 2210, known as The Price-Anderson Act, and the Atomic Energy Commission's document WASH-740, "Theoretical Possibilities and Consequences of Major Accidents in Large Nuclear Power Plants," March 22, 1957. Before reading these documents the reader should know that few congressional acts and few AEC documents have been as extensively reviewed as these. One should also be aware that safety criteria have been established on a national rather than a local level.

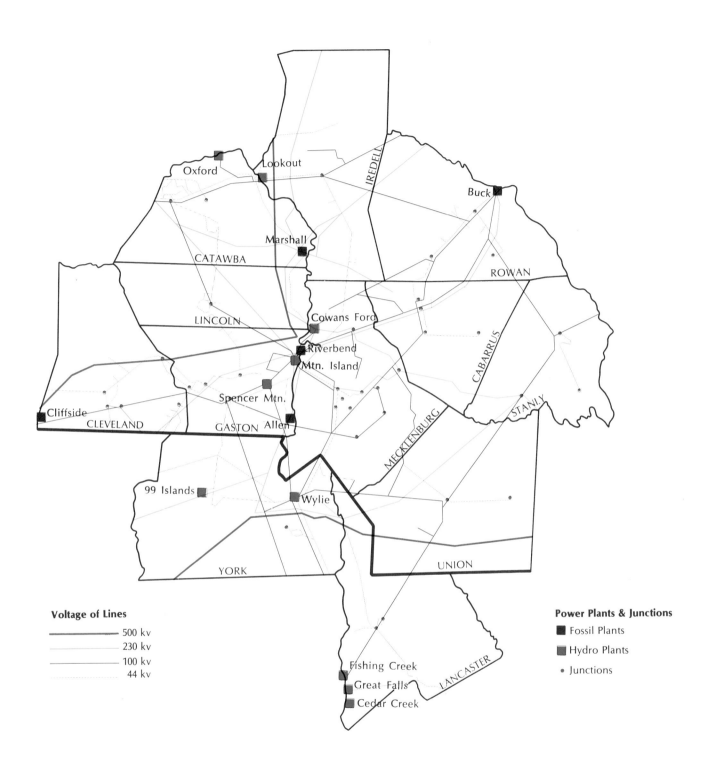

Voltage of Lines

———————— 500 kv
———————— 230 kv
———————— 100 kv
·············· 44 kv

Power Plants & Junctions

■ Fossil Plants

■ Hydro Plants

· Junctions

Fig. 6.16. Electric Power Stations and Transmission Lines in Metrolina

Waste Heat Disposal. Steam power plants have an over-all efficiency of about 40 percent in converting heat into electricity. Current nuclear power reactors are somewhat less efficient. The unused heat must be disposed of into the receiving waters by way of the generating plant's steam condensers. As future increased demands are made on the heat-receiving capacity of rivers and reservoirs, other means of cooling are called for in Metrolina as well as in much of the rest of the nation.

The Future. Since 1904 electric power demands in Metrolina have doubled on the average of each 10.8 years. Metrolina electric power demand is expected to double again during the next eight years and quadruple by 1985. It is obvious that enormous increases in generating capacity will be necessary. Because of the developing scarcity of fossil fuels it is likely that nuclear power will find increased application in and near Metrolina as well as in most of the rest of the nation.

A large portion of the Atomic Energy Commission's research and development money for nuclear power has been devoted over the last several years to a different type of reactor, known as the fast-breeder reactor. The utility industry has committed substantial funds to breeder-reactor technology. It is believed that this device will both generate power economically and at the same time convert currently unusable uranium (the uranium U238, which makes up 139 of 140 atoms in natural uranium) to plutonium 239. This artificially produced plutonium 239 is then available to produce power in a fashion similar to the naturally existing fissionable uranium 235. If more plutonium is produced than uranium 235 fissioned, it is a "breeder" system. There are important engineering, economic, and safety problems connected with the fast-breeder reactor, but none that appear beyond existing competence to solve. Thus it is believed a future nuclear fuel shortage should not occur.

There is much hope that a sustained fusion reaction can be developed in the more distant future. This process requires enormously powerful magnets of highly specialized design. With these it is hoped that certain of the lightest elements—isotopes of hydrogen, for example— can be welded together into helium with a simultaneous release of energy. The fusion fuel available from the ocean is known to be enormous by almost any standard. Although no sustained reaction has been reported, the result of practical fusion-reactor power-generating stations could have far-reaching implications for economic development throughout the world.

Carlos G. Bell, Jr.

Telephone Service

Telephone service in the Metrolina area is provided by eight separate telephone companies, one cooperative, and one municipally owned system. There are approximately 350,000 subscribers served by sixty-three exchanges located in the area with over 600,000 telephone connections. The latter include extension telephones and business-private branch-exchange service.

Metrolina subscribers place nearly 3.5 million long distance calls each month, including calls to overseas points, across the nation, or in some cases, to other exchanges within the Metrolina area where the interconnection is still on a long-distance basis. A substantial part of this volume of long-distance calling is between exchanges in the Metrolina region despite the fact that there are seventy-five different "extended-area service" arrangements joining selected individual exchanges together on a "toll-free" basis. An extended area service arrangement is one that permits calling between specific exchanges without a long-distance charge applying. The cost of the service is included in the basic monthly rate for local calling.

Each of Metrolina's sixty-three telephone exchanges and extended-area service arrangements is based on a "community of interest" set of criteria, encompassing various elements of regional economic-cultural homogeneity. Because community of interest ignores political boundaries such as county lines, the boundaries of the separate exchanges and the interconnecting extended-area service arrangements frequently cross county lines and even state lines. For instance, since the textile industry uses most of the exchanges in Gaston County and occupations and employment in this industry tie together the community of interest between telephone subscribers connected to these exchanges, nearly all the exchanges are connected by extended-service arrangements. Further, the easternmost of these exchanges, Belmont and Mount Holly, are interconnected to Charlotte and the westernmost, Kings Mountain, is interconnected to Shelby and Grover. But the community of interest between Kings Mountain and Charlotte and between Belmont or Mount Holly and Shelby is not sufficient to justify an extended-area service arrangement among them. The location of these exchanges and the extent to which they are interconnected by extended-area service arrangements are displayed in Fig. 6.17. The legend at the bottom of the figure shows the approximate area served by the different companies involved in providing service to Metrolina subscribers.

George K. Selden, Jr.

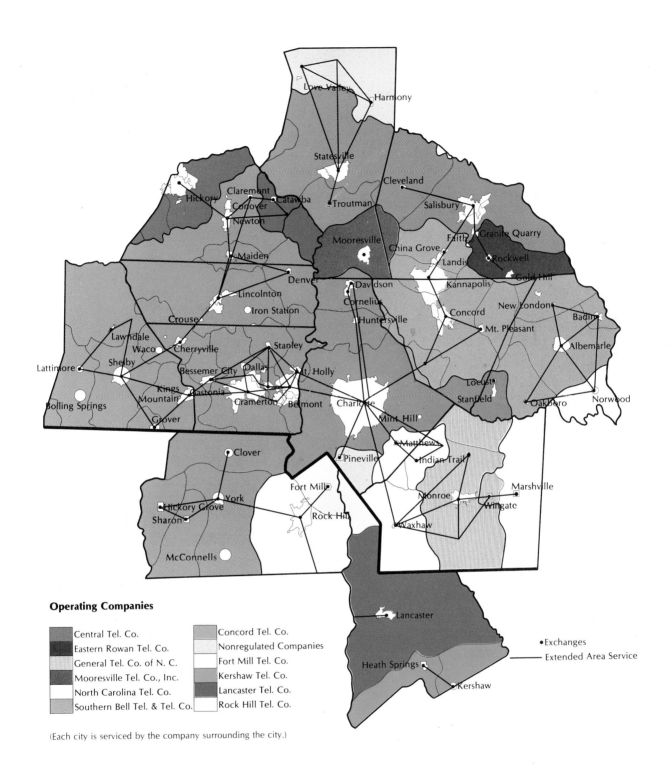

Operating Companies

Central Tel. Co.
Eastern Rowan Tel. Co.
General Tel. Co. of N. C.
Mooresville Tel. Co., Inc.
North Carolina Tel. Co.
Southern Bell Tel. & Tel. Co.

Concord Tel. Co.
Nonregulated Companies
Fort Mill Tel. Co.
Kershaw Tel. Co.
Lancaster Tel. Co.
Rock Hill Tel. Co.

• Exchanges
Extended Area Service

(Each city is serviced by the company surrounding the city.)

Fig. 6.17. Metrolina Telephone Exchanges

REFERENCES

Fleischer, G. A. "Effect of Highway Improvement on Travel
Time." *Highway Research Record* 12 (1963): 19-47.

Garrison, W. L.; B. J. L. Berry; D. F. Marble; J. D. Nystuen; and
R. L. Morrill. *Studies of Highway Development and Geographic
Change.* Seattle: University of Washington Press, 1959.

Haggett, Peter, and Richard J. Chorley. *Network Analysis in
Geography.* New York: St. Martin's Press, 1969.

Horton, F., ed. *Geographic Studies of Urban Transportation and
Network Analysis.* Northwestern University, Studies in Geography no. 16. Evanston, Ill.: Northwestern University, 1968.

Joint Committee on Atomic Energy, U.S. Congress. *Atomic
Energy Legislation Through 91st Congress, 1st Session.* Washington, D.C.: U.S. Government Printing Office, December 1969.

Kansky, K. J. *Structure of Transportation Networks,* Department
of Geography Research Paper no. 84. Chicago: University of
Chicago Press, 1963.

North Carolina Rural Electrification Authority. *Directory of Electric Power Agencies Serving Rural North Carolina.* Raleigh:
North Carolina Rural Electrification Authority, January 1971.

North Carolina Utilities Commission. *Third Statistical and Analytical Report, Data Through 1966.* Raleigh: The Commission,
March 1969.

Oi, W. Y., and P. W. Shuldiner. *An Analysis of Urban Travel Demands.* Evanston, Ill.: Transportation Center, Northwestern
University Press, 1962.

Smeed, R. J. "Road Development in Urban Areas: The Effect of
Some Kinds of Routing Systems on the Amount of Traffic in
the Central Areas of Towns." *Journal of the Institution of
Highway Engineers* 10 (1963): 5-26.

Smeed, R. J. "Traffic Studies and Urban Congestion." *Journal of
Transport Economics and Policy* 2 (1968): 1-38.

Southeast Regional Advisory Committee to the U.S. Federal Power
Commission. *Electric Power in the Southeast 1970–1980–
1990.* Washington, D.C.: U.S. Federal Power Commission,
April 1969.

U.S. Atomic Energy Commission. *Theoretical Possibilities and
Consequences of Major Accidents in Large Nuclear Power
Plants* (WASH-740). Washington, D.C.: U.S. Government
Printing Office, March 1957.

U.S. Federal Power Commission. *Statistics of Privately Owned
Electric Utilities in the United States, 1968.* Washington, D.C.:
U.S. Government Printing Office, October 1969.

U.S. Federal Power Commission. *Water Resources Appraisal for
Hydroelectric Licensing, Santee River Basin, North and South
Carolina.* Washington, D.C.: U.S. Federal Power Commission,
1970.

7. COMMUNICATIONS, TRADE, AND FINANCE

G. JACKSON BURNEY,
JERRY HENDRICK
THOMAS F. BAUCOM

"Commerce is a game of skill which every man cannot play, which few men can play well. The right merchant is one who has the just average of faculties we call common sense; a man of strong affinity for facts, who makes up his decision on what he has seen. He is thoroughly persuaded of the truths of arithmetic."—Ralph Waldo Emerson.

The people of Metrolina share the same TV stations, and in many instances, read the same newspaper. Depending on what he is shopping for, a person in Metrolina will frequently drive to other parts of the area for the best selection and bargains in retail stores. Interrelationship is further demonstrated by thousands of salesmen who fan out across Metrolina daily to sell goods and services to industry. Specialization of communications media has taken form in Metrolina as it has in many other parts of the country. Not only are radio stations specializing in format, so are radio networks. Seven different radio networks provide area residents with a variety of program fare coupled with an even more intensive variety of local programming. Three commercial television networks, four noncommercial networks, plus cable TV facilities, enable area TV audiences to choose from an assortment of programs.

In addition to major dailies, newspapers have sprung up to serve special interest and limited geographic markets, further expanding the color and variety of media available to Metrolina.

"Trade" is broadly defined to include not only retail and wholesale trade but also services. Metrolina has historically been an important trading center ever since the first white settlers began using the Great Trading Path of the Indians, a route that bisected the area from the northeast to the southwest in the 1700s. Today important new thoroughfares, including Interstates 40, 77, and 85, are reshaping the trading patterns in Metrolina. The availability of new products, rising income levels, and new patterns of living all affect this portion of the economy.

Almost twenty thousand persons earn their livelihood in finance, insurance, and real-estate activities in Metrolina. The financial institutions they work for aid the economy in a number of specialized functions. Because of their region-wide importance, banks and savings and loan institutions have been treated individually in this section. All other forms of financial institutions such as insurance companies, consumer-credit firms, mortgage banking, and stock brokers are grouped together under "Other Financial Institutions."

Newspapers

Metrolina's newspaper industry began in 1798 when the area's first paper, the *North Carolina Mercury and Salisbury Advertiser,* began publication. Today there are ten dailies and fifteen nondailies published within the twelve-county region. Eight Metrolina counties are "home" counties for at least one of the ten dailies. Nine are evening and one is a morning paper. The four largest nondailies are located in the remaining four counties.

The region's most widely circulated newspaper, the *Charlotte Observer,* has an extensive readership throughout twenty-one North Carolina counties and six South Carolina counties, in which at least 10 percent of the households in each county are reached. The *Observer*'s circulation outside its home county of Mecklenburg amounts to nearly 60 percent of its total circulation. It has the largest circulation of any newspaper between Atlanta, Georgia, and Washington, D.C.

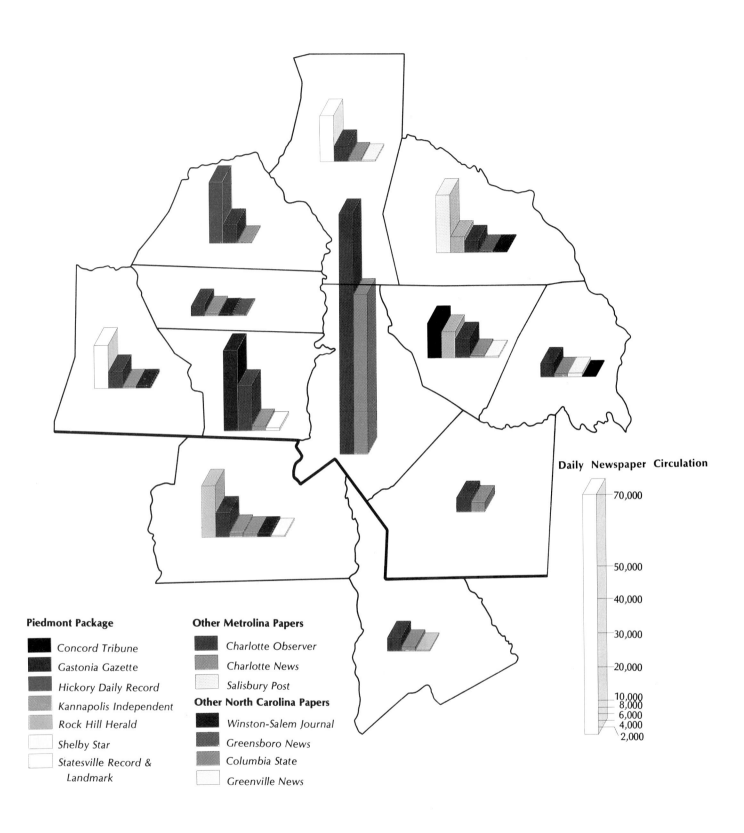

Piedmont Package

■ Concord Tribune

■ Gastonia Gazette

■ Hickory Daily Record

▨ Kannapolis Independent

▨ Rock Hill Herald

☐ Shelby Star

☐ Statesville Record & Landmark

Other Metrolina Papers

▨ Charlotte Observer

▨ Charlotte News

☐ Salisbury Post

Other North Carolina Papers

■ Winston-Salem Journal

▨ Greensboro News

▨ Columbia State

☐ Greenville News

Daily Newspaper Circulation

70,000

50,000

40,000

30,000

20,000

10,000
8,000
6,000
4,000
2,000

Fig. 7.1. Metrolina Newspaper Circulation

Fig. 7.1 reveals that although the *Charlotte Observer* is the major regional newspaper in Metrolina, local dailies are quite strong. Each local has the largest circulation of any paper within its home county with the exception of the *Charlotte News,* which nevertheless is the Carolinas' largest evening newspaper. The *Hickory Record* has a substantial circulation outside its home county of Catawba amounting to 27 percent of its total circulation, the highest such proportion of any local evening daily. In order to expand their regional advertising potential, seven of the local evening dailies along with three other dailies outside Metrolina formed the "Piedmont Evening Package," whereby an advertiser with a single order can run an ad in all participating papers.

Nondaily newspapers in Metrolina range in circulation from 1,300 to slightly over 10,000 per week. The four largest nondailies with their weekly circulations are the *Stanly News and Press* (10,300), the *Monroe Enquirer-Journal* (9,500), the *Lincoln Time-News* (7,600), and the *Lancaster News* (6,400). Each is situated in counties that are the least populated and the most rural. As these counties develop further, the large nondailies may eventually form the basis of strong local dailies.

Outside newspapers, surprisingly, do not have as much as a 10 percent household readership in any one Metrolina county. The largest penetrations occur in Iredell County where the *Winston-Salem Journal* has about a 5 percent readership and in Lancaster County where the *Columbia State* has almost a 9 percent readership. Parts of these two counties form the outermost extremities of Metrolina, which explains their greater penetration by outside newspapers.

There are marked differences in newspaper readership among the Metrolina counties. Mecklenburg has a 70 percent readership of morning dailies while the seven other counties with local dailies have an evening readership of over 50 percent. Cabarrus County leads with an 85 percent evening readership. Counties with no local dailies show a larger proportion of morning readership. For Metrolina as a whole, evening newspapers are read more than morning papers.

Television

The urban, suburban, and rural sections of Metrolina have been united more by television than by any other medium. The extent of Charlotte and Hickory TV broadcast areas is portrayed in Fig. 7.2 in terms of computed Grade B contours, which largely comprise three factors for each station: (1) effective radiated power, (2) antenna height, and (3) channel (frequency). Normally the higher the channel, the greater the required power to create an acceptable quality of picture. Grade B contours define a geographical area in which the quality of service is expected to be satisfactory to the median viewer at least 90 percent of the time for at least 50 percent of the receiving locations in the absence of interfering cochannel and adjacent-channel signals. As Fig. 7.2 shows, the Charlotte stations cover a radius of up to eighty-five miles.

Surveys made by the TV industry delineate TV market areas in terms of combinations of counties in which household viewing preference reflects a particular group of television stations. The Charlotte TV market area or "TV Area of Dominant Influence" is an elongated region (similar to the trade area of Charlotte newspapers, as defined by the Audit Bureau of Circulations). This shape results in part from the nearby adjacent-channel stations of Greensboro, High Point, Columbia, and Greenville, limiting the reception of Metrolina's TV stations in the northeast and to the southwest. The Charlotte TV market is economically viable, for of the six TV markets within the Carolinas Charlotte predominates in total time sales and broadcast income. TV-radio contrast is emphasized by the Charlotte TV stations, which receive thirty times the $196,000 total broadcast income of Charlotte radio stations. (See Tables 7.1 and 7.2.)

Radio

Although television is more regionally oriented, radio stations are primarily local. Radio's local role results largely from limited radio-clear channels plus transmitter power restrictions. Radio is quite competitive; there are seven radio stations in Metrolina for every TV station and over two radio stations for every newspaper.

Metrolina can boast the South's first radio station, WBT in Charlotte—Metrolina's 50,000-watt radio voice. There are at least five additional Metrolina AM stations whose wattage and programming combine to identify them as regional in character. In all there are forty AM and fifteen FM radio stations in Metrolina; twenty-three of the AM stations operate during the daytime only. As a group Charlotte's ten AM and AM/FM radio stations, when compared with those of six other major metropolitan areas in North and South Carolina in 1969, had the highest time sales and broadcast revenues yet were the second lowest in broadcast income. And the broadcast income average for Charlotte radio stations was slightly below the national average. This points to the sharp competition with which the Charlotte radio broadcasting industry must contend.

Radio provides an important service to the local community by offering a high degree of specialization. The radio listener has a wide range of program sources, particularly if his set receives both AM and FM. In a few cases listeners can also receive "carrier-current" radio stations which can be received within a few feet of the electrical wiring in the building housing the station. Such stations (which require no license) have become popular particular-

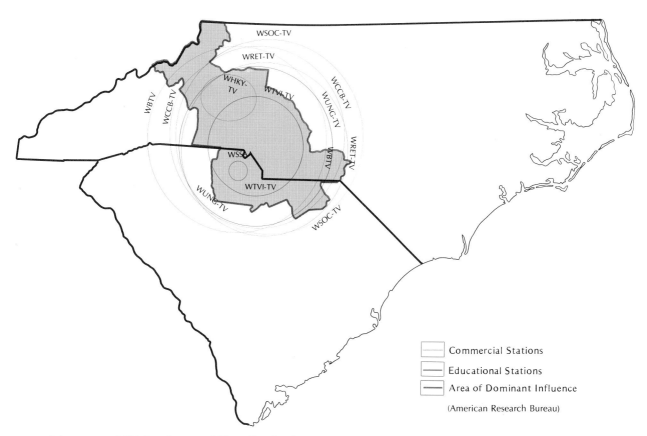

Fig. 7.2 (a). Range of TV Dominance of Metrolina Stations

Legend:
Commercial Stations
Educational Stations
Area of Dominant Influence
(American Research Bureau)

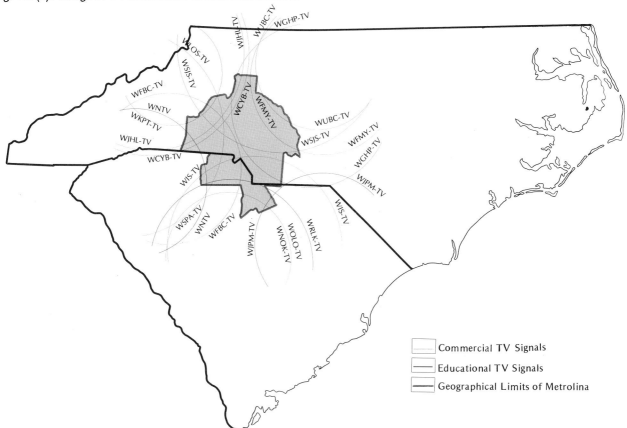

Fig. 7.2 (b). Reception of TV Signals from Stations Outside Metrolina

Legend:
Commercial TV Signals
Educational TV Signals
Geographical Limits of Metrolina

Table 7.1. 1969 TV Market Data: FCC Broadcast Expenditures by Advertisers

	Charlotte	Greensboro High Point Winston-Salem	Greenville Spartanburg Asheville	Greenville Washington New Bern	Columbia	Raleigh Durham
Total Time Sales (in millions)	$11.3	$8.4	$7.6	$3.8	$4.1	$6.9
Total Broadcast Revenues (in millions)	$9.8	$7.3	$6.7	$3.6	$3.8	$6.1
Source of Time Sales						
Network	19%	19%	19%	25%	18%	30%
National and Regional	52%	46%	60%	46%	50%	44%
Local	29%	35%	21%	29%	32%	26%
Total Broadcast Income (in millions)	$3.1	$2.4	$2.6	$0.7	$1.2	$1.9
Income As Percent of Revenues	32%	33%	39%	19%	32%	32%
Number of Stations	4	4	3	3	3	3

Table 7.2. Metrolina TV Log

Location	Station	Channel	Effective Radiated Power	Height Above Average Terrain	Height Above Mean Sea Level	Network
Charlotte, N.C.	WBTV	3 VHF	100 kw	1,090'	1,878'	CBS
	WSOC-TV	9 VHF	316 kw	1,190'	1,929'	NBC
	WCCB-TV	18 UHF	5,000 kw	1,295'	2,049'	ABC
	WRET-TV	36 UHF	1,330 kw	1,350'	2,049'	IND
	WTVI[a]	42 UHF	214 kw	450'	1,172'	PBS, SEN
Concord, N.C.	WUNG-TV[a]	58 UHF	550 kw	1,290'	2,049'	NCETV
Hickory, N.C.	WHKY	14 UHF	8.91 kw	600'	1,648'	IND
Rock Hill, S.C.	W55AA[b]	55 UHF	100 w	—	—	ETS

a. Educational/Public.
b. Translator of WRLK-TV, Columbia, S.C.
VHF—Very high frequency.
UHF—Ultra high frequency.
kw—kilowatts (w = watts).
CBS—Columbia Broadcasting System.
NBC—National Broadcasting Company.

ABC—American Broadcasting Company.
PBS—Public Broadcasting Service.
SEN—Southern Educational Network.
NCETV—North Carolina Educational Television Network.
ETS—Educational Television Station.
IND—Independent.

Table 7.3. Metrolina Radio Log

Location	Station	Frequency	Power Day	Power Night	Network	Directional Day	Directional Night
Charlotte, N.C.	WAME	1,480 kc	5 kw	5 kw	—	Yes	Yes
	WAYS	610 kc	5 kw	1 kw	ABC-C	No	No
	WBT	1,110 kc	50 kw	50 kw	—	No	Yes
	WBT-FM	107.9 mc	100 kw	100 kw	—	No	No
	WGIV	1,600 kc	1 kw	500 w	—	No	Yes
	WIST	1,240 kc	1 kw	250 w	Tobacco	No	No
	WRNA (FM)	95.1 mc	100 kw	100 kw	—	No	No
	WKTC	1,310 kc	1 kw	—	MBS	No	—
	WRPL	1,540 kc	1 kw	—	—	No	—
	WSOC	930 kc	5 kw	1 kw	NBC	No	Yes
	WSOC-FM	103.7 mc	100 kw	100 kw	ABC-FM	No	No
	WYFM (FM)	104.7 mc	3.8 kw	3.8 kw	—	No	No
Monroe, N.C.	WIXE	1,190 kc	500 w	500 w	MBS	No	No
	WMAP	1,060 kc	250 w	—	ABC-C	No	—
Albemarle, N.C.	WABZ	1,010 kc	1 kw	—	—	No	—
	WABZ-FM	100.9 mc	3 kw	3 kw	—	No	No
	WZKY	1,580 kc	250 w	—	Tobacco	No	—
Belmont, N.C.	WCGC	1,270 kc	1 kw	500 w	ABC-I	No	Yes
Cherryville, N.C.	WCSL	1,590 kc	500 w	—	—	No	—
Concord, N.C.	WEGO	1,410 kc	1 kw	—	Tobacco	No	—
	WPEG (FM)	97.9 mc	10 kw	10 kw	Tobacco	No	No
Dallas, N.C.	WAAK	960 kc	1 kw	—	—	No	—
Gastonia, N.C.	WGAS	1,420 kc	500 w	—	Tobacco	No	—
	WGNC	1,450 kc	250 w	250 w	ABC-E	No	No
	WGNC-FM	101.9 mc	11.1 kw	11.1 kw	—	No	No
	WLTC	1,370 kc	5 kw	—	—	No	—
Hickory, N.C.	WHKY	1,290 kc	5 kw	1 kw	ABC-E	No	Yes
	WHKY-FM	102.9 mc	14.8 kw	14.8 kw	ABC-FM	No	No
	WIRC	630 kc	1 kw	—	ABC-I	No	—
	WXRC (FM)	95.7 mc	27 kw	27 kw	Tobacco	No	No
	WSPF	1,000 kc	1 kw	—	—	No	—
Kannapolis, N.C.	WGTL	870 kc	1 kw	—	—	No	—
	WRKB	1,460 kc	500 w	—	—	No	—
	WRKB-FM	99.7 mc	10 kw	10 kw	—	No	No
Kings Mountain, N.C.	WKMT	1,220 kc	1 kw	—	—	No	—
Lincolnton, N.C.	WLON	1,050 kc	1 kw	—	Tobacco	No	—
Mooresville, N.C.	WHIP	1,350 kc	1 kw	—	—	No	—
Newton, N.C.	WNNC	1,230 kc	1 kw	250 w	—	No	No
Salisbury, N.C.	WSAT	1,280 kc	1 kw	1 kw	—	No	Yes
	WSTP	1,490 kc	1 kw	250 w	MBS Tobacco	No	No
	WRDX (FM)	106.5 mc	15 kw	15 kw	MBS Tobacco	No	No
Shelby, N.C.	WADA	1,390 kc	1 kw	500 w	Tobacco	No	Yes
	WOHS	730 kc	1 kw	—	MBS	No	No
	WOHS-FM	96.1 mc	2.6 kw	2.6 kw	—	No	No
Statesville, N.C.	WDBM	550 kc	500 w	—	—	No	—
	WDBM-FM	96.9 mc	3.6 kw	3.6 kw	—	No	No
	WSIC	1,400 kc	1 kw	250 w	ABC-C Tobacco	No	No
	WFMX (FM)	105.7 mc	52 kw	52 kw	Tobacco	No	No
Kershaw, S.C.	WKSC	1,300 kc	500 w	—	Tobacco	No	—
Lancaster, S.C.	WAGL	1,560 kc	10 kw	—	ABC-E	No	—
	WLCM	1,360 kc	1 kw	—	—	No	—
	WLCM-FM	107.1 mc	3 kw	—	—	No	No
Rock Hill, S.C.	WRHI	1,340 kc	1 kw	250 w	MBS	No	No
	WTYC	1,150 kc	1 kw	—	—	No	—
York, S.C.	WYCL	980 kc	1 kw	—	Tobacco	Yes	—

Note: The maximum power imposed upon radio stations is 50,000 watts for AM stations and 100,000 watts for FM stations.

w = watts.
kw = kilowatts.
kc = kilocycles.
mc = megacycles.
ABC-C = American Broadcasting Company-Contemporary.
ABC-E = American Broadcasting Company-Entertainment.

ABC-I = American Broadcasting Company-Information.
ABC-FM = American Broadcasting Company-Frequency Modulation.
NBC = National Broadcasting Company.
MBS = Mutual Broadcasting System.
Tobacco = Tobacco Radio.

ly on school campuses. Normally the distance at which a radio station can be received depends upon its frequency, power, and antenna array; but at night the ionosphere forms an invisible reflecting layer by which radio "sky wave" signals can reach far beyond the extent of their daytime "ground wave." (See Table 7.3.)

Postal Service

The United States postal system has experienced many changes since 1794 when mail was delivered in the Metrolina region by stagecoach in a biweekly Salisbury-Concord-Charlotte-Statesville route and back. Mail service improved with the beginning of railroads in the 1850s and expanded at the turn of the century by providing free city and rural delivery. Mail delivery in Metrolina quickened with the start of air-mail service at Charlotte in 1930 and with the introduction of the zip-code delivery system in 1963. On July 1, 1971, the United States Postal Service superseded the United States Post Office Department in a reorganization aimed at improving the quality of postal service.

In the Metrolina area the two postal sectional centers, Charlotte and Hickory, have acquired extended authority and responsibility. Formerly independent post offices are now functioning as associate offices directly accountable to either Hickory or Charlotte, both of which have been assigned more administrative duties. Problems beyond the control of each sectional center are referred first to the North Carolina District Office at Greensboro and then to the regional postal headquarters for eleven southern states located at Memphis, Tennessee.

During 1970 the Charlotte post office processed about two million pieces of mail a day of which only about one-third originated within the Charlotte delivery area. In fact, the majority of the mail passing through Charlotte originates outside Metrolina. Charlotte's area role is explained by its superior air service and partly because Charlotte is one of the few sectional centers having a mechanical mail sorter. The Charlotte post office expects all mail collected by its associate post offices to be sent directly to it for processing in order to reduce the time spent handling the mail. The large volume of mail handled at Charlotte is indicated by the fact that in 1970 Charlotte represented only about .1 percent of the nation's total population while the amount of mail processed through its post office was about .7 percent of the country's total volume of mail.

Fig. 7.3 is a generalized picture of the postal system in Metrolina in the form of a zip-code delivery-area map. Small areas with no delivery service are included within an adjacent delivery area and those that have overlapping delivery service are divided between the respective delivery areas. Revenues for each of the eighty-seven zip-code delivery areas (comprising a total of 114 different zip codes) portray the relative size and importance of mail delivery across Metrolina. The pattern closely resembles that of a 1970 population density map. Revenues in 1970 for all of Metrolina's 144 listed post offices totaled more than $25 million for an estimated total of 356 million pieces of originating mail annually.

Several private firms in Metrolina offer services competitive with the United States Postal Service. Those offering parcel-post service have been very successful in the region, especially United Parcel Service, which serves the whole South. Two more recently established firms offer both third- and second-class mail service.

Retail Market

Retailing had a rather unsettled start in Metrolina when in 1671 a merchant named James Needham was reportedly murdered by an Indian at Trading Ford on the Yadkin River in what is now Rowan County. From those times of "backwoods bartering," Metrolina has grown into a giant retail market drawing customers from areas far beyond the boundaries of the twelve counties. In fact, a slightly larger area that includes Metrolina has been identified by the New Yorker magazine as one of the top forty markets nationwide for sales of quality merchandise.

As shown in Fig. 7.4, Metrolina attracts considerably more dollars in retail sales than it loses to other retail centers, with a net annual gain of approximately $180 million. Mecklenburg County, as would be expected, has enjoyed the largest drawing power, but as Fig. 7.4 indicates this is for the most part not at the expense of other Metrolina counties. And whatever other Metrolina cities may lose to Charlotte by way of retail volume is apparently balanced by dollars coming in from elsewhere.

Historically the development of retailing in Metrolina has probably centered more around the "mill store" than in most other places. Large textile companies for many years operated the major retailing outlets within villages that were constructed for mill employees. This was a convenient method of extending credit, especially since eventual collection was assured as long as the customer was employed by the mill. J. B. Ivey, founder of the Ivey's stores (department stores and specialty stores in five Metrolina locations and eleven others in the Carolinas and Florida), had early merchandising experience in managing mill stores in Cleveland County.

One town in Metrolina still maintains the tradition of the mill store. The carefully planned central business district of Kannapolis exhibits the uniformity and scale of a shopping center. It is the result of a major project of the manufacturing company that dominates the town, Cannon Mills. Kannapolis remains a unique unincorporated "company town" to this day.

Retailing in Metrolina developed through substantial store branching. The twentieth century has seen many of

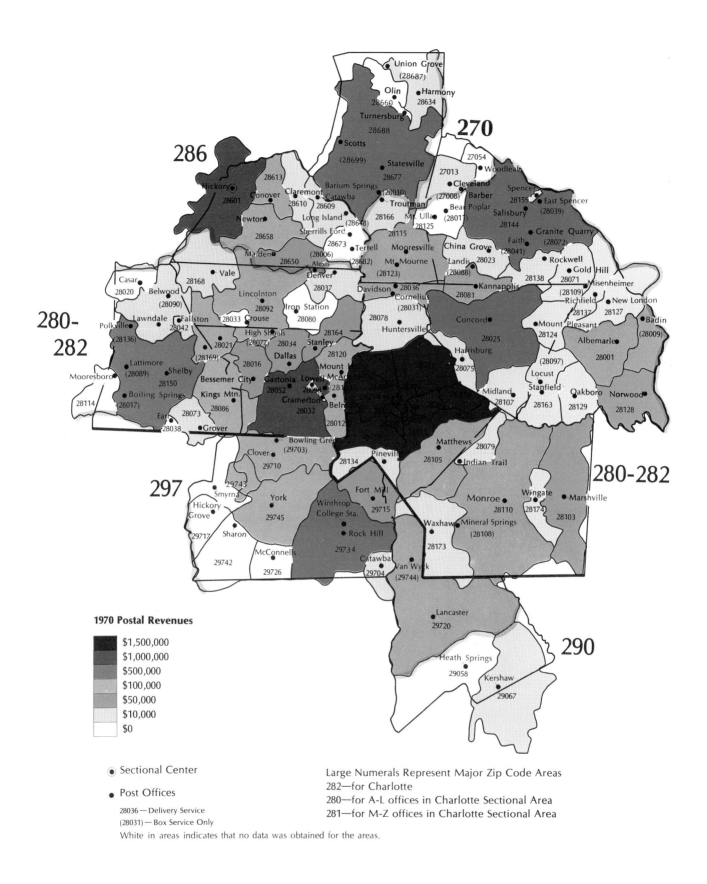

1970 Postal Revenues

- $1,500,000
- $1,000,000
- $500,000
- $100,000
- $50,000
- $10,000
- $0

◉ Sectional Center

● Post Offices

28036 — Delivery Service

(28031) — Box Service Only

White in areas indicates that no data was obtained for the areas.

Large Numerals Represent Major Zip Code Areas

282—for Charlotte

280—for A-L offices in Charlotte Sectional Area

281—for M-Z offices in Charlotte Sectional Area

Fig. 7.3. Metrolina Postal Zip Code Areas and Postal Revenues

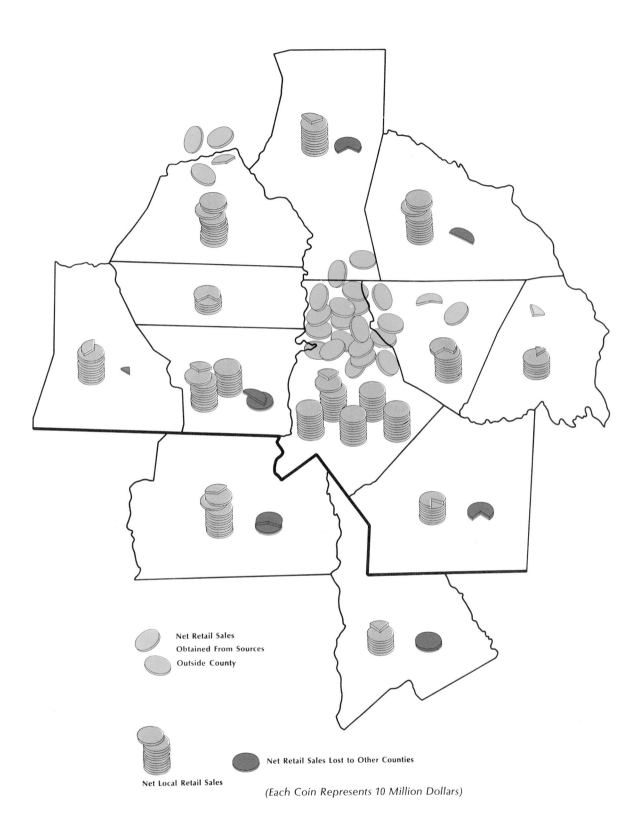

Net Retail Sales
Obtained From Sources
Outside County

Net Retail Sales Lost to Other Counties

Net Local Retail Sales

(Each Coin Represents 10 Million Dollars)

Fig. 7.4. Metrolina Retail Sales Drawing Power

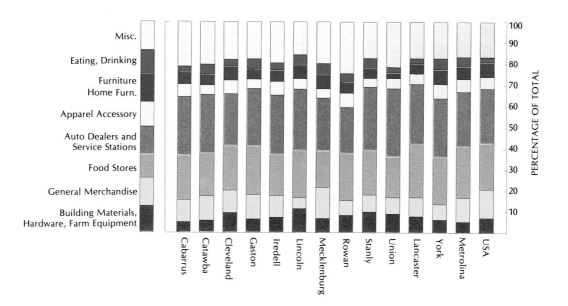

Fig. 7.5. Types of Retail Trade in Metrolina, by County

the most successful stores indigenous to the area branch into other Metrolina locations, the Carolinas, and adjoining states. Indicative of this tendency is the Belk group with a buying service located in Charlotte and over four hundred stores throughout the South. Belk stores originated in Monroe, and today a Belk store or a Belk partnership is the largest downtown store in almost every sizable Metrolina community.

A drive along the major highways of Metrolina reveals a world of retailing unheard of at the turn of the century. Today a major component of retailing, the shopping center, offers those time-honored goods found in department stores, apparel stores, furniture shops, and drug stores, along with specialty shops and, frequently, amusements and restaurants, all serviced with ample free parking. Along with the shopping center have come "strip developments," areas of specialization where automobile dealers, for example, have located near one another. Other types of "strips" include mobile home dealers and recreational equipment dealers.

In recent years large national retailers, most noticeably discount stores, have located in Charlotte and have also found key locations in the smaller cities of the region. Of the fifty largest retail groups in the country listed by *Fortune* magazine, twenty-one have some type of operation in Metrolina.

There are ninety-one shopping centers in Metrolina, and shopping malls have become increasingly popular. During the last ten years an average of five shopping centers has been added yearly to the Metrolina landscape. The lead-

ing example of a major regional shopping center is Charlotte's South Park, with over seventy-five stores. Offering one million square feet of retail space mostly on an internal mall, South Park opened in 1971 as the largest shopping center between Washington and Atlanta. Many of its five thousand parking spaces are located under the store area.

Nevertheless most central business districts in Metrolina's cities have remained attractive and active though declining in their proportion of total retail volume. Automobile dealers alone, by moving to strip developments, have accounted for a large part of the shift. Also, in recent years food stores have tended to avoid central business-district locations. But generally retail activity in downtown areas continues to be healthy, probably because Metrolina's cities are not so large that problems of accessibility and traffic congestion have become excessive.

By 1967 total retail sales for Metrolina had passed the $1.6 billion mark, an increase of 37 percent over the previous five years. As of that year there were 9,749 establishments employing 47,676 people. With retail sales per household at $5,180, Metrolina stands above the annual average for either North Carolina or South Carolina but still substantially below the figure for the nation as a whole, primarily because of an income level also less than the national average. (See Fig. 7.5.) In addition, the difference is accentuated by the fact that Metrolina contains a large rural nonfarm population whose grocery needs are met somewhat by home gardening. The contribution of food-store sales to total retail sales in Metrolina compared to the equivalent national percentage confirms this fact. The oppo-

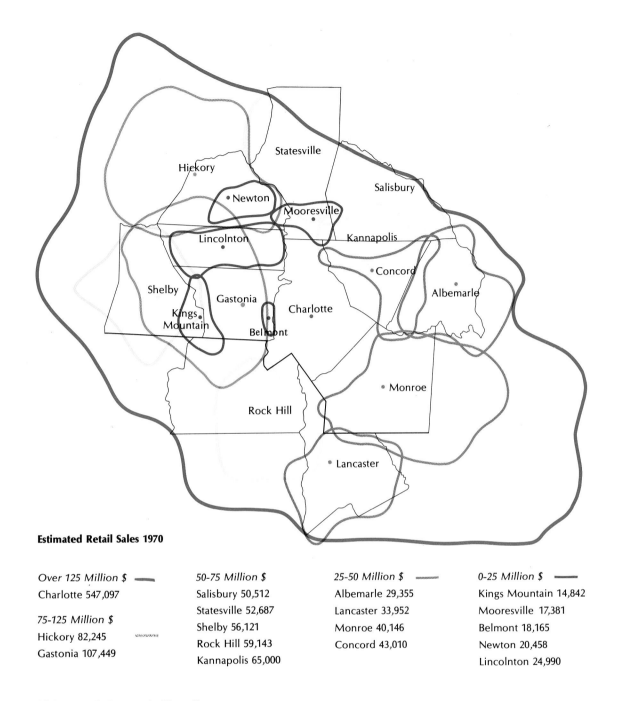

Estimated Retail Sales 1970

Over 125 Million $ ▬▬	*50-75 Million $*	*25-50 Million $* ══	*0-25 Million $* ▬▬
Charlotte 547,097	Salisbury 50,512	Albemarle 29,355	Kings Mountain 14,842
	Statesville 52,687	Lancaster 33,952	Mooresville 17,381
75-125 Million $	Shelby 56,121	Monroe 40,146	Belmont 18,165
Hickory 82,245	Rock Hill 59,143	Concord 43,010	Newton 20,458
Gastonia 107,449	Kannapolis 65,000		Lincolnton 24,990

Fig. 7.6. Major Retail Centers in Metrolina

site is true of automobile retailing, where Metrolina exceeds the nation proportionally. The area's dispersed population pattern has contributed to more commuting, hence a greater dependence upon the automobile.

A very generalized view of the trade areas of Metrolina's major retail centers (see Fig. 7.6) shows the geographic pattern of retail trade. None of the trade areas are as completely dominant as some that are frequently found in other regions in the nation. The numerous medium-sized trade centers in Metrolina are evidence of a rather well-dispersed urban region.

A trade area represents the theoretical retail outreach of an urban center according to the level of specialty goods it offers. It is an area in which most of the people are more likely to make a shopping trip to its retail center for items not so available in smaller communities nearby. The shopping trip varies from a weekly basis in and around the retail center to a seasonal basis near the fringe of the trade area where shoppers are less attached to any one retail center, hence the frequent overlapping of trade areas.

The size and shape of a trade area depends upon its consumer population and the nearness of competitive retail centers. For example, it might be assumed that Monroe has a greater volume of retail trade than Salisbury because of Monroe's larger trade area but the reverse is true because Salisbury serves a more populous urbanized area while Monroe draws upon a less dense rural setting. Charlotte's elongated trade area reflects the absence of large retail centers to the northwest and southeast and the presence of the large centers of Greensboro and Winston-Salem to the northeast and Greenville and Spartanburg to the southwest.

Services

Services, the fastest growing sector of the national economy and of the Metrolina economy as well, increased 72 percent in employment during the last ten years in the United States and 74 percent in Metrolina. It includes a wide variety of enterprises ranging from hotels and motels to advertising agencies, repair services, laundries and dry-cleaning establishments, architectural and engineering services, non-profit organizations (such as the Chamber of Commerce), and funeral homes. These enterprises present great possibilities for continued growth in Metrolina because of higher income levels, accelerating urbanization, and the increasing impact of educational training programs. Schools in the area, especially community colleges, are gearing courses of study to the skills required by service occupations. Receipts from services amount to over $250 million annually, and service establishments employ approximately 43,000 people. Catawba County led all the Metrolina counties in the last ten years in the rate of increase in services employment.

Outstanding among services is the photographic studio business, which in Metrolina accounts for over $10 million annually, a greater volume than that of any of thirty-three states. This is primarily because of the presence of large national photo-studio firms which contract with department stores to provide photo services, especially children's pictures. Although the photographs of these firms may be taken at any location in the nation, they are shipped to Metrolina for processing before being returned to customers. Added to this is a large volume of business done in school-yearbook printing which provides selections of photographs as a related part of the service. Barber and beauty shops also hold an important place in Metrolina since their national trade association, the Associated Master Barbers and Beauticians, is headquartered in Charlotte. Finally, Metrolina is also an important motion-picture distribution point.

Wholesale Trade

Metrolina exceeds each of twenty-seven states in volume of wholesale sales. Furthermore, wholesaling, with $4.6 billion in 1967, accounted for greater sales than is contributed by any other economic sector within Metrolina. Yet manufacturing and retailing both exceed wholesaling in employment. In Metrolina there are over two thousand wholesale establishments employing nearly thirty thousand people. The annual payroll for wholesale employees stood at roughly a quarter of a billion dollars in 1969.

Charlotte's position as the wholesale center of the Carolinas is the primary reason for Metrolina's wholesale volume (see Fig. 7.7). Mecklenburg County accounts for 83 percent of the total wholesale sales in the twelve-county region; in wholesale employment Mecklenburg accounts for 71 percent and in a number of wholesale establishments, 61 percent. Charlotte ranks high nationally as a wholesale center. Among the sixty metropolitan areas with an annual volume of one billion dollars or more, Charlotte ranks first in wholesale sales per capita, first in wholesale sales per employee, and during the period 1958-67 ranked first in the South and third in the nation in the rate of increase in sales volume.

Wholesaling in Charlotte is a result of Metrolina's industry rather than strictly Charlotte's industry. The Carolinas' textile industry centered in and around Metrolina makes Charlotte one of the nation's most important marketing centers for synthetic fibers, dyes, and other textile chemicals. Because synthetic fibers are technically classified as "chemicals," Charlotte ranks fourth in the United States in wholesale sales of industrial chemicals, trailing only New York, Chicago, and Philadelphia.

A characteristic of wholesaling in Metrolina can be highlighted by comparing from Census of Business reports the volume of business done by merchant wholesalers with "other operating types." Merchant wholesalers are those businesses typically thought of as wholesale establishments engaged primarily in buying merchandise from producers and reselling to retailers and industry. "Other operating types" include manufacturers' sales branches and sales offices. The volume of wholesale business in Metrolina is particularly attributed to the sales branches of nationally operating companies, since 71 percent of the total wholesale volume is accounted for by these "other operating types." Charlotte especially exemplifies this tendency. Although it is the home of a number of prominent regional merchant wholesalers, it ranks highest in the nation in the proportion of wholesale volume accounted for by manufacturers' sales branches.

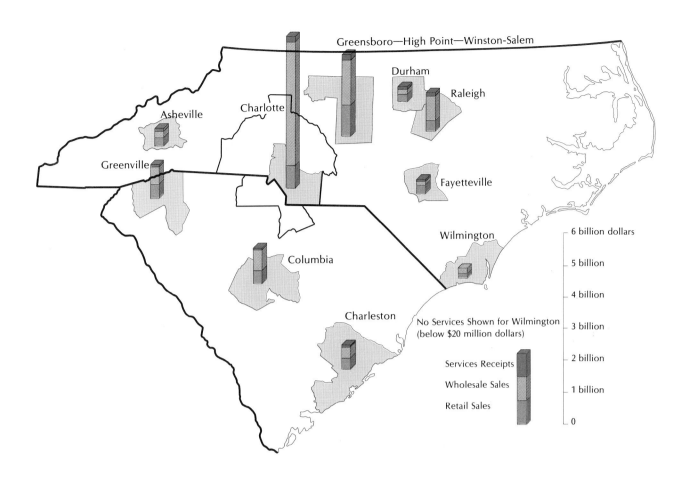

Fig. 7.7. Retail and Wholesale Sales and Services Receipts for SMSAs in North and South Carolina

Personal Income

Persons employed in Metrolina received $3.9 billion in personal income during 1969. Sources of income varied considerably from county to county.

For the size of their local economies, Lincoln and Rowan residents had a high income from real estate and investments, leading Metrolina in the percentage of local personal income derived from property. Only three Metrolina counties—Stanly, Lincoln and Cleveland—achieved a percentage of farm income equal to the average for the Carolinas. Each showed about 5 to 6 percent of its total personal income in farm earnings, excluding income of farm owners. The percentage of income from governmental earnings was higher in York and Rowan counties than in any of the other Metrolina counties; this income was undoubtedly boosted by the presence of Winthrop College in Rock Hill, which is state-supported, and the thousand-bed Veterans Hospital in Salisbury.

With over 40 percent of Metrolina's employees engaged in manufacturing, it is no surprise that manufacturing earnings represent such a high proportion of the total. For every hundred dollars of total personal income received in North Carolina, twenty-nine dollars came from manufacturing earnings while in Metrolina thirty-five dollars came from this source.

Manufacturing exceeds all other sources of personal income for Metrolina except for the Charlotte Standard Metropolitan Statistical Area (SMSA). In the Charlotte area wholesale and retail trade produced 17 percent greater personal earnings than manufacturing during 1969.

Fig. 7.8 shows the 1969 components of personal income for each Metrolina county. Mecklenburg and Union counties are combined into the Charlotte SMSA since the Department of Commerce does not separate the two counties for these compilations. During the ten-year span ending in 1969, total personal income grew by 128 percent within the twelve counties, a rate slightly higher than North Carolina's 123 percent.

In personal income per capita the Charlotte SMSA and Catawba, Cabarrus, Stanly, and Gaston counties exceeded the North Carolina estimated average of $2,934, and York

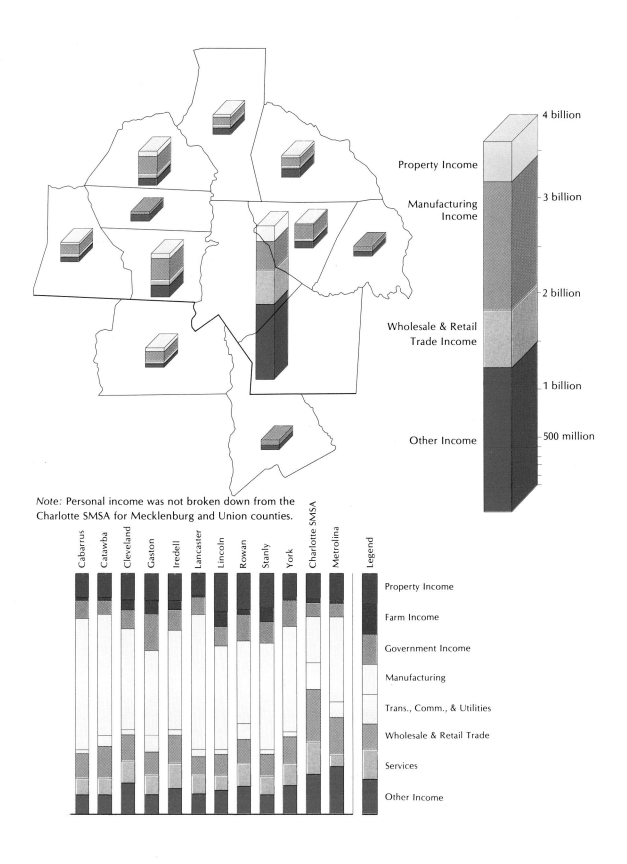

Note: Personal income was not broken down from the Charlotte SMSA for Mecklenburg and Union counties.

Cabarrus
Catawba
Cleveland
Gaston
Iredell
Lancaster
Lincoln
Rowan
Stanly
York
Charlotte SMSA
Metrolina
Legend

Property Income
Manufacturing Income
Wholesale & Retail Trade Income
Other Income

4 billion
3 billion
2 billion
1 billion
500 million

Property Income
Farm Income
Government Income
Manufacturing
Trans., Comm., & Utilities
Wholesale & Retail Trade
Services
Other Income

Fig. 7.8. Sources of Income in Metrolina, 1969

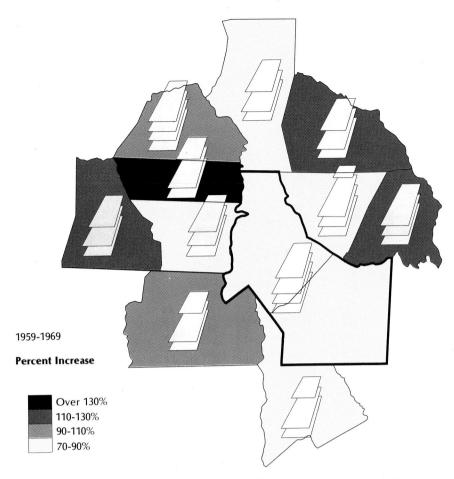

1959-1969

Percent Increase

- Over 130%
- 110-130%
- 90-110%
- 70-90%

Each Whole Bill Represents One Thousand Dollars

Fig. 7.9. Per Capita Personal Income in Metrolina

and Lancaster Counties were above the South Carolina estimated average of $2,537. However, only the Charlotte
SMSA and Catawba County had per capita incomes above
the national average of $3,955. Excluding the Charlotte
SMSA, these counties are strongly dependent on manufacturing as a source of personal income. On the other hand,
there appears to be a general tendency for counties with a
lower per capita income to exhibit a high dependence on
farm and governmental earnings as a source of income.
One curious situation is that of Lancaster County: it has
the highest percentage of county income from manufacturing earnings in Metrolina, yet it ranks as one of the lowest
in per capita personal income.

Banking

Metrolina is well served by banking institutions as evidenced
by its nearly three hundred banking offices, aggressive
bank-marketing programs, and numerous innovative ser-

vices offered the business community and the public. The
number of banking offices in relation to population in Metrolina is greater than that for the Carolinas as a whole.
With one bank for every 4,400 persons, Metrolina compares
favorably with the average for the Carolinas of one bank
for every 4,600 persons and the national average of 5,800
persons. In the last twenty years banking in Metrolina has
been characterized by mergers and rapid growth in deposits,
as well as extensive branching.

The national phenomenon of improved banking convenience is evidenced in Metrolina by increases in banking
offices and by the diversity of facilities such as those found
at airports, shopping malls, colleges, industrial parks, and
even an automated branch where customers can have, for
certain transactions, twenty-four-hour, seven-day-a-week
service. The last-named service is the first completely automated branch facility in the nation.

In 1970 banks in the twelve-county area held over 20
percent of the banking deposits of all North and South Carolina banks, even though Metrolina contained only 15 per-

Table 7.4. Metrolina Banking Profile, 1970

Category	Metrolina Counties	Carolinas	Metrolina Percentage of Carolinas		Mecklenburg Percentage of Metrolina	
Population	1,162,123	7,671,950	15%		31%	
Banking offices	264	1,667	16		33	
Population/Banking office	4,400	4,600	—		—	
			All Accounts	Accounts $100,000 Up	All Accounts	Accounts $100,000 Up
Deposits ($000)						
Checking accounts[a]	$836,251	$3,810,100	22%	33%	56%	78%
Savings accounts[b]	303,672	1,641,945	19	18	43	74
Other time accounts[c]	312,949	1,685,139	19	27	47	63
State, county, city[d]	153,580	809,783	19	20	53	62
All other accounts[e]	220,377	646,577	34	37	84	88
Total deposits	$1,826,829	$8,593,544	21%	30%	56%	77%

a. Individuals and businesses.
b. Individuals and nonprofit institutions.
c. Individuals and businesses.
d. Governments.
e. Correspondent banks, trust funds, etc.

cent of the population. The area possesses four of the nation's one hundred largest banks, two of which rank among the top three in the Southeast. Both Carolinas permit statewide branching, a fact that led substantially to these high rankings. (States are categorized as permitting statewide, limited, or no branching.)

Table 7.4 shows that Metrolina has nearly $2 billion in banking deposits. Banks in Mecklenburg County hold over half of this total. Mecklenburg's concentration is more evident in large corporate checking accounts where its banks hold nearly 80 percent of the twelve-county total and 88 percent of public funds, correspondent bank deposits, and trust funds.

Catawba County ranks second to Mecklenburg in size of banking deposits, but Mecklenburg's substantial concentration results in a six-to-one larger deposit level than Catawba.

The average Metrolina passbook-type savings account totals $900, whereas the average of all types of checking accounts in the area totals twice this amount. Though the average Metrolina savings account has the same amount as a typical savings account in the two Carolinas, checking

account balances, which include business accounts, average 40 percent above the two-state average, not an unexpected condition since Metrolina is more industrialized than coastal and mountain sections.

The Federal Reserve System located a branch of its Richmond bank at Charlotte in 1927. This facility serves most of North and South Carolina as the "banker's bank," thus providing faster check-clearing and other services for its members located throughout Metrolina. (See Fig. 7.10.)

Savings and Loan Associations

Savings and loan associations contribute substantially to the economy of the area since they represent the greatest amount of savings and credit related to home-buying and property ownership. Metrolina claims the Carolinas' oldest savings and loan, a Charlotte association which opened its doors in 1881. The majority of the existing associations were chartered in the late 1800s and early 1900s in a period that might be identified as the modern savings and loan movement. Generally speaking, the pace in the Carolinas

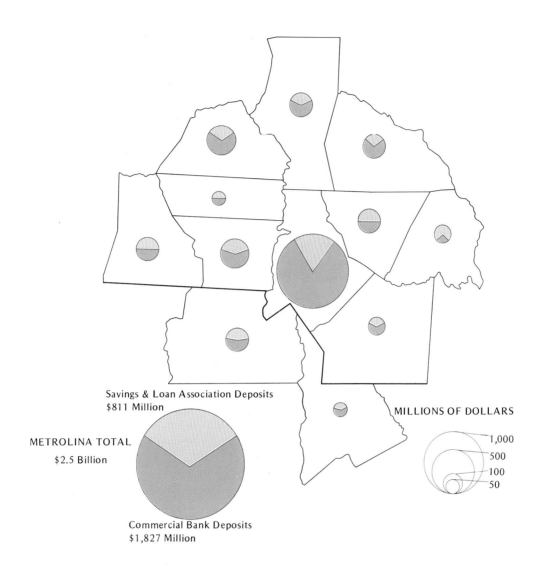

Savings & Loan Association Deposits
$811 Million

METROLINA TOTAL
$2.5 Billion

Commercial Bank Deposits
$1,827 Million

MILLIONS OF DOLLARS

1,000
500
100
50

Fig. 7.10. Metrolina Deposits by County, 1970

for the formation of savings and loan associations was somewhat behind that of the nation as a whole. These associations have grown phenomenally in recent years, however, following the pattern of increasing urbanization and branching.

The savings and loan picture in Metrolina is characterized by numerous associations rather than domination by a few giant operations. Compared to other markets of metropolitan character with about the same population base, Metrolina has an unusually large number of institutions of this type—forty-four savings and loan associations operating sixty-four offices. The region has thirty associations in the ranges of $10 million to $70 million in assets. Metrolina's savings and loan associations hold over $837 million in savings deposits. The largest portion of this is within Mecklenburg County yet this represents the smallest ratio of savings and loan savings deposits to bank deposits in Metrolina. On the other hand, Cabarrus, Cleveland, Lincoln, and Stanly counties have more savings and loan deposits than bank deposits. In fact, Stanly County, the home of Metrolina's largest savings and loan association, has almost three times the total savings and loan deposits as bank deposits.

Savings and loans in Metrolina have been characterized in recent years by rapid branching programs with a number of associations crossing county lines. The number of savings and loan investors in Metrolina totals almost a quarter of a million people and associations are extending over 75,000 loans within the area.

Other Financial Institutions

Although the insurance companies domiciled in Metrolina are not particularly large, the insurance industry in the area is notably active. A number of other counties in the Carolinas have home offices of larger insurance companies than are in Mecklenburg, but Mecklenburg leads all other Carolina counties in insurance employment. Charlotte alone represents 115 insurers who employ over 4,500 persons out of Metrolina's nearly 7,000 employees in the insurance sector.

Many national companies use Charlotte as a service center for North Carolina or the two Carolinas. Numerous insurance companies have played a major role in the area through participation in broadcast-company ownership, construction financing, and residential mortgage lending.

The New York Stock Exchange provides statistics only by state and SMSA. The reported 117,000 shareowners and 174 stockbrokers for the Charlotte SMSA represent the largest number for any SMSA in the Carolinas.

Metrolina has numerous consumer-credit organizations located in its retail centers. Three of the larger regional firms are located in Charlotte. Mortgage banking is another specialized financial service in Metrolina which is centered in Charlotte.

REFERENCES

American Newspaper Markets. *Circulation '70.* Northfield, Ill.: American Newspaper Markets, 1970.

American Research Bureau. *Coverage /69—Television County Viewing Share Study.* Beltsville, Md.: American Research Bureau, 1969.

Audit Bureau of Circulations. *Audit Report.* (Reports on individual newspapers.) Chicago: Audit Bureau of Circulations, 1970.

Bennett, D. Gordon, and Charles R. Hayes. *Factors of Spatial Interaction in North Carolina.* Raleigh: North Carolina Department of Administration, 1969.

Federal Communications Commission. *News.* Washington, D.C.: U.S. Government Printing Office, 1969.

National Research Bureau. *The Directory of Shopping Centers.* 12th ed. Burlington, Iowa: National Research Bureau, 1971.

Reilly, William J. *The Law of Retail Gravitation.* New York: G. P. Putnam's Sons, 1931.

Sales Management. *1971 Survey of Buying Power.* New York: Sales Management, July 1971.

Standard Rate and Data Service. *Daily Newspaper Rates and Data.* Skokie, Ill.: Standard Rate and Data Service, 1970.

Standard Rate and Data Service. *Spot Radio Rates and Data, January 1, 1971.* Skokie, Ill.: Standard Rate and Data Service, 1971.

Standard Rate and Data Service. *Weekly Newspaper Rates and Data.* Skokie, Ill.: Standard Rate and Data Service, 1970.

Television Digest. *Television Factbook 1970-71.* New York: Television Digest, 1971.

U.S. Department of Commerce, Bureau of the Census. *County Business Patterns, 1969.* Washington, D.C.: U.S. Government Printing Office, published annually for each state.

U.S. Department of Commerce, Bureau of the Census. *1967 Census of Business, Retail Trade.* Washington, D.C.: U.S. Government Printing Office, 1967. (Published for each state.)

U.S. Department of Commerce, Bureau of the Census. *1967 Census of Business, Selected Services.* Washington, D.C.: U.S. Government Printing Office, 1967. (Published for each state.)

U.S. Department of Commerce, Bureau of the Census. *1967 Census of Business, Wholesale Trade.* Washington, D.C.: U.S. Government Printing Office, 1967. (Published for each state.)

U.S. Department of Commerce, Office of Business Economics. "Personal Income," Washington, D.C.: The Department, 1970. (Computer printouts.)

U.S. Postal Service. *Revenues and Classes of Post Offices,* publication no. 4. Washington, D.C.: U.S. Government Printing Office, July 1, 1970.

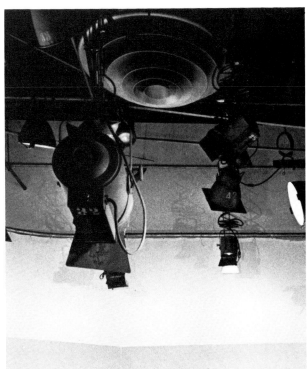

WBTV
Morning Report

8. POLITICS

SCHLEY R. LYONS
WILLIAM J. MCCOY

"Political questions in North Carolina have always been questions of east and west, of the upcountry against the lowlands, of crystalline schists and granites against the unconsolidated clays, sands, and gravels."—V. O. Key, Jr., Southern Politics, *1949.*

Metrolina is a part of North Carolina's rapidly growing Piedmont region. Its citizens are served by two state governments, North and South Carolina, and congressmen from the North Carolina Eighth, Ninth, Tenth, and the South Carolina Fifth Congressional districts. At the state legislative level there is no regional cohesiveness among the representatives serving the area. From the standpoint of political analysis Metrolina cannot be severed from the Piedmont nor from the state of North Carolina and studied in isolation; the political dynamics of the region are inescapably part of the broader context of North Carolina politics. On the other hand, Lancaster and York counties are not discussed in detail since they are part of another state. Although state boundary lines have little impact on some of the activities reviewed in this atlas, they are of fundamental importance in political analysis.

The focus of this chapter is the development of two-party competition within Metrolina and the state of North Carolina and the socioeconomic changes associated with that development. One of the most commonly used indicators to describe the politics of a region, state, or nation is the degree of competition among the existing political parties. Both theoretical and practical considerations support the use of this particular political measurement. First, a measurement of political competition is easy to acquire and involves few problems of interpretation. Second, it has been widely used in political research and lends itself to easy comparison from one region to another as well as from one period of time to another. Third, there are a number of socioeconomic characteristics that are usually associated with party competition or a lack of competition, and these variables can be taken into account in explaining political patterns. Fourth, and perhaps most important, it is assumed that governmental output in the form of policy positions is affected by the presence or absence of political party competition.

Traditionally North Carolina has been classified as a one-party Democratic state. To accept such a simple description of North Carolina politics, however, is to overlook the persistent Republicanism of many of the mountain counties and the substantial increase of Republican electoral strength in the urban, industrialized Piedmont. Politics in North Carolina is changing. Describing that change and attempting to account for it are the major objectives of the sections that follow.

Voting Trends: 1948-1970

V. O. Key in his classic study of southern politics observed that North Carolina had "more tender sectional sensibilities than any other state in the South." For most of the twentieth century a handful of western mountain counties were Republican territory. The inner coastal plain with its heavy concentration of blacks was the bastion of the Democratic party. Most of the rest of the state was securely in the Democratic fold, although Republicans did win on occasion in the western third of the state. In statewide races Republicans have experienced almost a total lack of success.

North Carolinians have expressed their approval of Republican presidential candidates twice in the twentieth

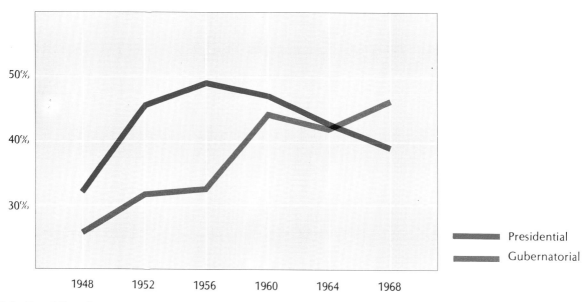

Fig. 8.1. Republican Percentage of Presidential and Gubernatorial Vote for North Carolina, 1948-1968

century. Herbert Hoover polled 54.9 percent of the vote in 1928 as the state Democratic party split over the candidacy of the "wet," Catholic, New-York-City-born Al Smith. Richard M. Nixon won a close three-way race in 1968 against Hubert Humphrey and George Wallace, polling 39.5 percent of the vote. Republican gubernatorial candidates have been even less successful during the twentieth century. Although the Democratic margin of victory has been steadily decreasing over the last twenty years, a Republican candidate has yet to win. (See Fig. 8.1.)

However, within Metrolina presidential elections since 1952 clearly show a Republican preference. In 1968 the Democratic presidential candidate failed to carry any of the Metrolina counties. Only Cleveland escaped the Republican column, casting a plurality for George Wallace. With the exception of the 1964 Goldwater candidacy, the Republicans have had a clean sweep in presidential elections since 1952 in Cabarrus, Catawba, Gaston, Iredell, Lincoln, Mecklenburg, Rowan, and Stanly counties. (See Table 8.1.) In gubernatorial races Catawba and Stanly counties had cast their votes for Republican candidates several times prior to the Hoover election of 1928. Since 1952 Republican candidates for governor have carried Cabarrus, Catawba, Rowan, and Stanly counties more frequently than the Democrats. In only Cleveland, Union, and Mecklenburg have the voters failed to provide a majority for a GOP gubernatorial candidate during the 1948-68 period. (See Table 8.2.)

Presidential and gubernatorial voting trends in Metrolina are similar to the patterns found over the whole Piedmont. The North Carolina GOP has either been firmly in control or at least competitive with the Democrats in presidential races since 1952. Republicans became competitive in gubernatorial politics in 1960. The voting pattern in the 1968 gubernatorial race suggests that support for Republicans is no longer limited to only the mountain and Piedmont regions but has spread to many of the coastal plain counties. Although North Carolina has lagged behind several of its neighboring states (for example, Virginia, Tennessee, and Florida) in delivering presidential electoral votes to Republicans, GOP strength in statewide elections appears sufficiently strong to exist independently of strong Republican coattails at the national level. Such a pattern indicates that North Carolina is on the threshold of a genuine two-party system. (See Figs. 8.2 and 8.3.)

Perhaps a more reliable measurement of increasing party competitiveness may be obtained by examining electoral contests of less visibility and intensity than presidential and gubernatorial elections. Statewide races that have relatively low visibility among the rank-and-file electorate—e.g., elections for state auditor, secretary of state, commissioner of agriculture—are less susceptible to special short-term impacts such as the appeal of exceptionally popular candidates. Controlling for the impact of candidate popularity is virtually impossible in highly visible presidential and gubernatorial races; an obvious case in point was the candidate appeal of Dwight D. Eisenhower. In analyzing aggregate data there is no way to separate party appeal from candidate appeal. However, since candidates for the Council of State offices are less well known, it can be assumed that party identification is a much stronger factor in determining how citizens will vote. The mean percentages of the Metrolina vote for the Republican candidates in nine statewide executive office races from 1948 to 1968 show a persistent increase in the

County	Percent Republican Vote in Presidential Elections					
	1948	1952	1956	1960	1964	1968
Cabarrus	33.4	62.2	66.8	64.4	52.5	52.3
Catawba	47.5	59.3	62.8	58.6	52.0	56.3
Cleveland	20.5	43.9	45.7	43.9	42.1	32.3
Gaston	32.5	51.9	53.7	51.4	45.9	43.8
Iredell	36.5	57.9	60.4	57.4	53.4	43.2
Lincoln	43.4	53.6	53.2	50.3	44.6	46.2
Mecklenburg	34.7	57.3	62.0	55.1	48.4	52.4
Rowan	36.4	60.8	64.3	57.8	49.8	46.8
Stanly	50.5	58.4	61.4	57.3	52.9	51.4
Union	14.3	33.8	34.5	35.3	37.0	38.7
Lancaster, S. C.	3.4	38.2	26.8	34.3	48.8	37.8
York, S. C.	10.6	41.3	33.9	38.8	46.6	37.5

Table 8.2. The Percentage of the Voting Population That Supported
Republican Gubernatorial Candidates in Elections from 1948 to 1968
in Metrolina Counties of North Carolina

County	Percent Republican Vote in Gubernatorial Elections					
	1948	1952	1956	1960	1964	1968
Cabarrus	28.9	45.0	42.2	60.6	52.5	53.7
Catawba	40.2	50.1	49.9	55.7	51.0	60.5
Cleveland	16.1	25.5	23.9	38.5	36.5	42.4
Gaston	23.8	36.5	32.9	47.6	46.5	52.7
Iredell	28.8	41.6	39.7	54.6	46.3	51.2
Lincoln	41.8	46.0	45.4	48.2	46.7	51.5
Mecklenburg	19.4	32.4	34.4	49.4	50.0	44.8
Rowan	31.7	45.5	43.7	54.9	50.6	51.0
Stanly	46.9	50.4	50.5	55.1	56.9	57.6
Union	9.8	18.4	17.4	32.0	32.0	41.9

electoral power of the Republican party. The trend, however, is the same in all parts of the state, towards greater interparty competition. (See Table 8.3.)

Within Metrolina counties there are sharp differences in level of party competition. Cleveland and Union are the most Democratic; e.g., in the nine executive office races 60 percent of the electorate in 1968 cast their ballots for Democrats. At the other extreme Catawba and Stanly counties were delivering 50 percent or more of the vote to Republican candidates in statewide races as early as 1952. To date, Mecklenburg and Gaston counties have not had a Republican candidate win in a Council of State race but have experienced several extremely close contests. Since the overall voting pattern is very similar for all nine executive office races between 1948 and 1968, the party split for lieutenant governor is presented to show electoral trends within the ten North Carolina Metrolina counties. (See Fig. 8.4.)

Even though the Republicans have become a serious threat in statewide elections, regarding party registration the citizens of North Carolina retain a lopsided Democratic identification. In 1970, 75.7 percent of the eligible voters

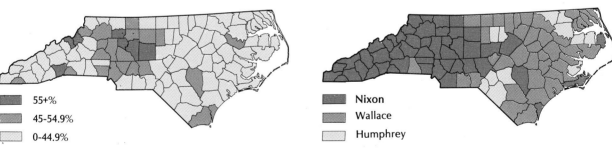

Percentage Republican Vote, 1948

55+%
45-54.9%
0-44.9%

Percentage Republican Vote, 1952

55+%
45-54.9%
0-44.9%

Percentage Republican Vote, 1956

55+%
45-54.9%
0-44.9%

Percentage Republican Vote, 1960

55+%
45-54.9%
0-44.9%

Percentage Republican Vote, 1964

55+%
45-54.9%
0-44.9%

Three Way Party Split, 1968

Nixon
Wallace
Humphrey

Fig. 8.2. Republican Percentage of Presidential Vote in North Carolina Counties, 1948-1964
(1968 election shown for three-way party split)

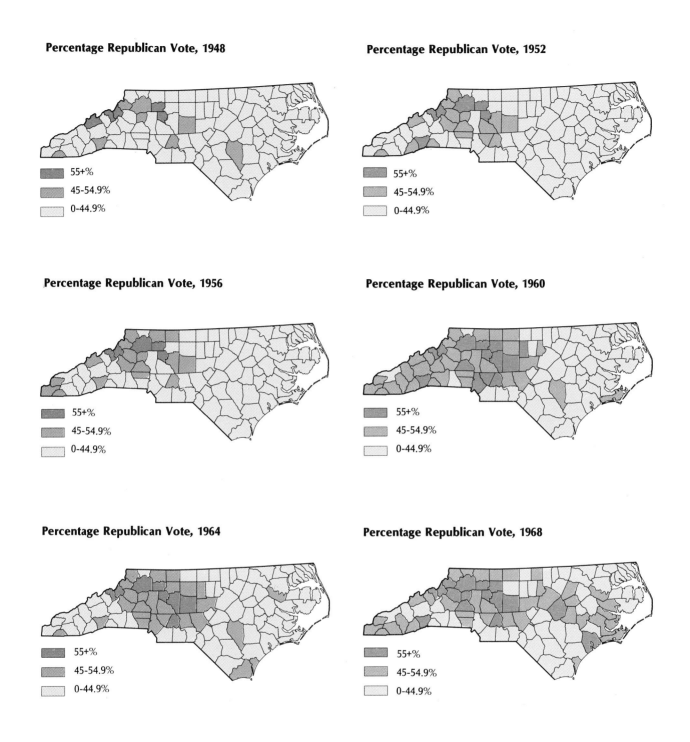

Percentage Republican Vote, 1948

55+%
45-54.9%
0-44.9%

Percentage Republican Vote, 1952

55+%
45-54.9%
0-44.9%

Percentage Republican Vote, 1956

55+%
45-54.9%
0-44.9%

Percentage Republican Vote, 1960

55+%
45-54.9%
0-44.9%

Percentage Republican Vote, 1964

55+%
45-54.9%
0-44.9%

Percentage Republican Vote, 1968

55+%
45-54.9%
0-44.9%

Fig. 8.3. Republican Percentage of Gubernatorial Vote in North Carolina Counties, 1948-1968

Table 8.3. Percentage of Republican Vote in Metrolina and the State for Nine Statewide Executive Offices, 1948-1968

Office	Area	1948	1952	1956	1960	1964	1968
Lt. governor	Metrolina	30	39	39	46	44	48
	State	26	32	33	41	39	45
Secretary of state	Metrolina	31	39	39	44	44	48
	State	28	32	33	39	38	45
State auditor	Metrolina	31	39	40	45	44	50
	State	28	32	33	39	39	45
Treasurer	Metrolina	31	39	40	44	44	49
	State	28	32	33	39	39	44
Attorney general	Metrolina	31	39	40	45	44	48
	State	28	32	34	39	39	44
Commissioner of agriculture	Metrolina	31	39	40	45	43	48
	State	28	32	33	39	38	44
Superintendent of public instruction	Metrolina	31	39	39	44	Democrat	48
	State	28	32	34	39	unopposed	44
Commissioner of insurance	Metrolina	31	39	42	44	45	49
	State	28	32	33	39	38	44
Commissioner of labor	Metrolina	31	39	40	46	44	49
	State	28	32	33	39	38	44

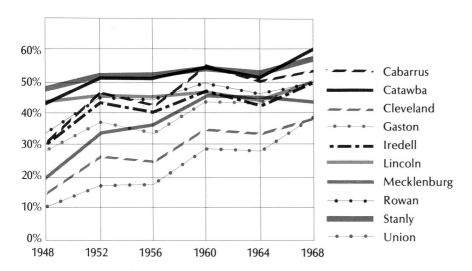

Fig. 8.4. Percentage of Vote for Republican Candidates in Lieutenant Governor Races in Metrolina Counties of North Carolina, 1948-1968

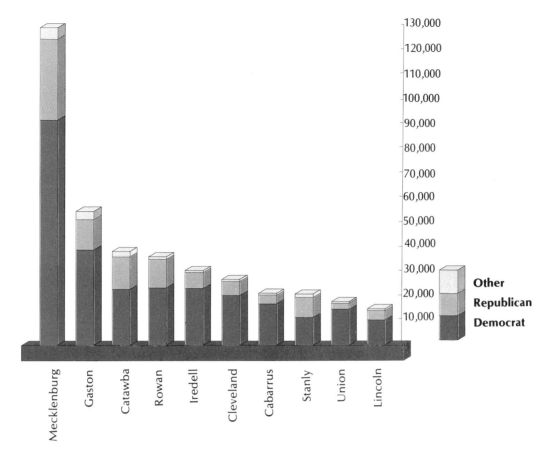

Fig. 8.5. Voter Registration in Metrolina by Political Party, 1970

in North Carolina were registered as Democrats compared to 21.5 percent registered as Republicans. In Metrolina the Republicans faired only slightly better, 67.9 and 24.9 percent respectively. (See Fig. 8.5.) Even in Catawba and Stanly counties, the most Republican of the Metrolina counties, only one out of three were registered as Republicans. On the surface this would seem to be an obstacle in making the Republicans competitive at all levels of the ballot. First, it would limit substantially the pool of candidates available for the Republicans and, second, it would retard party organizational efforts in the less visible races within the state—for example, state legislator, county commissioner, sheriff, solicitor, etc. The low Republican registration will probably act as a brake on any dramatic Republican upswing in these particular elections. The trend of party competition at the state legislative level tends to support such a hypothesis.

The North Carolina General Assembly currently consists of a 120-man House of Representatives elected from forty-nine districts and a Senate composed of 50 members elected from thirty-three districts.[1] In order for the

Republican party to be genuinely competitive, it must contest and win elections at this level of the ballot.

Within North Carolina there are no districts where the Democratic party is so weak it cannot offer to the electorate candidates for the state legislature. With only a handful of exceptions there has been a Democratic candidate in every legislative race over the past two decades. On the other hand, in 1970 the Republicans were unable to offer candidates for 30 percent of the state legislative seats. There is no question that the minority party finds it more difficult to offer qualified candidates to run for all available offices. Nevertheless the Republican party's capability to challenge the Democrats has improved over the last two decades. Contesting elections, however, has not led to a dramatic upturn in seats won. As of 1970 the Republicans controlled only 14 percent of the seats in the Senate and 20 percent in the House. Overall there were 31 Republicans serving in the 170-man General Assembly. (See Fig. 8.6.)

At the beginning of the 1970s Republican electoral strength at the state legislative level remained concentrated in a handful of mountain and Piedmont counties. Although the Republican party is increasingly showing signs of vigorous political life, it remains in its infancy at the state legislative level. Progress has been painfully slow in recruiting candidates and winning elections. (See Fig. 8.7.) The

1. Undoubtedly the most momentous impact on the character of the North Carolina legislature over the last twenty years was the judicially imposed requirement of "one man, one vote." Because of long-term population trends, the bulk of the state's population is now located in the Piedmont, which will have the effect of shifting a greater legislative voice to that region.

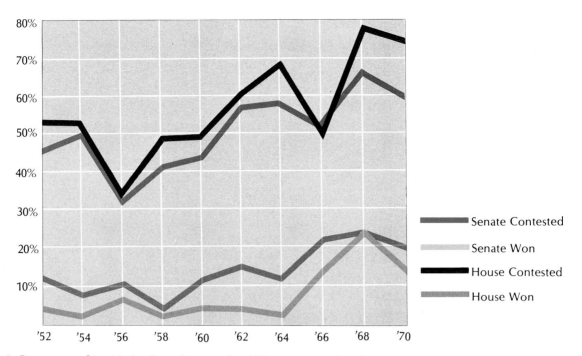

Fig. 8.6. Percentage of Legislative Seats Contested and Won by Republican Party in North Carolina, 1952-1970

drawbacks of being identified with the minority party and being on the outside in the legislative decision-making process is most keenly felt and is not an obstacle easily overcome. Party politics in North Carolina is changing but changing slowly in the state legislature.

At the congressional level recruitment is less of a problem; and the Republicans in 1970 offered candidates in ten of the eleven congressional races and won four—the Fifth, Eighth, Ninth, and Tenth North Carolina Congressional districts. In 1968 Republicans contested nine of the eleven congressional races while the Democrats were unable to find a candidate to face Republican Congressman Charles Raper Jonas. Congressman Jonas's Ninth Congressional District included three Metrolina counties: Iredell, Lincoln, and Mecklenburg. In the eight contested congressional races in 1968 and the ten contested races in 1970 Republicans received 47.5 percent and 46.1 percent of the statewide congressional vote respectively.

At the beginning of the 1970s the Republican party had demonstrated its capability to compete successfully in presidential and congressional elections, had become a powerful and threatening contender in gubernatorial and Council of State races, but still was weak and inexperienced at the lower levels of the ballot. It permitted the Democrats to take one-third of the state legislative seats by default and was electorally secure in a few mountain and Piedmont counties. Only slightly more than 20 percent of the electorate openly proclaimed themselves to be Republicans by registering with the party.

A Sociodemographic Analysis of Party Competition

What are some of the factors associated with the metamorphosis of North Carolina from a one-party Democratic state to one approaching a competitive two-party system? Since major social and economic changes often trigger corresponding political changes, it might be useful to review what has been occurring in North Carolina over the last two decades. The state has experienced massive technological changes and increased urbanization. Simultaneously there has been a major shift in the makeup of the state's population. The Negro has been moving out of the state and into the large urban centers of the North, while Caucasians from all parts of the country have been moving in to assist in the management of the new technology. In general the state's newcomers are much better educated and earn more than those who migrate northward. There has been considerable change in the political and economic lives of those Negroes who remain. In the following section the relationships, if any, between the above social and economic changes and the increasing competitiveness of the party system are explored.

The following six variables are used as indicators of the social, economic, and demographic systems and are referred to in the analysis as independent variables.

1. Percent urbanization—the percent of a county's population that resides in an urban place, which according to the Census Bureau's definition is any city with a population of 2,500 or more.

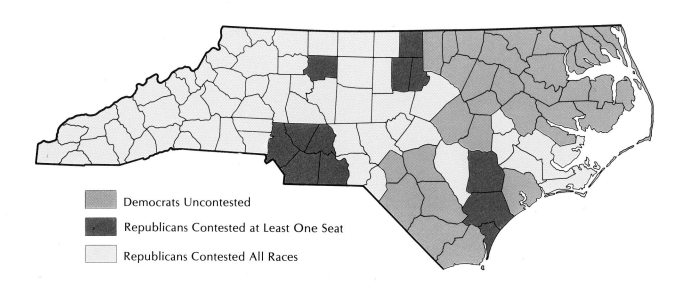

Fig. 8.7 (a). Contested State Senate Elections in North Carolina Counties, 1970

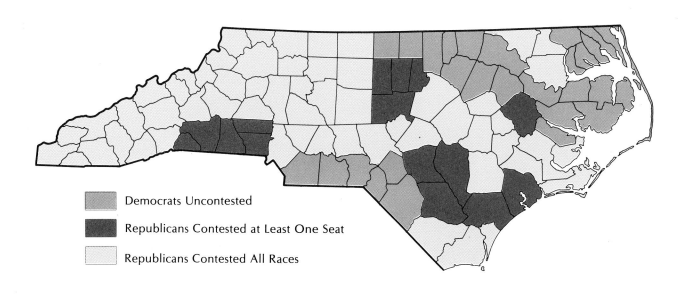

Fig. 8.7 (b). Contested State House of Representative Elections in North Carolina Counties, 1970

2. Percent nonwhite—the percent of a county's population that is Negro. At times in the following analysis this variable will be referred to as black concentration.

3. Percent manufacturing—the percent of a county's labor force engaged in manufacturing.

4. Population change—the percent of increase or decrease in a county's population from one census to another.

5. Median education—the median number of school years completed by the adult population of a county.

6. Median family income—self-explanatory.

The primary dependent variable is a measure of party competition. Competition is measured by computing the difference between the percentage of the vote cast for the Republican candidate and the percentage of the vote cast for the Democratic candidate; consequently a small number indicates a highly competitive situation while a comparatively large number indicates little competition. A second dependent variable used in portions of the analysis to follow is the percent of the total vote garnered by the Republican candidate. This variable is a direct measure of Republican electoral strength.

Certain expectations concerning the relationship of the sociodemographic variables with the political variables are postulated below. An increasing urbanism is an indicator of a more heterogeneous societal mix, which in turn is considered to be a prerequisite for a durable two-partyism. Although the percentage of North Carolinians living in urban places has shown a steady increase during the twentieth century, it still is relatively low compared to the national average, with only 45 percent of the population living in such areas in 1970. The rapid urbanization of some parts of the state and the persistence of extreme rurality in others accentuates the demographic contrasts. The Piedmont is urban; the eastern coastal plain is the stronghold of rurality; and the mountain region is typified by traditional folk rurality in which ownership of marginal farms is common. Because of these sharp regional differences the relationship that is expected between urbanism and competition could be obscured somewhat.

Twenty years ago V. O. Key, Jr. discussed the relatively progressive nature of North Carolinians on the race question, especially when compared to other southern states. He stated that the black man had already won his electoral spurs in some locales, and as black participation spread throughout the state, this event might not seem as traumatic to North Carolinians as it would to the citizens of other areas of the South. Nevertheless one would expect that in areas of high black concentration two-party competition would be depressed. The thesis for such an assertion is that when an issue takes on the highest level of importance for the leadership and its coterie, all other possible differences are absorbed within it. The racial composition of North Carolina has not remained static over the years, however. Blacks have been leaving the state, and their

percentage of the total population has decreased from 32 percent in 1910 to 22.4 percent in 1970.

Since North Carolina's growth rate has been relatively slow over the years, it is easy to assume that the state's population is stable. Change is constant, however, and in recent years North Carolina has been losing population to other states to an extent that many do not realize. The massive exodus of population from rural areas, brought on by agricultural mechanization and industrialization hits North Carolina particularly hard because the state has been heavily agricultural. In 1940, 33.6 percent of the state's labor force was employed in agriculture compared to only 8.6 percent in 1968. Whites and blacks have been leaving the state's agricultural regions in large numbers in about the same ratio. Between 1960 and 1970 thirty-six of the one hundred North Carolina counties lost population. Most of these counties are located in the east. (See Fig. 8.8.) Of major political significance, however, is the fact that while a large percentage of the white migrants are moving to towns and cities within North Carolina, most of the black migrants who usually identify with the Democratic party are moving outside the state. This general trend has been evident for at least the last thirty or forty years.

In-migration patterns since 1950 are also tending to erode the Democratic advantage. Philip Converse in commenting on population redistribution in the South as a whole stated: "Unlike the South-to-North migration, the new North-to-South stream is selective along partisan lines: it turns out that the non-Southerners moving into the South are actually more Republican than the non-Southerners they leave behind. This fact means that interregional convergence in partisanship is correspondingly speeded up, for the departure of these Republicans leaves the non-South more Democratic than it would otherwise be at the same time as the South becomes more Republican."[2] With traditionally Democratic identifiers leaving the state and a disproportionate number of Republicans moving into the state, there should be an association between population change and support for the Republican candidate as well as for two-party competition.

The percent of the labor force engaged in manufacturing, median education, and median income all tend to be highly related to the measurement of the more general characteristic, socioeconomic status. As these variables exhibit a relative increase, Republican voting and consequently two-partyism should show an increase. If there is a relative decrease in the socioeconomic indicators, the obverse should occur.

The determinants of party competition are examined

2. Philip Converse, "A Major Political Realignment in the South?" in *Change in the Contemporary South*, ed. Alan P. Sindler (Durham: Duke University Press, 1963), p. 210.

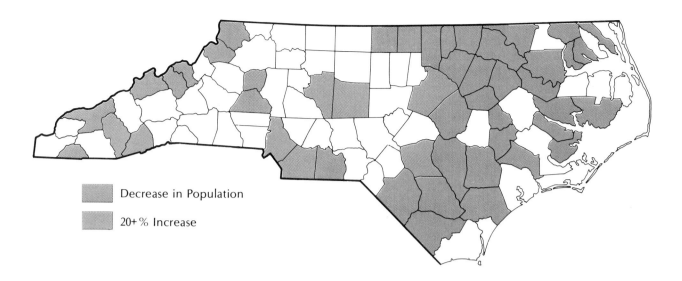

Fig. 8.8. Population Change in North Carolina Counties, 1960-1970

first at the state level; second, at the regional level, the Piedmont; third, at the subregional level, Metrolina; and fourth, at the urban level, Charlotte. Throughout this chapter the unit of analysis is the county or precinct. The data deal with the characteristics of counties, not individuals, and generalizing from the areal to the individual level is hazardous. It should be kept firmly in mind that because of the restrictions of the data nothing can be said about the individuals that comprise the units of analysis. The observations are derived from a statistical analysis of the relationships between the dependent variables (party competition and percent of Republican vote) and the social, economic, and demographic indicators. The particular research technique employed was correlational analysis.[3]

In North Carolina the Republican party has been unsuccessful in capturing many votes where there is a high concentration of blacks. There is a high negative relationship between percent nonwhite in a county and competition between political parties in all the presidential elections since 1948 with the exception of 1968—a result of the third-party movement of that year. On the other hand, the socioeconomic indicators—percent of the labor force engaged in manufacturing, median education, and median family income—have a weak to moderate positive relationship with party competition in most of the election years. Consequently, though black concentration has served to depress competitiveness, high socioeconomic status has

3. A correlation coefficient measures the degree of association between any two intervally measured and linearly distributed variables. Although correlation tables were not included in the *Atlas*, they are available on request from the authors. For a discussion of simple, partial, and multiple correlation see Dennis J. Palumbo, *Statistics in Political and Behavioral Science* (New York: Appleton-Century-Crofts, 1969), pp. 177-222.

enhanced two-party competition. Even after the influence of black concentration has been controlled or removed from consideration, socioeconomic factors show an independent and positive influence on party competition.

In 1948 the six sociodemographic variables accounted for 73 percent of the variance in the dependent variable of competition. At that time a very simple political system existed where the Republicans collected most of their votes in the traditional Republican areas of the mountains, and the Democrats and splinter Democrats got the remainder. However, the decreasing amount of variance in party competition explained by the sociodemographic variables (1952, 61 percent; 1956, 46 percent; 1960, 57 percent; 1964, 47 percent; 1968, 15 percent) indicates that presidential voting is becoming more complex.

At this point a disclaimer is necessary. The three-way presidential election of 1968 clearly obscures the trends, and it is assumed that the existence of the third party is primarily the cause of this breakdown. Part of the problem in the analysis of the 1968 presidential election is that the measure of competition does not discern the presence of the third party in the election. The difference figure was arrived at by subtracting the Humphrey vote from the Nixon vote or vice versa depending on which was the larger. This can account for the change in the relationship of black concentration with party competition. The counties where the difference between the Republican and Democratic vote was the narrowest were those in which a sizable black population was found. Since blacks overwhelmingly supported Humphrey, their very presence aided two-partyism.

Data on party competition at the gubernatorial level suggest that the election of 1960 signified a basic change in North Carolina state politics. All the relationships show a change, sometimes marked, in this electoral period. The relationship of urbanism with competition changed from negative to positive. The depressing influence of black concentration and the positive influence of manufacturing with competition began to decline. The relationships of population change, median education, and median family income with competition all increased. By 1968, however, all the relationships with the exception of urbanism and population change had decreased from their 1960 highs, suggesting that the GOP was appealing to a much broader segment of the electorate than ever before.

In the Piedmont all the indicators that have been suggested as possible factors related to the development of two-partyism are present. Manufacturing instead of agriculture provides the wage base, median education and median income are higher, blacks are less numerous, urbanism is much in evidence, and the rate of growth has been rapid. In other words, the Piedmont as a region is much more heterogeneous in its makeup than either of the other two regions.

Neither support for the Republican party nor two-party competition are new phenomena for the thirty-eight counties comprising the Piedmont. The percentage (and number) of the thirty-eight counties that gave a majority of their votes to Republican presidential and gubernatorial candidates from 1948 to 1968 is depicted in Table 8.4. From this table one can easily see the lift that Eisenhower gave to Piedmont Republicanism in 1952 and the burden of the Goldwater candidacy in 1964.

It is instructive to see that Nixon received a majority in the same number of counties as did Goldwater, although Nixon was in a three-party race instead of the traditional two-party election. Because of long-term voting patterns, it is safe to say that the Republican base in the Piedmont is composed of the following eleven counties: Alexander, Cabarrus, Catawba, Davidson, Davie, Iredell, Randolph, Rowan, Stanly, Wilkes, and Yadkin. The counties forming the base of Democratic strength during the span of elections covered in this study are the following: Caswell, Cleveland, Franklin, Granville, Person, Union, Vance, Wake, and Warren. Consequently, the heart of two-partyism in the Piedmont is the urban counties of Alamance, Durham, Forsyth, Guilford, and Mecklenburg. These clusters of strength are represented pictorially in Fig. 8.9.

Within the Piedmont region the relationships of the sociodemographic variables with the primary dependent variable of party competition are quite similar to those found statewide. Because of the fact that the 1968 presidential election obscures the trend in party competition, the percent of the Republican vote is also employed as a dependent variable. From 1948 to 1968 black concentration explained more about North Carolina and Piedmont voting patterns at both the presidential and gubernatorial levels than any other variable. If the black percentage of the total population was high, the propensity to vote Republican was low. This datum partially explains the existence of Democratic dominance in the Northeastern

Table 8.4. Piedmont Counties Showing a Republican Majority and Classification of Counties on Competition for Presidential and Gubernatorial Elections from 1948 to 1968

Republican Majority and Competition Classification	1948	1952	1956	1960	1964	1968[a]
Presidential						
Republican majority	13% (5)	50% (19)	66% (25)	63% (24)	26% (10)	26% (10)
Competition[b]						
Two-party	32% (12)	29% (11)	32% (12)	26% (10)	39% (15)	
One-party Democrat	55% (21)	34% (13)	24% (9)	32% (12)	50% (19)	
One-party Republican	13% (5)	37% (14)	45% (17)	42% (16)	11% (4)	
Gubernatorial						
Republican majority	8% (3)	18% (7)	16% (6)	50% (19)	37% (14)	45% (17)
Competition						
Two-party	11% (4)	26% (10)	24% (9)	39% (15)	45% (17)	37% (14)
One-party Democrat	84% (32)	66% (25)	68% (26)	32% (12)	39% (15)	39% (15)
One-party Republican	5% (2)	8% (3)	8% (3)	29% (11)	16% (6)	24% (9)

a. Competition in the 1968 presidential election was not included because the three-way race was not classifiable by the system utilized in the other elections.

b. The competition classification was derived from the difference in Democratic and Republican support. If the difference was nine or less, this was considered two-party competitive. If the difference was ten or more, this was considered a one-party county.

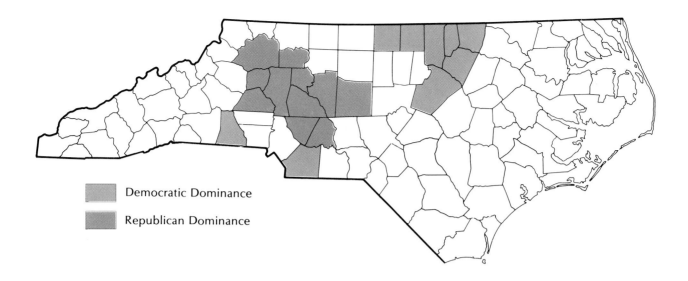

Fig. 8.9. Counties of One-Party Dominance in Piedmont

counties of the Piedmont—the part of the region with the highest concentration of blacks. But a closer look at the election statistics suggests that this reasoning is so simplistic that it results in covering up the actual change that is occurring. In the presidential election of 1968 Nixon received little support from the counties with a high black concentration, but that does not mean that these counties supported the Democratic ticket with total enthusiasm either. The nine counties that have formed the base of the Democratic support in the Piedmont gave Humphrey an average of 31.6 percent of their vote, but Wallace received an average vote in these counties of 43.3 percent. This indicates that the voters in these counties are not irrevocably wed to the Democratic party.

A review of the returns in the gubernatorial election of 1968 shows that Gardner, the Republican candidate, made inroads into the Piedmont bastion of Democratic strength. There was an average increase in Republican vote from the gubernatorial election of 1964 to 1968 of 11.9 percent in these nine counties. It is impossible to determine if the Wallace candidacy provided an opportunity for party switching or if this pattern is uniquely based on the kind of appeal made by the Republican candidate in this particular election. From 1964 to 1968 the eleven counties forming the base of Piedmont Republicanism increased their support of the party by an average of 3.1 percent. The eight counties with over 50 percent urban population actually decreased their support of the Republican candidate by an average percentage of 1.3. This decrease was most evident in Alamance (−10.5), Forsyth (−2.3), Guilford (−8.7), and Mecklenburg (−5.2).

With the exception of the 1968 election the sociodemo-graphic indicators other than race had a sizable independent influence on the Republican vote beginning in the presidential election of 1952 and the gubernatorial election of 1960. Overall, high median income within a county was the best predictor of Republican voting. In the gubernatorial election of 1968, however, Piedmont counties, regardless of their socioeconomic makeup, tended to be competitive; only three of the counties gave less than 40 percent of their vote to the Republican candidate and only five more than 60 percent.

The broad trends found in the entire state and the Piedmont are also evident in Metrolina with some extenuating exceptions.[4] First, black concentration has not been a major depressant to two-partyism in Metrolina, at least not in the most recent elections. Probably because of the Wallace candidacy, the percent nonwhite shows a positive correlation with competition in the presidential election of 1968. In the gubernatorial election black concentration was a negligible factor since it was not associated with party competition. Overall, there was very little patterning in the associations between the sociodemographic variables and presidential voting in Metrolina other than a tendency for the sociodemographic variables, other than race, to have a mild positive association with competition. Nevertheless support of Republicanism in Metrolina is greater than that provided in the entire state and in the Southeast region of the country, and is more comparable to nationwide support levels in presidential elections. These data suggest that

4. Analyzing political trends in Metrolina has two serious drawbacks: (1) the area does not form a distinct political unit, and (2) the number of counties is so small that correlational analyses cannot be definitive but only suggestive.

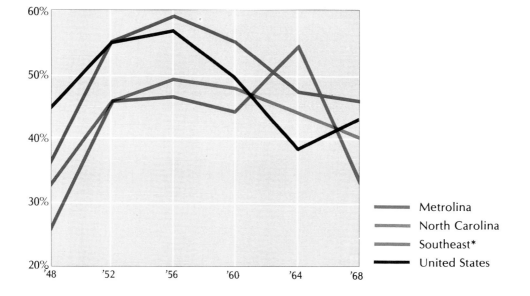

Fig. 8.10. Percentage Republican Vote in Presidential Elections from 1948 to 1968 in Metrolina, North Carolina, Southeast, and United States

Metrolina might be viewed as a microcosm of the nation at large. (See Fig. 8.10)

In Metrolina the major increase in Republican support in presidential elections occurred in 1952, as evidenced by the fact that the average county increase in Republican support over the preceding election was 21.2 percent.[5] This movement continued in 1956 but by the meager average county increase of .4 percent. From the election of 1960 through 1968 the Republican advantage has been eroding ever so slightly. The average county decrease in 1960 from the 1956 score was 2.0 percent; Republican support fell 2.6 percent in 1964 and 2.9 percent in 1968. This slight erosion of Republican strength may be explained by the short-term forces of the Goldwater candidacy in 1964 and the presence of Wallace in 1968, or the explanation may lie in a desire to return to the fold, so to speak—a return to support for the Democratic party.

Increased Metrolina support for Republican gubernatorial candidates seems to be more predictable. In the span of elections covered in this study the Republican party has shown three spurts of growth. In 1952 there was an average county increase of 10.4 percent over the 1948 figure; in 1960, an average increase of 11.7 percent over the 1956 figure; and in 1968, an average increase of 3.8 percent over the preceding election. After each of the

5. An index against which the growth of the Republican party in Metrolina might be assessed can be derived by taking the difference in the Republican vote from one election to another, summing it, and dividing the sum by the total number of counties in the analysis. This procedure provides a summary measure of the increase or decrease of Republican support. The raw data on which the summary measures are based may be found in Tables 8.1 and 8.2.

first two spurts, there was a small average county decrease—1.1 percent in 1956 and 2.5 percent in 1964. These small decreases seem to be reactions to the electoral convulsions of the preceding election period. In summary, the data indicate that a healthy and probably enduring two-partyism has developed in the Metrolina subregion.

Other analyses in this volume have portrayed the importance of Charlotte to the subregion of Metrolina, but politically there is no evidence to suggest that "as Charlotte goes, so goes Metrolina." The argument throughout this chapter suggests that whatever political movements might be afoot in Charlotte are also present in Metrolina, the Piedmont, and the entire state. Since Charlotte is the hub of Metrolina, however, a brief exposition of its voting trends might be enlightening.

An analysis of precinct voting behavior in Charlotte indicates nothing very startling in the way Charlotteans respond to the push and pull of political events. The response is quite similar to that of many other middle-size urban places in the United States. The blacks overwhelmingly support the Democratic party, while the upper socioeconomic levels support the Republican party. The bloc voting of Negroes for the Democratic candidate reached its apex at the presidential level in 1964 when Johnson received 99.6 percent of the vote in the all-black precincts. In the all-white precincts Republican support prevails in the upper income and better educated precincts, but this support declines as one moves down the socioeconomic ladder. At the presidential level the Democratic party has an appeal that elicits a favorable response from the "have-nots," while the Republican party enjoys the support of the

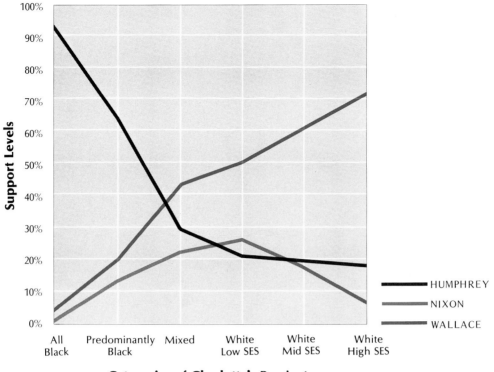

100%
90%
80%
70%
60%
50%
40%
30%
20%
10%
0%

Support Levels

All
Black

Predominantly
Black

Mixed

White
Low SES

White
Mid SES

White
High SES

HUMPHREY

NIXON

WALLACE

Categories of Charlotte's Precincts

Fig. 8.11. Support Levels for the Three Presidential Candidates in the Presidential Election of 1968 by Types of Precincts in Charlotte

"haves." In the electoral period covered in this analysis presidential Republicanism was at its peak in the Eisenhower elections (especially 1956) and dropped to its nadir in 1964. In a three-way race Nixon received a more favorable response from the citizens of Charlotte than did Goldwater in a traditional two-way race. In the 1968 presidential election Wallace received only nominal support in the Charlotte precincts, but his candidacy, based on a mixture of populist and racist appeals, was greeted with some favorableness in the all-white precincts of low socioeconomic levels and in those precincts that exhibited mixed traits on the racial and socioeconomic indicators. Humphrey fared very badly in the all-white precincts. (See Fig. 8.11.)

At the gubernatorial level Charlotte was clearly a one-party city until 1960. (See Table 8.5.) In the 1952 and 1956 gubernatorial elections very little difference in Republican support is found when the different categories of precincts are considered. In 1960, however, the Republican vote in the gubernatorial election began to approximate that received by the presidential candidate and began to vary concomitantly with socioeconomic levels. This trend continued in 1964, but the gubernatorial election of 1968 clearly deviates from this tendency. Republican support does not vary with socioeconomic levels—an aver-

age 48.7 percent, 50.0 percent, and 49.2 percent supported the Republican candidate in the white low, middle, and high socioeconomic categories of precincts. At the presidential level the corresponding support levels in these same categories of precincts were 51.6 percent, 61.5 percent, and 73.0 percent. Something brought about massive ticket-splitting in the middle and upper socioeconomic areas, and the cause of this phenomenon is elusive. Some possibilities come to mind: (1) these precincts are returning to their voting habits of the 1940s and 1950s; (2) the Democratic organization was especially effective in its 1968 campaign; (3) the Republican candidate, Gardner, in an effort to capture the Wallace supporter became associated in the voter's mind with the kind of appeal that Wallace was making, which reduced his support among the upper-class voters. The data on the presidential and gubernatorial elections of 1968 show that at the precinct level, there is no evidence to suggest that ticket-splitting was occurring in the all-black, predominantly black, mixed, and low socioeconomic precincts. Ticket-splitting occurred in the middle- and upper-class precincts. At this level the voters are normally better informed and more interested than in the other categories of precincts. The voters in these precincts would be more capable of discerning the type of appeal being made, and at the same time would be more likely to react nega-

Table 8.5. Percent Republican Vote in Charlotte in Presidential and Gubernatorial Elections from 1952 to 1968

Election Years and Type of Election	Black[b]	Predominantly Black[c]	Mixed[d]	Low SES White[e]	Middle SES White[e]	Upper SES White[e]
1952						
Presidential	17.8	48.3	59.3	37.4	60.6	75.2
Gubernatorial	12.1	24.7	31.3	34.8	36.4	35.7
1956						
Presidential	38.7	45.9	61.9	51.8	61.6	73.3
Gubernatorial	49.9	39.1	35.1	28.0	32.9	33.4
1960						
Presidential	11.1	32.2	48.5	44.3	56.7	69.3
Gubernatorial	8.2	25.6	44.1	37.6	51.2	62.9
1964						
Presidential	.4	22.8	46.8	44.1	51.9	64.1
Gubernatorial	10.6	24.8	45.9	40.6	52.5	64.4
1968						
Presidential	5.9	21.0	44.3	51.6	61.5	73.0
Gubernatorial	6.1	22.9	42.1	48.7	50.0	49.2

Classification[a]

a. The classification is based on forty-two precincts in 1952, thirty-three precincts in 1956, forty precincts in 1960, fifty-three precincts in 1964, and fifty-seven precincts in 1968. This number is not the same as the total city precincts in each of these years, with the exception of 1956. Certain precincts had to be dropped because of the difficulty in matching census tract information to them.

b. Precincts in which the population is over 90 percent black.

c. Precincts in which the population is 50 to 89 percent black.

d. Precincts of mixed characteristics; most of them have over 10 percent black population.

e. Precincts composed of over 90 percent white population: low SES—lower educational and income levels; middle SES—medium educational and income levels; and upper SES—higher educational and income levels.

tively to the racist and populist connotations of that appeal. In the upper-class precincts Wallace received only 7.3 percent of their vote.

The Wallace Phenomenon

The presidential candidacy of George Wallace has seriously complicated the analysis of North Carolina and Metrolina political trends. Wallacite electors garnered 31.2 percent of the popular vote, eight percentage points behind the slate of Republican electors and two percentage points ahead of the Democratic slate. The Wallace appeal was a strongly concentrated one, centered almost entirely in a wide belt of eastern counties stretching from the Virginia to South Carolina border. Only one county in the western

part of the state, Cleveland, a Metrolina county, was carried by Wallace.

The sectional pattern of the 1968 vote is interesting in at least two aspects. First, the distribution of the vote indicates that loyalty to the Democratic presidential candidate in the eastern counties rests on very precarious grounds. All of the counties won by Wallace in 1968 were carried by the Democrats in 1964 and, with the exception of Alamance, in 1960. Humphrey received a substantial portion of his support from black voters. On the other hand, white voters generated enthusiasm for Wallace partially because of his racist appeal. If the above propositions are correct, and the evidence is persuasive, then the white-black Democratic coalition is on shaky ground in its last remaining bastion of strength.

Second, it is not at all clear that the Republican party

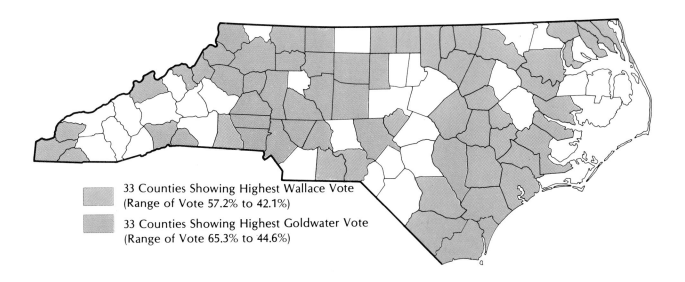

33 Counties Showing Highest Wallace Vote
(Range of Vote 57.2% to 42.1%)

33 Counties Showing Highest Goldwater Vote
(Range of Vote 65.3% to 44.6%)

Fig. 8.12 (a). Comparison of Goldwater and Wallace Vote in North Carolina Counties

can successfully advance its position through a similar racist appeal in the absence of a third-party candidate such as Wallace. This observation derives from a comparative analysis of the 1964 and 1968 election returns. There had been widespread speculation about a so-called "southern strategy" in the Republican presidential campaign of 1964 with some commentators equating the Goldwater voters with those who would have supported Wallace had the latter candidate entered the 1964 race. Even though survey data are needed to test this proposition directly, aggregate data supply strong evidence that refutes such a relationship. The accompanying map identifies the upper third (by percentages) of Goldwater's strongest counties in 1964 (which includes a substantial number of the Metrolina counties) and of Wallace's strongest counties in 1968. There is absolutely no overlap; the two candidates were appealing to different clientele. This interpretation is buttressed by more recent national survey data gathered by the Survey Research Center, which points out that, if anything, Wallace was a "poor man's Goldwater." His demogogic appeal was attractive to the "redneck"-populist electorate but somewhat repugnant to the more educated and middle-class conservative. Although the racist appeal of a Wallace may indirectly aid the Republican cause by bringing about a deterioration of Democratic strength, a similar Republican appeal may not be equally successful, because of the creation of internal tensions among potential Republican voters who cannot opt for an out-and-out demagogue. (See Fig. 8.12 (a).)

For the purpose of time-period comparisons, one may examine the strength of the Thurmond third-party move-

ment in 1948. The Dixiecrat candidacy of the South Carolina senator was markedly unsuccessful in North Carolina as a whole, with the best showing coming in Metrolina's Cabarrus County where 27 percent of the vote was won by the Thurmond ticket. Identification of the upper quartile of those counties where the Dixiecrats made their greatest impact reveal a pattern that might be best characterized as a "friends and neighbors" vote. Except for a few Piedmont counties in the north, all of the "strongest" Dixiecrat counties were located on the South Carolina border or contiguous to border counties. Most of the Metrolina counties fit into this category. The major observation to be made is that the Dixiecrat division of the vote bears no resemblance to that which emerged twenty years later in the Wallace candidacy. (See Fig. 8.12 (b).

Several explanations can be offered to demonstrate the differential impact of the Thurmond and Wallace candidacies. First, in 1948 the South had not yet experienced the traumatic political repercussions of the Supreme Court's *Brown* decision nor any of the subsequent desegregation rulings leading to the busing controversies rampant in the 1968 campaign. Second, the Republican party in North Carolina in 1948 was still in its infancy and the state was in the process of developing the social, economic, and political configuration that in the 1960s nurtured a growing Republicanism. Third, party loyalty among the electorate eroded significantly over the last twenty years in the face of a mass media revolution. Candidate orientation is now a more important determinant in presidential elections than party identification. Whatever the reason or combination of reasons for the substantial Wallace vote, the 1968 elec-

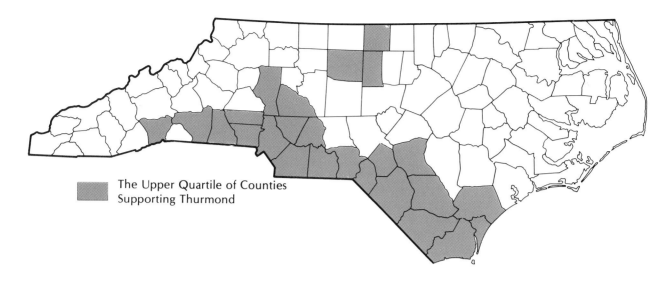

Fig. 8.12 (b). Thurmond Presidential Vote in North Carolina Counties, 1948

tion revealed the extent to which Democratic dominance of North Carolina politics had eroded. At the beginning of the period covered in this analysis it would have been unthinkable for the Democratic candidate for president to run third in a three-way race.

Black-White Registration Patterns

The vote is widely considered to be the Negro's most important weapon in his struggle for social and economic equality. In a sense political rights pave the way for all others. Since in North Carolina race explained more about the state's electoral patterns than any other variable, changes that take place in the registration of whites and blacks are of fundamental importance.

During the 1960s there were significant shifts in the proportions of whites and blacks registered in North Carolina. Between 1960 and 1968 there was a 44.6 percent increase in the number of Negroes registered compared to a decrease of 15.2 percent among white registrants. The decrease in the white registrants reflects greater care in purging the registration lists of people who have moved to other localities or to the local cemeteries. Overall, however, the black-white composition of the state's electorate changed only slightly. In 1960, 89.9 percent of the state's registered voters were white and 10.1 percent nonwhite; in 1968 the proportions had changed to 83.9 percent white and 16.1 percent nonwhite. (See Table 8.6)

In 1960 there were twenty-five counties with fewer than 21 percent of the eligible Negroes registered to vote.

By 1968, because of legal pressure on registrars, registration drives, abolition of poll taxes and similar legal and political reforms, only three counties had fewer than 21 percent of the eligible Negroes registered, including Graham County, which had no Negroes listed among its population. (See Figs. 8.13 (a) and 8.13 (b).)

The map that follows shows that Negroes remain concentrated in the coastal plain region and urban centers within the Piedmont. As has been the case for decades, there is an especially heavy concentration of blacks in a band of counties located in the northeastern portion of the state. In the past there has been a pattern where those counties with the larger proportions of Negroes in the population had the smallest proportion of Negroes registered to vote. It has been suggested that "the larger the proportion of Negroes in an area, the more intense the vague fears of Negro domination that seem to beset southern whites."[6] (See Fig. 8.14)

Although the area of the state showing the most dramatic upturn in Negro registration during the 1960s was that band of northeastern counties with a high black concentration, the counties with the highest percentage of blacks registered still tended to be those with the smallest percentage of Negroes. Of the fourteen counties with 75 percent or more of the Negroes registered, twelve had Negro populations of 10 percent or less. Sampson County, with a black population of 34.5 percent, was the only major exception, with 94.7 percent of the Negroes registered.

6. Donald Matthews and James Prothro, "Social and Economic Factors and Negro Voter Registration in the South," *The American Political Science Review* (March 1963): 28.

Table 8.6. Statewide Registration, 1960-1968, by Race

	1960	1968	% Change
Total registrants	2,071,780	1,883,389	−9.1
White registrants	1,861,330	1,578,984	−15.2
Nonwhite registrants	210,450	304,405	44.6

Generally the shifts in registration between 1960 and 1968 appeared to "even out" nonwhite registration throughout the state.

There were three counties in which less than 50 percent of the adult whites were registered in 1968—Craven, Cumberland, and Onslow. The presence of large military bases in these counties probably explains their deviancy. On the other hand, there were thirty-six counties in which the number of names on the registration lists exceeded 90 percent of the white adult population. In 1960 there had been seventy-four counties that claimed to have 90 percent or more of their eligible white voters registered; in fact, fifty-seven counties had over 100 percent of the eligible citizens registered. By 1968 the number of counties still carrying on the registration rolls more names than white adult citizens residing in the county had declined to nineteen, ten of which were located in the western mountain region. (See Fig. 8.15.)

In the Metrolina counties of North Carolina the Negro proportion of the population ranged from a low of 10.3 percent in Catawba to a high of 23.8 percent in Mecklenburg. Proportionately, fewer Negroes registered than whites. Statewide in 1968 it was estimated that 78.7 percent of the white and 55.3 percent of the black population were registered. In Metrolina the comparable percentages were 75.4 and 56.3 respectively. Metrolina followed the state trend in that the blacks comprised a higher proportion of the electorate in 1968 than in 1960, 12.2 percent compared to 8.5 percent. (See Fig. 8.16.) Much of this percentage change can be explained, however, by the "cleansing" of the registration lists rather than by population shifts. Between 1960 and 1968, 83,990 white adults were removed from the county registration lists while 6,597 Negro names were being added. Nevertheless it is apparent that the overall racial composition of the electorate changed little in Metrolina during the 1960s. Fig. 8.16 shows that the Negro voter represents only roughly 15 percent of the eligible electorate in urban Mecklenburg and declining percentages in the surrounding Metrolina counties. With the exception of Catawba and Cleveland counties, there were no substantial increases in the proportion of Negroes registered during the decade of the 1960s in Metrolina.

The South Carolina Counties: Lancaster and York

In South Carolina there was a tendency for those counties with a high percentage of Negro population to revolt against the national Democratic party ticket between 1948 and 1968. The probable explanation for this statistical relationship is the same as offered above for North Carolina: as the percent of Negro population increases, white resistance to Negro registration and voting increases, resulting in an inverse relationship between percent of Negro population and rate of Negro registration. With the normal black Democratic vote depressed and whites reacting against the national Democratic party's racial and economic policies, third-party movements such as the Dixiecrats in 1948, the Byrd phenomenon in 1956, and the Wallace candidacy in 1968 are warmly received by many South Carolinians.

On the other hand, the center of Democratic strength in South Carolina has been the upper-state or Piedmont region, including Lancaster and York counties. Compared to the rest of South Carolina, the Piedmont counties have relatively small percentages of Negro population, high median family incomes, high levels of education, and large numbers of industrial workers. As Donald L. Fowler has observed, this presents something of an illusion or impression of upper-income groups voting Democratic. Examination of the upper-income precincts of cities and towns in the Piedmont, however, discloses a substantial and continuing affinity for Republican candidates; a similar examination of working-class precincts discloses strong Democratic sentiment. Only in contrast to the rural, coastal counties does the Piedmont appear to be "upper income."[7]

From 1948 to 1964 Lancaster and York counties consistently provided Democratic presidential candidates higher levels of support than they received statewide. In 1964 the Democratic margin of victory began to erode and Lyndon Johnson was provided a scant majority. With the entrance of George Wallace into the 1968 presidential race the voting pattern in Lancaster and York altered substantially.

7. Donald L. Fowler, *Presidential Voting in South Carolina: 1948-1964* (Columbia: University of South Carolina, Bureau of Governmental Research and Service, 1966), pp. 114-15.

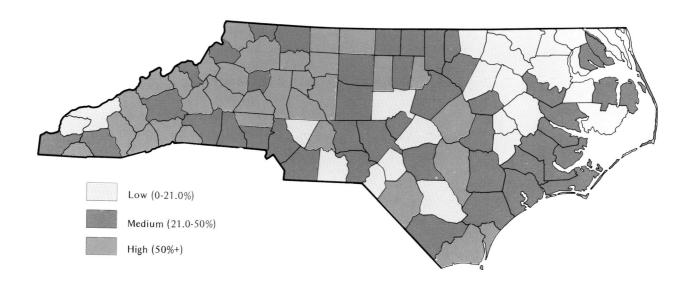

Fig. 8.13 (a). Nonwhite Potential Voters Registered in North Carolina Counties, 1960

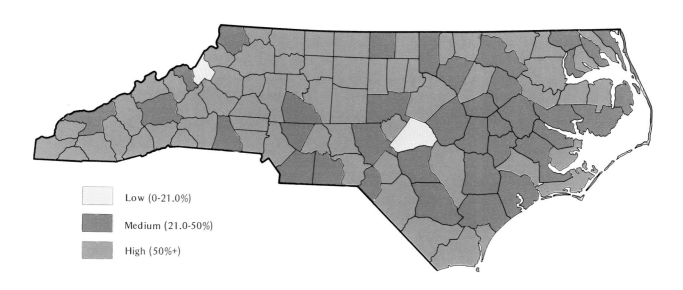

Fig. 8.13 (b). Nonwhite Potential Voters Registered in North Carolina Counties, 1968

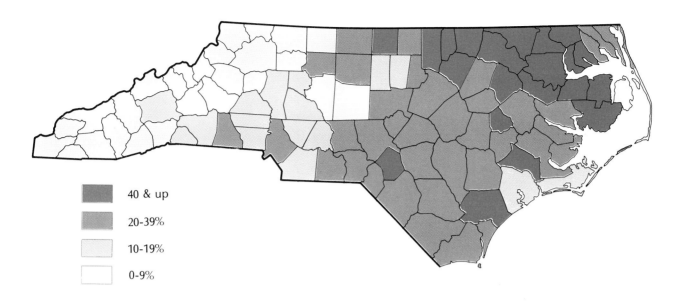

Fig. 8.14. Concentration of Nonwhite Population in North Carolina Counties, 1970

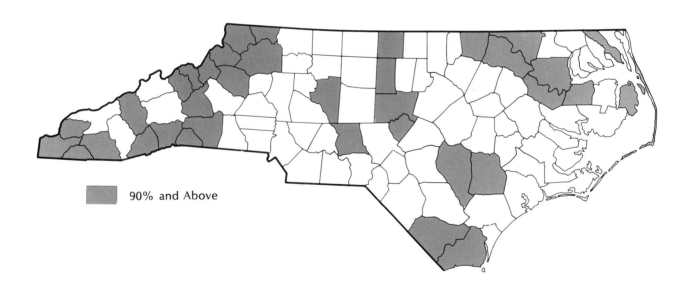

Fig. 8.15. North Carolina Counties in Which 90 Percent or More of Adult Whites Are Registered, 1968

The Democratic percentage of the vote shrunk to approximately one-quarter of the turnout while Nixon and Wallace almost evenly divided the remainder. For the first time in the period covered the Democratic percentage of the vote in Lancaster and York counties lagged behind the statewide count. (See Fig. 8.17.)

Compared to the North Carolina counties in Metrolina, Lancaster and York counties are politically similar to Cleveland and Union. In general, these counties seem to react to the force of events much like the areas of the Deep South rather than like the other counties of the region. All of these counties except Cleveland responded to the Goldwater appeal with increased Republican support, while none of the other Metrolina counties showed an increase in Republicanism between 1960 and 1964. These four counties also gave the candidacy of George Wallace its major support

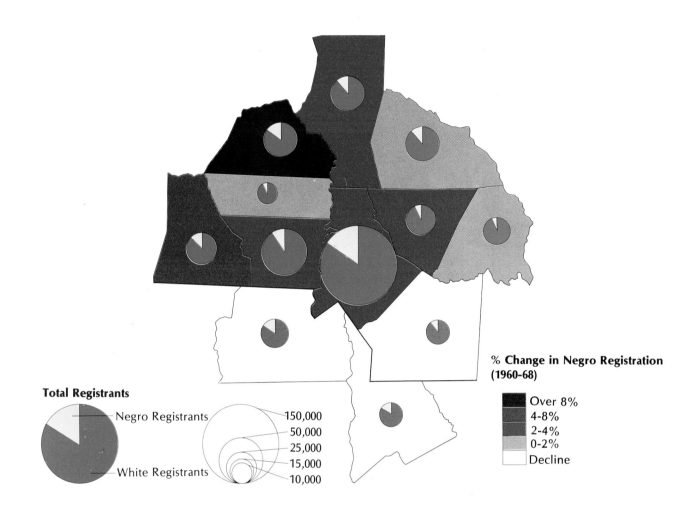

Total Registrants

Negro Registrants

White Registrants

150,000
50,000
25,000
15,000
10,000

**% Change in Negro Registration
(1960–68)**

Over 8%
4-8%
2-4%
0-2%
Decline

Fig. 8.16. Potential Voters by Race in Metrolina, 1968

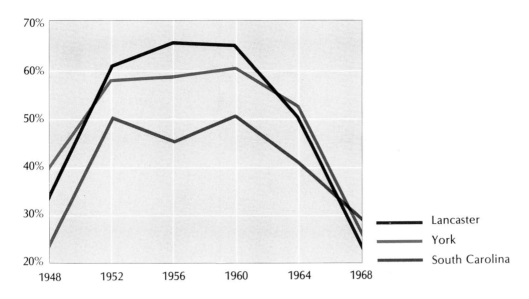

Fig. 8.17. Percentage of Democratic Vote for President, 1948-1968, in Lancaster, York, and South Carolina

with Cleveland and Lancaster being carried by the American Independent party. Whether the Republican inroads of 1964 in Lancaster and York will endure, recede, or perhaps be accelerated by a Wallace-to-Republican movement over the long term is too complex to predict at this point. Nevertheless the dominance the Democratic party once enjoyed at the presidential level is apparently over, and Lancaster and York are probably on a political path traversed earlier by most of the Metrolina counties north of the border.

A Speculative Summary

Since the forces that move politics in Metrolina are the same ones that are active at the regional and state levels, the observations that follow are stated for the most part in general terms; Metrolina is segmented out for special consideration only when the need for emphasis is evident. Earlier in this chapter the statement is made that "politics in North Carolina is changing." Evidence has been presented that documents the validity of such an assertion. Change in the political world is rather easily described, but explaining the change—why it happened, what the results will be—is more perplexing. We attempted the task of explanation through studies based on correlation analysis. In this concluding section, rather than restating the many examples of change in the politics of North Carolina, we will speculate about the relationship of previous change to probable future trends.

The rise of the Republican party has to rank near the top

of the list of events having the greatest impact on North Carolina politics. What this impact might mean for the future of Tar Heel politics, however, is difficult to foresee. There is no denying that the Republican party in the last two decades has moved from the position of a minority party unable to compete for the plums of political office to that of a serious contender for state office. This movement to competitive status has resulted in remarkably little success at the ballot box, however. The GOP became competitive with the Democrats in 1952 at the presidential level but did not gain the electoral votes of the state until 1968 in a three-way race. At the gubernatorial level the Republicans moved to a competitive status in 1960 but have not yet elected a governor. The Council of State elections were competitive in 1968, but no Republican was elected. To date, for all practical purposes, the two United States Senate seats have been safe for the Democrats. At the state legislative level the Republican record is improving in some respects. The party is contesting more of the elections (70 percent in 1970) than ever before, but its winning percentage has shown relatively little advancement over the last two decades. On the other hand, the major success story of the Republican party is at the congressional level. In 1970 the party offered candidates in ten of the eleven districts and elected four.

The Republican party in North Carolina is at the threshold of achieving parity with the Democratic party. Nevertheless, moving across the threshold to capture control of the governor's mansion, the state legislature, and lesser political offices is not necessarily inevitable. The data presented in this chapter support the notion that the

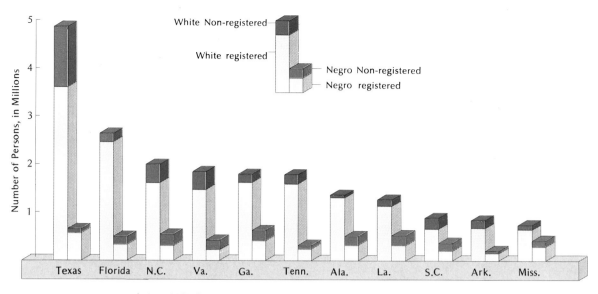

*VAP - Voting Age Population, 1960 Census.

Source: Voter Education Project, Inc., as reproduced in Congressional Quarterly *(Dec. 11, 1970), p. 2952.*

Fig. 8.18. Voter Registration in the Southern States, Spring-Summer, 1970

Republican party has a fairly firm base of about 45 percent support in statewide and national elections. To add the five or six percentage points to gain an electoral majority, in all likelihood, will be more difficult for the party than accomplishing the past documented gains.

In its effort to gain an electoral majority, the Republican party must be aware not only of its deficiencies but also of the dynamic elements afoot in North Carolina politics. Two fairly sizable groups of voters have recently been or are in the process of being added to the electorate. From 1960 to 1968 there was a 44.6 percent increase in black registration although North Carolina trailed all of the other southern states in the registration of blacks with only 54.8 percent registered. Comprising 16.1 percent of the electorate, the Negro has recently been providing Democratic candidates with a bloc vote. If such a practice continues, the GOP will be faced with a serious disadvantage in achieving parity. (See Fig. 8.18.)

In the past the Republican party has provided little appeal to the black man. In fact, some recent electoral contests seem to suggest that the party does not wish to appeal to the newly enfranchised black but instead seeks to take advantage of his presence by appealing to the white voter in the areas of high black concentration. This "southern strategy" was supposedly a strong component in the Goldwater candidacy in 1964, and it seemingly worked well in some southern states. In North Carolina, however, its success was nominal. North Carolina responded to this appeal much like the states of the Upper South (Kentucky,

Tennessee, and Virginia) rather than like the states of the Deep South. In the 1968 election Wallace's mixture of racist and populist appeals generated a favorable white response in counties of high black concentration. At the same time the Republican candidate for governor, James Gardner, fared extremely well in these same counties. Nevertheless a vexing problem for the Republicans at the state as well as the national level is what to do about the black vote. Can the party win consistently in the future if it allows the black vote to go to the Democrats by default?

The lowering of the voting age to eighteen will increase the size of the electorate and concomitantly present the Republican party with other problems. Recent nationwide polls have shown that new voters are decidedly liberal and register overwhelmingly as Democrats or Independents. These young voters probably view the Republican party as the party of the old, the rich, and the "Establishment." Therefore, to appeal to this new voter the party is faced with having to reshape its image.

Then too the stigma of being a long-term minority party is difficult to overcome. Most North Carolinians are registered as Democrats, primarily because in the past the "real" election was the Democratic primary. Although evidence has been presented above showing that voting behavior does not necessarily coincide with nominal party membership, candidate recruitment and party organization are adversely affected by the low levels of Republican registration. Leaders of both parties as well as political observers feel that the biggest problem facing the GOP is

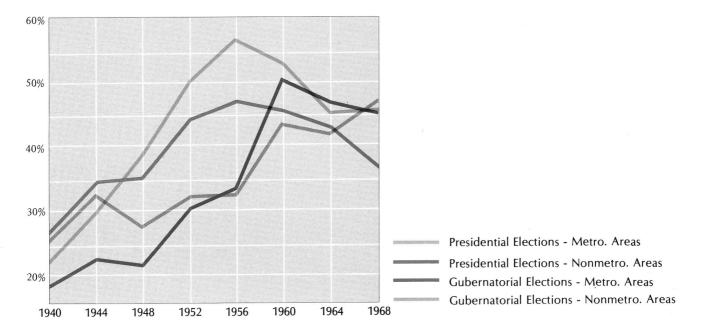

*The metropolitan vote includes returns from the six largest urban areas.

Source: The 1940-64 data are taken from Jack D. Fleer, *North Carolina Politics: An Introduction*, p. 134.

Fig. 8.19. Republican Percentage of the Total Vote in Presidential and Gubernatorial Elections in Metropolitan and Nonmetropolitan Areas, 1940-1968

the difficulty in getting attractive, viable candidates running under its banner. Generally, citizens in a traditional one-party state who wish to enter politics must join the majority party if they are to have any hope of success. Only time and political victories by the minority party can erode this tendency.

The future of the Republican party and consequently two-party competition in North Carolina is not as bleak as it might appear from the preceding discussion. Republicans also are advantaged by several phenomena. The migration patterns have led to increased Republicanism, because traditional Democratic identifiers are leaving the state while those moving in tend to be Republicans. This pattern in all likelihood will continue in the 1970s.

Growing Republicanism in North Carolina is no longer limited to the urban areas of the state. A few years ago political observers were referring to the growth of the Republican party in the New South as primarily an urban phenomenon. It is true that growth occurred initially in urban areas but since that burst of energy Republicanism has spread into the nonmetropolitan areas as well. The apex of urban Republicanism occurred in the presidential election of 1956 and the gubernatorial election of 1960. Since 1960 the appeal of the Republican party has "evened out" between metropolitan and nonmetropolitan areas. (See Fig. 8.19.)

The Republican party is also advantaged in an off-handed way by the woes of the Democrats. First, support for the majority party is declining—a psychological disadvantage. Second, the Democratic party has been so accustomed to winning in an almost effortless manner in North Carolina that it may be difficult for the party to adjust itself to a new situation. Third, long-term dominant parties tend to be ridden by factionalization. One measure of this is the number of aspirants in major office primaries. Currently there seems to be no decline in the number of candidates in the Democratic primaries. At some point in the future, however, Democrats must come to an understanding that they must defeat Republicans rather than one another for political office.

At this juncture in the political development of North Carolina and Metrolina it is particularly difficult to forecast political trends. The powerful third-party movement of George Wallace is an obscuring factor. The greater tendency for split-ticket voting complicates analysis and enhances such short-term ad hoc phenomena as candidate appeal and campaign intensity. The impact that the eighteen-year-olds will have on the electoral process is unknown. Whether blacks will remain wed to the Democratic party or become more of a swing group over the next decade or two is an open question. Some predictions, however, appear to be fairly safe. Complete Democratic dominance of North

Carolina politics is over. Party loyalty among Tar Heel voters appears to be less important now than it was previously. As the more highly visible electoral contests such as the presidential, congressional, and gubernatorial races are increasingly decided on the basis of issue and candidate appeal, the rate of ticket-splitting will increase. Elections will be less predictable, margins of victory narrower, and at the top of the ballot an "every man for himself" political style will probably develop. It is altogether possible that at the very time the Republican party has almost closed the gap between itself and the Democrats the importance of party in highly visible elections is on the decline.

REFERENCES

Campbell, Angus; Philip Converse; Warren Miller; and Donald Stokes. *Elections and the Political Order.* New York: John Wiley & Sons, 1965.

———. *The American Voter.* New York: John Wiley & Sons, 1960.

Converse, Philip; Warren Miller; Jerold Rusk; and Arthur Wolfe. "Continuity and Change in American Politics: Parties and Issues in the 1968 Election," *American Political Science Review* 63 (December 1969): 1083-1105.

Cosman, Bernard. "Presidential Republicanism in the South, 1960," *Journal of Politics* 24 (May 1962): 303-22.

Fleer, Jack D. *North Carolina Politics: An Introduction.* Chapel Hill: University of North Carolina Press, 1968.

Fowler, Donald L. *Presidential Voting in South Carolina: 1948-1964.* Columbia: University of South Carolina, Bureau of Governmental Research and Service, 1966.

Key, V. O., Jr. *Southern Politics in State and Nation.* New York: Random House, Inc., 1949.

Lefler, Hugh Talmage, and Albert Ray Newsome. *North Carolina.* Chapel Hill: University of North Carolina Press, 1963.

Leiserson, Avery, ed. *The American South in the 1960's.* New York: Frederick A. Praeger, Publishers, 1964.

Matthews, Donald R., and James W. Prothro. "Social and Economic Factors and Negro Voter Registration in the South," *The American Political Science Review* 57 (March 1963): 24-44.

Orr, Douglas M., Jr. *Congressional Redistricting: The North Carolina Experience.* Chapel Hill: University of North Carolina, Department of Geography, 1970.

Sindler, Allan P. *Change in the Contemporary South.* Durham: Duke University Press, 1963.

Strong, Donald S. *Urban Republicanism in the South.* University, Ala.: Bureau of Public Administration, University of Alabama, 1960.

Zoph, Paul E., Jr. *North Carolina, a Demographic Profile.* Chapel Hill: Carolina Population Center, 1967.

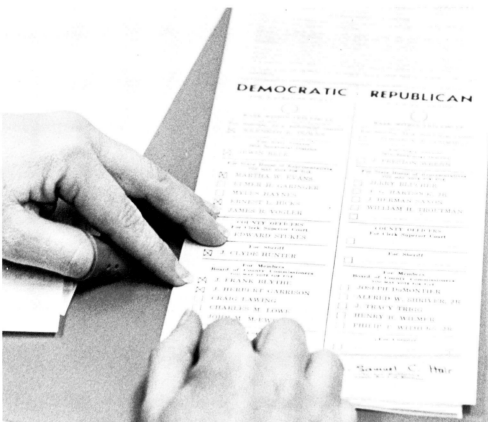

9. EDUCATION

J. NORFLEET JARRELL

"A complex society is dependent every hour of every day upon the capacity of its people to read and write, to make complex judgements and to act in the light of fairly extensive information. When there is not this kind of base on which to build, modern society and economic developments are simply impossible."—*John W. Gardner,* Excellence

No issue is more important to the quality of life in Metrolina than the status of its educational system. The availability of a good education for all the region's citizens is fundamental to the development of the wisdom and understanding necessary to deal with present and future problems. Metrolina possesses several assets for meeting this goal: a public-school system availing itself of recent innovations in education, a new and promising system of community colleges and technical institutes providing intermediate post-high-school educational opportunities, a system of well-established, private junior and senior colleges, and a new and rapidly expanding public university in Charlotte.

As is the case in much of the South, Metrolina does not rank very high according to national standards in terms of median educational level. A substantial part of the region's tax dollar is allotted to public education, but the median salary level is well below the national average. Long-resisted public-school desegregation has occurred rapidly over the last five years, costing money and administrative energy, but toward the goal of equal educational opportunity. Education is becoming an increasingly expensive business at all levels as funds have become tight in the late sixties and early seventies.

The facilities of the Metrolina educational system consist of a large complex of public elementary, middle, and high schools employing 11,361 teachers in 1970; four technical institutes; two community colleges; four private junior

colleges; twelve private four-year colleges; a branch of the University of South Carolina in Lancaster; a branch of the University of North Carolina in Charlotte; and thirteen teaching hospitals.

THE PUBLIC SCHOOL SYSTEM

Public-School Administration

The administrative designs of Metrolina's various public-school systems are not consistent (see Fig. 9.1). The Mecklenburg and Gaston city and county systems are consolidated, with single administrative units presiding over city and surrounding county school populations. Lancaster County, in South Carolina, also operates under a single division of school administration. In all of the other systems, however, the city and county divisions are separate. York, the other South Carolina county in Metrolina, is the most fragmented system, with four divisions centered around the four largest cities of that county—York, Clover, Rock Hill, and Fort Mill. The Cabarrus County system operates separately from those of both Concord and Kannapolis; the Catawba County system is distinct from those of Hickory and Newton; the Kings Mountain and Shelby city schools are administered separately from each other and from Cleveland County; the Iredell County system is separate from Mooresville and Statesville; and separate systems exist for Lincolnton City and Lincoln County, Salisbury City and Rowan County, Stanly County and Albemarle City, and finally Monroe City and Union County.

Overall, the public-school administrative organizational structures of Metrolina favor separate city and county school operation, with only three instances of consolidation.

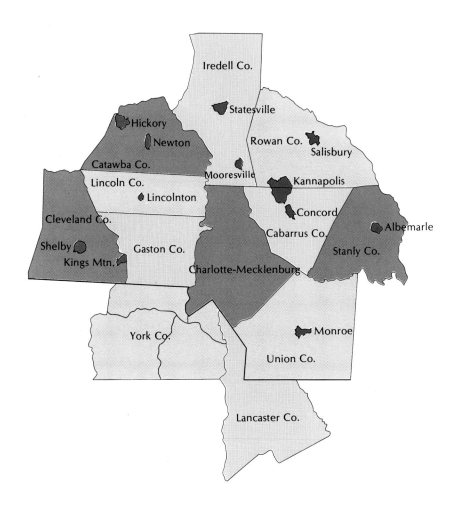

Fig. 9.1. Location of All Metrolina Public School Systems

Public-School-System Assessment

Public education should come under particular scrutiny in
an area such as Metrolina, which has a median educational
level significantly short of a high-school diploma. Many
estimates and comparisons may be used to analyze the
area's school systems. Some of these have primarily a financial basis and thus are related to the input of money a
system receives and how that money is used. For example,
what does a system pay its teachers and what is the per-
pupil expenditure for its student population in comparison
to other systems? Other estimates may involve different
measurements: How has school desegregation progressed?
What is the median educational level of the populace served
by a particular public-school system?

Student-Teacher Ratio. The public-school student-teacher
populations and ratios for 1969-70 are shown in Fig. 9.2.
Only the Salisbury system shows a ratio less than the national average of 22.7 students per teacher.

The student-teacher ratio is an important index to the
evaluation of a school system, indicating the total number
of students per staff member within that system. The student-teacher ratios depicted in Fig. 9.2 should be viewed
with caution, however. The ratios usually show a smaller
number of students than those actually in the classroom.
Calculation of a student-teacher ratio takes into account
the entire professional staff of a school, including supervi-
sors, counselors, librarians, and others, who have only
limited contact with students during the school day.

The vital area of special education also tends to inflate
the student-teacher ratio, since it demands more money,
uses more teacher time with small numbers of students, and
therefore draws teachers away from the standard classroom.
Special education within each school system takes on different organizational structures using varying amounts of
teaching energy. Charlotte-Mecklenburg, for example, involves fourteen hundred of its students in special-education
programs for the educable mentally retarded in grades one
through twelve and eighteen hundred students in speech-

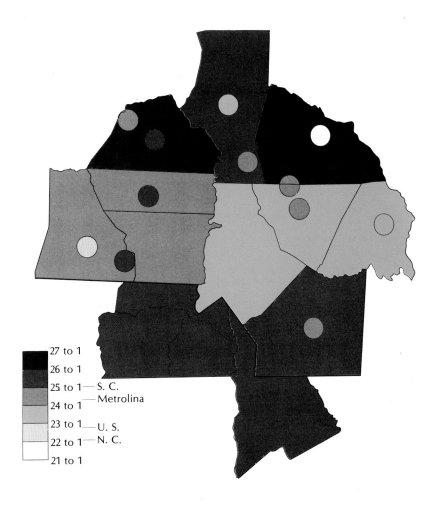

27 to 1	
26 to 1	
25 to 1	S. C.
24 to 1	Metrolina
23 to 1	U. S.
22 to 1	N. C.
21 to 1	

Fig. 9.2. Metrolina Public-School Student-Teacher Ratio

therapy programs in grades one through six. These efforts, along with others such as programs for trainable mentally retarded children and hospital-bound students serve a total of nearly four thousand students in this system.

Parents and teachers probably agree that the pupil-teacher ratio in Metrolina or, more importantly, operational class size, is in most cases not yet at a level allowing for optimum teaching and learning efficiency. At the same time it has become apparent during the last few years that there is no longer a teacher shortage. Overcrowded classrooms therefore reflect a shortage of funded positions, not a lack of available teachers.

Per Pupil Expenditure. Money for public-school systems is highly variable because of differences in federal funds made available to the schools, and especially because of supplements from metropolitan areas of high population density. Fig. 9.3 shows the great differences in per-pupil expenditures for each of the Metrolina school systems.

State funding is of course basic to the operation of any

school system in the Carolinas. The state provides the basic teacher-pay scale, and in areas where there is no local aid state money is the only source of funds for teachers' salaries. State appropriations provide salaries for administrative and paraprofessional personnel, along with money for the operation and maintenance of school buildings and buses. They also provide teaching materials, equipment, and supplies.

Federal funding is largely distributed through the Elementary and Secondary Education Act (ESEA). The amount of federal money received by a system is essentially a response to proposals submitted by the administrators of a public-school system. These proposals are reviewed by ESEA committees, and funds are allocated to systems submitting the most worthy proposals. For example, money is currently being awarded to child-development centers under Title I, ESEA, Title II funds are still largely spent for library books, and Title VI resources are currently being allocated for programs involving learning disabilities. The amount of federal funds utilized in a particular school

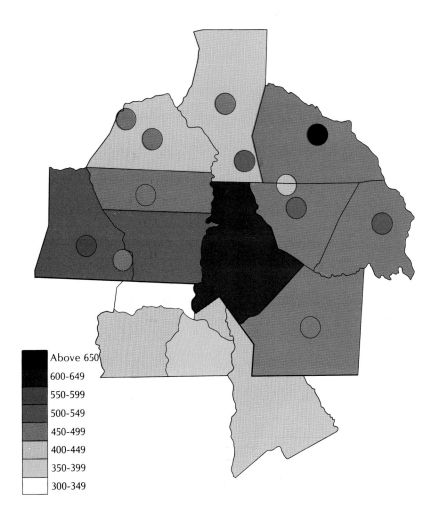

	Above 650
	600-649
	550-599
	500-549
	450-499
	400-449
	350-399
	300-349

Fig. 9.3. Metrolina Public-School Per-Pupil Expenditure, 1968-69

system is determined by the amount of money allocated for a specific title program, by the submission of a request by the school system for the money that is available, and by the quality of the submitted proposal.

Local funds are used largely to supplement teacher, administrative, and paraprofessional salaries. These funds may be used also to provide additional teaching or administrative staff positions, and to some degree must contribute toward the operation of buildings and other basic school-system expenses. Local supplements for a school system are derived from the tax structure of a city and/or county and are approved by public referendum.

In 1968-69 the per-pupil expenditure as a national average was $680. An increase of 14 percent brought the national average to $773 in 1969-70. The National Education Association projects this figure to $839 per pupil for 1970-71, an additional increase of 12 percent.

Fig. 9.3 shows the amount of federal, state, and local funds expended by each of the public-school systems of Metrolina, divided by each system's student enrollment

for the 1968-69 school year in each respective unit. These averages have not increased proportionately with national averages since 1968-69.

There was little variation in state funds allotted on a per-pupil basis; the average was $480.86 per pupil for the North Carolina systems of Metrolina in 1968-69. Federal funds averaged $49.31 and local funds, $90.35. The two administrative units with the greatest input of local funds were Salisbury City with an allotment of $224.71 per pupil and Mecklenburg Consolidated with $215.04 per pupil. Mecklenburg, however, had the highest percentage of total per-pupil expenditure from local funds of any Metrolina system—35.4 percent. Salisbury's local funds provided 32.5 percent of the total school bill. Both of these percentages were among the highest in the Carolinas.

Teachers' Salaries. There is some diversity in the methods for determining teachers' salaries throughout the twenty-seven school systems in Metrolina (see Fig. 9.4). Four systems offer only the state's pay scale at both the baccalaure-

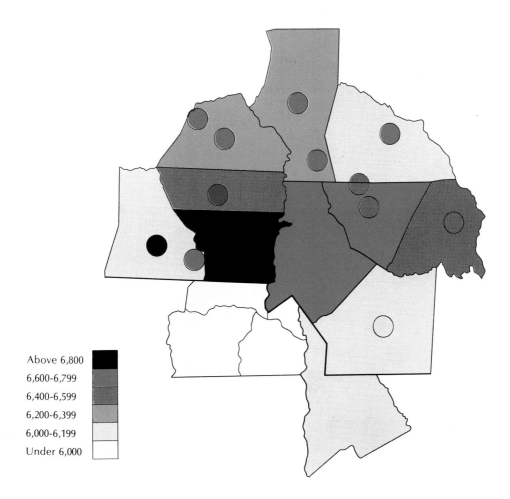

Above 6,800
6,600-6,799
6,400-6,599
6,200-6,399
6,000-6,199
Under 6,000

Fig. 9.4. Teachers' Salaries in Metrolina's Public Schools

ate and master's level of preparation. All the rest offer some kind of supplement either in the form of a flat monthly or yearly amount that does not vary with years of teaching experience, or a rate of supplemental pay that increases with experience. An example of the latter is Mecklenburg, which pays on a scale that increases pay regularly with experience so that after two years of teaching experience teachers in this system make the highest salaries of any in Metrolina and continue to receive maximum pay after fifteen years' experience.

The South Carolina base for a beginning teacher with a B.A. degree was $4,961 compared to North Carolina's $6,050 in 1970-71. The maximum amount a teacher with a master's degree could make in South Carolina was $8,372, and in North Carolina $9,158. Only state base salaries are considered in these pay rates, but the districts of York and Lancaster counties have partially closed this gap in pay scales by offering large supplements. Lancaster's consolidated system paid an additional $1,100 per year to teachers with B.A. degrees and $1,200 to those with M.A. degrees in 1970-71. York County's York, Clover, and Fort

Mill districts paid a supplement amounting to 20 percent of state aid, while the Rock Hill District is unique in Metrolina in that it has a form of merit pay, based on the scores recorded on the National Teacher's Examination. The following 1970-71 figures compare average pay rates for beginning teachers with a baccalaureate degree and average maximum rates for holders of master's degrees in all systems having over six thousand students:

Metrolina	$6,406	$9,419
North Carolina	6,153	9,343
South Carolina	6,192	8,949
United States	6,850	11,813

Median Educational Level. The 1960 census showed a national educational level of 10.5 school years completed. By 1970 this figure had risen to 12.1. In addition, 75.9 percent of American citizens had a high-school education or better in 1970.

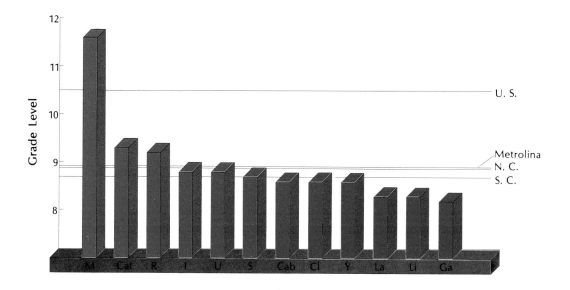

Fig. 9.5. Median Educational Level for Metrolina, North Carolina, South Carolina, and the United States, 1960

Although median educational level statistics are not yet available for 1970 on the county level, as shown in Fig. 9.5 the average grade level completed in Metrolina in 1960 was slightly higher than the North Carolina or South Carolina average, yet 1.57 grade levels below the national norm for 1960. The figures are as follows: Metrolina, 8.92; North Carolina, 8.90; South Carolina, 8.70; United States, 10.50. The 1960 census revealed that North Carolina ranked forty-third in school years completed and South Carolina ranked forty-ninth. When grade levels completed by Metrolina's population are compared to those of other states, Metrolina ranks forty-third.

Percentage of Fifth-Grade Enrollment Graduating from High School. Fig. 9.6 provides some insights into the school dropout rate, or the "holding power" of the schools. The available data are by county unit only. Mecklenburg, Catawba, and Rowan counties lead the list in the percentage of fifth-grade students to graduate from high school seven years later.

Percentage of Population Twenty-Five Years of Age and Over Who Have Graduated from High School. Fig. 9.7 reveals the percentage of the population twenty-five years old or older who have completed four years of high school or more. The 1960 data is from the 1960 census. The 1967 and 1980 data are both projections made by the Research Triangle Institute of Chapel Hill—Durham—Raleigh. The projections were made for North Carolina counties only; the South Carolina projections are based on average percentage increases for North Carolina counties. For all three sets of data, Mecklenburg County shows the greatest percentage of graduates, followed by Catawba and Rowan

counties. Gaston, Lancaster, and Lincoln counties have and are predicted to maintain the lowest levels.

Metrolina's Educational Attainment. An examination of the educational attainment of Metrolina's public-school population as shown in Figs. 9.5, 9.6, and 9.7 reveals areas that need improvement. In 1960 Metrolina had a median educational level of only 8.92 grade levels completed, with only one school system (Mecklenburg) having a grade-level attainment exceeding the national norm but still short of the high-school diploma. The percentage of fifth-grade enrollment graduating from high school in 1968-69 was 63.7, with no system equivalent to the national norm of 75.9. Of those students graduating from high school, less than 44 percent went on to an institution of higher learning in 1969. The Research Triangle's 1980 projection of the Metrolina population twenty-five years of age and over who will have completed high school is 57 percent, only 6 percent higher than the national norm of 1960. One very important problem that the public-school system cannot ignore is the disposition of the more than one-third of the students who drop out. Some of these dropouts of course reenter the educational system later in life. Others enter military service. But most of the dropouts are the unmotivated students for whom public education seems to have little relevance. Public education is charged with the incredible responsibility of designing an educational program relevant to the needs of each child within the system. Because of the almost impossible nature of this task, a large percentage of students suffer from "underachievement"—performance and classroom involvement beneath the level of the child's ability. Underachievement is often related to complex family and home problems the child brings to school with

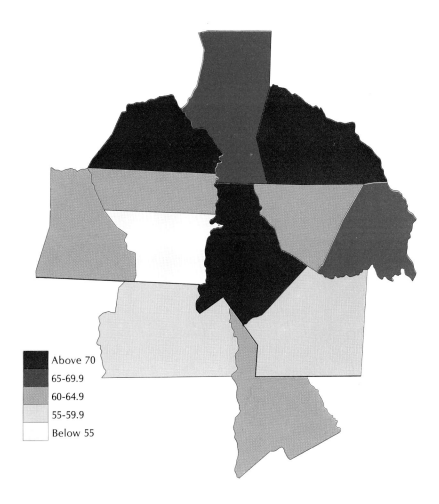

Fig. 9.6. Percentage of Metrolina Fifth-Grade Enrollment Graduating from High School, 1968-69

him. A study made in 1967 at the North Carolina Advancement School in Winston-Salem (an experimental residential school for eighth-grade boys from all over the state who were classed as underachievers) attempted to categorize underachievers in the hope of finding some cure for the several types of underachievement. The results were discouraging but not really surprising. Although the student body was analyzed carefully so that it would represent a typical group of potential dropouts, the researcher found nearly as many groups of underachievers as there were underachievers themselves. The program that worked best involved small groups, much individual attention, almost constant counseling, and educational programs having an action orientation.

There has been a comparatively larger percentage of Negro students dropping out from school than whites. It will be interesting to observe whether the recent complete desegregation of public schools at all levels, producing a school learning environment of greater equality, will lower the dropout rate among Negro students.

Administrative awareness, with the help of local and federal funding, is beginning to supply greater motivation in the public schools for other types of potential dropouts. For example, there has been a reawakening to the need for occupational education to provide students lacking the desire or ability to enter college or even to finish high school with job skills in addition to the high-school diploma. Many school systems in Metrolina give some of their students at the junior-high and senior-high levels an opportunity to learn a skill. The Gaston County system, for example, has a high dropout rate and has designed a curriculum with this problem in mind. In 1960 Gaston had the lowest median educational level of any county in Metrolina; it also exhibited the lowest percentage of fifth-grade enrollment graduating from high school and the lowest percentage of population twenty-five years of age and over who had completed high school. Yet the percentage of high-school graduates who entered college was quite high. Gaston County has a high dropout rate, it seems, partly because it is a heavily industrialized county, with textile manufacturing

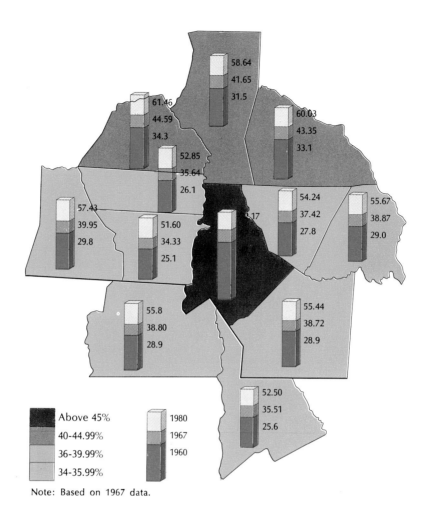

Fig. 9.7. Percentage of Metrolina Population Twenty-five Years of Age and Over That Has Completed High School

in the cities of Cramerton, Gastonia, and Belmont. Job availability to a sixteen-year-old dropout in Gaston County is therefore relatively high. Funds provided by the federal Vocational Educational Act of 1963 and 1968 have allowed the county to develop occupational opportunities for its junior- and senior-high-school students in cooperation with local industry. Approximately 40 percent of Gaston's high-school population has become involved in occupational educational programs—a group that surely would have had a high dropout potential in the past. Industry has provided equipment and instruction in many cases, and the school system has obtained assistance from the North Carolina School of Textiles in Belmont. Since the dropout rate is greater after the ninth grade, which is beyond the compulsory school-attendance age, junior- and senior-high schools have provided programs in cosmetology, auto mechanics, graphics, masonry, textiles, and other fields of work. The school system is thus equipping some of its potential dropouts with job readiness or the opportunity to continue

with a sequential program at Gaston Community College.

Other systems, Charlotte-Mecklenburg, for example, also have well-developed occupational training programs. The Cleveland system has begun a program utilizing occupational education teachers provided by local industry.

Some systems are developing "career awareness" programs in the middle grades (six, seven, and eight). New courses are designed to stimulate a student's thinking about his future occupation in life, and to some degree instruct him in the kinds of jobs and salaries available at different levels of educational attainment.

The "EMRs," or educationally and mentally retarded, comprise another group of students easily lost in the large classroom. In Charlotte-Mecklenburg these students are enrolled in a program beginning in grade one and continuing through grade twelve that features individualized instruction and small classes. In Shelby such students remain in regular classrooms and are taken to resource centers during part of the school day for special instruction in

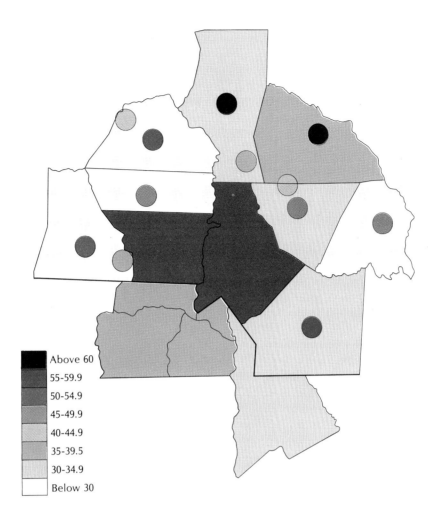

Fig. 9.8. Percentage of Metrolina High-School Graduates Enrolled in College

reading and learning skills related to occupational programs. Virtually every system in the Metrolina area has availed itself, to some degree, of available federal money to design a specialized program for this group of potential dropouts.

There is not yet an across-the-board effort on the part of school systems in Metrolina to provide students with the most recent and innovative instructional techniques, but as in the area of occupational and special education there are some encouraging beginnings. Iredell County, in a novel experiment, conducts an entire grade-one through grade-eight program in a building constructed to facilitate team teaching. There are no walls within the building and the students are not assigned to any specific grade level. Instead, there are fourteen attainment levels in each subject area through which a student progresses at his own individual pace. Instruction is carried out with mixed ages at all levels within flexibly designed areas defined by movable bookshelves, partitions, and blackboards. The heart of the system is the open library or learning-resources cen-

ter along with the team-teaching technique. Team teaching is providing new learning opportunities to these students while using a smaller number of teachers accompanied by teacher aides. It is hoped that this kind of instruction, which is tailored to the specific needs of students, will provide its learners with the greater stimulation and lessened frustration required for a child to remain in school.

Percentage of High-School Graduates Enrolled in College. What happens to Metrolina students educationally after graduation from high school? An average of 43.5 percent enter a college, university, or technical institute. Of this percentage, 30.5 percent enroll in a senior college and 12.7 percent enroll in a junior college or two-year school. Fig. 9.8 shows that an unusually high percentage of Statesville's high-school graduates enter a junior college as opposed to a four-year school and that Salisbury leads the region in college entrance, with 60.5 percent of its students enrolled in an institution of higher learning after high-school graduation. Mecklenburg and Gaston also have high percentages of college enrollment, with 57.8 and 56 percent respectively of their high-school graduates continuing their education. Nationally the figure is approximately 60 percent.

Public-School Desegregation. The school systems of Metrolina have had no issue in the past few years more significant than that of effecting desegregation in the public schools. The problem has not been unique to Metrolina, however, since courts throughout the nation have handed down rulings requiring each school's Negro-white enrollment to reflect the racial balance of the entire community. In the eleven southern states the number of Negro pupils attending public schools with white majorities doubled during the period from the fall of 1968 to the fall of 1970. And in terms of percentage change the increase was also dramatic. In the South the percentage of the desegregated school population that is Negro rose from 18.4 percent in 1968 to 38.1 percent in 1970.

The mechanics of desegregation have been given high priority by the administrative units of the schools of Metrolina. School systems have responded to court orders and promoted desegregation quickly. The pattern of desegregation presents a very rapidly changing picture in the region even now when most systems are nearly completely desegregated. School district lines are changing from year to year to assure a more equal distribution of Negro and white students in the public schools, but not without resulting confusion to parents, students, and the administrative hierarchy.

The upheaval in the larger systems has been somewhat more drastic because of large-scale busing, particularly in the complex Mecklenburg system of over a hundred schools. Court orders, followed by appeals from school boards, the formation of parent groups, threats of loss of federal money to systems not complying, and general unrest in junior- and senior-high-school student bodies have all been a part of the changing scene in Metrolina's Mecklenburg system.

By 1971, of the 344 schools in Metrolina, 334 were desegregated (97 percent), compared to 304 desegregated schools of 357 in 1968 (85 percent). The loss of schools during a period of desegregation, thirteen in this case, often happens when an all-Negro school in a Negro neighborhood is closed and its students bused out into the surrounding predominantly white areas. This process of school-plant deactivation has thus caused some overcrowding in Metrolina schools.

As is the case with the rest of the South, Metrolina counties have shown a rapid advance in the percentage of the desegregated school population that is Negro, from an average of 18 percent in 1968 to 22 percent in the spring of 1971. During this period the region's South Carolina systems have experienced a sharper increase, mainly because they had a lower percentage in 1968 than the Metrolina counties of North Carolina.

J. Norfleet Jarrell

HIGHER EDUCATION

In 1971 there were, in the twelve-county region of Metrolina, thirteen senior institutions offering the baccalaureate degree, seven two-year institutions offering vocational training and/or college-parallel work leading to the Associate in Arts degree, and four technical training institutions granting certificates to students completing specified programs (see Fig. 9.9). Only eight of these twenty-four institutions were supported by public funds.

Although education is their primary role, these institutions also contribute significantly to the economic development of the region. The twenty-four institutions employ a total of 4,481 people whom they pay approximately $30.3 million in annual salaries, and they enroll approximately 51,000 students, though not all on a full-time basis.

When translated into practical terms, these figures are of enormous import. One researcher, Warren Rovetch, has stated that "translating a full-time-equivalent student (FTE) into a unit of measure that also includes faculty and staff and their families and the families of married students, our studies show, on the average, that one daytime FTE represents an expenditure of $5,000 per year apart from education and housing costs and apart from buying by the college."[1] Thus, according to Rovetch's study, an FTE of 11,000 would mean $55 million in personal buying per year. No such study is known to have been conducted in the Metrolina region, but the implications are clear.

In addition to the enormous purchasing power represented by individuals associated with post-secondary and technical institutions, the total operating budgets of the institutions themselves amounted to $47.4 million in 1970-71. Furthermore, the value of their combined capital assets was in excess of $159.4 million. These figures suggest that the twenty-four post-secondary and technical institutions constitute a major consumer of goods and services.

The direct economic impact of the institutions is only a portion of the picture. The region's institutions produced over 4,200 graduates with terminal degrees, representing a variety of professional and technical fields. Although no precise data has been collected concerning the mobility patterns of these individuals, the figures available suggest that the vast majority of them remain in the region after graduation.

The institutions have from their inception influenced the physical development of adjacent areas, but within the past half decade city and regional planners have become much more actively involved in planning and allowing for appropriate boundary relations between post-secondary institutions and their host communities. This type of planning is most dramatically illustrated by the cooperative ef-

1. Warren Rovetch, "Architecture for the Urban Campus," in *Agony and Promise: Current Issues in Higher Education,* ed. G. Kerry Smith (San Francisco: Jossey-Bass, 1969), p. 80.

The term "full-time equivalent student" means all full-time students plus the total number of credit hours taken by all part-time students divided by the number of credit hours considered to be a full load.

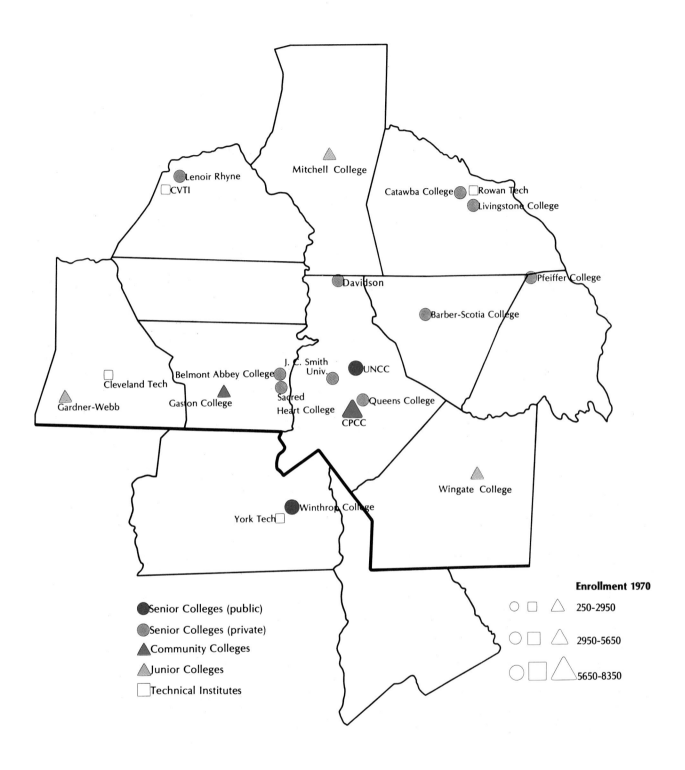

Mitchell College

Lenoir Rhyne
CVTI

Catawba College Rowan Tech
Livingstone College

Davidson Pfeiffer College

Barber-Scotia College

Cleveland Tech

Belmont Abbey College J. C. Smith Univ. UNCC

Gardner-Webb Gaston College Sacred Heart College Queens College

CPCC

Wingate College

York Tech Winthrop College

Senior Colleges (public)
Senior Colleges (private)
Community Colleges
Junior Colleges
Technical Institutes

Enrollment 1970

○ □ △ 250-2950

○ □ △ 2950-5650

○ □ △ 5650-8350

Fig. 9.9. Location of Metrolina Community Colleges, Technical Institutes,
Junior Colleges, and Senior Colleges and Universities

forts of the University of North Carolina at Charlotte and the Charlotte-Mecklenburg Planning Commission toward blue-printing a university city complete with shopping centers, churches, schools, recreational areas, and other facilities. This is by no means the only such cooperative arrangement in the region, but it is, to date, the most ambitious project of this nature.

Several of the institutions are participating in planning efforts with region-wide implications. The Institute for Urban Studies and Community Service of the University of North Carolina at Charlotte is serving as the Secretariat of the Piedmont Urban Policy Conference. Another example of regional-institutional cooperation in planning may be seen in North Carolina's policy of requiring its community colleges and technical institutes to conduct studies of regional need before implementing new programs.

The twenty-four post-secondary and technical institutions exert many other influences on the region in more subtle ways. The use by business, industry, and service organizations of faculty members as consultants and resource persons is one example. Another is the service-learning program in which students from Johnson C. Smith, Queens, Davidson, and UNCC work in a number of public and private agencies. The institutions' contributions to the cultural life of the region are discussed in Part 10 of this atlas.

Of course no discussion of regional-institutional interaction would be complete without reference to the contributions of the individuals, civic groups, businesses, and industries to Metrolina's post-secondary and technical schools. Not only are millions of dollars in gifts granted each year, but individuals from the community serve as part-time instructors in a number of the institutions, and some civic organizations, such as the Charlotte Chamber of Commerce, have formed special committees whose charges include assisting local higher educational institutions in a variety of ways.

Junior and Community Colleges and Technical Institutes

Within the past fifteen years both North and South Carolina have established state-supported networks of community colleges and/or technical institutes.

Through legislation enacted in the 1957 and 1963 General Assembly a system of community colleges and a system of industrial education centers or technical institutes were established in North Carolina. In the Metrolina region there are two community colleges (Central Piedmont Community College and Gaston College) and three technical institutes (Catawba Valley Technical Institute, Cleveland Technical Institute, and Rowan Technical Institute) that are affected by this legislation.

Both types of institutions offer adult and continuing education and vocational and trade programs of as much as a year's length, plus one- and two-year technical pro-

grams with certificates and diplomas appropriate to each. Some of these institutions also provide college preparatory programs for those whose high-school preparation has not enabled them to meet minimum college-admissions standards. In addition to these programs and services, the community colleges offer two-year-college parallel curricula in the arts and sciences leading to the associate degree. Recipients of this degree may apply to four-year colleges or universities for admission with a maximum of full junior standing.

In 1962 South Carolina established a system of adult technical education centers. Of twelve such centers in the state, one (York County Technical Institute) lies within the Metrolina region. Its program is comparable to the programs of the technical institutes described above. The region also contains one other public, two-year institution. During their freshman year students at the University of South Carolina at Lancaster choose between a college parallel program or a two-year terminal program. The campus is governed as a two-year branch of its parent institution in Columbia.

There are four private junior colleges in the Metrolina region. Mitchell College and Wingate College in North Carolina and Friendship College and Clinton Junior College in South Carolina offer two-year college parallel programs which prepare students to transfer to senior institutions.

Special Programs and Services. It is impossible to do justice to all the special programs operating in the region's two-year institutions in a work of this nature. The programs presented here are selected by virtue of their uniqueness within the region and/or their implications for practice beyond the region.

In 1969 Central Piedmont Community College was invited to become a member of the "League for Innovation in the Community College," an organization composed of fifteen outstanding community colleges in the United States. These pioneering institutions exchange information on pilot projects, teaching techniques, and new instructional material. Central Piedmont's work in developing individualized-instruction methods has earned it a reputation as a leader in that field. Much use is made of audio-visual and programmed instruction, and students are allowed to work at their own pace by using learning-activity packages that include video tapes, slides, film presentations, and programmed texts.

Gaston College offers more discrete engineering technical programs (six) than any other institution in North Carolina or the region. It also provides an Advancement Studies Program which annually enrolls sixty high-school graduates who have experienced limited academic success but who have demonstrated some intellectual potential. Through team-teaching, which, as mentioned earlier, emphasizes motivation as well as subject matter, these individuals are exposed to psychologists, counselors, reading specialists,

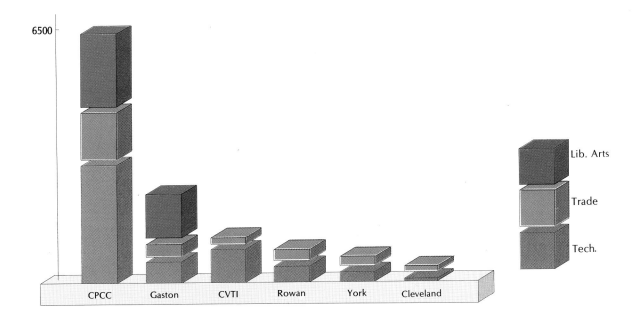

6500

Lib. Arts

Trade

Tech.

CPCC   Gaston   CVTI   Rowan   York   Cleveland

Fig. 9.10. Metrolina Curriculum Profile by Enrollment, Community Colleges and Technical Institutes

and sociologists. Upon completing the program (which has no rigid time limits but normally lasts one year) the students are moved directly into sophomore-level work, and the experience to date has been excellent. A number of individuals who have entered this program have graduated with honors, and these successes have attracted the attention of educators from throughout the East.

Mitchell College, within the past two years, has begun an instructional program that has as its base the practice of teaching by specific behavioral objectives. The teacher using this method is required to state explicitly the knowledge and skills to be mastered by the students in a given course. Thus the student has a clear knowledge of what is expected of him and the teacher is guided in his selection of subject matter and instructional techniques. Grades and progress are based on the level of mastery attained by the student.

Curriculum Profile by Enrollment. The data presented in Fig. 9.10 reflect the extent to which the community colleges and technical institutes have been successful in extending their services into the community. The "nondegree" category includes students enrolled in both on-campus and off-campus courses, which may be special workshops and seminars taught for industry, high-interest courses such as ceramics or art, or courses designed to assist an individual in a particular area, e.g., electronics. Also included in this category may be courses designed to lead to the high-school equivalency certificate, remedial reading, and other types of adult education. Without exception the in-

stitutions listed enroll more students in these nondegree courses than in any other single category of courses and programs.

The comparatively high percentage (26 percent) of Gaston College's students who are working toward the liberal-arts degree probably reflects the institution's original status as a community college, although it has since incorporated technical programs into its curriculum.

Enrollment Trends. Fig. 9.11 presents enrollment trends in the region's community colleges and technical institutes from 1963 through 1975. The importance of the need that these institutions are meeting is reflected in the continuous on-campus enrollment increases observed in the past and projected at least until 1975. Central Piedmont Community College and Rowan Technical Institute predict average enrollment increases of over one thousand per year and thus will be the fastest-growing institutions of this type in Metrolina. The remaining schools predict a more gradual but continuous increase in enrollment. Central Piedmont's rapid growth can be attributed to Charlotte-Mecklenburg's burgeoning population. Rowan Tech, on the other hand, is surrounded by four counties that do not have technical institutes or community colleges: Iredell, Davie, Stanly, and Cabarrus. As a result, roughly 40 percent of its students come from these surrounding counties.

Geographic Origin of Students. Fig. 9.12 highlights the intended function of the community college and technical institute: to serve the local population. Three of the tech-

page 193

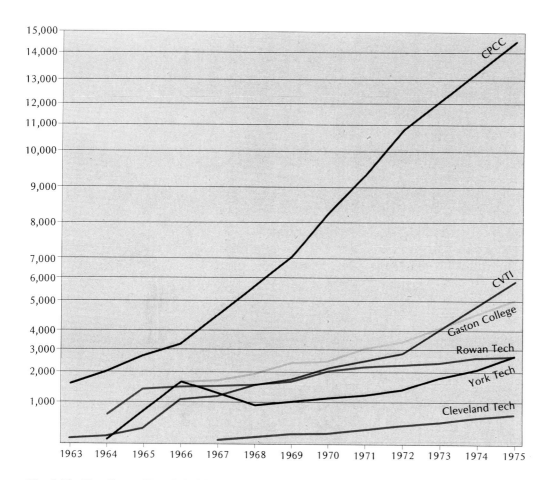

Fig. 9.11. Enrollment Trends in Metrolina Community Colleges and Technical Institutes

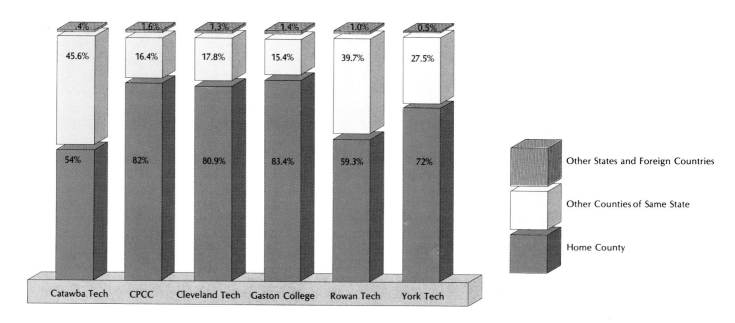

Fig. 9.12. Origin of Students in Selected Higher Education Institutions in Metrolina, 1970

nical institutes—York, Rowan, and Catawba—serve a broader geographic area. This reflects the lack of similar facilities in neighboring counties and also the more dispersed population pattern in those parts of the region. The consistently localized origin of students in all Metrolina community colleges and technical institutes is encouraged by the fact that no dormitory facilities are provided and all are therefore commuter schools.

Senior Institutions

The thirteen senior institutions of the region offer a number of programs leading to Bachelor of Science and Bachelor of Arts degrees in a wide variety of liberal-arts areas. They also offer teacher-training programs with specialities in several areas within the field of education or with majors in a liberal-arts discipline, and undergraduate professional programs including business administration, nursing, architecture, and engineering. One institution, UNCC, offers a Bachelor of Engineering Technology degree through a special program designed to provide the last two years for transfers from community colleges and technical institutes.

Special Programs and Services. As in the case of the two-year institutions, it would be impractical to describe all the noteworthy programs and services of the region's senior institutions. The four programs presented here have been selected for their uniqueness and to demonstrate the variety of innovative programs available in Metrolina.

In 1968 Davidson College revised its curriculum to provide undergraduates a number of unusual opportunities to expand their perspectives. The new program emphasizes the exploration of various value systems, largely through interdisciplinary programs, and features courses of independent study in which the student "contracts" with guiding faculty members to engage in work and research outside the classroom. Other exciting aspects of the new program at Davidson are the opportunities for students to become involved in the community through "extended studies" and "career-service" courses and the special foreign-study programs that now take students to Europe and will soon be expanded to include India.

Pfeiffer College offers its students a choice of three routes to a B.A. degree. Each of these routes is extremely flexible, but in all there is sufficient structure to insure that students are exposed to subject matter in a variety of fields. In addition to providing maximum freedom for its students to tailor their own academic programs, Pfeiffer features an evaluation-of-progress system based on units earned rather than on the traditional grading system. The number of units earned in a given course is determined by the quality of the student's work and the number of hours per week the class meets. A student needs 1,000 units to graduate. Some of these units may be earned by attending certain cultural events such as dramatic productions, lectures, poetry readings, and art exhibits. Most students earn approximately 125 units each semester, but that rate may be accelerated or reduced depending on the student's wishes and his performance.

The Charlotte Area Educational Consortium includes Barber-Scotia, Belmont Abbey, Davidson, Johnson C. Smith, Queens, Sacred Heart, and UNCC, plus three two-year institutions—Central Piedmont, Gaston, and Wingate. Through the consortium a student enrolled in any of the participating schools may take courses at any of the other schools with credit being granted by the student's institution. Faculty exchanges have also been arranged through the consortium as well as special programs and conferences such as the Writers' Workshop held at Belmont Abbey in 1971.

During the summer of 1971 Johnson C. Smith sponsored a program that provided an opportunity for Negro and white Charlotte-Mecklenburg public-school students to come together in a living-learning experience. The program, which ran for seven weeks and included approximately a hundred students per week focused on the problems and opportunities of human relations. The primary thrust was toward fostering interracial understanding and reducing tension in the school system.

The College of Human Development and Learning at UNCC has developed a teacher-education program that concentrates on developing in prospective teachers skills in recognizing, diagnosing, and clinically involving themselves in behavioral manifestations of physical, emotional, and/or mental handicaps. The teachers-in-training, through a combination of course work and exposure to actual classroom situations (in inner-city, small town, and rural settings), are taught to identify developmental needs, talents, and individual learning problems and to develop personalized learning experiences after assessment and diagnosis. The program also emphasizes educational planning through research and stresses the importance of translating research results into practical application.

Enrollment Trends. Fig. 9.13 reveals that UNCC has had the fastest growth rate of any higher educational institution in Metrolina. Indeed, UNCC's 31.9 percent increase from 1969 to 1970 was among the largest increases in the nation.

There are a number of reasons for UNCC's rapid growth. It is the only coeducational state-affiliated university of moderate size in Metrolina. Metrolina is a densely populated area, and students do not have to travel far to attend the college and may do so conveniently even if they choose not to live on campus. Also, the cost of attending a state university is relatively low as compared to that of private institutions.

Many private schools throughout the nation are experiencing declines in enrollment. Locally Belmont Abbey, Sacred Heart, and Livingstone have experienced enrollment declines of more than 10 percent. These declines relate in

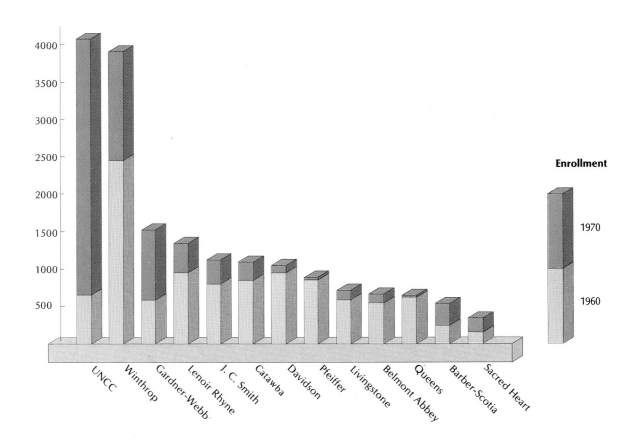

Fig. 9.13. Higher-Education Enrollment Trends in Metrolina, 1970

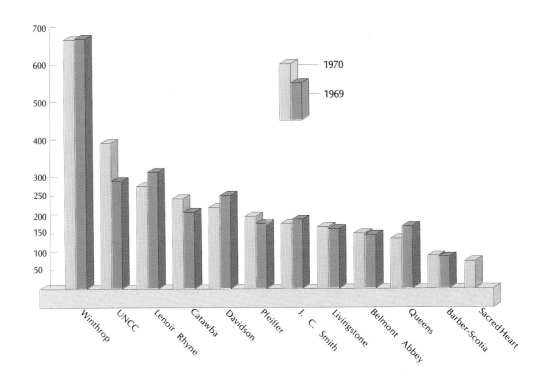

Fig. 9.14. Bachelor's Degrees Conferred in Metrolina, 1969-70

part to the fact that the less expensive state universities, technical institutes, and community colleges are drawing off some of the private schools' student bodies. A number of these schools, including Sacred Heart and Belmont Abbey, are modifying their curricula in order to produce more unique educational experiences and thus attract more students.

Several of the private colleges (Davidson, Pfeiffer, Queens, and Catawba) have made it their policy to maintain a constant student enrollment and have been relatively successful in doing so. Nevertheless the greater tuition and fee costs of these as well as many other private institutions have recently resulted in a decline in student applications.

Bachelor's Degrees Conferred. Fig. 9.14 indicates that in 1969-70, 2,766 B.A. degrees were conferred by Metrolina colleges and universities, an increase of 7.2 percent from the 2,576 degrees awarded in 1968-69. Winthrop College in Rock Hill, South Carolina, has granted the largest number of B.A. and B.S. degrees, followed by UNCC, Lenoir Rhyne, and Catawba.

Graduate Degree Programs. Two institutions in Metrolina are currently offering graduate work. Winthrop College offers Master of Arts, Master of Arts in Teaching, Master of Education, Master of Music, and Master of Science degrees, with seventeen departments offering graduate courses and ten departments offering master's degrees. Winthrop granted fifty-seven master's degrees in 1970 and forty-two in 1969. Graduate work at the master's level is also available at UNCC. The College of Human Development and Learning (Education) offers the option of a Master of Education or the Master of Arts in Education with a concentration in English, history, or mathematics. The College of Business Administration offers a master's program leading to the Master of Management degree.

Geographic Origin of Students. Fig. 9.15 reveals that Davidson, Queens, Johnson C. Smith, Belmont Abbey, Sacred Heart, and Catawba have student bodies composed of over one-half out-of-state students. UNCC, with residence halls for less than one-fourth of the student body, has drawn more than 50 percent of its students from Mecklenburg County and thereby has a larger commuter enrollment. Winthrop College draws almost 90 percent or more of its students from South Carolina.

Student Cost and Per-Pupil Expenditure (1970-71 Academic Year). The data in Fig. 9.16 present per-student expenditures and student costs at Metrolina colleges and universities for the 1970-71 academic year, excluding the cost of room and board. Average student costs increased 16 percent from 1969-70 to 1970-71 for the private schools shown in the table and 11 percent for the public institutions. Inflation accounts for about 6 percent of this rise.

shown in the table and 11 percent for the public institutions. Inflation accounts for about 6 percent of this rise. The remaining increase may be accounted for by extended services and in some cases the necessity for a smaller student body to support programs that were not substantially cut back over the previous year.

The smaller, private institutions require larger budgets for their size than the public institutions and therefore show a larger per-pupil expenditure. Because of the lower tuition and fee structure at the public schools, however, students at the public institutions are much more heavily subsidized than those at private colleges. An index that reflects this situation is shown in the last column—the ratio of institutional expenditure to student expenditure. This is calculated by dividing total tuition and fees into per-pupil expenditure. The higher the index shown, the greater the degree to which the institution subsidizes the student's education.

Library Resources. One measure of the learning resources of an educational institution is its library resources. Fig. 9.17 presents the total number of bound volumes in the library collections of each institution, and the number of bound volumes per full-time equivalent student.[2] As might be expected, the smaller, well-established, private four-year schools such as Davidson and Queens show a high number of bound volumes per full-time equivalent student, while some of the larger institutions, despite substantial collections, have a much lower ratio.

The most rapidly expanding library facility on any college campus in Metrolina is the recently completed eleven-story library tower on the campus of UNCC. This glass and concrete structure will increase the potential number of volumes housed to 500,000. The building opened 100,000 square feet of new space for library operations and 20,000 square feet for other campus offices. Current library services will be expanded and new services added.

Davidson College also plans to build a new library to expand as well as relocate its current collection. To be situated next to the major classroom building, it will thereby become a more focal part of the daily life of the college.

Paramedical Education. Of the high-school graduates in Metrolina entering post-secondary education, approximately 18 percent enter a technical institute or a health-careers program. Degrees in medicine and dentistry are not awarded by any institute of higher learning in Metrolina. There is, however, ample opportunity for training in several paramedical programs. In areas having a college or technical institute much of the academic training is carried on within that facility and hospitals are made available for practical experience and instruction. This is particularly true of nursing programs.

2. See note 1 in this section.

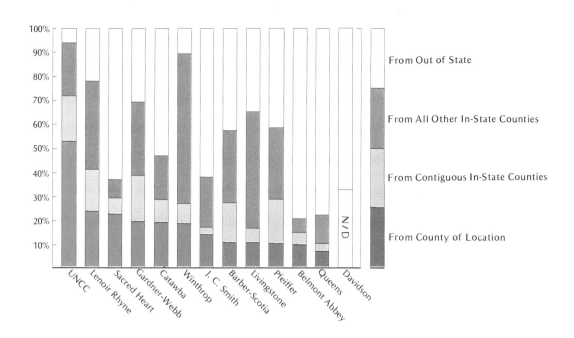

From Out of State

From All Other In-State Counties

From Contiguous In-State Counties

From County of Location

Fig. 9.15. Geographic Origin of Students in Metrolina Higher-Education Institutions, 1970-71

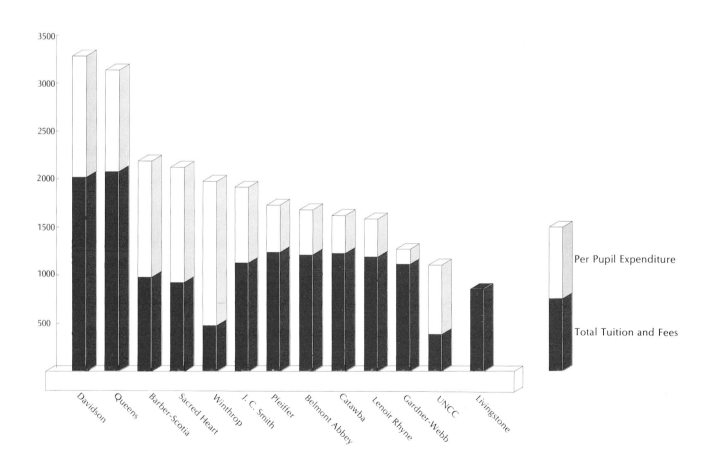

Per Pupil Expenditure

Total Tuition and Fees

Fig. 9.16. Metrolina's Per-Pupil Expenditure and Student Cost, Higher Education, 1970-71

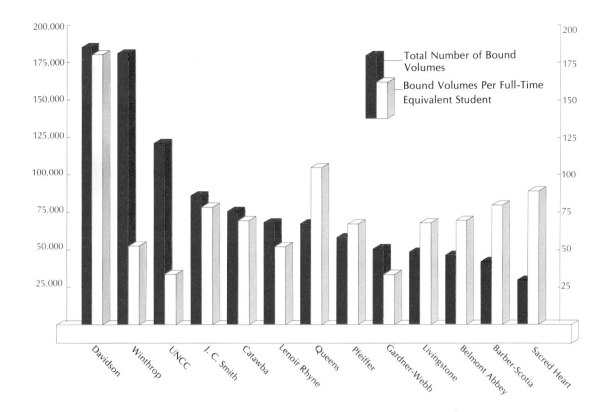

Fig. 9.17. Library Resources in Metrolina's Institutions of Higher Education, 1970

The paramedical training available within the region varies from a B.S. in Nursing (UNCC, Lenoir Rhyne) to such specialized technical training programs as X-ray technology and operating-room technology. All twelve Metrolina counties have some form of paramedical training, although Mecklenburg County, with its extensive hospital facilities, provides a large portion of these services.

Higher Education Summary

Community colleges and technical institutes are currently reaching about 30,000 students in Metrolina with their educational programs as compared with about 21,000 students enrolled in the private and public junior and senior colleges. A very high percentage of the community-college and technical-institute student bodies is comprised of Metrolina residents whereas a greater portion of the enrollment of junior and senior institutions is from out of state. The majority of students in the senior institutions and the private junior colleges are enrolled in degree programs whereas the largest numbers of the community college and technical institute students are enrolled in nondegree programs.

The number of private colleges in Metrolina is far greater than that of the public institutions, but most of them have small enrollments, usually less than fifteen hundred.

Furthermore, many of the small schools are beginning to experience enrollment declines due to spiraling costs and necessary increased tuition rates and fees.

A general correlation can be noticed between the educational attainment of a county's population and the presence of a college or university. As an example, four out of the top five counties in Metrolina in median educational level all have senior colleges within the county (Mecklenburg, Catawba, Rowan, and Cleveland). On the other hand, Gaston County, with a community college and two four-year schools, has the lowest educational attainment level of the North Carolina Metrolina counties. Examination of the enrollment for that county's two four-year schools reveals a large percentage of out-of-state students who, ostensibly, leave the state upon graduation.

The contributions of Metrolina's post-secondary institutions to the region are extensive. Culturally, economically, and educationally they change the complexion of the twelve-county area. The extent and true nature of their contribution is yet to be fully studied and appreciated.

Benjamin H. Romine, Jr.
J. Norfleet Jarrell

REFERENCES

Brubacher, John S., and Willis Rudy. *Higher Education in Transition.* New York: Harper & Row, 1968.

Harris, Seymore E. *Challenge and Change in American Education.* Berkeley, Calif.: McCutchan Publishing Co., 1965.

Harris, Seymore E. *Education and Public Policy.* Berkeley, Calif.: McCutchan Publishing Co., 1965.

Jencks, Christopher, and David Reisman. *The Academic Revolution.* New York: Doubleday & Company, 1968.

Mayhew, Lewis B. *Colleges Today and Tomorrow.* San Francisco: Jossey-Bass, 1969.

National Education Association. *Salary Schedules for Teachers—1970-71.* Washington, D.C.: The Association, 1971.

North Carolina Board of Higher Education. *North Carolina Board of Higher Education—Biennial Report, 1967-69.* Raleigh: The Board, 1969.

North Carolina Board of Higher Education. *Planning for Higher Education in North Carolina.* Special Report 2-68. Raleigh: The Board, 1968.

North Carolina Board of Higher Education. *Statistical Abstract of Higher Education in North Carolina, 1970-71.* Raleigh: The Board, 1971.

North Carolina Department of Public Instruction. "Comparison of High School Graduates with Appropriate Fifth Grade Enrollment." Raleigh: The Department, 1970 (unpublished).

North Carolina Department of Public Instruction. *Follow-up Survey of N.C. High School Graduates.* Raleigh: The Department, 1970.

North Carolina Department of Public Instruction. *1968-1969 Current Expenditures by Source of Funds.* Raleigh: The Department, 1970.

North Carolina Department of Public Instruction. *1969-1970 Instructional Personnel.* Raleigh: The Department, 1970.

North Carolina Hospital Association. *Educational Programs for Health Careers.* Raleigh: The Association, 1969.

Renetzky, Alvin, and John S. Greene, eds. *Standard Educational Almanac.* Los Angeles: Public Academic Media, 1970.

Rovetch, Warren. "Architecture for the Urban Campus," in *Agony and Promise: Current Issues in Higher Education,* ed. G. Kerry Smith. San Francisco: Jossey-Bass, 1969. Pp. 78-81.

"Schools, Colleges and Universities." *The Charlotte Observer,* January 24, 1971.

South Carolina Board of Education. *Annual Report—100th Year.* Columbia: The Board, 1967-68.

U.S. Bureau of the Census. *Statistical Abstracts of the United States.* Washington, D.C.: U.S. Government Printing Office, 1970.

U.S. Department of Health, Education and Welfare. *Statistics of Public Elementary and Secondary Day Schools, Fall 1969.* Washington, D.C.: The Department, 1970.

U.S. Office of Education. *Digest of Educational Statistics.* Washington, D.C.: U.S. Government Printing Office, 1962-70.

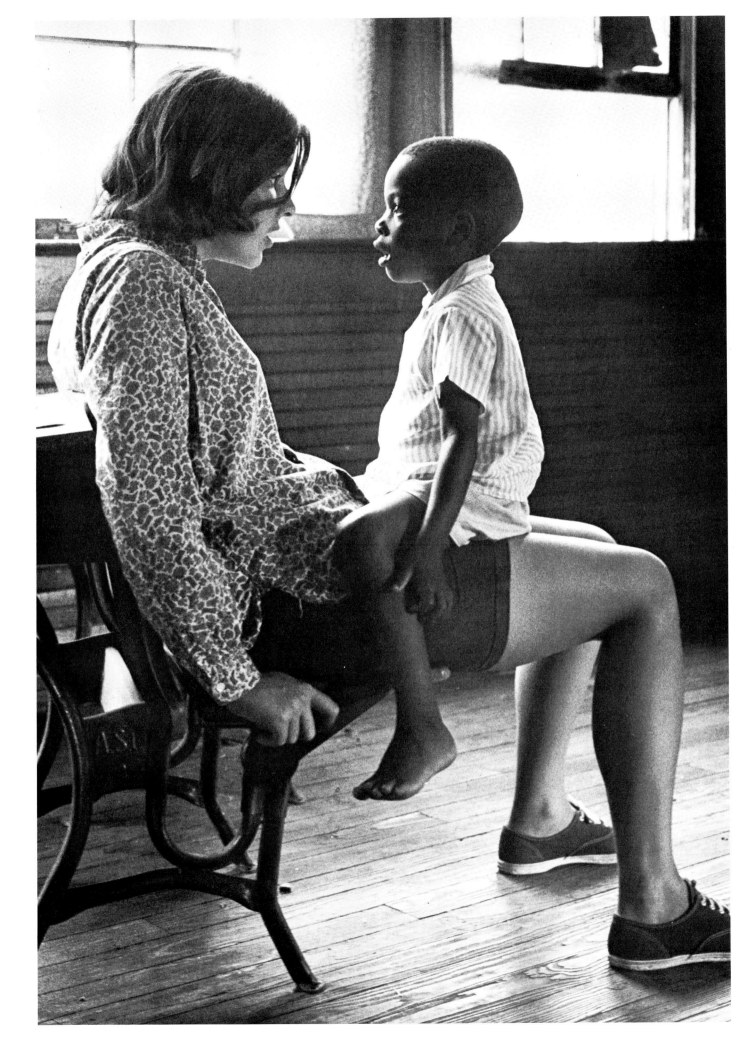

10. CULTURAL AMENITIES

DOUGLAS M. ORR, JR.

"The amenity factor should be kept in mind in predicting future regional development; the predictor, however, is under special obligation to be objective, because most of mankind thinks his own region best. . . ."—Edward L. Ullman, The Geographical Review, *vol. 44, 1954.*

One measure of a civilization, whether on a national or local scale, is the quality and availability of cultural amenities. A society's cultural amenities are in a way a mirror of the successes of other elements in its life-style: its history, physical environment, economy, politics, and education. In the sequential order of themes in this book, the amenities are to some degree a culmination of all the rest. A regional society that protects its natural environment, affords its people a viable livelihood, and governs and educates itself should also be able to provide good health care and meaningful leisure opportunities.

The challenges to good regional health care are abundant and constantly changing. Not only must health facilities and personnel keep pace with new medical breakthroughs, but they must also adapt to the changed characteristics, distribution, and growth patterns of a population. The dynamics of change is an omnipresent fact of life for modern medicine.

Another basic change in the nature of a society as it advances relates to time. Today the average individual has more leisure time through a combination of shorter working hours, longer vacations, later entry into the labor force, and earlier retirement—all reinforced by the broader range of options that increasing wealth can provide. One recent study categorized the average person's time into four activities: subsistence, free time, commuting, and work. Free time was calculated to be 34.8 percent of the total. And of course this figure has been continually rising. What to do with our increasing leisure time is a question that is fundamental to a society's value system. "Having to decide what we shall do with our leisure," said Julian Huxley in *The Future of Man,* "is inevitably forcing us to re-examine the purpose of human existence, and to ask what fulfillment really means . . . this involves a comprehensive survey of human possibilities and methods of realizing them; it also implies a survey of the obstacles to their realization."

A wide variety of leisure-time activities is being pursued throughout the nation. It has been estimated, for example, that fifty million Americans are amateur artists and that thirty-two million are musicians. Many millions are attending amateur and professional sports events, yet many more are becoming participants, from the golf courses to the lakes to the backpacking trails. In seeking out opportunities for leisure-time activities, the inhabitants of an urban region such as Metrolina amply demonstrate their footloose and fluid quality.

Hospitals

In order to discern the availability and quality of health care in Metrolina, it is useful to begin with a review of the existing hospital facilities. In late 1971 Metrolina had a total of thirty nonfederal hospitals, staffed by more than ten thousand employees, and one federal hospital. Control of the operations of the nonfederal facilities rests with a variety of organizations, the most common being the non-profit association that controls fourteen of the hospitals throughout Metrolina. Since 1961 four Mecklenburg County hospitals—Charlotte Memorial, Charlotte Community, Charlotte Rehabilitation, and Huntersville—have been governed by a Charlotte-Mecklenburg Hospital Authority. Other controlling organizations in Metrolina include four counties, three churches, two corporations, one partnership, one

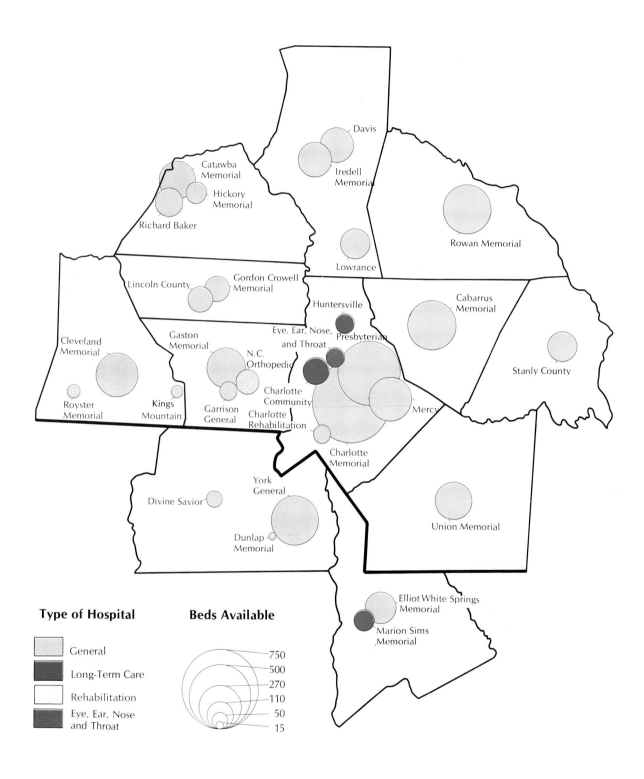

Type of Hospital

General
Long-Term Care
Rehabilitation
Eye, Ear, Nose
and Throat

Beds Available

750
500
270
110
50
15

Fig. 10.1. Size and Type of Hospitals in Metrolina

individual, and the state. In terms of type of service, twenty-four of the hospitals are classified as general, three offer long-term care (Charlotte Community, Huntersville, and Lancaster County's Marion Sims Memorial), two are rehabilitation centers (Charlotte Rehabilitation and North Carolina Orthopedic in Gastonia), and one is a specialty hospital (the Charlotte Eye, Ear, Nose and Throat). Of course, many special functions may be included within the types of service available at general hospitals. A good example is mental care. Although there is no mental institution in Metrolina, the closest being the large Broughton Hospital at Morganton in neighboring Burke County, the following Metrolina hospitals maintain a number of beds for mental care: Charlotte Memorial (forty-eight), Cleveland Memorial (nineteen), Catawba Memorial (fifteen), and Gaston Memorial (ten).

Fig. 10.1 shows that although a rather even dispersal of hospitals exists throughout Metrolina, there is a heavy "clustering" around Charlotte. Four of Metrolina's six special hospitals are located here, plus the region's two largest nonfederal facilities, Charlotte Memorial (749 beds), the largest nonfederal facility between Richmond and Atlanta, and Presbyterian (504 beds). All of the communities of Metrolina refer complicated and diagnostic problems to Memorial, a regional medical center, in which more open-heart surgical procedures are performed annually than appendectomies. And although neither Charlotte nor Metrolina possesses a medical school, Charlotte Memorial has a significant medical-education program. In 1965, for example, an affiliation was established with Central Piedmont Community College and the University of North Carolina at Charlotte to provide clinical experience for students in their nursing-degree programs. In 1966 a teaching affiliation with the University of North Carolina in Chapel Hill was begun as part of the training program for medical students. Charlotte Memorial is also the nation's only community hospital (not part of a medical school) to be able to fill its intern quota on a consistent basis—every year since 1962. Most United States hospitals do not get all the interns they need, and some fail to get any. Memorial's unparalleled success has been attributed in part to the number of private practicing physicians who work with members of the full-time teaching staff.

Another notable medical facility in Metrolina is the new Elliot White Springs Memorial Hospital in Lancaster, South Carolina. Although this 149-bed facility is not one of Metrolina's larger centers, it does offer the area residents one of the most highly automated hospitals in the nation. For example, the $8.5 million structure includes an automated system for distributing and processing foods and materials; single rooms for all patients; a patient-communications system which enables the patient and nurse to remain in constant contact; and a radial plan for the nursing floors which allows duty nurses to have visual control of the corridors.

A unique kind of planned expansion of the Charlotte Rehabilitation Hospital will be a first in the Carolinas. The $2.2 million addition will add thirty-three beds for vocational rehabilitation services and is to serve as a model for other such centers throughout North Carolina. Since often people must change an occupation or vocation because of illness or injury, this center will be a breakthrough in filling the need for simultaneous medical and vocational rehabilitation. Included in the vocational training plans are work evaluation, work adjustment, job training, and job placement.

The major medical facility currently under construction in Metrolina is a five-hundred-bed hospital in Gastonia, to replace Gaston Memorial Hospital. Approved in 1967 by Gaston County citizens in a $15-million-bond referendum, this substantial facility should be completed in 1973. Salisbury is the location of the largest hospital in Metrolina and the region's only federal facility: the thousand-bed Veterans Hospital primarily for neuropsychiatric treatment.

The total size of Metrolina's hospital facilities is best measured by the bed complement, that is, the number of beds available for use. In September, 1971, the bed complement (nonfederal) for the region was 5,316 beds with a net addition of 756 beds under construction.

A more significant consideration than simply the total number of beds, however, is the question of how adequately the hospital facilities of the region are meeting the health-care needs of the populace. Two indices that give an approximation of the general hospital-bed status for the counties of Metrolina are (1) the number of beds per thousand population and (2) the hospital-use rate, which measures the total annual days of care per thousand population (see Table 10.1). According to the North Carolina Medical Care Commission, the hospital-use ratio is generally considered to be the most appropriate measure of hospital-bed needs, although as the figures indicate, the number of beds per thousand population usually has a direct relationship to the hospital-use rate. In other words, the greater the number of beds per thousand population, the higher the use rate is likely to be. Yet the county rates do not give a complete picture of bed needs because hospitals serve area rather than strictly county demands. This helps to explain why the need for more hospital space in a county like Mecklenburg is much greater than the figures indicate. For example, Charlotte Memorial Hospital, a regional referral center, draws 24 percent of its patients from outside Mecklenburg County. The regional role of the Charlotte facilities seems to be indicated by the "dampening" effect on hospital use rates of at least two adjacent counties, Gaston and Union. In addition, even though the total number of beds available in a particular locale may appear adequate, there can be a critical shortage of beds (and related care) to meet specialized needs. This is especially true in the case of acute and long-term care in a regional referral center like Charlotte. Thus periodic "standing-room-only" crises have be-

Table 10.1. Status of Hospital Facilities in Metrolina Counties, Metrolina, and the United States

	No. of Beds per 1,000 Population	Hospital-Use Rate
Cabarrus	4.7	1,518
Catawba	4.2	1,122
Cleveland	5.6	1,647
Gaston	3.5	538
Iredell	4.2	1,475
Lincoln	5.8	1,213
Mecklenburg	4.8	1,415
Rowan	3.8	940
Stanly	3.3	851
Union	2.3	672
Lancaster	3.2	890
York	3.7	865
North Carolina	4.2	1,067
United States	5.0	—

come rather frequent in that city, especially at Charlotte Memorial.

Major urban centers throughout the nation seem to be experiencing a similar crush on existing hospital facilities. This trend is most often explained by pointing to the continued large-scale population growth around urban centers, and most recently, the effects of Medicare and Medicaid in permitting more people to take advantage of hospital services. The latter factor may stimulate a closer and harder look by the various hospital review boards at hospital utilization methods. One possible suggested form of relief may be a greater stress on ambulatory "outside" care in the future.

On balance, most medical authorities believe that the people of Metrolina are endowed with a good array of hospital facilities. In number and diversity of treatment centers, hospital care seems to be a notable asset of the region. Problems do exist, however, particularly that of the lack of accessibility of medical facilities to some parts of the very diffused population of Metrolina. This is exemplified in the largest population center, Mecklenburg, where medical facilities are not keeping pace with the sprawling

population growth. The result has been a bitter controversy over the location of a proposed new $23 million hospital, a facility that would help relieve the pressures on Charlotte Memorial and others. An interim solution, and one that may become more widespread in other parts of the region as well as the country, would be to build satellite community hospitals serving outlying population centers. Such a solution might at least reduce some of the damaging sectional rivalries that surface in the demand of each locality for accessible as well as quality health facilities.

Douglas M. Orr, Jr.

Health Care

Health Manpower. Health manpower is the keystone to the maintenance of health care. Even with the best medical facilities available and unlimited resources, without the necessary health manpower, medical care cannot be effected. Generally physicians, dentists, and nurses are considered to be the key personnel in the health-care system. Health manpower can be evaluated by comparing the manpower available to the population being served, but usually such statistics are dated by the time they are available to the public. This will continue to be a problem until a more sophisticated method of data collection and distribution is developed at the local, state, and national levels.

In 1970 the twelve Metrolina counties had a total of 905 physicians, 373 dentists, and 3,462 registered nurses (not including public-health nurses or licensed practical nurses). Fig. 10.2 shows the ratio of available health personnel to the area's population.

Several obvious conclusions can be drawn from the data presented in Fig. 10.2. Urbanized Mecklenburg County exhibits the best ratio of physicians per 1,000 population when compared to Metrolina as a whole or to its constituent counties. Estimates for the United States indicate a higher ratio than that of Mecklenburg County, but these figures are only approximate. Union County appears to have the lowest ratio of physicians per 1,000 population of all counties within Metrolina.

The statistics indicate also that Mecklenburg County has the highest ratio of dentists per 1,000 population and Lincoln County the lowest. Figures for the United States show a much higher ratio when compared to either North or South Carolina and to the Metrolina counties. Historically the ratio of dentists per 1,000 population has always been lower than that of physicians.

The ratio of registered nurses per 1,000 population for Metrolina counties shows that Union County has the lowest ratio within Metrolina. Figures for Mecklenburg County indicate the highest ratio of registered nurses per 1,000 population in Metrolina. South Carolina as a whole has a registered-nurse ratio close to the highest reported in Metrolina.

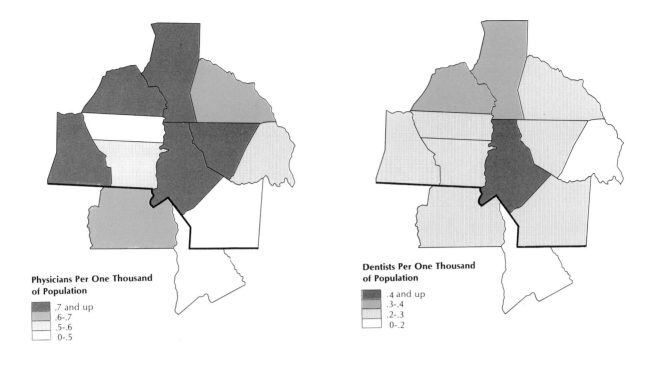

**Physicians Per One Thousand
of Population**

- .7 and up
- .6-.7
- .5-.6
- 0-.5

**Dentists Per One Thousand
of Population**

- .4 and up
- .3-.4
- .2-.3
- 0-.2

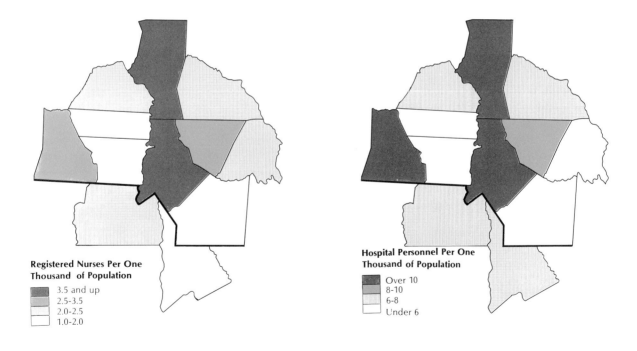

**Registered Nurses Per One
Thousand of Population**

- 3.5 and up
- 2.5-3.5
- 2.0-2.5
- 1.0-2.0

**Hospital Personnel Per One
Thousand of Population**

- Over 10
- 8-10
- 6-8
- Under 6

Fig. 10.2. Metrolina Health Manpower, by County

One major factor appears to influence the distribution of health manpower in Metrolina: urbanization. Generally the more urbanized an area, the more adequate its health-manpower resources will be.

In the past, and more so in recent times, physicians, dentists, and other health-care personnel have tended to flock to urban areas, probably because of the existence in urban areas of better job facilities, more lucrative salaries, and easy access to cultural activities. This problem of attracting and keeping health manpower in rural areas must be solved or the time will come when many of the rural areas will have little or no health-manpower resources available. Some rural communities that have lost their only physician, through death or out-migration, have been unable to attract another physician to take his place. It is possible that a major reason for Union County's low health-manpower ratios is its proximity to heavily urbanized Charlotte, which has a large number of such personnel.

Data relating to the number of hospital personnel per 1,000 population for Metrolina counties show a wide variation of ratios from county to county. Mecklenburg, Iredell, and Cleveland counties have the highest ratios of hospital personnel to population. The figures for Gaston and Lincoln counties indicate that these counties have the lowest ratios of hospital personnel to population. There appears to be no correlation between the size of a county's population and the number of hospital personnel per 1,000 population, but there is a correlation between the ratio of hospital personnel to population and the Metrolina counties' per-capita expenditures for hospital services.

The figures for hospital-operating expenditures on a per-capita basis as shown in Fig. 10.3 indicate that Mecklenburg County spends more dollars for hospital services than any other Metrolina county and that Gaston spends the least. However, Gaston's status will no doubt change when its 500-bed hospital now under construction is completed.

Again there appears to be no correlation between the size of a county's population and per-capita expenditures for hospital services. One fact that may affect both per-capita expenditures and personnel ratios is the type of procedures being carried out in a particular county's hospital. The more sophisticated procedures most likely require more personnel and individuals who have advanced skills. These kinds of personnel generally will receive a higher salary than other hospital personnel. Therefore Metrolina counties that act as medical catchment areas, i.e., counties with hospitals that receive a large number of referrals and undertake sophisticated medical procedures, will tend to have a higher per-capita expenditure for hospital services and a higher ratio of hospital personnel to population than other Metrolina counties.

Public Health. Data on the per-capita expenditure for public health in Metrolina again indicate substantial differences among counties (see Fig. 10.4). There seems to be no cor-

relation between the size of the population and the per-capita expenditure. Although the two most densely populated counties, Gaston and Mecklenburg, spend the most, York and Catawba counties, also two comparatively densely populated areas, spend the least. The per-capita figure arrived at by each county administration is probably no more than an arbitrary figure based on available revenue and probably bears no relation to the need for health services. There may be some relationship between the per-capita figure and the availability of health and health-related services, however. In other words, in the more urban areas of Gaston and Mecklenburg counties there are more doctors, nurses, technicians, and other health-care personnel, which may somehow influence the amount of public expenditure for health services.

In addition to a county's public-health-department director, the two basic manpower resources for public health are the public-health nurse and the public-health sanitarian. These two types of personnel perform the majority of all public-health services. In order to achieve some perspective on their availability in Metrolina, ratios of public-health nurses and sanitarians to population have been developed.

Fig. 10.5 indicates that the ratios of public-health nurses and sanitarians per 1,000 population for the majority of Metrolina counties are nearly the same as those for North and South Carolina. South Carolina shows a slightly higher public-health-nurse ratio compared to that of North Carolina. Cleveland County exhibits the lowest ratio of public health nurses per 1,000 population and Mecklenburg shows the highest. The data for public-health sanitarians indicate that there is a wide variation among counties within Metrolina in regard to the number of sanitarians per 1,000 population; the county with the lowest sanitarian ratio is York and the highest is Mecklenburg.

Selected Causes of Death. Fig. 10.6 shows heart disease as the leading killer in both North and South Carolina and all Metrolina counties. The death rate for this disease ranges from a high of 399.1 per 100,000 population in Cleveland County to a low of 271.9 deaths per 100,000 in Mecklenburg County. About half of the counties listed had rates lower than those indicated for both North and South Carolina as a whole.

Cerebrovascular-disease (stroke) death rates ranged from a high of 157.9 deaths per 100,000 population in Lincoln County to a low of 76.5 deaths per 100,000 in Mecklenburg County. Again, about half of the counties have death rates lower than those of North and South Carolina.

Figures for deaths due to cancer (malignant neoplasms) for 1969 indicate that Stanly County had the highest rate and that the counties of Catawba and Cleveland had the lowest rates.

Since heart disease, cerebrovascular disease, and cancer are chronic diseases which usually attack individuals in their later years of life, high death rates for these diseases

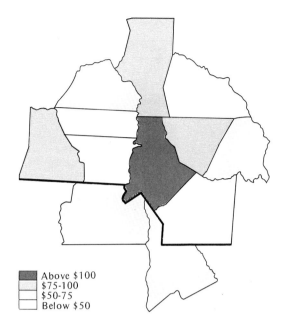

Above $100
$75-100
$50-75
Below $50

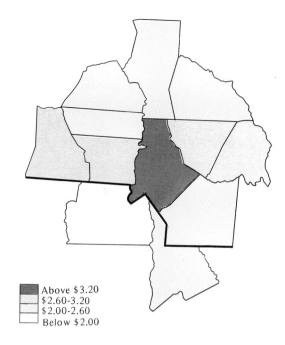

Above $3.20
$2.60-3.20
$2.00-2.60
Below $2.00

Fig. 10.3. Metrolina Hospital Operating Expenditures Per Capita

Fig. 10.4. Metrolina Public Health Expenditures Per Capita

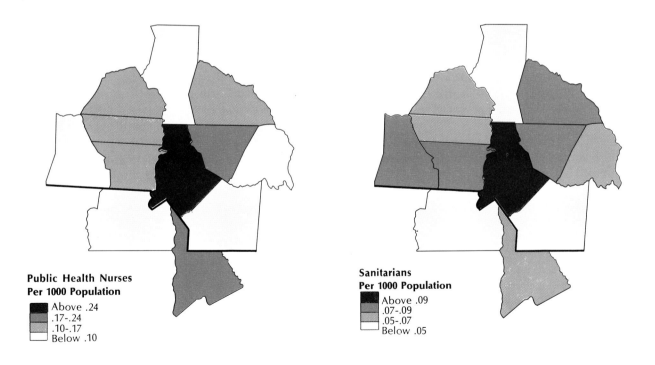

**Public Health Nurses
Per 1000 Population**

Above .24
.17-.24
.10-.17
Below .10

**Sanitarians
Per 1000 Population**

Above .09
.07-.09
.05-.07
Below .05

Fig. 10.5. Public Health Nurses and Sanitarians Per 1,000 Population in Metrolina

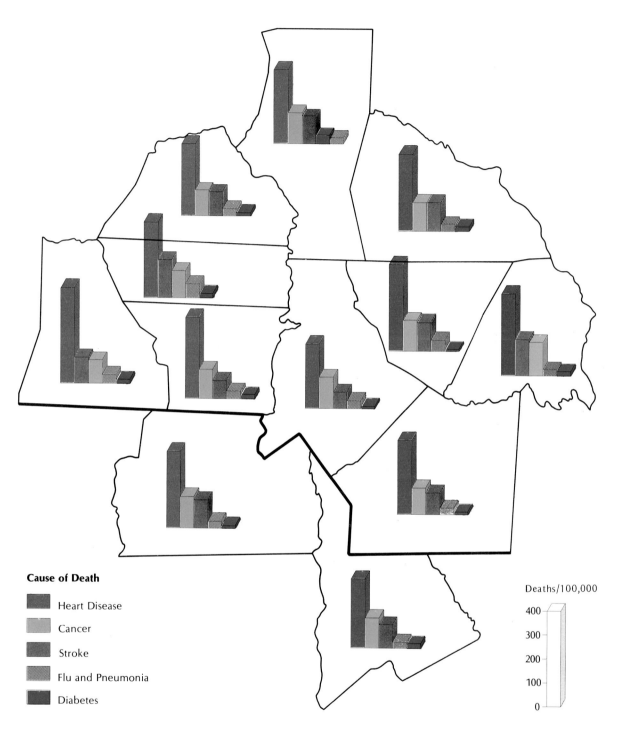

Cause of Death

■ Heart Disease

▨ Cancer

▨ Stroke

▨ Flu and Pneumonia

■ Diabetes

Deaths/100,000

400
300
200
100
0

Source: N.C. and S.C. State Boards of Health, 1969.

Fig. 10.6. Selected Causes of Death in Metrolina

indicate that an area probably has a large old-age population.

Data for deaths due to influenza and pneumonia show that Lincoln County experienced the highest death rate per 100,000 population and Union County the lowest.

Figures for deaths due to diabetes indicate that Cabarrus County had the lowest rate for 1969 and Iredell County had the highest rate of deaths per 100,000 population. Deaths due to diabetes have been reduced to some extent in recent years through early detection and better treatment.

The Future. There are several innovations that can greatly influence health-care services in the region and the nation in the future. In many respects health-care services have changed very little during the past century, but medical knowledge has accelerated tremendously during the most recent decades. Several authorities within the health field have suggested that the ability to treat illness has far exceeded the ability of the health system to provide adequate care.

A major factor in this inability to maintain pace with the demand for health care has been the inefficient utilization of health facilities and health manpower. One of the most recent innovations in health care is the reorganization of our somewhat fragmented system of health-care services. This reorganization is being accomplished through the formation of "health-maintenance organizations." This kind of health organization is not entirely a new idea. One of the prototype health-maintenance organizations was begun in Washington, D.C., in the mid 1930s. Basically the health-maintenance organization usually provides health care on a prepaid basis to a defined population through group practice. At the present time over eight million Americans are being served via either a health-maintenance organization or a medical society foundation. The health-maintenance organization appears to make more effective use of health manpower and more selective use of appropriate health facilities.

Another innovation that may have a tremendous effect on the provision of primary health care is the use of new types of paramedical professionals, such as "physician assistants." Physician assistants are now being trained to do many of the things physicians are currently required to do. This frees the physician from performing many relatively simple procedures and allows him more time for dealing with complex medical problems.

The role of local public-health departments has been rapidly changing during recent decades. For example, health departments have been moving into new areas of concern, such as family planning. Some problems have intensified, such as the potential threats to public health from air and water pollution. Stanly County's health department recently conducted a preliminary study which found a possible relationship between birth defects in babies and the drinking of polluted water by the mother. The survey, among women who delivered babies in Stanly County in 1970, indicated that the birth-defect rate for infants born to mothers living in homes with polluted drinking water was 10 percent higher than that for infants born to mothers who lived in homes with nonpolluted water. Such findings are no doubt an indication of future possibilities for the field of public health.

The health field is changing, and will continue to do so. The health of our population has been improving with every passing decade. Through innovations and technical advancements in the health field, higher levels of health care can be expected and achieved.

Robert E. Randolph

Visual Arts

The visual arts in Metrolina have become a firmly established part of the cultural growth of the area. And with the advent of many new developments such as museum exhibitions, galleries, university programs, and professional schools, the region may become one of the most significant visual-arts centers in the Southeast. An important asset is that Metrolina is ideally located in regard to already existing art centers; for example, it is close enough to New York City to feel the influence of avant-garde trends and at the same time established enough in its own right to maintain a strong regional quality that is growing more rapidly every year.

The visual arts in Metrolina may be divided into three areas: programs for the visual artist, educational opportunities in the visual arts, and visual-arts events and activities.

Programs for the Visual Artist. The Metrolina area has many programs for the visual artist. There are a number of private galleries located throughout Metrolina that continually exhibit a broad range of graphic styles as well as sponsor invitational shows for the regional artists of the area. The number of privately owned galleries appears to be increasing every year, which is a healthy sign of the continued growth of the visual arts in the region.

The Mint Museum of Art in Charlotte sponsors four major competitive shows a year: the Piedmont Crafts Exhibition, the Piedmont Drawing and Graphics Exhibition, the Piedmont Painting and Sculpture Exhibition, and the Experimental Film Exhibit. These shows are open not only to Metrolina but to an eleven-state area of the southeastern United States. They are juried by outstanding artists and museum curators throughout the nation, and purchase awards amount to an attractive sum, given by the Mint Museum, the North Carolina National Bank in Charlotte, and the University of North Carolina at Charlotte. In 1971, for example, a total of $3,750 was given in purchase awards for the Painting and Sculpture Exhibition. In addition to sponsoring competitive and invitational shows, the Mint Museum also has an active rental and sales gallery on the second floor of the museum. This gallery is designed for the sale of all types of art works (ceramics, graphics, painting, sculpture) and for small special shows and one-man exhibitions.

The Spring Mills Show in Lancaster, South Carolina, is probably the next largest competitive exhibition in Metrolina. Sponsored by the textile mills in Fort Mill, South Carolina, this show hosts a large number of regional artists with a substantial cash-purchase gift heading the list of several awards. This show takes place annually, and the number of artists entering is increasing each year. Various campuses throughout Metrolina also sponsor invitational shows which provide good opportunities for one-man and group shows of local as well as nationwide artists. Davidson College's sponsorship in 1972 of a national print and drawing exhibition marks the first national competition in Metrolina. And Metrolina hosts many active art clubs and guilds which provide exhibiting programs for their membership in shopping malls and banks. These clubs have become more sophisticated since their inception and some support large memberships and active visual-arts programs.

Opportunities such as these offer a broad scope of visual-arts programs that are well suited to the needs of the producing artist in Metrolina. These programs are enhanced by the fact that Metrolina is centrally located in relation to three of the most notable museums in the South: The State Museum of Art in Raleigh, the Gallery of Contemporary Art in Winston-Salem, and the High Museum in Atlanta.

Visual-Arts Education. Education in the visual arts is growing at a rapid pace in Metrolina. Most elementary and secondary schools have a directed art program for students, and some, especially at the secondary level, have outstanding art programs and faculties. At the higher-education level, many Metrolina colleges and universities have well-established programs in the visual arts. The following institutions provide art programs and course work: Belmont Abbey College (Concord, North Carolina), Catawba College (Salisbury, North Carolina), Central Piedmont Community College (Charlotte), Davidson College (Davidson, North Carolina), Gardner-Webb College (Boiling Springs, North Carolina), Gaston Community College (Gastonia, North Carolina), Lenoir-Rhyne College (Hickory, North Carolina), Pfeiffer College (Misenheimer, North Carolina), Queens College (Charlotte), The University of North Carolina at Charlotte, and Winthrop College (Rock Hill, South Carolina). These schools offer studies in the visual arts ranging from introductory course work to a B.A. degree in art and teacher certification, qualifying graduates to teach art at the elementary and secondary levels. Many of these institutions also have active programs in such areas as film, traveling exhibits, invitational shows, and faculty and student

exhibitions. The college campus provides Metrolina with some of the most exciting and contemporary art in the region.

Visual-Arts Activities and Events for the Public. In addition to the museum and gallery exhibitions already mentioned, there is an excellent permanent collection on view at all times at the Mint Museum, ranging from Renaissance art to twentieth-century European and American painting. Also, cosponsored by the Mint Museum and by Queens College, is the Kino Film Series, which presents outstanding foreign and American films throughout the year.

Civic and community organizations in Metrolina sponsor small shows of various types, including art lectures and studio workshops. For example, the North Carolina National Bank has been a long-time supporter of the visual arts by offering purchase awards in regional shows and sponsoring invitational and traveling exhibits. Various campuses in Metrolina have visiting lecture programs open to the public year round. One of the more noted of these events was R. Buckminster Fuller's 1971 appearance at The University of North Carolina at Charlotte.

There are also many festivals, sidewalk sales, and auctions taking place in various communities during the summer months. These events are generally sponsored by local art groups and community organizations within Metrolina and prove to be both profitable and interesting. In short, the Metrolina area offers a wealth of opportunities to view year-round shows and exhibitions covering the entire visual-arts spectrum: crafts, ceramics, graphics, painting, sculpture, and photography. Schedules of the various activities can be obtained easily by the organizations sponsoring the events.

As a part of Metrolina's rapid growth, the visual arts should continue to grow and flourish in proportion to the energies and creative talents of its citizens. As beneficiaries of the region's growth, however, artists and art lovers should help set the tone of a changing regional life style. The pell-mell rush to urbanization with all its unattractive accouterments is only too evident in many parts of the country. The visual arts and the esthetic awareness of the populace can be a foundation element in a regional growth that is not only viable but an artistic success as well.

R. Eric Anderson

Literary Activity

Metrolina has had a rich and varied literary history. Some of the area's authors have attained national and even international prominence—names such as W. J. Cash, Thomas Dixon, Marion Hargrove, Harry Golden, and LeGette Blythe, immediately come to mind—but scores of less well-known writers have created literary works of value during the past hundred years or so and are continuing to do so to-day.

Before surveying the contemporary scene in Metrolina a brief retrospective glance at some of the older literary figures who were born or who lived in Metrolina is in order.

W. J. Cash (1901-41), whose *Mind of the South* (1941) became a classic study of southern mores, was associate editor of the *Charlotte News* for four years and grew up in Cleveland County.

Thomas Dixon was born in Cleveland County in 1864 and died there in 1946. Dixon was a voluminous writer of historical novels and religious tracts, including *The Clansman* (1905) and *The Leopard's Spots* (1913). The screenplay for *The Birth of a Nation* was made from *The Clansman*.

Marion Hargrove's *See Here, Private Hargrove* (1942) was an extremely popular comic exposition of one soldier's problems during World War II. Hargrove attended Charlotte's Central High School and later worked as a reporter for the *Charlotte News*.

Other successful but less well-known published writers from Metrolina and a representative work of each include John Charless McNeill (*Lyrics from Cotton Land,* 1907); H. E. C. Bryant (*Tar Heel Tales,* 1910); Andrew Hewitt (*Traveler to April,* 1949); Sarah T. A. McCorkle (*Old Time Stories of the Old North State,* 1903); Tim Pridgin (*Tory Oath,* 1941); Walter Spearman (*Death of the Swan,* 1932); John V. A. Weaver (*In American,* 1921; enlarged edition, 1939, with a foreword by H. L. Mencken); Anne Blackwell Payne (*Released,* 1930); James Ross (*They Don't Dance Much,* 1940); Fred Ross (*Jackson Mahaffey,* 1951); Marion Sims (*The City on the Hill,* 1940); Stewart Atkins (*The Halting Gods,* 1952); Zoe K. Brockman (*Heart on My Sleeve,* 1951).

Within the past two decades literary activity in Metrolina has flourished. Published authors are serving as writers-in-residence at a number of the area's colleges. Poets and fiction writers appear to dominate the scene, with dramatists seemingly a very rare commodity.

Certainly the most famous author, from the viewpoint of national prominence, now living and writing in Metrolina, is Harry Golden. Golden, who has resided in Charlotte for some thirty-odd years, has enjoyed particular success with his stories and anecdotes about growing up on the Lower East Side of New York City. Most of these brief tales were originally recounted by Golden in the pages of his newspaper, *The Carolina Israelite*. The best of them were then arranged according to a general thematic pattern and, with the help of Golden's son, published in book form. Some of the more popular of these works have been: *Only in America* (1958), *For 2¢ Plain* (1959), *Enjoy, Enjoy!* (1960), *You're Entitle'* (1962), *So What Else is New?* (1964), and *So Long As You're Healthy* (1970). Golden's other works include *Mr. Kennedy and the Negroes* (1964), a study of President Kennedy's attitudes and attempts to eliminate segregation in America; *A Little Girl Is Dead* (1965), a study of religious prejudice and hysteria leading to the lynching of an innocent Jew in 1913 for the murder of a young girl; and *Carl Sandburg* (1961), a fine biography and personal reminiscence of the great poet.

LeGette Blythe, of Huntersville in Mecklenburg County, has had innumerable books published over a period of fifty years and is still an active writer. His works cover an astonishing variety of subjects, only some of which can be enumerated here. In the field of drama Blythe has written and has had produced *Shout Freedom* (1948), *Voice in the Wilderness* (1955), and *The Hornet's Nest* (1968). Some of his historical novels include *Alexandriana* (1940), *Bold Galilean* (1948), *A Tear for Judas* (1951), *Hear Me, Pilate!* (1961), and *Brothers of Vengeance* (1969). His biographies include *Miracle in the Hills* (1953), which had sixteen American printings and eleven foreign printings during a period of fifteen years; *James W. Davis: North Carolina Surgeon* (1956); *Thomas Wolfe and His Family* (1961); and *Meet Julia Abernathy* (1970). Blythe has published two histories: *Hornet's Nest* (1961) and *38th Evac* (1966), as well as dozens of articles, short stories, and book reviews in magazines such as *Look, Time, Life,* and *The Saturday Review*.

A host of writers from Metrolina have published poetry, fiction, biographies, histories, and other types of literary works in the past decade or two. The following paragraphs include a cursory account of these authors together with a representative example or two of their published works. The account is divided into three categories: poetry, fiction, and nonfiction.

Paul Newman, at Queens College in Charlotte, has published three volumes of poetry: *The Cheetah and the Fountain* (1968), *Dust of Snow* (1969), and *The Ladder of Love* (1970). Robert W. Grey, at UNCC, has had poems published in *Western Review, Southern Poetry Review,* and *Poet Lore,* among others. Zoe Kincaid Brockman, of Gastonia, published *Heart on My Sleeve* in 1951. William Harmon was the winner of the Lamont Poetry Prize in 1970. Howard G. Hanson's *Future Coin or Climber and Other Poems* was published in 1967. Ed Godsey's *Cabin Fever* was published posthumously in 1967. Heather Ross Miller, primarily a novelist, published a book of poems, *The Wind Southerly,* in 1967. Sallie Nixon won the John Masefield Award from the Poetry Society of America in 1971. Harriet Doar, book editor of the *Charlotte Observer,* has had poems in *North Carolina Poetry 1970* and *Appalachian Harvest*. Bertha Harris's poetry has appeared in *Greensboro Review* and *Coraddi*. Amon Liner has published in *The Red Clay Reader* and *Folio*. The work of T. J. Reddy has appeared in *Southern Poetry Review* and *Galaxy of Black Writing*. Julie Suk's poems have been published in *Goliards* and *Poetry Ireland*. The former editor of *Red Clay Reader,* Charleen Whisnant, has published poetry in *Prairie Schooner* and *Southern Poetry in the Sixties*. Other published poets in the area include William Browne, Claude Davis, Christine Sloan, Marian Cannon, Joy Durham Rorie, Margaret B. Woodruff, Betty R. Ford, Eleanor Rigney, and Stanley Burns.

Writers of fiction from the area who have had novels or stories published in recent years are perhaps not quite as numerous as published poets, but their number includes some very distinguished names. Although some of the following writers no longer reside in Metrolina, they were born or lived there for some time. Heather Ross Miller's novels are *The Edge of the Woods* (1964), *Gone a Hundred Miles* (1968), and *Tenants of the House* (1966). Doris Betts has published one novel, *The Scarlet Thread* (1964), and two short story collections: *The Astronomer and Other Stories* (1965) and *The Gentle Insurrection and Other Stories* (1954). Ben Haas has had a number of novels published, including *Look Away, Look Away* (1964) and *The Troubled Summer* (1966, a children's book). Bertha Harris, who teaches creative writing at UNCC, published a novel, *Catching Saradove*, in 1969; her second novel, *Confessions of Cherubino*, is scheduled for publication in the spring of 1972. Robert Bristow, at Winthrop College, has written many short stories and two novels, *Night Season* (1970) and *Time for Glory* (1968). Burke Davis, former editor of the *Charlotte News*, wrote a novel, *Whisper My Name*, which was published in 1949. Evan Brandon, of Gaston County, had his novel, *Green Pond*, published in 1955. Finally, two authors of popular children's books should be included here: Helen Copeland, author of *This Snake Is Good* (1968) and *Meet Miki Takino* (1963), and Mary Gillett, author of *Bugles at the Border* (1968), who also has written an adult novel, *Shadows Slant North*.

Biography, history, philosophy, and general essays come under the rubric of nonfiction works, and Metrolina boasts a number of well-known writers in this category. Burke Davis won the North Carolina Mayflower Cup, an annual award for the best nonfiction work of the year, in 1959 for *To Appomattox*. Chalmers Davidson, professor of history at Davidson College, has written many biographies and historical novels, including *Major of Rural Hill* (1943), *Cloud Over Catawba* (1949), *Friend of the People* (1950), and *Piedmont Partisan* (1951). Katherine Springs published *The Squires of Springfield* in 1965, a historical account of a prominent local family. The husband-and-wife team, Bruce and Mary Roberts (Bruce is a photographer, Mary the writer) published *David* in 1968, a moving account of their retarded child. Bruce Roberts collaborated on two other nonfiction works: *The Face of North Carolina* (1962) and *You Can't Kill The Dream* (1968). Fred T. Morgan of Albemarle wrote *Ghost Tales of the Uwharries* in 1968. *The Camellia Treasury* and *Japanese Garden and Floral Art* by Viola W. Kincaid both have received international acclaim. Dwayne Walls, a reporter for the *Charlotte Observer*, has received several awards for his reporting of rural poverty in the Carolinas. In *The Chickenbone*

Special (1970), Walls chronicles the economic decline of small Southern tobacco farms and the resultant flow of migrants from the tobacco country to northern cities by relating the poignant personal story of a young Negro South Carolinian who takes a train to New York seeking new opportunities. Lastly, Rabbi Israel Gerber's *Immortal Rebels* (1963) and *The Psychology of the Suffering Mind* (1951), works of religious philosophy, have also been widely circulated.

Two annual writers' forums in Metrolina bring prominent North Carolina writers to the public eye and give writers and public alike an opportunity to exchange views and ideas. The North Carolina Writers' Forum, sponsored by UNCC, the *Charlotte Observer*, and the Junior Woman's Club of Charlotte, meets every fall. And the Carolina Writers and Readers Conference, sponsored by the Charlotte Area Consortium, is an annual spring affair.

Very few independently published literary journals are available to local writers. *The Red Clay Reader*, edited by Charleen Whisnant, has been the most exemplary journal of recent years, but it expired in 1970. Other independent outlets at present are *Aim*, edited by T. J. Reddy, and *Charlotte* magazine, which publishes stories and poems sporadically. In 1971 a collection of poetry by local writers entitled *Eleven Charlotte Poets*, edited by Charleen Whisnant and Robert Waters Grey, was published.

Aside from these few independent journals, there are a number of college- and university-sponsored literary magazines in the area. These, of course, cater primarily to student writing. Some of the more prominent magazines in this category include: *Miscellany* (Davidson), *Sanskrit* (UNCC), *The Treewell* (Johnson C. Smith), *Agora* (Belmont Abbey), *Counterpoint* (Wingate), *One Little Candle* (Gardner-Webb), and *The Phoenix* (Pfeiffer).

Metrolina urgently needs a good literary magazine to serve as an outlet for the writers of the area. *The Red Clay Reader* fulfilled this purpose admirably for seven years (1964-70), but since its demise nothing of equal distinction has appeared. The college and university literary magazines provide valuable exposure for student writers, but not, as a general rule, for others. It is to be hoped, however, that with more and better-published writers serving student needs as writers-in-residence and teachers of creative writing new outlets will appear in the future.

Morton Shapiro

Music

Charlotte dominates the musical scene in Metrolina, although there is considerable musical activity throughout the area. The Charlotte Symphony Orchestra, the Oratorio Singers of Charlotte, and the Charlotte Opera Association, perform to sell-out houses in Ovens Auditorium and thus constitute a focal attraction for music lovers from the entire Metrolina area. The main reason for Charlotte's preeminence in the field of music is that a full-size symphony orchestra, a large, highly trained choral group, and an opera association that imports nationally known singers for its lead roles all require considerable expenditures of money in order to flourish. Charlotte, with an urban population of almost a quarter of a million, is the only center in Metrolina that can support such groups financially.

The Charlotte Symphony Orchestra was organized in 1932. Now under the direction of Jacques Brourman, the orchestra performs with internationally renowned artists as guest soloists and increased the number of its concerts during the 1971-72 season to seven. Each of its concerts in Charlotte's Ovens Auditorium is repeated in neighboring communities and the orchestra also gives concerts for young people who attend the Performing Arts Series sponsored by the Symphony Women's Association.

The Charlotte Symphony Chamber Orchestra was formed in 1971 and gave its first public performance in January, 1972, at Queens College. The Chamber Orchestra is scheduled to give eighty performances in the Charlotte public schools during the 1971-72 academic year.

The Charlotte Symphony Youth Orchestra, composed of talented young musicians, presents two concerts each year.

The Oratorio Singers of Charlotte, organized in 1951, is composed of 155 members and performs choral works such as Bach's *St. Matthew Passion* and Honnegger's *King David*. In 1965 the group appeared in Washington, D.C., for the lighting of the national Christmas tree. In 1971 it joined the Charlotte Symphony in a performance of Beethoven's Ninth Symphony.

The Charlotte Choral Society, organized in 1953, is a 115-member chorus which presents three concerts each season, culminating in "The Singing Christmas Tree" with five performances each December.

Organized in 1949, the Charlotte Opera Association presents three operas each season, utilizing leading artists from the Metropolitan and other major opera companies for its lead roles. The Youth Matinee Program, free to school children in the Metrolina area, is a splendid means of developing interest in opera in young people.

The American Guild of Organists is a national professional organization which is represented in chapters throughout the United States, including one in Charlotte. Every week members of the Charlotte Chapter perform to more than 25,000 people in Metrolina. The city of Gastonia also has a chapter of the guild, which was formed in 1967.

The Charlotte Music Club presents recitals throughout the year, culminating in the annual community performance of Handel's *Messiah*.

The Community Concert Association of Charlotte brings to the area internationally acclaimed artists of the stature of Leontyne Price and the London Symphony Orchestra.

The association presents an annual program of five attractions.

On a smaller scale, colleges in Charlotte present outstanding musical groups and personalities as part of their Artist Series. For example, the Munich Chamber Orchestra performed in 1971 under the auspices of the Queens College Artist Series. Johnson C. Smith University presents nationally known figures too, such as the Patterson Singers of New York. UNCC, through the efforts of the University Center and its Fine Arts Department, also attracts foremost musical artists to its campus annually.

Local churches throughout Metrolina present concerts of religious music; the Covenant Presbyterian Church of Charlotte, for example, gave a performance of Mozart's *Vesperae Solemnes de Confessore* and Bruckner's *Te Deum* recently.

An unusual musical organization is The Queens Community Orchestra, composed of sixty-five musicians drawn from the Queens College student body and citizens from the Charlotte area. This newly organized amateur group, formed in 1970, gave a performance of Mozart and Telemann in the spring of 1971 together with the Queens Concert Choir.

Finally, Charlotte's main-branch library has an excellent and extensive collection of monoaural and stereophonic classical recordings which may be borrowed by patrons.

A number of other communities in Metrolina have concert series that sponsor very prominent musical groups. The Hickory Community Concert Series, for example, presented the National Opera's production of *Die Fledermaus* in Monroe Auditorium in 1971. The Gastonia Community Concert Association, organized in 1961, sponsors four performances a year by internationally known musical figures. The Statesville-Iredell Community Concert Association is also quite active. Colleges such as Winthrop, Gardner-Webb, Belmont Abbey, Wingate, Davidson, and others, also sponsor well-known musical artists through their own Artists Series.

Many of the schools in Metrolina have music departments whose faculties and students present recitals throughout the academic year. Colleges such as Winthrop, Queens, UNCC, Mitchell, Gardner-Webb, Wingate, Pfeiffer, and Davidson are quite active in this area.

In addition to the Charlotte Symphony Orchestra, there are two other symphony orchestras in Metrolina that perform on a regular basis for area patrons: the Piedmont Orchestra, under the direction of Igor Buketoff, and the Hickory Symphony Orchestra. Both groups serve a valuable function for those music-lovers in the area who cannot attend the Charlotte Symphony concerts.

Special notice should be given to the Gastonia Music Education Foundation, Inc., which was founded in 1950. This foundation was organized for the purpose of providing financial aid and encouragement to gifted young musicians and is the only organization of its kind in the United States.

Its membership is composed of professional musicians and others especially interested in young people's musical education.

Musical activity in Metrolina is not confined to the classical forms. Folk and country music indigenous to a particular area may be heard at annual fiddlers' conventions in many counties of Metrolina, although Iredell County seems to be the heart of these colorful festivals. Certainly the best known and oldest convention is the Union Grove Old-Time Fiddlers' Convention of Iredell County, held annually on Easter weekend since 1924. Over five-hundred musicians come from all parts of the country to compete for the "World Championship" before an appreciative audience that has grown into the thousands. Nationally known and respected too is the Rock Hill, South Carolina, Elks Club Quartet. Other nationally prominent country-music personalities from Metrolina include Earl Scruggs, Arthur Smith, and the Carter family.

In summary, then, musical activity in Metrolina is reasonably varied. Classical music lovers in the area would be well served also by the inception of an FM radio station emphasizing classical music. WYFM in Charlotte programmed such music throughout the day at one time but now limits its classical format to one or two hours in the late evenings. Finally, Metrolina's classical-music buffs might wish for more contemporary music than they are used to getting; the traditional eighteenth- and nineteenth-century composers constitute almost the only fare at concerts here.

Morton Shapiro

Drama and Dance

Except for Charlotte's semiprofessional Mint Museum Drama Guild, drama in Metrolina is confined primarily to various "little theaters" (amateur companies) and college drama departments. Although there is a fair degree of dramatic activity throughout the area, productions of a purely experimental nature or of the work of avant-garde writers are noticeably rare.

The Mint Museum Drama Guild of Charlotte under the long-time direction of Mrs. Dorothy Masterson is the only semiprofessional dramatic organization in the area. In 1967 the Drama Guild, which utilizes some of the latest and most sophisticated equipment, moved into its new theater-in-the-round location in the Mint Museum, and attendance over the past several seasons has increased at a healthy rate. In recent years the Drama Guild has produced traditional plays such as Arthur Miller's *All My Sons*, Noel Coward's *Private Lives*, and Euripides' *Trojan Women;* but it has also included some contemporary works such as *The Night Thoreau Spent in Jail* (a pre–New York production) and *Feast*, a UNC-student production about the problems of

growing up in the last two decades.

Charlotte's Little Theatre presents about eight plays per season. Although its actors are primarily drawn from local amateur talent, its director is a full-time professional. During the 1970-71 season the Little Theatre staged plays such as *The Importance of Being Earnest* and *Inherit the Wind*. An interesting innovation of the Little Theatre is its Sunday-afternoon "Four O'Clock Theatre," which presents experimental drama. In these productions a minimum of scenery and props is used, and the performance is followed by an audience discussion with director and actors. Recently, for example, the Davidson College Drama Department staged two short plays by the Polish dramatist, Slawomir Mrozek: *Charlie* and *Out at Sea.*

Charlotte's Children's Theatre is also a very active amateur group, presenting four plays for children each season.

Other "little theaters" in Metrolina include those at Rock Hill, Gastonia, and Statesville. At Rock Hill two Children's Theatre productions are staged each year by Winthrop College students, using local children as actors. Recent productions have included *Heidi* and *Rumpelstiltskin*. The Gastonia Little Theatre, Inc., averages four performances a year and also sponsors a Children's Theatre as well as theatrical workshops. Statesville's Little Theatre is also very active throughout the season.

Quite a large number of colleges and universities have very fine drama departments which stage major productions each year and which sponsor touring professional and amateur companies. In Charlotte Queens College recently produced T. S. Eliot's *Murder in the Cathedral*, employing experimental production techniques that included black strobe lights, slide projections, and audience involvement. In the past the UNCC Drama Department has had to operate under trying circumstances, since there has been no theater on campus. But the university's new Fine Arts building, which opened in the summer of 1971, houses two theaters, one of them a small experimental theater. Under the directorship of Catherine Nicholson, UNCC's Drama Department now has exciting prospects for the future. Within Charlotte and Mecklenburg County other excellent college drama departments are found at Johnson C. Smith University, Central Piedmont Community College (whose director, Tom Vance, coordinates the Charlotte Little Theatre experimental programs with plays originating at area colleges), and Davidson College.

Other Metrolina college theater groups and some of their productions include The Lenoir Rhyne Playmakers (Shakespeare's *Twelfth Night*, Brecht's *Threepenny Opera*); Catawba College's Blue Masque Players (*The Masques of Barbara Blomberg*); Gardner-Webb College's Theatre Arts Department (three major productions each year); Winthrop College's Theatre (Samuel Beckett's *Endgame*); Wingate College's Theatre (Archibald MacLeish's *J. B.*); Pfeiffer College's Playmakers (*The Subject Was Roses*).

Two major drama festivals took place recently in Metrolina. In the spring of 1971 the Carolina Drama Association District Festival was held at Central Piedmont Community College in Charlotte and the Palmetto Drama Association Festival (now in its sixteenth year) was held at Rock Hill. Both are three-day competitive festivals at which schools are invited to present plays, either of a traditional or an original nature. The encouragement and fostering of drama are of course the motivating principles behind such festivals.

Touring dramatic and dance companies are often sponsored by Metrolina colleges or local civic groups. The National Players (a renowned touring repertory group) has been sponsored by Winthrop College's Artist Series, which also sponsored the famous Paul Taylor Dance Company in 1971. The Gastonia Fine Arts Council has sponsored The North Carolina School of the Arts' dance group in a ballet performance as well as that same school's production of *John Brown's Body.* The Charlotte Community Concert series usually includes a professional touring dance group among its five events each season. Johnson C. Smith University's Lyceum Series sponsors various dramatic and dance groups, mostly black, throughout the year. And UNCC brought in the Shaw University Players' production of *In White America.* The New York Touring Company (a professional drama group) recently presented *Forty Carats* and *Plaza Suite* in Charlotte's Ovens Auditorium. Finally, perhaps the most unique of touring groups, "The Alliance Francaise," presents a play in French each year at Ovens Auditorium; a recent production of this organization was Moliere's *Tartuffe.*

Theater in Metrolina also includes a somewhat unusual kind of dramatic production: the "dinner theatre." Two dinner theatres in the region are the Pineville Dinner Theatre and the Playhouse Dinner Theatre, both in Mecklenburg County. As its name indicates, the dinner theatre is a restaurant and theatre combined. The main theatrical roles are played by professional New York actors.

Outdoor dramas, spectacular affairs whose themes are drawn from the history of the locale where the plays are presented, have not fared well in Metrolina, at least in recent times. Three outdoor plays by local author LeGette Blythe have, however, been received quite well over the years: *Shout Freedom* (1948), *Voice in the Wilderness* (1955), and *The Hornet's Nest* (1968).

Another type of dramatic production that has grown increasingly popular during the last two decades is the "art film," a movie created and produced with the same painstaking care and professional standards as a legitimate play. Because there are no commercial theatres in the area specializing in art films, especially those produced in foreign countries, the outlet for such films has devolved upon the colleges. Schools such as Winthrop College, Sacred Heart College and Belmont Abbey College (joint sponsors), Davidson College, UNCC, and Queens College present series of fine films by world-renowned directors each year.

To date Negro involvement in drama in Metrolina has been slight. Except for some performances at Johnson C. Smith University in Charlotte and those of a few scattered touring dance and dramatic companies, there has been a paucity of productions of Negro playwrights and choreographers. And dance, a form of drama, has also been sadly neglected in Metrolina. The largest urban center, Charlotte, does not have a resident dance company and has not had one in recent history. Finally, it is to be hoped that more experimental drama will be offered to theatergoers of the area in the near future. There is some experimental theater, as noted above, but for the most part the stock-in-trade plays have been traditionally staged, even by the various college drama departments.

Morton Shapiro

Outdoor Recreation

For some time now there has been a rapidly increasing tendency for Americans to seek out and spend more time in various forms of recreative leisure. Outdoor recreation, one form of recreative leisure, has had a particular attraction for many people, and this trend appears as if it will continue unabated. For example, the utilization of public park and wilderness areas has been increasing at an annual rate of over 10 percent, and the Outdoor Recreation Resources Review Commission has predicted a tripling in the overall demand for recreation by the year 2000.

Various reasons have been given for this tendency: increasing income, more leisure time, and a greater mobility. Yet there is still another kind of attraction to the open spaces. The intense pace and confining dimensions of the urban (and even suburban) setting heightens the desire of many for recreation away from metropolitan areas. In a certain sense, we are returning to our past; away from the exceedingly complex lives most people live to places where nature is still intact or where the historical integrity of past cultures has been preserved.

Metrolina offers a good example of this pattern. Each municipality of course has its own array of public parks and recreation facilities that provide widespread opportunities for outdoor recreation at the local level. The major regional outdoor recreational sites, however, are located predominantly within the two river basins—the Catawba and the Yadkin—that centuries before served as the major avenues for settlement into Metrolina (see Table 10.2 and Fig. 10.7). Therefore in an almost literal as well as figurative sense these river basins allow the Metrolina resident's past to overtake him, just when he needs it most.

The Catawba Basin. Of the two basins, the Catawba is the larger and is more centrally located in the Metrolina counties. The river, named after the Indian tribe that once domi-

Table 10.2. Metrolina Lakes on the Catawba and Yadkin

	Date Completed	Shoreline in Miles	Surface Acres at Full Elevation
Catawba			
Hickory	1927	105	4,100
Lookout Shoals	1916	39	1,270
Norman	1964	520	32,510
Mountain Island	1924	61	3,235
Wylie	1904	325	12,455
Fishing Creek	1916	61	3,370
Yadkin			
High Rock	1927	360	15,180
Tuckertown	1962	75	2,560
Badin	1917	115	5,353
Falls	1919	run of river	204

nated the area, has its headwaters on the Blue Ridge Escarpment in the western extremity of McDowell County. This historic watercourse has a basin in North Carolina of over three thousand square miles and keeps the name "Catawba" until it flows into South Carolina's Wateree Lake. The waters flowing from that lake become the Wateree River and eventually the Santee River before emptying into the Atlantic Ocean fifty miles to the northeast of Charleston, South Carolina.

The Catawba River has been altered considerably during this century by Duke Power Company's construction of nine hydroelectric impoundments along the course of the river. These facilities evolved from J. B. Duke's idea for providing electric power throughout this entire section of the Carolinas' Piedmont. An indirect benefit was a string of lakes along the Catawba that have been developed for recreational purposes. Although Duke Power owns most of the shoreline and watershed lands around all of its lakes, it makes the lakes available for boating and fishing by providing access areas. Individual tracts can frequently be leased for private recreational use and cottage sites. In addition, the company has leased a total of 165,000 acres to wildlife commissions for game-management purposes.

The first of Duke Power's lakes on the Catawba—Lake

James and Lake Rhodiss—are located in counties to the west of Metrolina. The Catawba begins its course through Metrolina as Lake Hickory, which forms the northern boundary of Catawba County. Completed in 1927, the lake's 4,100 surface acres and 105-mile shoreline provide good opportunities for swimming, boating, and fishing, and are especially accessible to residents of the Hickory metropolitan area.

The Catawba then swings to a southeasterly direction and continues its broad course by becoming the elongated Lookout Shoals Lake. Although Lookout Shoals is not a large lake (1,270 surface acres and 39 miles of shoreline), it is one of the oldest on the Catawba, since Lookout Dam was completed in 1916.

The Catawba's flow thereafter leads into the largest manmade lake in North Carolina—the "Inland Sea" of Lake Norman (see Fig. 10.8). Metrolina's major outdoor recreational feature is relatively young. It was created by the construction of Cowan's Ford Dam, begun in 1959 and completed in 1964, at the site of General Davidson's heroic defense against Cornwallis during the American Revolution (see Part 2). The more than mile-long dam and hydroelectric station has as its primary purpose of course the generation of electric power (372,000 kilowatts total capacity). The reservoir created, however, has been a boon to recreation in Metrolina. Its surface area of 32,510 acres (when full) and 520 miles of shoreline borders on four counties: Catawba, Iredell, Lincoln, and Mecklenburg. The "Inland Sea" extends nearly thirty-four miles in length and is eight miles in width at its widest point.

As indicated in Fig. 10.8, a large number of recreational facilities, from marinas to camp grounds, are available on Lake Norman. All types of boating can be found, although sailing seems particularly popular. With a season that runs approximately from March through October frequent regattas are sponsored by the yacht clubs of the area. The largest, the Lake Norman Yacht Club, was organized before the lake was even filled and today includes over one hundred sailboats registered.

Fishing on Lake Norman is considered to be as good as can be found in North Carolina. The reason is related to Lake Norman's youth. New lakes follow a rather standard biological pattern in that excellent aquatic food conditions exist on the youthful and fertile lake bottom. Lake Norman includes among its fish species the same types that exist on most of the Catawba's lakes in the Metrolina area: game fish such as largemouth bass, crappie, striped bass, white bass, sauger, yellow perch, plus catfish, carp, and threadfin shad. The largemouth bass is one of the most popular sport fish, and Lake Norman has a reputation for being one of the better largemouth-bass fishing lakes in the country. Catches of over ten pounds of this fish are no longer unusual on this still young body of water. It is the crappie, however, that is fished for the most, no doubt because catches of up to two hundred daily per fisherman are

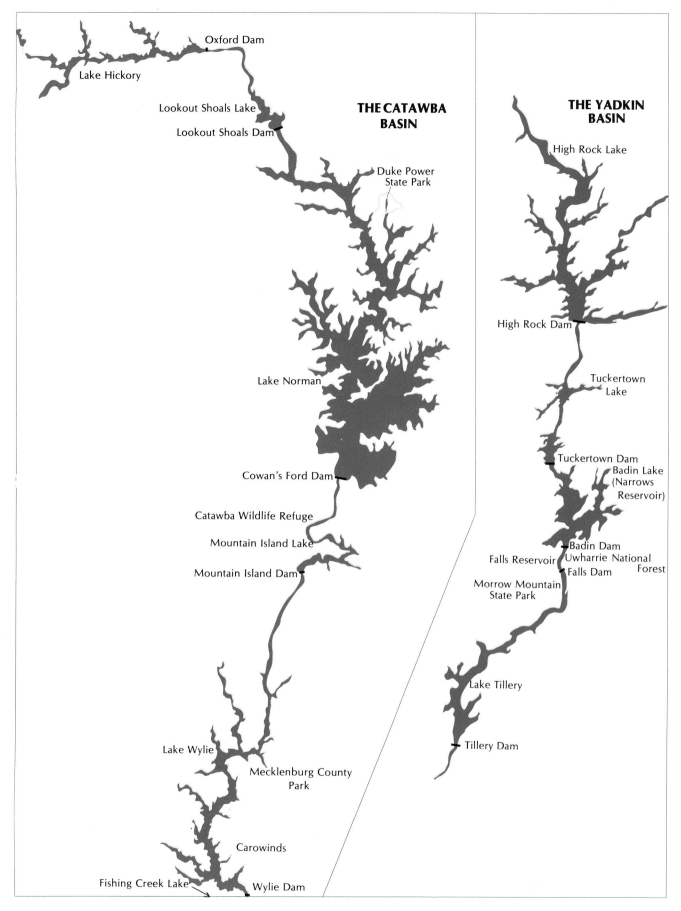

Fig. 10.7. The Catawba and Yadkin Basins Recreational Sites

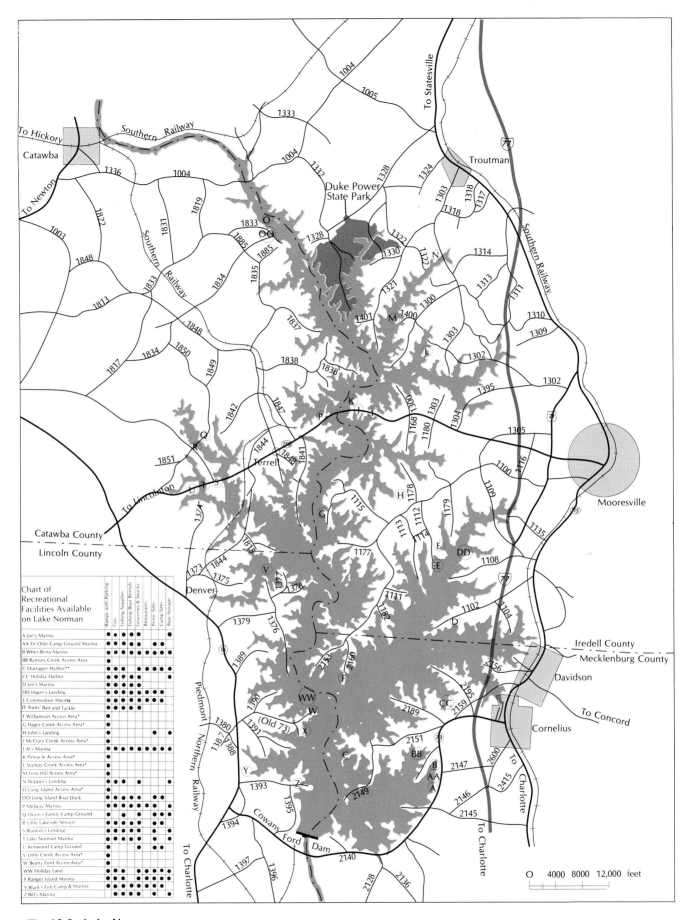

Chart of Recreational Facilities Available on Lake Norman

	Ramps with Parking	Gas	Fishing Supplies	Fishing Boat Rentals	Groceries & Snacks	Restaurants	Picnic Sites	Camp Sites	Boat Storage
A Joe's Marina	●	●	●	●					
AA Ye Olde Camp Ground Marina	●	●	●	●			●	●	●
B Wher-Rena Marina	●	●	●	●	●				●
BB Ramsey Creek Access Area	●								
C Outrigger Harbor**	●	●	●	●	●	●	●		●
CC Holiday Harbor		●	●	●					●
D Jim's Marina		●	●	●	●				●
DD Hager's Landing	●	●	●	●	●				●
E Commodore Marina		●	●	●	●				●
EE Stutts' Bait and Tackle	●	●	●	●					
F Williamson Access Area*	●								
G Hager Creek Access Area*	●								
H John's Landing	●						●	●	
I McCrary Creek Access Area*	●								
J Al's Marina	●	●	●	●	●				●
K Pinnacle Access Area*	●								
L Stumpy Creek Access Area*	●								
M Fern Hill Access Area*	●								
N Skipper's Landing	●	●	●		●				
O Long Island Access Area*	●								
OO Long Island Boat Dock	●	●	●	●			●	●	●
P Midway Marina	●	●	●	●	●				●
Q Drum's Family Camp Ground		●	●		●		●	●	
R Little Lakeside Service	●	●	●	●	●		●		
S Blanton's Landing	●	●	●	●					
T Lake Norman Marina	●	●	●	●	●				●
U Kenwood Camp Ground	●	●	●					●	
V Little Creek Access Area*	●								
W Beatty Ford Access Area*	●								
WW Holiday Land		●	●		●	●	●	●	
X Ranger Island Marina	●	●	●	●			●	●	●
Y Black's Fish Camp & Marina	●	●	●	●	●				●
Z Bill's Marina		●	●	●	●	●			

Fig. 10.8. Lake Norman

page 220

not uncommon.

Lake-front property around Lake Norman has been so popular that available sites are now extremely difficult to find. Duke Power owns approximately 50 percent of the land surrounding the lake and has leased some 2,700 lots averaging three-fourths acres apiece. Most of these sites have been leased to individuals, therefore cottages, trailers, and homes continue to spring up along the lake shore. But the company has no more land it is willing to lease at present, and a waiting list of five thousand is said to exist. Other Duke Power property is being retained as possible sites for future steam plants. Additional large parcels of land still remain, but these are owned by farmers who are reluctant to sell. Although adjacent property not fronting the lake has been much less in demand, by the time construction of I-77 is completed (1975-76), connecting Charlotte with the length of Lake Norman, there may be a building boom in the entire lake area. So far such building has been slow because of inaccessibility and the fact that finance companies believe it is a poor risk to invest in homes there.

One of Metrolina's two state parks is located at the northern end of Lake Norman. The Duke Power State Park is a 1,328-acre tract on the Iredell County shore of the lake. The park includes camping and picnic areas, a boat-launching ramp, and a thirty-three acre constant-level swimming lake with swimming facilities and bathhouses. A sizable portion of the tract is still to be developed. During 1971, 92,188 people visited this park, making it the eighth most frequented of North Carolina's fifteen state parks. Yet the park has not experienced the popularity originally envisioned for it. Perhaps its inaccessibility to major population centers is one reason. On the other hand, during 1971 there was a 9 percent increase over the attendance rate for 1970. And the completion of the unfinished portions of I-77 should increase its popularity in the future. Ironically, the Duke Power State Park area is one of the most scenic parts of the entire Lake Norman shoreline, densely forested and with a hilly topography.

The most frequently heard complaint about Lake Norman concerns the fluctuation of its water level. As is the case with any reservoir used for hydroelectric generation, the level of the lake fluctuates according to generation needs as well as the amount of rainfall. Duke Power reports that the maximum drawdown for any one week is rarely more than two feet and that seasonal fluctuation, during an average rainfall year, is about eight feet during a period of three or four months. It is usually in the late summer that the demand for electricity becomes so great that the company must put its hydroelectric turbines into operation. This process uses water and the water level consequently drops. If accompanied by a dry spell, the water level may drop drastically. This happened during the summer of 1970. During August of that year the water level dropped rapidly to such a low level that many floating docks were sitting on the lake bottom. The experience of the past several years seems to indicate that Lake Norman has a water-level fluctuation greater than that for other lakes on the Catawba and the Yadkin. Duke Power officials point out, however, that by the latter part of the decade the water level will become much more stable. By that time the mammoth McGuire nuclear station is to be in operation and the hydroelectric turbines at Cowans Ford Dam should not have to be used as often.

Just downstream from the Cowans Ford Dam, the Catawba broadens into Mountain Island Lake, a meandering body of water with sixty-one miles of shoreline and 3,235 surface acres. Four access areas provide public recreational opportunities. The water supply for the city of Charlotte comes from this lake, which was completed in 1924 by the dam at Mountain Island Station. On both banks of the upper portion of Mountain Island Lake, and extending up the Catawba to Cowans Ford Dam, is the Catawba Wildlife Refuge. This tract of about a thousand acres is leased by Duke Power to the North Carolina Wildlife Commission for management purposes. The refuge is maintained in its natural wilderness state, and hunting is prohibited within one-half mile of the refuge boundary. Planted as well as purchased grain has been set out in order to attract migratory waterfowl. During the last several years an increasing number of waterfowl have been attracted to the area, with several thousand ducks and approximately 250 Canadian Geese now coming there each year. The migratory arrivals begin in the fall and a peak population exists from about January to February. Public viewing stands are provided for bird-watchers.

As the Catawba reaches the state line, it becomes Lake Wylie, the oldest lake on the Catawba. The original dam construction was in 1904 and was called the Indian Hook Shoals Station. The lake itself was simply known as Catawba Lake. In 1925 the present dam was built over the old one, increasing the spillway and enlarging the lake to its present 325 miles of shoreline and 12,455 acres. The name "Lake Wylie" was established in 1960 in honor of Dr. W. Gil Wylie, who organized the Catawba Power Company, a predecessor of Duke Power. This lake is a good reflection of the interstate nature of Metrolina as the state line runs through the middle of most of its course, separating Mecklenburg County from South Carolina's York County. Because of its age and proximity to Charlotte and Rock Hill, Lake Wylie for some time has offered a broad array of recreational facilities. There are six public access areas and a number of piers, marinas, and boat landings. As is the case on Lake Norman, boating is extremely popular and a number of sailing regattas are held throughout the warmer months. The Mecklenburg County Park covers a sixty-acre wooded tract that extends as a peninsula into a portion of the lake. This park is only about five years old but its activities include swimming, boating, camping, and picnicking.

A special kind of recreational facility that will capitalize on the attractiveness of the Lake Wylie area is under development in the vicinity of the state line. To be known as Carowinds, this amusement, resort, and development complex is a ten-year project that will eventually cost $250 million. The first phase of the project is a $20-million, 250-acre amusement park that will straddle the state line next to the location of I-77 and just three miles from Lake Wylie. Tentatively scheduled to open in 1973, the park will feature a wide variety of the "magic kingdom" types of rides and amusements. It will emphasize also the history and culture of the Carolinas. For example, there will be an exhibit re-creating the culture of the Catawba Indians, plus a southern plantation, a colonial exhibit, a miniature farm in operation, and areas reflecting Old Charleston and Old Wilmington. Later phases of Carowinds will be developed nearby on a six-mile stretch of Lake Wylie shoreline and will include a resort community and residential area.

The Catawba's last reservoir, Fishing Creek Lake, is completely in South Carolina, running along the Lancaster County line. The lake was filled in 1916 and includes sixty-one miles of shoreline and 3,370 surface acres. The entire shoreline along the Lancaster side is under the management of the South Carolina Wildlife Resources Department. There is a substantial deer population in this area, and deer hunting is permitted on a seasonal basis.

The Yadkin Basin. The Yadkin River rises on the Blue Ridge Escarpment in Watauga County near Blowing Rock and flows for about one hundred miles in a northeasterly direction to a point near Winston-Salem. From there it veers to the southeast and joins its major tributary, the South Yadkin, along the northern boundary of Metrolina's Rowan County. It expands into a string of lakes along the eastern border of Metrolina, becoming the Pee Dee when joined by the Uwharrie River just below Falls Dam. The Pee Dee River empties into the Atlantic Ocean through Winyah Bay near Georgetown, South Carolina.

Along the Metrolina border, the river and its lakes can be divided into two sections. The upper portion is the Yadkin River section and includes four lakes, each being a hydroelectric impoundment of Yadkin, Inc., a wholly owned subsidiary of the Aluminum Company of America. Construction of the first dam and reservoir began in the early 1900s when a French combine, seeking to harness the flow of the Yadkin to produce the electrical power necessary to produce aluminum, began construction of the Narrows Dam. Alcoa acquired the French interest in 1915 and formed the Tallassee Power Company to finish building the dam and power station in order to power the company's aluminum smelter at Badin. The dam and the new Badin Reservoir (called the Narrows Reservoir by the company) was completed one year later. The Falls Dam and reservoir were finished in 1919 and the High Rock Dam and its reservoir were completed in 1927. Eventually the

Tallassee Power Company became the Carolina Aluminum Company, which in 1958 became Yadkin, Inc. The final reservoir was established in 1962 by the construction of the Tuckertown Dam.

Recreation opportunities are provided at each of the lakes, except for the Falls Reservoir, where the steep surrounding slopes make that area generally inaccessible. Public access areas are furnished by Yadkin, Inc. and operated by the North Carolina Wildlife Commission. Boating, fishing, swimming, picnicking, cottage sites, and other recreational uses are popular on all three lakes. The most common fish catches include largemouth bass, white bass, crappie, bream, and catfish. In a few of the surrounding areas large- and small-game hunting is permitted under the regulations of the North Carolina hunting laws.

The northernmost and by far the largest of the four Yadkin, Inc. reservoirs is High Rock Lake. With a sprawling shoreline of 360 miles and a surface area of 15,180 acres, this reservoir was constructed mainly for water storage. Since the water level of High Rock is at the mercy of watershed rainfall, drawdown could pose a serious problem to recreation use. In order to reduce extensive drawdown during the recreation season, however, Yadkin, Inc. has agreed to maintain higher elevations at this reservoir.

The Tuckertown and Badin lakes, although much smaller than High Rock, are located within an especially scenic stretch of the Yadkin's course. The Uwharrie National Forest is tucked up against the eastern shore of most of the two lakes, providing a heavily wooded and rolling topography of natural scenic beauty. Badin Lake in particular has a large portion of its diffused 115-mile shoreline and 5,353 surface acres within the national forest.

After the Yadkin River leaves Falls Dam, it enters the second section of its Metrolina course. Not only does the river change its name when met by the Uwharrie River but it moves out of the Yadkin, Inc. domain into the Carolina Power and Light Company's Lake Tillery hydroelectric impoundment. The company finished construction in 1928 of the Tillery dam and generating plant, some twenty-five miles above its Blewett Falls Plant. Although the company does not provide recreational facilities at Tillery except for some picnic areas, it has allowed free public access for the purpose of full utilization of lands and waters for recreation, including fishing and hunting. It has worked with the North Carolina Wildlife Commission in providing four public access areas. One recreational asset to Lake Tillery is the fact that the water level drawdown is minimal. This is primarily because Tillery is a "run of stream" plant and a contract was negotiated long ago with Tallassee Power Company to stabilize the river flow upstream. Also, the lake provides an excellent natural recreational setting because its elongated 104-mile shoreline (and 5,000 surface acres) winds its way between the scenic Uwharrie National Forest and the Morrow Mountain State Park area.

Morrow Mountain, Metrolina's second state park, is lo-

Fig. 10.9. Metrolina Points of Interest

Fig. 10.10. Charlotte Points of Interest

cated in Stanly County on the western side of Lake Tillery. It is seven miles east of Albemarle and accessible by state highways 27, 73, and 740. Morrow Mountain is a part of the Uwharrie Mountains, which forms a portion of what remains of the Ocoee Mountains, one of the oldest mountain ranges on the North American continent. There is a sharp difference in elevation between these ancient mountains and the surrounding Piedmont. From Morrow Mountain's summit one can get a beautiful panoramic view of the adjacent hills, farmlands, and the curving course of Lake Tillery stretching to the south. Within the 4,135 forested park area are deer, raccoon, turkey and other native animals.

Many recreational activities are possible at Morrow Mountain State Park because of the great variety of facilities available. These include sixty-five tent and trailer camp sites, six fully equipped vacation cabins, boating, a swimming pool, picnic shelters, and a refreshment stand. Extensive hiking and nature trails allow a closer observation of the diversity of plant and animal life as well as the unusual geologic history. Indian lore is abundant. The park also has a Natural History Museum that is open daily throughout the summer season. A park naturalist is on duty June through August.

Morrow Mountain is North Carolina's second most popular state park (Fort Macon ranks first). A total of 409,068 persons visited this park in 1971, representing an approximate doubling of attendance over the past decade.

Douglas M. Orr, Jr.

REFERENCES

American Hospital Association. *Journal of the American Hospital Association, Hospitals, Guide Issue,* Parts 1 and 2 (1971).

American Public Health Association. *American Journal of Public Health.* (Published monthly.)

Division of Recreation, North Carolina Department of Local Affairs. *1971 North Carolina Inventory of Outdoor Recreation Areas.* Raleigh: The Division, 1971.

Duke Power Company. *Lake Norman, the Inland Sea.* Charlotte: Duke Power, n.d.

Duke Power Company. Maps of Duke Power reservoirs on the Catawba. Charlotte: Duke Power Company, n.d.

Dunn, O. J. *Basic Statistics: A Primer for the Biomedical Sciences.* New York: John Wiley & Sons, 1967.

Fabun, Don. *The Dynamics of Change.* Englewood Cliffs, N.J.: Prentice-Hall, 1967.

Haar, F. B., and J. Smolensky. *Principles of Community Health.* Philadelphia: W. B. Saunders Company, 1961.

Lilienfeld, A. M., and A. J. Gifford, eds. *Chronic Diseases and Public Health.* Baltimore: Johns Hopkins Press, 1966.

MacMahon, B. *Epidemiologic Methods.* Boston: Little, Brown and Company, 1960.

Mustard, H. S., and E. L. Stebbins. *An Introduction to Public Health.* New York: MacMillan Company, 1965.

North Carolina Department of Conservation and Development. *State Parks Public Use Record.* (Published monthly.)

North Carolina Medical Care Commission. *A Complete Listing of North Carolina Hospitals* (nonfederal). Raleigh: The Commission, April 1, 1971.

North Carolina State Department of Administration. *Outdoor Recreation Planning* (December 1967).

North Carolina State Department of Water Resources. *Catawba River Basin: Pollution Survey Report.* Raleigh: The Department, 1961.

Outdoor Recreation Resources Review Commission. *Action for Outdoor Recreation for America.* Washington, D.C.: Citizens Committee for the ORRRC Report, 1964.

Piedmont Area Development Association. Raleigh: The Association, n.d.

Somers, A. R., and M. D. Somers. *Doctors, Patients and Health Insurance.* Washington, D.C.: Brookings Institute, 1967.

South Carolina State Board of Health. *South Carolina State Plan for Construction and Modernization of Hospital and Medical Facilities* (Hill-Burton Program), 1969-70. Columbia: The Board, 1970.

Stipe, Robert E. *County Recreation in North Carolina.* Chapel Hill: Institute of Government, University of North Carolina at Chapel Hill, 1967.

Yadkin, Inc. *The Yadkin Story.* Badin, N.C.: Yadkin, Inc., n.d.

11. REGIONAL OVERVIEW

JAMES W. CLAY
DOUGLAS M. ORR, JR.

"If you do not think about the future, you cannot have one."—John Galsworthy

The trends depicted in the preceding sections of this book suggest that Metrolina, like many other emerging urban regions throughout the nation, is experiencing a momentum of urbanization that is indeed irreversible (see Fig. 11.1). Yet the new spatial order raises many questions concerning the future quality of life for the citizens of the region. Will expanded growth and urbanization overcome the self-cleansing capacity of the environment? Will service facilities such as schools, parks, and utilities be adequately revised and enlarged to accommodate the new order? What will this growth mean in terms of rush-hour, commuter traffic? And can public administration and governing bodies keep pace with this expanded scale of operations? In short, will such a region offer more opportunities or will it be simply more confining?

A danger is that Metrolina's regional evolvement will lack order and purpose and simply become the all-too-familiar "urban sprawl." The dictionary defines "sprawl" as a "spreading out ungracefully." The landscape seems to take on a gray, formless, fragmented appearance that lacks esthetic or functional value. There are some evidences that Metrolina's continued urbanization is leading to urban sprawl, although on the whole, the region has more opportunities than problems. Yet the evolvement of the urban region is certainly not something that is inherently undesirable. In fact, it can be a very positive development, affording the people of the area new horizons and the chance to live fuller lives. Urbanization may be the most heterogeneous social and economic system that has ever been produced by man. A lack of understanding of this diversity, however, and the failure to direct and control it can be fatal.

Challenges to Metrolina

Certainly Metrolina exemplifies the varied opportunities of the urban region. Each of the previous sections has offered numerous illustrations of this, from which certain challenges to the region's future can be surmised.

History has given the modern delimitation of Metrolina a justifiable raison d'etre. The historical corridors of transportation and settlement, from the Great Trading Path to today's expressways, have endowed Metrolina with a focus and an axis on which to build. The historical symbols of the region's past, from Kings Mountain to the Charlotte Mint Museum, are important bases of opportunity for enhancing the region's sense of heritage and esthetics.

The section on Metrolina's physical environment emphasizes what is readily apparent to most of the region's inhabitants: the endowment by nature of a particularly moderate climate, plentiful and high-quality water resources, and an interesting diversity of topography and geology. Yet these favorable conditions are currently being threatened by such byproducts of civilization as the high emission and low dispersal tendency of air pollutants; the existence of polluted stream tributaries due to industrial and municipal wastes; the possible uncontrolled mining exploitation of some of the most scenic topographic features; and a frequent deterioration in the unique natural qualities of the landscape as a result of haphazard urban growth. Unlike some more intensely developed urban areas, however, Metrolina's natural setting is not yet blighted beyond preservation. Herein lies the opportunity and challenge that Metrolina is fortunate enough to still have.

Yet some of the same tendencies characteristic of other urbanizing areas may be observed in Metrolina: a more rapid population growth and a higher population density than that of the surrounding area, state, or nation; a net

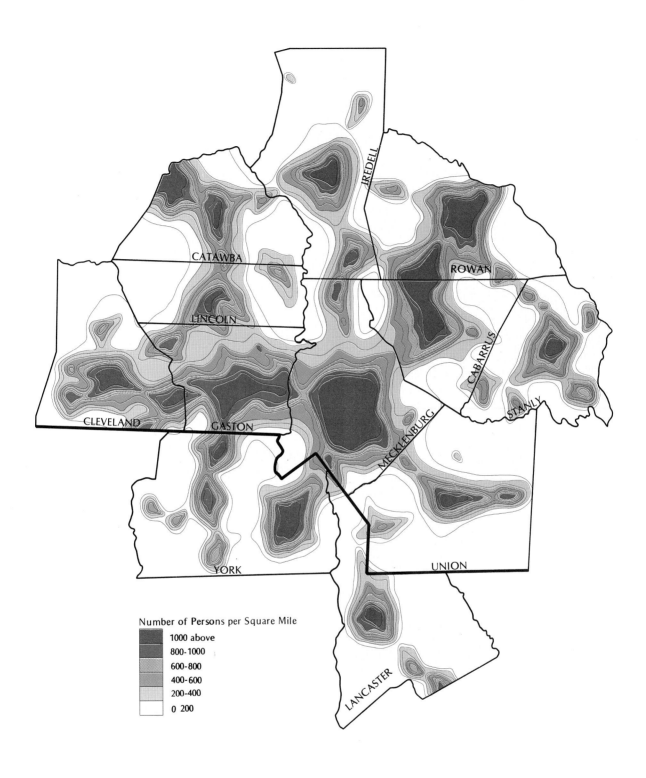

Fig. 11.1. Metrolina Population Density Pattern

in-migration of population; a movement of Negroes from rural areas to the city, and, as is the case in other parts of the South, a net out-migration of Negroes from the region; migration of whites to the suburbs; declining fertility; a younger population; and so on. Transcending each of these individual features is a general diffusion of the population distribution pattern and the pervading influence of urbanism in molding life-styles.

Metrolina was shown to be a major manufacturing region within the nation, yet the region has been more dependent on textiles than either North or South Carolina as a whole. The challenge now facing Metrolina is to make the conversion to economic diversity without undue dislocation or disruption of the economic well-being of the population, and to diversify into industries that offer attractive wage and employment opportunities. It is important to remember also that manufacturing often stimulates a portion of a suburbanized, low-density urban development that constitutes urban sprawl. As one possible planning solution, the clustering of such activities into industrial districts can allow for linkages with ancillary goods and services, create the population concentration necessary for the channeling of commuter traffic through public transportation, and thereby inhibit the possibility of fragmented industrial sprawl.

Even a brief review of the figures in the transportation section gives the reader an impression of the great magnitude of transportation flow into and out of the region, particularly concentrating on Charlotte. The early development of key transportation corridors plus a strategic mid-Atlantic location between Washington and Atlanta have made Metrolina a transportation center. The statistics given for the magnitude of Charlotte's trucking industry are one indication of this centrality. Of particular concern however, is the inadequacy of intercity and intracity routes within Metrolina. It is too often tempting to try to solve the transportation problem by simply providing more facilities when alternative uses of existing facilities may be a better answer. But when more facilities are the only solution one must take into consideration the consequences of the new routes for the type of adjacent land-use patterns that will follow.

Although Metrolina does not revolve around an overpowering central city, the region's communication, trade, and finance are strongly oriented toward its regional capital, Charlotte. Activities such as wholesaling, financial and commercial headquarters operations, and major communications media require the economies of scale that only the larger central city can provide. Charlotte's ever-rising skyline is proof that the city's importance is increasing. Metrolina's challenge in communications, trade, and finance is to allow for the continuation of healthy competition within the area but to avoid resistance to regional cooperation on the part of the smaller communities because of the dominant role of the largest city.

The changing political voting patterns in Metrolina counties reflect to a large extent the evolving characteristics of the region's life-style as depicted in other sections of this atlas. Demographic patterns, urbanization, and industrialization, plus new groups of eligible voters have meant the continued development toward a genuine two-party competition but also the evolution of an electorate that is more issue oriented. The politics section reveals too that Metrolina, a prototype of the lower-density urban region, may also be a small-scale model of the nation's voting habits. Particularly in presidential elections, the region as a whole has been an almost perfect microcosm of the national pattern. Metrolina can capitalize on this more viable and responsive electoral tendency by choosing those political programs and representatives that can best provide farsighted regional planning and development.

Perhaps in no other area is the challenge to the people of Metrolina greater than in the educational system. It is the basis for the development of the region's most important natural resource—its people. Although there are many promising new educational programs in the Metrolina school systems, the constant lag behind national averages in nearly every educational index is a gauge of the challenge still ahead. What does the reality of the urban region mean for education? The apparent demise of the neighborhood-school concept, with all the accompanying confusion and turmoil, highlights a basic fact of life in an urban society that would have become obvious eventually even without the court mandates: we are indeed all neighbors in this new environment. It is a closed system, in human as well as physical terms, and the complex interactions within require a responsive educational mainspring to foster human development in the face of regional development. Those involved in teacher training, for example, must consider the learning and living environment of the urban area. Administrators of higher education can further recognize that learning is a life-long process and permit more opportunities for continuing adult education. Curricula should include courses on the social contact of different cultures, the land-use problem—private and public—and, as an interdisciplinary study, the nature of the environment. Most of all, education must stretch the mind and overcome student parochialism, which is out of step with the fluidity of urban society.

Finally, the cultural amenities of Metrolina are a telling commentary on the quality of the region's life-style. Despite the provincialism that many associate with the South, Metrolina exhibits a significantly varied and substantial array of amenities. The combination of major urban centers, higher educational institutions, and scenic physical features is the principal foundation for this variety. A continuing problem, however, is that with increases in population and incomes the desire for the amenities of life grows at an almost revolutionary pace. Perhaps this is as it should be. Greater affluence and opportunities mean changing values and a search for new meanings in life. The result is the need for a better availability of and accessibility to health-care facilities, the cultural arts, and outdoor recreational opportunities. Again, the challenge will be to devise ways of better using space in a closed system of finite usable land area.

The foregoing themes, each a section in this book, represent the life-style of Metrolina. In order to fit these elements together harmoniously for the future, a great deal of planning is necessary. Recently the Charlotte-Mecklenburg Planning Commission, in releasing a report on community land-use planning, pointed out that a plan should rest on two foundations: first, it should reflect the kind of community the people want, and second, it must be sound and realistic. What do people want? Basically we already have the answer by simply looking at urban growth and development patterns throughout the country. They want what is often called the "broad acres city," which allows plenty of room for people to live as and where they wish with easy accessibility to job, cultural, and recreational opportunities. The outward spreading of the nation's cities and living areas long ago impressed a visiting French geographer, Vidal de la Blanche, to such an extent that he called it the most perfect expression of Americanism. Freedom of preferences and movement has been an indigenous part of the American scene. Abundant space could always be taken for granted. But is this desire still realistic? Some planners point out in their projections that as a population doubles and incomes rise, the use of space at least quadruples because the drive to attain the good life makes a wider life space necessary for each individual. But because of more people and greater activity, land use can be fragmented and full of contradictory purposes. The broad-acres city becomes extremely difficult to control and develop properly.

The common denominator to these desires and realities is regionalism. The desire of the population for acres of opportunity and freedom of movement is not realistic if only the local perspective prevails. Comprehensive regional planning, which incorporates the broad mosaic, seems to be the only possible way that the wishes of the people and the realities of the landscape can be effectively blended.

Problems in effective regional planning today are compounded by the large number of existent political units. For example, the United States has over eighty thousand such units—states, cities, counties, and townships, plus scores of special-purpose districts, many of them created to focus efficiently on narrow problems that include everything from airports to garbage. More than half of these units contain less than two thousand inhabitants. The spread of population outward from a central core has brought about a corresponding decentralization of government and a preponderance of new political entities. This fits well into human desires, since people generally tend to associate with individualistic local elements such as school boards, various social groups, and the PTA, rarely linking local problems with the region or envisioning regional solutions. Larger governmental units are distrusted. The fact that city-county consolidation is usually voted down—as in the case of Charlotte-Mecklenburg—exemplifies this distrust. Although students of government may continue to debate the practicality of metropolitan government, the necessity for more governmental cooperation among existing units is becoming obvious.

Efforts at Regional Cooperation

There are some promising indications that counties, municipalities, and organizations within Metrolina are voluntarily coordinating their activities in a number of ways. For example, though the Metrolina concept itself is only a geographic framework for studying the region, an area-wide Metrolina Coordinating Committee has been established by the Metrolina Committee of the Charlotte Chamber of Commerce. Representatives from each county work through the Metrolina Committee in pinpointing elements of mutual concern.

The Metrolina Environmental Concern Association. Another recently created organization that has chosen the Metrolina grouping as its area of concern is the Metrolina Environmental Concern Association, Inc. MECA is a nonprofit citizens' action group composed of individuals and organizations seeking to achieve a quality environment in the Metrolina region. It has committees working in the areas of land use, air, water, population, consumer ecology, wildlife, natural areas, solid waste systems, and electric power. Its methods include educational efforts and litigation.

The Centralina Council of Governments. Since intergovernmental efforts have not developed into region-wide government, a new concept in metropolitan organization has evolved. The councils of governments (COGs) are voluntary organizations of local governments formed for the purpose of fostering cooperation in resolving problems, policies, and plans that are common and regional in nature. In the United States there are approximately one hundred such voluntary regional councils of governments or councils of elected officials. The limitations of the COGs help to explain their current popularity. They lack the legal means to implement programs, cannot regulate local functions or pass ordinances, and cannot levy taxes. Despite these shortcomings, however, the federal government is supporting them as an ideal channel for increased federal involvement in urban regional affairs. Within the Metrolina area, such a Council of Governments was created in 1968. Now named the Centralina Council of Governments, the local COG includes a membership of twenty-six counties and municipalities as shown in Fig. 11.2. In addition, Catawba County and the city of Shelby in Cleveland County are affiliate members. Lancaster and York counties were expected to join initially but an enabling constitutional amendment failed to be ratified by the South Carolina legislature even though it was approved in a referendum by the voters. There is a likelihood, however, that these counties may also work out an affiliate status, thereby giving the Centralina COG some sort of representation from every Metrolina county.

The local COG has a professional staff with an office in Charlotte. Operating expenses come from a ten-cents-per-citizen assessment of each member government plus federal funding. Each member jurisdiction sends delegates to council meetings, which are held in Charlotte every three months. When a specific council plan or recommendation is proposed, each member governing unit, acting on the advice of its delegate to the council, votes to adopt or reject the particular action. After a gradual beginning, the council is developing regional planning on a number of fronts. The first accomplishment, typically, was in overcoming the suspicions of some members that the council represented an effort to implement another level of government with enforceable powers. One program in particular, the "895 Review," does allow the council some degree of power. It gives the council the responsibility for reviewing most applications for federal money that originate in the local region. Although the council does not have veto power, its favorable action is usually necessary for approval by the federal government. A related development has been the council's recent release of a regional development plan. The plan, designed by private consultants, will be used by the Department of Housing and Urban Development as a basis for deploying federal water and sewer funds in the region. As such, the plan can have a substantial impact on future regional development. It attempts to channel the region's urban development into a large number of different-sized urban centers separated by open space. It adheres to a basic planning philosophy of the council that a more densely populated central city (Charlotte) is not necessarily a better city, and that orderly population dispersion throughout the region is a desired goal. Other programs being formulated by the council include a region-wide airport system, plus regional air-quality and water-quality control boards.

The Lake Norman Marine Commission. Housed within the Centralina COG's offices is the Lake Norman Marine Commission. It involves the four Metrolina counties bordering Lake Norman and so far has concerned itself with regulations regarding lake use. Soon to be released, however, is an environmental impact study worked out with COG which will recommend land-use policy for the lake and surrounding land area.

North Carolina Planning Region F. Paralleling the development of the Centralina COG is the creation of a local state-planning region (Region F) that is one of seventeen new multicounty planning regions in North Carolina. Legislation enacted by the 1969 General Assembly greatly increased the responsibilities of the State Planning Division and committed the state to the development of comprehensive regional land-use planning. As an outgrowth of this action, on May 7, 1970, the governor issued an executive order establishing the seventeen multicounty planning regions throughout the state. According to the State Planning Division, the several roles of these new districts are (1) to better identify and judge the regional trends, problems, and opportunities that are not well perceived by local government officials, who are concerned mainly with the local perspective; (2) to allow the pooling and sharing of scarce planning resources and expertise; (3) to provide an effective channel of communication to the state and federal government and serve as a means for identifying and obtaining needed state and federal assistance. Although these district boundaries can be altered in the future according to changing conditions and trends, the future implications of these regions as delimited were demonstrated when the Centralina COG adjusted its county membership to correspond to the eight counties in Planning Region F.

Metropolitan Charlotte Interstate Air Quality Control Region. Ten Metrolina counties are included within the twelve-county Metropolitan Charlotte Interstate Air Quality Control Region. In accordance with the provisions of the national Clean Air Act of 1970, the state of North Carolina is divided into eight air-quality-control regions. Only the Metropolitan Charlotte Interstate Air Quality Control Region crosses a state line, as it encompasses four South Carolina counties plus the eight North Carolina counties in state Planning Region F. These regions provide a framework of operation for the Environmental Protection Agency, as directed by the Clean Air Act, to implement enforcement of its regulations regarding national primary and secondary ambient air-quality standards.

North Carolina Soil and Water Conservation Area 8. The North Carolina Soil and Water Conservation Committee of the new Department of Natural and Economic Resources coordinates planning in eight soil and water conservation "areas" in the state. All of the North Carolina counties of Metrolina except Catawba are located in Area 8 of this grouping, which as of January 1, 1972, was reorganized to include state Planning Districts F and C. Although the eight areas exist primarily as an administrative structure for the Soil and Water Conservation Committee in Raleigh, the county representatives in each area meet twice a year to discuss and coordinate projects and activities. There is no

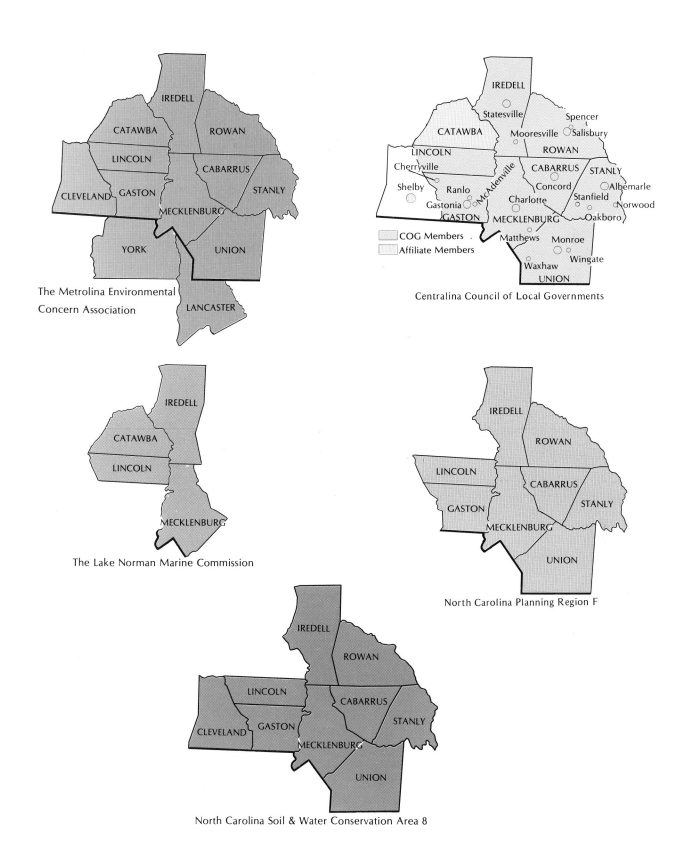

The Metrolina Environmental Concern Association

Centralina Council of Local Governments

COG Members
Affiliate Members

The Lake Norman Marine Commission

North Carolina Planning Region F

North Carolina Soil & Water Conservation Area 8

Fig. 11.2. Regional Organizations in the Metrolina Area

Metropolitan Charlotte Interstate Air Quality Control Region

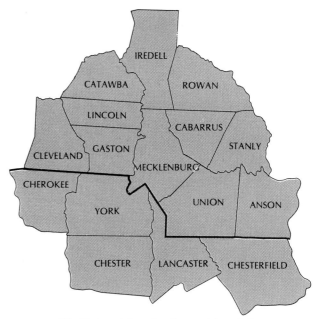

The Piedmont Area Development Association

Fig. 11.2. Regional Organizations in the Metrolina Area (continued)

permanent area headquarters office but an area chairman is chosen annually.

The Piedmont Area Development Association. The oldest and largest of the Metrolina-area regional groupings is the Piedmont Area Development Association. Founded in 1958, it is comprised of sixteen counties, extending across the state line to include five counties in South Carolina. There are thirteen of these voluntary local-area groupings throughout North Carolina, which exist to promote regional development programs principally through educative rather than action-oriented programs. The Piedmont Area Development Association attempts to accomplish this objective through four functioning committees—Community Development, Recreation, Agriculture, and Housing.

The Piedmont Urban Policy Conference. This organization was founded as a nonprofit corporation under the laws of North Carolina in 1970. Although it covers an area—the Carolinas' Piedmont—far larger than the Metrolina territorial limits, it provides Metrolina organizations with a means for outside linkages with other urban centers in the Piedmont. The conference is comprised of a group of private citizens who share a common interest in and concern for the urbanization of the Carolinas' Piedmont region. It meets each fall and holds a series of related day-long sessions during the spring months. The members participate regularly in conferences, seminars, and workshops on sub-

jects of general interest to those engaged in public or private activities that influence the quality of life and the urban process in the Piedmont region.

Each of the Metrolina counties has a local planning board or commission which oversees the particular land-use and planning activities within that county's boundaries. Though these agencies have an extremely important role, their efforts often lack region-wide coordination.

On the whole, a great deal is being attempted concerning regional coordination in the Metrolina area. A potential danger is that each of these individual regional efforts might begin to compete with and duplicate one another. Although not all of the regional organizations have the same objectives, there is obviously considerable overlap. As long as there is a close and open working relationship between each, however, they all should fulfill a useful purpose.

Planning for the Future

The Metrolina urban region has much of value to preserve and a promising potential to work toward. As is the case in most regional settings, however, comprehensive regional planning has been slow to materialize. Perhaps Americans are just not used to thinking on this particular geographic scale. Yet the previously mentioned regional organizations hold great promise for Metrolina-area planning, even though most are in their infancy and are not yet fully understood or accepted by the populace.

In today's changing society events can shape the future sometimes faster than the future can be planned. This happens almost unconsciously, with every bond issue, every new building permit, every new road authorized, and every public school action. These events can manifest themselves in the haphazard pattern called urban sprawl or they can become a part of a more orderly form that corresponds to a regional plan.

Urban sprawl is the sum of a number of uncontrolled forces. The great mobility of today's population—one out of every five Americans moves every year—certainly helps make it possible, although rapid turnover alone does not produce sprawl. But as people move out of cities, the central core and contiguous areas often seem to decay. The direct causes are more related to such things as shortsighted zoning and taxing policies, land speculation, land hoarding, fragmentation, poor market information, and either archaic or nonexistent land-use policies. Outward growth can frequently occur through a "leapfrogging" process, as farms and rural communities are overrun or outflanked by land investors and developers, thereby diminishing the integrity of the rural community but not giving it viable urban underpinnings either. Commercial land users will follow the movement of the population, seizing upon random suburban locations wherever land might be available and cars can be parked. What emerges are bands of suburban "gray zones," a customary feature of urban sprawl. Another kind of "leapfrogging" sprawl is seen in the encirclement of a city by a noose of incorporated suburbs. The city of Charlotte, for example, has been threatened by this phenomenon on the part of some of its surrounding communities, each wanting to protect itself from annexation. It has already happened to some cities elsewhere, such as Chicago. Finally, unabated sprawl can extend its tentacles out farther, eventually coalescing cities and towns in fragmented fashion.

There are several key ingredients of an urban regional plan; principally they consist of the movement system, the array of urban centers, and the pattern of open spaces. Local planners have presented three concepts of regional planning based on these features: the trend concept, the urban-center concept, and the corridor concept. The trend concept consists of reacting to past trends (as well as reflecting current development policies) and projecting those trends for future planning. Since it requires the least change it is the easiest to accomplish, but it confines development to patterns of the past. Ideally, the best of past trends would be selected and incorporated into one of the other plans. A twofold challenge exists: conserving and building up the old centers, and promoting in the outer areas a rational pattern of development in concentrated sites (ur-

ban-center concept) or along major transportation arteries (corridor concept). Whatever blend of these concepts is selected, a desirable plan for an urban region should create opportunities without destroying the localized sense of community and personality. Diversity between centers would be promoted, so that the overall region would not take on the monotony that already brands many areas. For example, in Metrolina the uniqueness of a McAdenville or a Monroe would be preserved and new centers could be planned around natural features, such as the Charlotte-Mecklenburg Planning Commission's suggestion that a series of small but self-contained riverfront communities might be created along the Catawba River.

In any event, it is hoped that many new planning suggestions will be forthcoming in Metrolina. At the same time, tomorrow's plan involves far more than just a plan; it demands an awakened citizenry that is willing to think and act on a regional scale. And it calls for more than pure emotion and negative criticism of urbanization. The land-use plans presented by planners can only succeed if accompanied by meaningful land-use controls and commitments to allow implementation of planning at all levels. There is no question that Metrolina possesses the means to act for the future; the critical question is whether it can manifest the will. If such a willingness exists, the future evolvement of the Metrolina urban region may avoid the misfortunes of urban sprawl and grow gracefully, functionally, and esthetically.

CREDITS FOR PHOTOGRAPHS